# TUG OF WAR

# TUG OF WAR

## Ottawa and the Provinces Under Trudeau and Mulroney

DAVID MILNE

James Lorimer & Company, Publishers

Toronto     1986

Design: Brant Cowie/Artplus Ltd.
Cover illustration: Maureen Paxton

---

**Canadian Cataloguing in Publication Data**

Milne, David A., 1941-

Tug of War
Includes index.
ISBN 0-88862-978-8 (bound) ISBN 0-88862-977-X (pbk.)

1. Federal-provincial relations — Canada.* 2. Canada — Politics and government — 1980-84.* 3. Canada — Politics and government — 1984- .* I. Title.

JL27.M55 1986 320.971 C86-094527-8    69045

---

James Lorimer & Company, Publishers
Egerton Ryerson Memorial Building
35 Britain Street
Toronto, Ontario M5A 1R7

Printed and bound in Canada

5 4 3 2 1     86 87 88 89 90

# Contents

# Preface

I began research on this book shortly after the completion of *The New Canadian Constitution* in 1982. At that time, although my principal preoccupation was with the unfolding of constitutional events, it was already clear that a much more expansive federal strategy across a variety of policy fields was being deployed and that a single book was needed to bring these elements together and provide a critical overview. This book, consequently, starting as a spinoff from constitutional subject matter, has roamed over a daunting range of politics and policy in pursuit of that federal horizontal strategy.

With the election of the Mulroney government in 1984, the plan of the book was enlarged to take into account the Tories' rise to power at the national level, a result shaped in part by the political fallout from the Liberals' horizontal strategy. As it turned out, the policy fields affected by the Liberals' strategy — from energy to broad economic development and from fiscal to constitutional policy — have also been the primary areas in which the federal Conservatives have chosen to act, often in "reactive" fashion, during their early years in office. Therefore, the chapter plan, giving play to each of these policy fields, serves equally well as a ground for the exploration and analysis of the federalism and policy priorities of the federal Tories.

I am grateful to the Social Sciences and Humanities Research Council for the assistance provided this project and to the Senate Research Committee of the University of Prince Edward Island for its encouragement and ongoing support. Grants from these research agencies permitted me to draw on the skills of several able research assistants. I salute them all: Patricia McQuaid, who for two years began to prepare and compile source material and to conduct interviews on my behalf; Wanda Wood, who tracked down and assembled many items; and Lisa Addis, who relentlessly pursued bibliographic leads and cleaned up footnote citations. I am, however, especially indebted to Scott Sinclair, who over three years not only worked on bibliographies for several chapters, summarized and introduced me to much of the research literature, assisted with footnote citations and interviewed officials on my behalf, but who also acted as a friend and sounding board for many of the ideas developed in this book. His was a special contribution, particularly valuable for strengthening the political economy analysis throughout the book. Indeed, his work and ideas were so important a part of chapter 4 that his name appears as a supporting author.

The manuscript is stronger too because of the kindness of many academic readers and specialists who gave generously of their time to offer corrections, criticisms and suggestions. They have added much to this book, though they bear no responsibility for any lingering flaws and failings. I thank them all — Larry Pratt, Robert Young, Donald Smiley, Peter Russell, Stefan Dupré, Raisa Deber, Steven Heiber and Phil Resnick — even when their wise counsel was sometimes not followed. There were also numerous people who graciously acceded to my requests for interviews over the years, many of whom, as officials of provincial or federal levels of government, cannot be named. In every government capital, they invariably provided insight and stimulation and I thank them for their assistance.

I am also grateful to my department secretary Brenda Young for all of her thoughtful and conscientious work on my behalf, to Nancy Smitheram for careful proofing, and to the staff of the UPEI Computer Centre, especially Blair Vessey, for splendid professional service often during harried times. For sensitive and meticulous copyediting, I thank Judith Turnbull. My editor Ted Mumford was of course as unruffled and perceptive as ever, and I thank him for his patience and advice.

Finally, I wish to thank my wife, Frances Gray, and my daughter Kyla for bearing with me in this project over several years.

Charlottetown 1986

# Introduction

Canadians witnessed the closing of an important phase in Canadian federalism in the decisive federal-provincial tug of war that developed during the last electoral mandate of the federal Liberals under Pierre Elliott Trudeau. Although short in duration, this was a period of intense political conflict around themes and issues that had dominated the imagination of Canadians for almost a quarter century. At the centre of those preoccupations lay the question of the future of Quebec, a now receding subject that nonetheless gripped the attention of a generation and was painfully played out in the 1980 referendum and the constitutional events that flowed from it. In a curious fashion, the political struggle over the issue of Quebec independence brought the country a new Charter of Rights and Freedoms it might otherwise not have acquired, at least for a long time. This was only the most spectacular illustration of how the working through of the dynamics of federalism could lead to startling policy innovations.

These were also years when the long-simmering struggle between regionalism and the forces of centralism truly broke out into open political combat across a broad range of policy fronts. The most important confrontation arose over the National Energy Program (NEP), a dramatic centralizing policy initiative announced by the Trudeau government in late October 1980, only weeks after it had decided to take unilateral action over the constitution. That policy forced a direct confrontation between the oil-producing provinces in the West under Alberta's leadership and a government in Ottawa, openly backed by Ontario. Analysts had anticipated some resolution of this fundamental dispute over energy and power, especially after 1973 when the interests of these governments began to diverge more sharply. But when it finally came to a head, in the form of a comprehensive and daring federal political package, it left most economists and business leaders, untrained in the politics of federalism, somewhat dumbfounded. This confrontation, personalized in the bitter relations between Premier Peter Lougheed of Alberta and

Prime Minister Trudeau, was, in its own way, almost as profound as that which divided Trudeau from Premier René Lévesque, the leader of separatist forces in Quebec.

When the Trudeau government began simultaneously to initiate other important policy changes challenging the provinces in the fields of industrial policy and economic development, and of financial relations and social policy, it was becoming clear even as early as 1981 that the government was deliberately using public policy instruments both to extend its own state-building program and to constrain if not roll back provincial power.[1] In that respect a common political thread became apparent in a variety of important government actions, ranging from an overhaul of the regional economic development program and a new "national" approach to the economy all the way to the Canada Health Act and increased federal monitoring of provincial goals and expenditures in postsecondary education. Although all of these actions were invariably wrapped in defensive nationalist terms, which often deceptively drew public interest groups onto the federal policy train, they were on closer examination best understood as planned elements in a federal state-building program. The nationalism sustaining these measures was therefore calculated primarily with an eye to federal power, interest and visibility, and that fact shaped from the start both the nature and the limits of this Liberal nationalism.

This comprehensive horizontal strategy, the ideological centre of the Liberals' so-called "new federalism" as expressed and applied in a variety of policy areas, is the starting point for this book and forms the basis for the chapters that follow. After a brief preliminary exploration of the meaning and history of federalism in Canada, covering particularly developments prior to 1980, the origins for this kind of global strategy are traced in the thought of Pierre Elliott Trudeau in chapter 1. His idea of using nationalism both to heighten the relevance and attraction of the central government in the eyes of Canadian citizens and as a separatist-fighting plan at the service of federalism is shown to antedate his accession to power in Ottawa; it provides the logical foundation and best early evidence for this species of federal state nationalism. The idea of making public policy a servant of that nationalism is clearly anticipated in Trudeau's writings in the 1960s. Nationalism's powerful electoral and political appeal as a shield against separatism (or other fissiparous movements or tendencies) is well understood and recognized. Chapter 1 concludes with an examination of the reasons why that strategy was finally put in place after the 1980 Quebec referendum. Subsequent chapters provide extensive treatment of each of the major centralizing prongs in the strategy of the Trudeau government: its constitutional goals and plans in chapter 2; energy policies in chapter 3; industrial and economic policies in chapter 4; and social and fiscal policies in chapter 5. The concluding chapter pulls these elements together in a comprehensive overview of the meaning, aims, failures and achievements of those final active years in the prime ministership of Pierre Trudeau.

Yet, since those actions turned out to be the closing gestures of a particular era in Canadian federalism, each of the chapters in this book also explains the consequences of this centralizing policy, especially in the subsequent rise of a different federalism with the Progressive Conservatives under the leadership of Brian Mulroney. The meaning of this change is explored across the whole range of policy from constitutional to economic matters, including the Mulroney government's historic decision to pursue a comprehensive free trade agreement with the United States. Indeed, in most cases, virtually half of the analysis in each of the areas touched on in this book is concerned with initiatives of the Mulroney government or with related issues of current interest. Here the aim has also been to grasp and analyze the essential threads of Mulroney's federalism through a comprehensive treatment of the language, ideology and policy priorities of the new government.

An examination of these matters suggests that the Mulroney government, largely unconcerned with questions of the relative balance of power of the two orders of government in Canadian federalism, may have impaired the capability of the federal state in the pursuit of a neoconservative program within the framework of cooperative federalism. In the early stages of the government's mandate, with a friendly cast of supporting premiers, these appeared to be mutually compatible goals. However, provincial encroachments on federal power were substantial even during the government's honeymoon period, and relations would doubtless become much less friendly as the government's neoconservative project proceeded and the cast of provincial premiers changed rapidly in party and political complexion.

The preoccupations of these two governments in Ottawa also led to rather different approaches to the question of foreign ownership of the Canadian economy and to Canada-U.S. relations. The Trudeau program of deploying nationalism in defence of federalism invariably caught in its net American multinational companies in Canada and their government in Washington, while the Mulroney program appeared to be aimed at correcting those irritants and the two economies even more closely. These matters are taken up especially in chapters 3 and 4 on energy and economic policy, and they are integrated into a broader and more encompassing understanding and definition of the meaning of federalism for these two governments. In effect, this work underlines the need to extend our horizons beyond the frequent constitutional or institutional approach to Canadian federalism and to take into account the complex interplay of state and private actors in this field.

While certain subjects, such as the constitutional area, lend themselves rather better to a traditional approach, that is clearly not the case with policy analysis in the fields of energy or economic development. Here political economy is indispensable, and the challenge for students of federalism is to work through this literature in order to give a prominence to issues of federalism often either lacking or not highlighted in the original. There are other important reasons for broadening our perspective in this way, not the least of which is the need to place intergovernmental conflict in Canada within the context of changing trends in international political economy. An illustration of that approach can be found in chapters 3 and 4.

At many points these conditions and constraints in the national and international political economy will be shown to limit or structure the nature of the policy options available to the state at one time or another, but they do not by any means dictate policy. Indeed, a study of this kind underlines how sharply the state's own agenda (its desire for a strong revenue base, for access to information, for defending its turf and maximizing power, and/or for achieving electoral or political advantage) as defined by bureaucrats or party leaders can crucially shape the pattern of Canadian federalism. Many of these factors come into play in the development of public policy at any time, but they were particularly prominent under Prime Minister Trudeau when the federal elite was more than usually self-conscious about its position in the country, indeed about the very integrity and survival of the Canadian state itself.

There is doubtless a price to be paid for the adoption of this comprehensive and eclectic approach — notably a loss of parsimony or of overall methodological unity and simplicity — but given the diverse range of policy to be analyzed by methods best suited to subject matter, that is probably unavoidable. In all cases, however, the analysis draws upon a rich variety of current research sources, including some of the studies completed for the recent Macdonald Commission (Royal Commission on the Economic Union and Development Prospects for Canada). While the chapter framework is dictated partly by the chronological flow of events, each policy chapter can be read as a separate unit or in a different order if desired.

Readers should not expect to find a consistent "provincialist" or "centralist" line of argument developed over these pages. The intention is to provide a critical commentary on the central themes and practices of the Trudeau and Mulroney governments and to reflect a balanced concern for regionalism and nationalism. Neither the Trudeau nor the Mulroney brand of federalism in the 1980s, each activated by a narrow collection of policy concerns and interests, managed to reconcile adequately these competing forces. So often such nationalism as we have witnessed over this decade has been fatally flawed by centralism, while a "cooperative federalism" approach has frequently lacked any wider compelling sense of collectivity and purpose. This is an old story, and perhaps from that perspective it is not so surprising that current governments have not fused the two much more successfully than in the past. Yet history may record that the country has not been entirely without some grand integrating synthesis over these years, especially concerning language and rights questions.

As its title suggests, the book draws upon the competitive dynamics of federal-provincial relations in Canada. That is fair enough, not only because such competitive tugging and pulling is always part of the normal dynamics of this system of government, but because these tensions have been unusually prominent in recent years, especially during Trudeau's final period in office. Moreover, one of the flaws in the Mulroney government's understanding of federalism is its apparent innocence about these competitive dynamics and how to deal with them. Even so, there remain numerous examples of cooperation between the governments even during the worst points in those years, often unnoticed in the heat over other issues of intergovernmental conflict.

It may well be that the country is now moving beyond the fashionable fixations upon the competitive dynamics around federalism that preoccupied Canadians for almost the last quarter century. With the forces of Quebec separatism and western and eastern regionalism so active during those years, these matters were of consuming academic and public interest, but they may now lose some of their lustre if the apparent decline in these movements persists. Although these questions will always be important in Canada, it would no doubt be passé to write about current matters primarily or exclusively in these terms.

Critics are already suggesting that even the conventional models for analyzing the dynamics of intergovernmental relations in Canada, such as the "loaded" competitive images of province-building or nation-building, have obscured as much as they have revealed about federalism in recent years.[2] They have pointed to important patterns of cooperation as well as conflict and to different variations in the pattern of federal-provincial conflict and cooperation, depending on the province and the time, and have urged a more specific and careful approach. However, the traditional dependence upon competitive imagery to convey the meaning of federalism cannot be dispensed with, though it does require cautioning and correcting from time to time. The competitive dynamic must be recognized as the pre-eminent feature of Canadian federalism, especially during the extensive intergovernmental tug of war under Prime Minister Trudeau in the 1980s and even, surprisingly, as an important if carefully suppressed theme in the Mulroney retrenchment period.

# CHAPTER I

# The Origins of the Liberals' "New Federalism"

Defining federalism is always in part a question of metaphor or imagery and thus can never be an exact or easy undertaking, even if all that is sought is some practical definition to use in writing about recent Canadian politics rather than a treatise in political theory. Moreover, the subject, as suggested by the imagery and metaphors built around it, is always emotionally and ideologically charged. Many of the questions raised by debates over federalism go to the roots of political philosophy, especially to the question of the appropriate pattern of political organization for a modern people who wish to live the good life in large and pluralistic societies. These are not matters on which reasonable people must all agree. But difficult as these questions remain, there are vested interests, both private and public, who will wish to enter the debate over federalism because they have material or ideological axes to grind. It is just as well to warn readers that when they begin a book on federalism, they must expect to encounter not only scientific information, but also profound ideological and political debate, often with loaded metaphors and images.

Canadians may remember former prime minister Trudeau's dismissal of Joe Clark's vision of Canada as a "community of communities" in 1979 with the derisive "shopping plaza federalism" tag, or the Conservatives' use of the loaded adjectives "centralist" or "dictatorial" for Trudeau's brand of federalism. Moreover, it is not at all uncommon to find in academic works on federalism literally hundreds of images and modifiers used either to advance arguments for a particular philosophy of federalism or merely as heuristic devices to convey and explain the subject matter. A recent book on this topic presents an entertaining catalogue of federalism descriptors; the use of the most engaging of figurative language is shown to be the stock-in-trade of political scientists around the world. Federalism metaphors include, for example, an awesome variety of cakes (birthday, marble, fruitcake, layer, upside down) and fences (bamboo, masonry wall, picket), as well as a barrage of value-loaded terms such as "coercive," "imperial" and "feudal."[1] Such descriptors are frequently employed in Canada, though our metaphorical taste tends more to ships (watertight compartment federalism) and construction (province-building and nation-building).

Both the extraordinary dependence on metaphor and the ideology and emotion built around federalism flow from this complex bifurcated system of government. Sovereignty itself is divided in a federal polity, with two governments charged with final power to make law over the same people with respect to discrete subject matters (or the same subject matter with rules of precedence or paramountcy in the event of conflict) as contained in a written constitution. It is in effect a system of limited government, in which neither order of state has the power to abolish or diminish the legislative jurisdiction of the other under the constitution. This coexistence of two independent levels of state (usually with similar executive, legislative, judicial and administrative structures) governing the same people and territory according to a master list of legislative functions (a division of powers) normally works only with the support of the courts as constitutional umpires. It has been from the beginning, in the United States and in countries such as Canada that subsequently adopted federalism, an uneasy compromise taken by a people who wished at once the benefits of larger political, economic and military union and the freedom to retain local communities and identities.

This inventive system of government, whether embraced by a people as a matter of principle or of necessity, must necessarily reflect and sustain polarities within the state. As analysts have long noted, a federal rather than unitary system of government has arisen only because of the prior existence of a federal society where a rich diversity of localized units often reflecting distinct economic, geographic, linguistic, religious, social and/or psychological identities is already in place. The leaders and peoples of these units, such as those in Upper and Lower Canada and in each of the Maritime provinces prior to Confederation, have been strong enough to demand continuing recognition of their distinctiveness as orders of state. Once so constituted, they are able to reinforce these initial identities not only symbolically but also in a myriad of practical ways. With a considerable range of constitutional responsibilities and with the ability to pursue these aggressively with their own policy goals and instruments, the provinces as governments are quite able to build upon any prior set of communitarian loyalties and to sustain themselves as vital institutional expressions of their people.[2]

Hence, two constitutionally entrenched systems of order to which the same citizens look for satisfaction of their different public needs and to which they will therefore pay taxes and owe some measure of allegiance will necessarily be the logical outcome of a federal arrangement. Such governments must always find their relations to one another a peculiar mix of conflict, ambition and competition. This dynamic will, of course, be restrained to some degree by the need for cooperation and bargaining over matters of mutual concern, as well as by the integrating bonds of history and a common political nationality.

The adversarial or cooperative properties may be intensified by the accidents, issues, events and personalities that are cast upon the federal system. In many federal countries, these forces over their history have moved the balance of federal and provincial power much more sharply toward the centre and reduced the level and seriousness of initial territorial divisions and antagonisms. The acquisition of a new nationality and the operation of national political institutions and practices may over time work against the continuing power of subnational governments to make countries, such as the United States, much less federal in practice than their formal constitution would suggest. In other cases, federations have simply fallen apart as a result of the strains and initial divisions that could not be successfully contained by federation.

Canada has moved in neither of these directions, although the Quebec government's referendum of 1980 to seek sovereignty-association with Canada suggested how perilously close the country had come to the second option. Instead, Canada has over its short history managed to preserve if not expand upon its essentially federal character while, almost as a corollary proposition, failing to create a particularly strong sense of national identity and purpose. Hence, the most important conflicts in the country have most often seen regions and provinces pitted against one another and/or the federal government, rather than social or class cleavages. As the Quebec referendum indicates most graphically, and the signs of alienation in the east and west of the country also show, citizen loyalties continue to form the complex and ambiguous pattern of a still vigorously federal country.[3]

There is also an intricate political economy around federalism that complicates the already murky field of state–private sector relationships. In a federal state, there will naturally be aggregations of private interests drawn to each level of government. Since business, labour and other private parties must align themselves with the state level that seems most capable of protecting and maximizing their own interests, while standing ready to change sides or straddle the constitutional fence as the occasion requires, they add yet another level of conflictual dynamics to those created by history, sentiment and the political order itself. So intertwined can some of these private interest–state coalitions become that they form almost an inescapable definition of the meaning of a state regime, a crucial part of a particular axis of power upon which a national government or provincial regime actually operates. This is perhaps best illustrated on the federal level by the Macdonald government's links with strong central Canadian business interests under the National Policy in the nineteenth century or by the modern Alberta state's alliance with aggressive domestic and foreign oil interests during the 1970s and 1980s.[4] These alliances are not likely to be struck forever and will change according to the interests and directions of the players and of the overall national and international economic environment, but they do add an essential element to our understanding of the dynamics of federalism.[5]

Then there are the bureaucracies that grow up around these constitutional polarities in a federal state. Not only must officials tend to the functional concerns of departmental business, but they must also act in relation to another whole cast of players at the other level of government. There may be requirements to coordinate policy initiatives and to consult with one another on a frequent and regular basis. With the development of specialized intergovernmental departments for the relations with other governments in the federation, it is easy to see how preoccupied senior officials in these quasi-diplomatic bureaus can become with the constitutional turf and power of the particular government they serve and from which they derive their sense of personal authority and prestige.[6] These powerful bureaucrats also become part of the dynamics of federalism, adding their own power-seeking and/or power-defending behaviours to the operation of the system.[7]

Given these dynamics and the powerful pull of interests, emotion and philosophy associated with them, it is not surprising that the field of federalism is littered with colourful if loaded descriptors and metaphors. Self-interested agents in government and the private sector will naturally be thrown into the fray and invited to pronounce on the particular brand of federalism that suits them. Academics have been drawn into these dynamics either as the hired guns of one party or another, or as researchers and/or staff of task forces or royal commissions, notably the recent massive Macdonald Commission. Even without these distractions from the intellectual life, scholars have naturally been highly sensitive to the material and ideological conflicts surrounding federalism, and apt to create their own images of these dynamics. One of the most powerful established versions — "province-building" and its federal counterpart — has been a recent parallel constructionist image where provincial (and recently the federal) governments are seen to be relentlessly "building" up power in a governmental equivalent to the self-interested laws of motion in a market economy.[8] While this picture of federal-provincial relations has been attacked for exaggerating the uniformly competitive nature of these relations, no one should seriously anticipate a departure from these or alternate kinds of competitive binary images.[9]

Despite all the differences between provinces and the nature of diverse political regimes and personalities in Canada, the tendency to think of federalism in terms of these two abstract polarities of power is still an overwhelming preoccupation. Therefore, the temptation will be exceedingly strong to collapse the multivarious dimensions of a real federation into essentially binary but repelling universals. Federalism descriptors almost always come in universal opposing pairs of relations — centrifugal (or decentralized) versus centripetal (or centralized) federalism, imperial versus classical federalism, cooperative versus competitive federalism, provincial versus federal state-building and so on. This preoccupation with dual images carries forward to the root metaphor of federalism itself as a polar balance of power, which is thereafter studied carefully by federalism specialists for changes in the original binary division over time.[10]

Whatever the expectations of the founders of federal states about the more or less permanent fixing of the boundaries of federal and provincial legal power, the political balance of power between central and local governments in any state undergoes constant change over time. Conditions of war, for example, can so shift the balance that a virtually unitary state can result; economic depression can sometimes accomplish a similar swing in the balance. The growth of urbanization, the welfare state, or changes in national or international capitalist modes and relations of production can also profoundly affect the balance of federal and provincial power. Nor is the play of federal and provincial power unaffected by the emergence of widely held conceptions of the role of the state in public opinion, a social consensus that may support and sustain the political pre-eminence of one order of government over another for considerable lengths of time.[11] These factors can bring about strong if often temporary shifts in power from one order of government to another, often achieved through political circumvention of the written division of powers rather than formal legal amendment. These processes have fascinated students of federalism in Canada and many countries, pushing them increasingly into the discipline's equivalent to the science of taxonomy and evolutionary explanation.

For example, in a classic essay on what he called the "Five Faces of Federalism," James Mallory reviewed the remarkably different stages of Canadian federalism over the first hundred years of its existence.[12] After naming, classifying and describing these five kinds of federalisms, and linking them briefly to their approximate historical periods, Mallory showed how variously the Canadian federal state had adapted to different political conditions. Although of an earlier time and with a different set of policy concerns, much the same exercise was completed by the Rowell Sirois Commission on Dominion-provincial relations in the late 1930s.[13] It too attempted to trace the evolution of Canadian federalism and to track the shifting balance of federal and provincial power, paying much more attention to the evolving political economy of the country and its effects on the balance of power in the federation. Here changing staples and trade

## Table 1-1

## THE EVOLUTION OF CANADIAN FEDERALISM

| Classification Name | Nature and Emergence in Time |
| --- | --- |
| *Quasi-Federalism | A term used to suggest the dubiousness of Canada's "federal" system under John A. Macdonald and for some time afterward. Federal powers to strike down provincial legislation, reserve legislation through instruction to provincial lieutenant governors, and retain control over western public lands until 1930 showed the "imperial" (mother country to colony) relationship Ottawa enjoyed in relation to the provinces. Clearly, though there remains a division of powers, this is legally a highly centralized system. |
| *Classical Federalism | Term used to denote a system and division of power between equally autonomous central and provincial governments whose disputes over jurisdiction would be settled by the courts. This version of federalism, it was said, was imposed on the Canadian federal union by legal decisions of the Judicial Committee of the Privy Council in London, England, especially from the 1880s until the end of the 1930s. It was also said to be more consistent with the realities of the federation by the turn of the twentieth century with a powerful Ontario, a determined and independent-minded Quebec, and a Liberal party in power highly sensitive to provincial rights. |
| *Emergency Federalism | As a direct spinoff of the role of the courts in the federation, an emergency doctrine had been created that justified virtually the surrender of provincial powers to the federal Parliament during the temporary prosecution of a war. Such a doctine was probably implicit in the defence power of the federal government anyway, but it permitted and justified the sharply centralized form the Canadian federal system took during the period of both world wars (1914-18; 1939-45) in this century and for some period afterward. |

| Classification Name | Nature and Emergence in Time |
| --- | --- |
| *Cooperative Federalism | This tag is meant to refer to the growth of administrative cooperation between the two orders of government over joint programs, the agreed delegation of powers to regulatory agencies of another order of government, and regular fiscal negotiations. This system is driven by federal willingness to use its spending power to prod provinces into desired programs (of health, welfare, etc.) in return for the maintenance of certain national minimum standards. This system emerged sharply in the post-1945 period and continued with growing expressions of provincial resistance through to the late 1960s. This was a centralizing phase in the balance of power in the federation, where federal control over the purse permitted a *de facto* (though not *de jure* except in the provincial transfer of unemployment insurance and pensions to Ottawa) rearrangement of constitutional responsibilities and political powers. |
| *Double-Image Federalism | This picture of federalism draws out the divisions between the French- and the English-speaking peoples in the federal union as reflected in the fight for constitutional language guarantees in the West and elsewhere in Canada, and in the growing alternative program of defending Quebec as the "fortress" of French power. Quebec's "opting out" practices against federal centralization under cooperative federalism, the discussion of a "special status" for Quebec as distinct from the other provinces, and ultimately Quebec separatism may flow from this idea. This imagery was a prominent feature of Canadian federalism throughout but acquired much more saliency after Quebec's "Quiet Revolution" in the 1960s. |

patterns, government-business projects and alliances, and differential patterns of growth, constitutional responsibilities and tax yields added their own logic to the evolution of the Canadian federal state.

Whatever the methodology or the particular imagery used by the evolutionary taxonomist, the focus is always on the binary balance of power.

In fact, as Canadian federalism moved on in the 1960s and 1970s to new images of "executive federalism," "province-building" and "centrifugal versus centripetal federalism," the preoccupation with the balance of federal-provincial power became even more pronounced. This question was put in stark relief by the rise of Quebec separatism, especially after the Parti Québécois (PQ) took power in 1976. Then the "crisis" of Canadian federalism, dwelt on extensively by every writer on the subject at that time, was the preservation of any kind of federal arrangement with the people of Quebec.

The issue of the balance of federal-provincial power also assumed more prominence in the light of the growing administrative and executive power of the provinces over these years, of the increasing drive to build provincial states and economies, if necessary at the presumed expense of other provinces and the nation. This relentless and threatening provincialism was first exemplified by petroleum-rich Alberta after the 1973 and 1979 international oil price shocks, but according to the Trudeau government and to many scholars on federalism, it later came to characterize the other provinces. Province-building had taken them all into "province-first" economic strategies that allegedly undermined the integrity of the national economic union, into gang-ups on the constitutional powers and authority of the federal government, and into massive spending and persistent demands on the federal treasury. The framework of "executive federalism," it was argued, captured best in the regular summit meetings of first ministers complete with flags, high-flown rhetoric and rows of supporting ministers and officials, appeared to conform increasingly to the cold image of self-seeking diplomatic bargaining between independent states. There was always some over-simplification in these images, but by the end of the 1970s the attention of the whole nation was drawn to such matters as the forces of Quebec separatism worked to overthrow federalism, and those of provincialism to redefine the balance of power in the country. These in turn provoked an Ottawa counterreaction: first, consternation, defensiveness and a search for accommodation; later, in the spirit of Canadian defensive expansionism, a vigorous counterattack.[14]

In short, developments over the 1960s and 1970s, especially as interpreted by governmental players and in academic imagery, had the effect of telescoping the actual complexities of political life in Canada into fundamental opposing binary dynamics. That may have been a somewhat misleading picture, particularly when applied outside the context of the federal-separatist battle in Quebec, but by 1980 it had become natural to see change in the intergovernmental balance of power as the acid test for the future. Was there to be a breakup and state realignment along linguistic lines, an apparently endless centrifugal federalism, or some eleventh-hour restoration of centripetal federalism? Was the balance to be destroyed, fundamentally realigned or merely restored? Where would the pendulum of power swing? This image of federalism as a pendulum swing, as a precarious and perpetually shifting balance of power, has long fascinated Canadians, but never more so than during the early 1980s. In fact, this conception of a shifting pendulum carrying with it, willy-nilly, the federal balance and the future of the Canadian state was an image around which the Trudeau government consciously rallied its political troops and prepared to take action as a new majority government in the spring of 1980. Hence, the delicious irony of a national program of political centralization being prepared purportedly to "save federalism," to stop the presumed excessive swing of the pendulum toward provincial capitals, to preserve a balance of powers upon which the future good of Canada was assumed to rest. That view of the state of the nation drew upon the theory and experience of the previous two decades in federal-provincial relations, as well as upon the prior philosophy of the prime minister.

### Separatism, Provincialism and the Federal Balance of Power

Trudeau mused in late 1981:

> There was a slippage of Canada towards, is it a community of communities or is it ten quasi autonomous states? That slippage has been going on for, perhaps a couple of decades now and I feel that they've had to be reversed and I think at least the swing of the pendulum has been stopped with the energy agreements, with the constitutional agreements. There is now, I hope, a line of policy which will keep Canada strong and won't keep it sliding towards this highly decentralized position which it's in and which people don't even realize that it's in....By just about every standard, whether it be economic, whether it be fiscal, whether it be legislative, whether it be administrative, power has been shifting to the provinces.[15]

This judgment about the recent decentralizing pendulum swing in Canadian federalism was supported by most academics, even though some pointed to the vigorous and often unilateral expansion of federal power and politics in energy policy, wage and price controls, bilingualism, constitutional reform under a national Charter of Rights, and the expansive moves in cultural policy, foreign ownership and regional economic development as illustrations of countertrends. It was noted that the pendulum image, which suggested only a single directional swing in power, might itself be misleading, since it excluded the possibility of simultaneous and contradictory operation of both centralizing and decentralizing trends. But the evolutionary taxonomists appeared to be essentially in agreement that the immediate postwar centralization of power in Canada, flowing out of the war, tax rental agreements, and a social consensus around Keynesian economics and the building of the welfare state under federal leadership, had been gradually replaced by a provincializing counterswing. Some were as convinced as Trudeau that the new trend had already gone too far, threatening the viability and integrity of the Canadian state.[16]

The pendulum reversal could first be seen, it was argued, in federal willingness in the 1960s to accept the principle of provincial opting out of shared-cost programs with full compensation. While most provinces did not take advantage of this option, Quebec proceeded to use it to withdraw from several federally led social programs, including hospital insurance, health grants, vocational training, unemployment assistance and old age assistance, choosing to run its own programs instead. Although this move appeared at one level to be merely symbolic, since all the usual federal terms and conditions attached to the programs continued to apply to the opting-out province, it was significant, since the political attention of Quebecers shifted increasingly to their own provincial capital for these services. In that respect, a *de facto* special status appeared, while federal visibility and power were gradually reduced. This retreat indicated the first federal acceptance of the provincial argument that the use of federal dollars in the form of conditional grants to the provinces for programs in provincial areas of jurisdiction was an invasion of provincial jurisdiction and an infringement of the spirit of the constitution.[17]

This decision ultimately led to even more important concessions when in 1969 a federal constitutional offer was made by Prime Minister Trudeau to limit the federal spending power. Here Ottawa proposed that any new federal shared-cost programs must first be supported by a broad provincial consensus of the legislatures of three of the four regions of Canada, with guarantees of financial rebates to the taxpayers of the opting-out provinces.[18] Since the relatively unrestricted use of the federal spending power was certainly one of the most important sources of federal authority, and virtually the single constitutional basis on which it had managed to erect the modern welfare state in Canada, this was no small retreat.

Similarly, after almost a decade of direct federal grants to universities during the 1950s, the payment of which the Duplessis government had blocked for institutions in his province at considerable expense to them and Quebec taxpayers, Ottawa permitted that province to take over as the dispenser of these grants in 1960.[19] This agreement, together with the return of all the higher education funds held in trust for Quebec over the previous eight years, indicated another political retreat away from Ottawa's unrestricted ability to make direct payments to whomever it wished within the provinces. Thereafter, federal support of higher education in Quebec was politically camouflaged, and a presumed consequent drop in federal visibility and relevance to Quebecers followed. As provincial objections grew to the use of these payments elsewhere in Canada and as the anomaly of Quebec's special relationship became increasingly apparent, the federal government took this reversal further and accepted the proposition that it ought not to circumvent provincial governments when making payments to institutions within and under provincial jurisdiction. In 1967 all federal dollars for institutional support of higher education were funnelled through provincial capitals. Although tempered by direct federal programs in the fields of student aid and research (and by continuing federal income support systems and direct payments to individuals), these pullbacks indicated a weakening of the direct links between the federal state and institutions and citizens within the provinces.[20]

Since these funds were, however, offered to the provinces on a 50-50 shared-cost basis, the provinces continued to be restricted in their fiscal and spending policy by these linkages, while the federal government found its own expenditure in this area tied to provincial spending decisions. The Established Programs Financing (EPF) arrangements of 1977 gave the provinces an assured annual source of increasing federal money nominally designated for health and postsecondary education without any requirement that it be spent on these areas. While the federal government received merely the budgetary assurance of a known mechanism — GNP (gross national product) and population increase — under which the level of its increase for these programs over the following five years would be set, the move to block-funding represented for the provinces a highwater mark of fiscal decentralization and the strongest repudiation of the earlier intrusive postwar practice of conditional grants.

Finally, on the fiscal front, the federal government and other analysts of federalism saw the pendulum swing toward the provinces in the aggregate statistical distribution of spending and revenue share in the federation. In a 1981 federal publication on this subject, the increasingly decentralizing effect of the fiscal system was given very extensive treatment.[21] The trend away from conditional shared-cost programs toward straightforward transfers to the provinces for established programs in health and higher education, the increasing growth of unconditional equalization payments, and the flexibility and higher provincial take of the income tax system were all noted. The scale of fiscal decentralization was also shown in the sharply declining federal share of total government revenues over the thirty years prior to 1978. It was calculated that from its earlier dominant position at the end of the Second World War, the federal government had slipped so far that "two-thirds of total government revenues after transfers accrued to the provincial/local sector."

Comparative data also showed that the fiscal position of Canada compared unfavourably to that of most other leading federal states. It was not a very significant leap from these figures to the claim that Canada was the "most decentralized federation in the world." The problem was, however, that using these figures in this way was a highly complex exercise in measurement and interpretation. Such an undertaking, warned Richard Bird, "was always misleading and generally useless," especially if the fiscal index was intended to be treated as "a proxy for decentralization in some profound sense of decision-making power."[22]

Whatever the validity of this approach, the fiscal dilemma was also claimed to be considerably exacerbated by the new revenue accruing to the oil-producing provinces as a result of the pricing policies of the Organization of Petroleum Exporting Countries (OPEC). While those provinces were piling up massive surpluses, building investment pools for their economic development as well as loan ties to have-not borrowing provinces, the federal government was by virtue of the same facts forced to assume higher and higher costs for energy imports and exploration and for equalization payments. Moreover, the costs for federal support of social programs through intergovernmental transfers continued to mount. These developments were causing what the federal government called a "fiscal imbalance" in favour of the provinces, and they were weakening the fiscal ability of the national government to meet its responsibilities. The long-term consequence, it was argued, was a growing federal deficit that sapped the strength from one of the federal government's most important sources of power and authority: its ability to finance both its own operations and the whole intergovernmental support structure upon which postwar federal pre-eminence had been built.

The economic dimension of Canadian federalism was also said to add its own logic to the provincializing swing of the pendulum. Although the federal government remained in both macropolicy terms and size the most important government in the federation, economic province-building was increasingly moving that order of government into the politically significant areas of microeconomic policy. Provincial governments' relations with business through joint investment ventures, the provision of incentive grants and tax inducements, the sponsorship of research, and their own experiments with public corporations for economic development, ownership and investment seemed to add to centrifugal pressures.[23] This kind of hands-on experience with specific firms, in part stimulated by federal incursions into microeconomic policy through the Department of Regional Economic Expansion (DREE), was fuelling a new confidence in provincial economic management and increasing pretensions to equivalence with the national government in national economic policymaking. Indeed, as the federal government wrestled with an increasingly difficult international economic environment during the 1970s, and as the need for intergovernmental economic cooperation was rising, there were more frequent demands by the premiers for a formal role in national economic policymaking. Typically, these demands emerged in First Ministers' Conferences, and they appeared to constitute a steady extraconstitutional threat to the jurisdiction, relevance and power of the federal government.

Even more disturbing from the federal point of view was the growing movement toward restrictive "province-first" economic measures: restrictions, for example, on the free flow of labour between provinces with Quebec's ban on the entry of Ontario construction workers or Newfoundland's and Nova Scotia's attempts to monopolize the offshore for their own labour force; the restrictions on the ownership of land by other Canadians in Saskatchewan and Prince Edward Island; obstacles to the free flow of professionals through differential, provincially created standards; barriers to the free movement of goods by provincial marketing boards; distortions to the market through provincial procurement policies or "buy provincial" campaigns; or regulatory obstacles to commercial operations by the erection of a jungle of differential standards in transportation, products and so on. These and other measures appeared to demonstrate the country was balkanizing, moving in economic terms toward Trudeau's derisive image of a "confederation of shopping plazas."

Meanwhile, the provinces were seen to be unusually well armed for the intergovernmental wrangling over these kinds of issues by their recent achievements in building up well-qualified and powerful bureaucracies. While this growth was certainly not true of all provinces, being largely the work of the larger and more aggressive provincial players such as Quebec, Ontario and Alberta, these developments did at least equalize the level of expertise between the two orders of government. If knowledge is power, there was no reason to presume that the provinces were in an uneven contest, as had existed before the 1950s. To a large extent, much of this province-building in administrative and development terms was, ironically, encouraged by federal policy, including regional development programs, equalization payments and the like — a curious development commented on by Albert Breton in his dissenting statement to the Macdonald Commission. But it was the later development of intergovernmental bureaus in provincial governments, as well as the growing horizontal executive grip that provincial governments exercised over all functional, "normal" interdepartmental business with the federal government, that prompted more concern. Increasingly, these appeared to be drawn into a coordinated "diplomatic" program of provincial state-building.

These dynamics reached their ultimate expression in the constitutional wrangles between the two orders of government over the previous two decades. Here too the pendulum was said to be moving dramatically in a provincialist direction. The swing began in Quebec after the Quiet Revolution of the 1960s with a seemingly endless string of constitutional demands for more power over social policy, cultural policy, immigration, representation abroad and economic policy; and demands for checks on federal powers, including the spending power, the declaratory power authorizing Ottawa to take over provincial works in the national interest, the power to disallow provincial legislation and so on. In fact, one of these claims, namely for more power over social policy, became the declared cause for Premier Bourassa to pull out of the earlier unanimous Victoria agreement to patriate the constitution with a Charter of Rights in 1971. After that, as Prime Minister Trudeau said, "when the provinces caught onto that, that jeez they can bargain more rights for themselves, well then the cat was out of the bag. What was good for Quebec in '71 became good for everybody in '75, '76, '77."[24]

It was principally the western provinces after the mid-1970s that began to accelerate the other provinces' demands for constitutional change. These included the strengthening of the provinces' powers over natural resources, particularly since these had now become so valuable after the spectacular petroleum price increases of the 1973 oil crisis. After losing two important cases in the Supreme Court over its regulatory and taxation measures, Saskatchewan wished to see secured in the constitution the provinces' power to regulate interprovincial and international trade in these resources and to apply indirect taxes on them.[25] The defensive side of the same preoccupation emerged with demands for curtailing the federal declaratory power over provincial works, for removing the federal disallowance powers, for restraining the use of the wide federal powers over emergencies, and for limiting the spending power, together with the unilateral federal power over important regulatory commissions affecting the provinces. Increasingly, these constitutional aims widened into a campaign to restructure the Senate into a true House of the Provinces, which would operate under the direction of the premiers and hence protect provincial interests in important federal legislation and appointments.

As for Quebec, as its constitutional demands evolved beyond the aggressive nationalism of premiers Lesage and Johnson in the 1960s, it moved steadily toward the goal of independence. After the accession to power of the PQ under Premier Lévesque in 1976, there was the demand that a constitutional right to national self-determination be written into the Canadian constitution — to secure, as it were, a formal authorizing instrument prior to the subsequent referendum in Quebec on sovereignty-association. This was a constitutional position that could hardly be described as business-as-usual or merely reformist, and it set off alarm bells in the national capital. Even the Quebec Liberal party under the leadership of Claude Ryan, while not advocating the independence option, was developing an aggressive program of constitutional decentralization that would have put the nationalists of the 1960s to shame.[26]

The dynamics within the federal capital seemed to demonstrate that the provincializing swing of opinion had taken a firm grip on many in the federal parties. At the end of the 1960s, the Conservatives and the New Democratic party had both toyed with the idea of national self-determination for Quebec, considering such political options as special status for that province. Only after a vigorous campaign by Prime Minister Trudeau and the subsequent passing of the Official Languages Act did these parties accept bilingualism and biculturalism as the appropriate federal policy response to Quebec nationalism. By the end of the 1970s, under opposition leader Joe Clark, the Progressive Conservatives had adopted much of the western case against Liberal federalism, however, and were preaching a more decentralized vision of Canada as a "community of communities." They supported many of the constitutional objectives of the provincial premiers, especially provincial control over natural resources, including Newfoundland's recent demand for control of the rich oil fields of Hibernia in the north Atlantic. This party came to power in 1979 as a minority government and was proceeding to put its constitutional program in place when its budget was unexpectedly defeated by the joint opposition in November 1979.

The state of thinking about the federation could also be seen in public opinion and in the many sympathetic academic treatments of the idea of provincialism and Quebec independence.[27] These were reflected in submissions to many government commissions and task forces looking at the constitutional issues over the 1970s. Perhaps none of these expressed the prevailing sentiments as well as the Trudeau government's own task force on the federation in 1979.[28] Its report, under the joint chairmanship of former Ontario premier John Robarts and former federal minister Jean-Luc Pepin, was nothing if not an eloquent panegyric to provincialism. Not only did its chief recommendations accept only statutory protection for minority language rights provincially, but they also enshrined many of the constitutional objectives of the provinces, including limits to the federal declaratory power, spending power, disallowance power, the provincialist version of Senate reform and the shift of residual power to the provinces.

It appeared that by the late 1970s Canada was moving progressively in a provincialist direction, although many of these matters were then only prominent trends and tendencies, not accomplished realities. Moreover, the provinces themselves could not be said to be uniformly enthusiastic at the prospect of a weakened federal state: neither have-not provinces, especially in the Atlantic region, which required a strong federal redistributive role, nor Ontario, which required the retention of federal control over the national market in its own long-run interest, were inclined to support wholeheartedly such a course of action. Even in Quebec there was considerable ambivalence around this question, particularly where practical matters of economic security were weighed in the equation. Hence, there was always a strong pattern of countervailing trends within the provinces despite constitutional pressures, the drive toward Quebec independence, the provincialist politics of oil, seemingly unrestrained economic province-building, and the apparent sympathies of public opinion.

In any case, these provincializing trends could not effect permanent changes in the nature of the Canadian federation without confrontation with and defeat of opposing political tendencies or counterweights operating from the centre. In any real federation these are likely to be considerable, even if obscured by provincialist rhetoric and politics. Certainly, after more than a decade of activist federal leadership under Trudeau, it would be a foolish analyst who would have written off the strength of these counterweights and the political determination of the federal government to exercise them. Despite the apparent fiscal and other accommodations to provincialist demands, Ottawa had hardly ceded the field to the forces of provincial autonomy. Instead, it had prepared its own constitutional counterattack to Quebec nationalism with the entrenchment of bilingualism under the Charter of Rights and Freedoms, had moderated and restrained the transfer of power to the producing provinces after the 1973 OPEC oil crisis, had asserted its right to direct and tame the Canadian economy, especially with the 1976 imposition of wage and price controls, and was actively using pan-Canadian nationalism in support of the federal state and its institutions against both the provinces and foreign multinationals. While many doubted both the effectiveness and tenacity of these countermoves, it was certainly not clear in what direction the country might actually go.

The matter was now an electoral question as the national Liberals and Progressive Conservatives squared off on these alternative federal futures, with the latter party (supported by heavy western representation under Joe Clark from western Canada) prepared to decentralize more power to the provinces in the name of "cooperative federalism" and the former (supported by heavy central Canadian representation under a leader from Quebec) adopting an increasingly harder line. Those divisions came out before the 1979 election of the Progressive Conservatives and were sharpened as the Conservatives pursued their program of accommodation with the provinces during their eight-month period in office in 1979-80.

## The Emergence of the Liberals' "New Federalism"

Even before 1980, the Liberals' program, as befits the party's historic position as the "government party," was considerably more turf-conscious than was the Conservatives'. With the Liberal party's strong pro-federal representation in Quebec, its first objective was to contain and defeat Quebec separatism, if necessary by making some modest accommodations to regional demands. There was considerable willingness to respond to provincial fiscal concerns, especially with the introduction of EPF at the urging of Ontario and Quebec. Further, in the closing year of its mandate and just before facing electoral defeat in 1979, the Trudeau government appeared willing to contemplate even more substantial concessions to the provincial premiers on constitutional matters, including the ceding of much of the western premiers' case over natural resources. But as Trudeau later put it, even that was not enough — there were only more demands and no deal. As the referendum on Quebec's sovereignty-association proposal drew nearer and the evidence of a strong provincialist swing of the pendulum continued to mount, this party moved toward a more nationalist centralizing program to restore the balance. In the words of Trudeau:

> I think that the turn of the pendulum or the swing back of the pendulum [toward centralism] happened probably sometime between '78 and '81. I don't like to be too partisan, but I think that we had that short period of the Conservative party that was preaching the community of communities and I think it brought forth rather clearly when even Mr. Clark couldn't reach an agreement with Alberta, after he'd given up Loto Canada, after he'd given away the offshore and after he'd been making many other promises to decentralize to that community of communities, I think it became obvious to more and more people that that was going too far and then I began to feel that I had support for stopping the pendulum.[29]

That pendulum-restraining or pendulum-redirecting program became the essential preoccupation of the federal Liberal government in the 1980s.

It was easy enough for opponents to accuse the Trudeau government of trying to buck the natural evolution of Canadian federalism toward a decentralized state or of favouring a restoration of unbridled centralism in the federation. But that would hardly square with the prime minister's known admiration for a balanced federalism or with his earlier attempts in the 1950s to buck the postwar centralizing measures of the federal government, especially the "misuse" of the federal spending power to direct federal grants to universities in defiance of provincial jurisdiction under the constitution. This latter-day change of sides could be written off either as opportunism or merely as the corrupting seductions of power once Trudeau had entered political life on the federal side of the balance. But neither of these postures will do. The federal Liberal program under Trudeau became obsessed with the idea of defending Canada by preserving federalism's balance of power because this had always lain at the heart of Trudeau's own philosophy of state. And, as everyone familiar with the idea of maintaining any balance of power will know, a true belief in the politics of political balance or equilibrium entails taking sides, applying counterweights, whenever the balance is threatened and against whoever is temporarily predominant. This is a better explanation for the paradoxical politics of Pierre Elliott Trudeau, as he himself always insisted.

As early as 1967, that commitment to equilibrium under federalism was clear in his foreword to *Federalism and the French Canadians:*

> The theory of checks and balances [in parliamentary and federal systems], so acutely analysed by these two writers [Montesquieu and de Tocqueville], has always had my full support. It translates into practical terms the concept of equilibrium that is inseparable from freedom in the realm of ideas. It incorporates a corrective for abuses and excesses into the very functioning of political institutions. My political action, or my theory — insomuch as I can be said to have one — can be expressed very simply: create counterweights. As I have explained, it was because of the federal government's weakness that I allowed myself to be catapulted into it.[30]

Like all dynamic systems of power, a federal arrangement of government is constantly subject to disequilibrium by the changes through which the country evolves. These may cause, as in Canada, a "radical" evolution over a hundred years without requiring any fundamental constitutional reform. This evolution often will take the form of alternating sequences of imbalance, with one order of government predominating over another according to a complex variety of extra-legal causes. Trudeau was quick to recognize that process and to point out well before other analysts that the postwar period of centralization fuelled by the liberal use of the federal spending power had by the 1960s begun to evaporate with a provincializing swing in the other direction.

> In our history, periods of great decentralization have alternated with periods of intense centralization, according to economic and social circumstances, external pressures, and the strength or cunning of various politicians. A recent factor in politics, which is also a verifia-

ble law in most industrial countries, is that the state must nowadays devote an ever increasing proportion of an ever increasing budget on purposes that in Canada are the constitutional responsibility of provincial governments. In other words, Canadian federalism is presently evolving in the direction of much greater decentralization.[31]

This trend in government activity could be read, he thought, in the consequent shifting pattern of federal-provincial expenditure in favour of the provinces. Unless the federal government intervened in an illegitimate way by taxing and distributing money for purposes under provincial jurisdiction, such as with direct grants for higher education, the "natural operation of demographic, social, and economic forces were transferring an enormous amount of power to provincial governments without the necessity of amending a single comma of the constitution."[32] While Trudeau acknowledged that this transformation in the balance was hardly a sinister plot but "a natural occurrence," by the 1980s he had come to the view that it was "the duty of those who believe in national politics, in politics for the whole nation to sense at which point the slide [toward provincialism] should stop."[33] At that point, a line of policy at the federal level must be deployed to restore the balance.

This commitment to preserving federalism as a real balance-of-power system that ensures citizens unity with diversity, order with freedom, and room for social and political experimentation at different levels of state was not a light undertaking for Trudeau. As a thinker as well as political actor, he gave federalism a critical role in preserving and enhancing democracy, particularly in multilingual states that would otherwise be torn apart by divisive nationalist passions. As an instrument of government, federalism was a compromise arrived at by reason, providing unity in the face of emotional, linguistic, territorial, religious and other divisions. Canada was in that respect a model for the future of mankind, "a brilliant prototype for the moulding of tomorrow's civilization"; its breakup, he told the American Congress, would be "a crime against human history."[34]

This same commitment to federalism as a real balance of power with consequent room for progressive experimentation in the furtherance of "the cause of democracy,...of healthy competition for self government" among regional communities at different levels of political maturity, and of the improvement of Canadian government through "creative tensions" between orders of state led him to scold socialists in 1961 for their centralist leanings and their failure to accept the challenge and possibilities of federalism.[35] By definition, to seek to escape these polarities would be inherently self-defeating. To move deliberately toward centralism would subvert the diversity of the federation and undermine the leavening quality of political life that directly arises from the presence of strong regional communities; to seek refuge in the other extreme polarity would, in his view, necessarily be a regressive step. The preservation of balance in these dynamics became the declared centre of the Trudeau government's policy, especially during the nation-building period from 1980 onward, a theme elaborated upon in scores of speeches of dutiful federal ministers at the time. Perhaps the closing lines of a speech by Jim Fleming put it best:

> The nature of Canada's federalism implies a constant tension between the goals of the nation and the regions. It's a compromise between nation-building and province-building, between the claims of unity and diversity, two seemingly opposite aspects of truth.
>
> Judging by recent political utterances, too many political partisans believe what poet Carl Sandberg said about a paradox: "two concepts that stand on opposite hilltops and call each other liars." Yet I'm sure it must be apparent to the great bulk of Canadians that opposite concepts needn't be opposed. It's not a question of either-or, all or nothing, right or wrong. The more diversity we have, the more unity we need. And the more unity we have, the more diversity we can afford. The two concepts are opposite sides of the same coin, interdependent, like the provinces.[36]

It was in that accommodative spirit, particularly during and after the period of minority government from 1972-74, that Trudeau proposed to limit the intrusiveness of the federal spending power, to refrain from new federal excursions into provincial jurisdiction, including housing and urban policies, to decentralize the fiscal system and, by 1979, even to materially reduce federal constitutional subject matters in return for a deal over the Charter of Rights. The latter concessions included limits to the federal declaratory and spending powers as well as an acceptance of the primacy of provincial resource ownership over the federal trade and commerce power except in cases of "compelling national interest." These accommodations were balanced against the many national programs designed over the decade to raise the visibility and relevance of the federal order of government in the country, including regional economic development programs, expansive nationalist cultural measures, improved income security programs, inflation-fighting wage and price controls, foreign ownership legislation, the creation of a state oil company and so on. That kind of functionalist federal spirit remained difficult for the prime minister to maintain, however, especially as he increasingly confronted the Quebec separatists' attacks on Canadian federalism and the aggressive assertion of regionalism during the 1970s.

In fact, it was the federal government's view that these forces were reinforcing each other in a general ground swell of provincialism that reached its zenith in the Quebec referendum of May 1980: "If there is a bottom line to the referendum debate ... it surely is provincial self-interest. Premier Lévesque has, if nothing else, provided the catalyst the premiers needed to make their own pitch for more power, control, and independence from Ottawa. The winds of decentralization are blowing with particular vigor."[37] The collapse of separatist and regionalist motives was also increasingly seen in their perceived mutual conceptions of the federal state as the mere "agent of the provinces." At the constitutional conference in September 1980, Trudeau charged that more premiers were coming to share "the concept of Canada put forward by Mr. Lévesque;" regionalism had by then become in the eyes of the Trudeau government hardly more than a variant of Quebec separatism.

### Defensive Expansionism: Nationalist Glue in the Service of Federalism

We have tried governing through consensus, we have tried governing by being generous to the provinces ... and that was never enough. So we have changed that and we have said on the constitution, as we are doing on the economy, there is not much point short of shifting powers and resources to the provinces because there is no stop. The pendulum will keep swinging.... I thought we could build a strong Canada through co-operation. I have been disillusioned.[38]

This conclusion compelled the Trudeau government to consider unilateral approaches to the question of the federal balance and to seek wherever possible to expand and protect the ability of the national government to speak for all Canadians. The emergence of this country-centred model of federalism, in direct competition with its province-centred rival, has been extensively described by many analysts, especially Richard Simeon.[39] This campaign was on one level merely an extension of the government's anti-separatist propaganda war. At a minimum it was aimed at the constitutional entrenchment of bilingualism, namely, of the right of French Canadians to feel symbolically and officially a part of the whole country and to enjoy rights to government services, including minority language education, in all provinces in Canada. These rights, as well as others contained in a broad liberal charter, were the very least the federal Liberals could offer Quebecers in the way of "renewed federalism," of a different conception of dualism from sovereignty-association, of a different outlet for francophone pride and the new Quebec middle class.

But on a wider level, this new vigorous assertion of the importance of the centre in federalism, of membership in Canada as something larger than and superior to provincial or regional loyalties, carried over from the campaign into the Trudeau government's "new federalism." Again and again, Trudeau and his ministers insisted that when there was a conflict of interests or a conflict of loyalties, the national interest and the common good must prevail over the provincial or regional interest. This view was perhaps most succinctly stated by Trudeau thus: "The time has come to reassert that Canada is one country and can move with unity and purpose toward shared goals....When there is conflict the national will must prevail. Otherwise we are not a country."[40] Those who preach otherwise, he contended, are the "enemies within," those who sow discord by exploiting regional alienations, questioning loyalties, implanting suspicions and doubts about the fairness of Canada:

> That is the enemy within — when loyalties are no longer to the whole but there is a conflict in loyalties; when we seek protection of our wealth, our rights or our language not in the whole country but in a region or a province of that country. That is how we come to shut doors in each other's face, because we feel we will not get a fair share in every part of the country.[41]

When this pan-Canadian vision was translated into institutional terms, it led to a much more heightened role for the Parliament of Canada, not as one legislature among eleven, but as the senior order of government.[42] Only the Canadian Parliament could "speak for every Canadian," "express the national will and the national interest" and ensure that it prevails in a conflict of interest (not laws) with the provinces.[43] This Ottawa-centred construction of the Canadian state was also a necessary element of the defence for the program of federal unilateralism that was to follow over the constitution, energy policy, fiscal policy and so on.

This country-centred view also extended into the economic and social fields. The special federal responsibility to protect and defend an integrated national economy against both internal barriers and foreign threats became an important part of the Liberals' new federalism on constitutional matters as well as in policy terms.[44] In social policy, the country builders stressed the importance of protecting national standards of social services, especially in health and higher education, and of redistributing wealth via equalization payments and income-support programs between have and have-not provinces and regions.

There was even a new nationalist element injected into the foreign ownership problem in the Canadian economy, for example, in the proposals to tighten the Foreign Investment Review Agency (FIRA), to improve Canadian ownership levels in the economy, and to repatriate the energy sector of the economy. Ministers regularly included this element in their speeches in the early 1980s as one part of the new program of

Liberal nation-building. John Roberts gave an early expression to that vision:

> If we are to resist the forces of assimilation and integration into the North American continent, ... then all Canadians, including Quebecers, have an interest in preserving a strong federal government which has the capacity to protect that identity. To sap the federal economic power wouldn't lead to a strengthening of regional identities, but rather a weakening of our capacity to withstand the pressures for integration into the North American market....Ten separate provincial economies, or five regional ones, or even shattered into two economies — they would be in a situation of such disproportion that they would become mere appendages to the economy of the United States and our natural resources would be less likely to be exploited with Canadian interests first in mind.[45]

The same defence for the federal state came forward strongly in the Liberals' country-centred program after it won a majority government in February 1980. Jim Fleming again reminded Canadians that

> the primary job of the state in Canada, as Lord Durham pointed out, is not to guarantee safety, but to aid economic growth. This has always been the role of the national government in the country. It has always been the fulcrum of the economic process, the means by which we have managed to keep our country distinct and united while prospering through our proximity to the U.S. — as you know, a very delicate balancing act.[46]

The problem, Fleming continued, is that "now some provincial governments want to take over much of this job" within a "looser federation." The result has been the erection of many nontariff barriers within the Canadian economic market affecting the movement of goods, capital and labour and making "our economic union in some ways less of a free trade area than the common market of Europe." On the external front, the provinces had already moved into foreign policy agreements in the fields of education and culture and were well along in conducting international economic agreements, notably in natural resources. Resource companies, many of foreign origin, had aligned politically with the provinces over the previous three decades and had "less need for the federal government," thus "sapping federal bargaining power."[47] While technically Ottawa could have exercised its economic powers over many of these areas earlier in the name of the national interest, its hands were tied, Fleming argued, by the combined opposition of Quebec separatism, the provinces, the multinationals and the U.S. government. This was an extraordinary public confession from a Liberal minister.

> Until the energy crisis, the provinces had almost a free hand in exporting resources as they saw fit. Ottawa didn't want to stand — didn't even *appear* to want to stand — in the way of western development. It didn't want to weaken national unity while separatism was gaining ground in Quebec. Nor could it afford a confrontation with the combined power of the provinces, the multinationals, and the government of the United States. And power unused is power abdicated.[48]

Ironically, it was this "weakness of English Canadian nationalism vis-à-vis the United States that worried francophone nationalists and spurred the growth of separatism."[49] Hence, accommodation with these interests had not in the long run been an appropriate strategy for the national government, any more than had the earlier policy of concessions to the provincial governments. In the end, there was only a continuing erosion of the status of the federal order of government.

> Clearly, the federal government has lost some credibility. But if it can be blamed for Canada's problems, it's not for asserting too much control but too little. Not for too much confrontation but too much accommodation. Not for too much centralization but too much decentralization.
>
> The more the federal government tries to appease the provinces by the piecemeal surrender of its power, the less able it is to manage the economy ... to finance energy subsidies and dispel discontent by equalizing social services ... to ensure that the provinces work together and not at cross-purposes ... and to withstand the pressure of our American-controlled industry, our American-controlled unions, and foreign governments.
>
> Decentralization is a catch-22 situation. The more we try to ease discontent by giving more power to the provinces, the more we weaken the national government and the economy, thus heightening the discontent that creates more provincial demands for power.[50]

Out of this frank analysis came the new Liberal program of economic nation-building in the National Energy Program of 1980, in the promised strengthening of FIRA, and in a national industrial strategy that never got off the ground. Both the defensive character of these initiatives and the rationale they provided for the federal state should not be ignored. In retrospect, the Trudeau government's program of expansionism in 1980, particularly its attempt to wrest control and direction of the Canadian economy from both American interests and provincial or regional elites, would appear to be entirely in the Canadian tradition of what Hugh Aitken has called "defensive expansionism."[51] That tradition, beginning with Confederation itself, had found the federal state squarely involved in the "political integration of widely separated regional economies ... the provision of indispensable transport facilities" and the "containing of the expansionism of the stronger and more aggressive economy of the United States and of preserving a distinct political sovereignty over the territory north of the present international boundary."[52] It was to that tradition the Trudeau government returned to find a logic and modern program for what had been earlier described as Canada's emerging Third National Policy.[53]

In fact, Trudeau had already written much of this federal script when he declared, almost twenty years earlier, that such political and economic nationalism might, ironically, well have to be drawn upon by a federal state like Canada's to fight fissiparous tendencies inherent in another nationalist tradition that encouraged the "natural" formation of peoples' states based on a common language, race or sense of distinctive identity. Such a doctrine made little sense for most modern states without homogeneous or ethnically concentrated populations, but it was especially threatening to multilingual countries like Canada, where geography had conspired to reinforce this "natural" definition of statehood for the distinctive province of Quebec. As Trudeau put it:

> Very few nations — if any — could rely on a cohesiveness based entirely on "natural" identity, and so most of them were faced with a terrible paradox: the principle of national self-determination which had justified their birth could just as easily justify their death. Nationhood being little more than a state of mind, and every sociologically distinct group within the nation having a contingent right of secession, the will of the people was in constant danger of dividing up — unless it were transformed into a lasting consensus.[54]

Against that threat of continuous separation, "a new glue had to be invented which would bind the nation together on a durable basis" so that "no group within the nation [would] feel that its vital interests and particular characteristics could be better preserved by withdrawing from the nation than by remaining within." Since "a (modern) state needs to develop and preserve this consensus as its very life" and since it cannot "persuade continually by reason alone," it must reach out for the emotional support of nationalism to sustain itself. And "if the heavy paste of nationalism is relied upon to keep a unitary nation-state together, much more nationalism would appear to be required in the case of a federal nation-state." Wherever separatism has seriously taken hold in such a state, the deploying of countervailing political nationalism at the federal level will be necessary — an inclusive "living" nationalism with a broad policy base carrying in the end "a national image which has immensely more appeal than the regional ones."[55] As a determined federalist, Trudeau was not at all reluctant to employ nationalism in this defence.

Therefore, there is no warrant for casting Trudeau as an arch anti-nationalist or in conflating his well-known attacks on ethnic nationalism with the broader, often positive and indispensable role of nationalism in a liberal pluralistic state.[56] While Trudeau always argued that "in the last resort the mainspring of federalism cannot be emotion but must be reason," he also recognized, if somewhat reluctantly, that a federal state required a shoring up of citizens' loyalties through nationalist emotion and policy. His short sketch of the elements of such a strategy, written in 1964 before his move into federal politics, is a revealing picture of past and would-be future elements of Canadian nationalism in the service of federalism.

> One way of offsetting the appeal of separatism is by investing tre-mendous amounts of time, energy, and money in nationalism, *at the federal level.* A national image must be created that will have such an appeal as to make any image of a separatist group unattractive. Re-sources must be diverted into such things as national flags, anthems, education, arts councils, broadcasting corporations, film boards; the territory must be bound together by a network of railways, high-ways, airlines; the national culture and the national economy must be protected by taxes and tariffs; ownership of resources and indus-try by nationals must be made a matter of policy. In short, the whole of the citizenry must be made to feel that it is only within the frame-work of the federal state that their language, culture, institutions, sa-cred traditions, and standard of living can be protected from external attack and internal strife.[57]

### The Federal Line of Policy

It would be difficult to find anywhere a more comprehensive and com-pelling statement of the idea of defensive expansionism in the service of a federal state than in the above. Here not only is the classic idea of eco-nomic interventionism by a threatened and highly activist state recog-nized, but the wider state-supported practical and symbolic bonds of nationhood involving images and culture are drawn into the defensive net. Many of the elements of this defence of Canadian sovereignty against both external and internal threat were already in place at the time of Trudeau's writing — the continental-sized publicly owned transporta-tion systems, the publicly owned broadcasting system, the Canada Coun-cil and the National Film Board, the national flag and the tariff protections for Canadian industry. There were, however, few laws to protect and extend domestic ownership of the economy except in the fields of transportation and banking.

Partly as a consequence of this oversight and of the protectionist blindness of the country's original National Policy to ownership concerns, more and more of Canada's economy was becoming controlled and directed by foreign interests, most notably through direct investment by American multinationals. By the mid-1970s many analysts argued that this level of foreign investment reduced Canadian control over external trade, industrial policy, domestic research and development, employment and investment targets, monetary and fiscal policy, and the nation's balance of payments. In short, the scale of foreign ownership in the country appeared to be as serious a potential threat to the integrity of the Canadian state as the centrifugal forces of regionalism and Quebec separatism. In fact, in the opinion of most writers on Canadian federalism in the 1970s, these three constituted something of a "holy trinity," a three-pronged crisis to the continued viability of Canada.

As the following chapters will show, the line of policy the Trudeau government decided in 1980 to deploy "to rebalance the federation" attempted to tackle all three of these crises simultaneously. There would be a vigorous, and if necessary unilateral, settlement of the constitutional dispute with the provinces, a settlement that would entrench minority language rights for francophones and anglophones everywhere in Canada and fundamental human rights for all other citizens, without at the same time "giving away the store" to the provincial premiers. There would be new simultaneous demands for stronger federal powers over the economy. Both provincial supremacy over energy and the power of multinational oil companies would be directly challenged with a massive national energy program that, unlike earlier national policies, would take account of "ownership of resources and industry as a matter of policy." In the face of the increasing obsolescence of the old tariff-driven National Policy, plans would be laid for a mildly dirigiste industrial policy, with the issue of stronger domestic ownership and control of the economy once again a matter of national concern. National economic development under federal leadership would be restored.

Other chapters will trace the same strategy of rebalancing the federation through the fields of fiscal federalism and social policy. This program was nothing if not ambitious, and it indicated that if, as Trudeau had earlier said, the balance of power in the federation could be shifted by "the cunning of politicians," rarely would history appear to have offered as golden an opportunity to federal forces as after the defeat of the PQ in the May 20, 1980, Quebec referendum. It remained, however, a deeply ironic exercise, since the strategy of centralization was mounted, as then justice minister Jean Chrétien insisted, not to seek "a highly centralized state or a quasi-unitary state" but "to rebalance the federation."[58] That reflected accurately enough the theory and complex motivation for this program, but it could hardly change the fact that these were unusually centralizing policy initiatives.

As later chapters will show, there was some question about how a political program of centralism might be developed and sold in the context of the 1980s. The federal state's use of public interest groups and private capital in this exercise is a highly revealing and interesting part of this story of state-building. So too is the link many of these policies have to earlier historical periods of federal leadership, from which they often draw their inspiration. These parallels, toward the federalism of John A. Macdonald for some purposes, toward postwar patterns of federal dominance for others, are discussed. These illustrations are obviously not meant to suggest that the Liberal brand of federalism in the 1980s is simply a reversion or in any sense directly parallels the motives and practices of these regimes; they merely demonstrate the Trudeau government's selective incorporation and updating of some comparative patterns and elements from earlier periods.

The study on this line of federal policy will also question vigorously the Trudeau government's rather easy identification of the "national interest" with federal state-building vis-à-vis the National Energy Program and several other matters. Such a presumption underlay the government's use of nationalism in defence of the federal state, but that claim becomes increasingly strained as the details and elements of these policies are analyzed. Since the federal Liberals' program required a tilting of policy to support both federal state interests and those of its political allies, these did not invariably add up to a rationally defensible idea of the national interest.

This program of federal state-building ostensibly in the name of "rebalancing" the federation did not go without challenge in Ottawa, Washington and the provinces. These opposition forces responded to the initiatives with unusual vigour, often succeeding in checking or moderating the federal strategy at the time, while preparing a long-run counterattack for the next federal election in 1984. The story of this struggle and of the working out of these interests, often in a highly unpredictable national and international environment, will be taken up in each policy chapter, providing insight into the later rise to power of the Progressive Conservatives under Brian Mulroney. Some gauge of the Mulroney government's approach to these interests, and to the broad question of federalism in general, can be taken from the policy review of the Conservative government appearing in each chapter. That review will show that the Mulroney government's policy agenda was to some extent merely "reactive," composed and structured of interests injured by the Liberals' "new federalism." Yet there is an overall coherence in the Conservative program, even if the prospects for a continuation of federal-provincial harmony do not appear encouraging. In the conclusion, these and other elements of the Conservative government's policy program and approach to federalism will be extensively reviewed. At that point, there will be ample opportunity to reflect on the meaning of this current period in Canadian federalism and to speculate on the future balance and direction of the Canadian state.

# CHAPTER II

# Constitutional Politics

By 1980 the constitution was the most important arena for the playing out of all of the developing federal-provincial tensions and conflicts discussed in chapter 1. After more than a decade of intergovernmental discussions, the arrival of the Quebec referendum and its aftermath brought many of these issues to a head. At the centre lay the fight over Quebec independence, a political struggle that necessarily called into question the power and adequacy of Canadian state arrangements set against the dream of a new Quebec homeland. Here normal legal skirmishes were being entirely bypassed by reopening the debate about fundamentals — whether the people of Quebec would continue to live within the Canadian state at all and, if so, under what new promises and conditions. The PQ's idea of an independent French-speaking Quebec state, of a distinct people finally assuming control over its own destiny after years of colonial entanglements, was a powerful modern variant of nationalist ideology that challenged the logic and appeal of federalism for Quebecers. In that subsequent battle of images, of politicians' portraits of people living in different patterns of association, the constitution was a symbol of possible new beginnings, and constitutional politics a way of taking stock of one's collective experience and attempting to redefine it either through renewal or revolution.

The federal-separatist war, which began in earnest after the PQ's electoral victory in 1976, could not be prosecuted without drawing on different meanings of community and of the good life. For the the Parti Québécois, sovereignty-association, as the final extension of a long drive for increased Quebec legal powers since 1960, was advanced as a communal value of great importance. National self-realization through the achievement of an independent Quebec state was to be the fulfilment of every Quebecer's need, an essential precondition for a people's dignity, maturity and sense of itself. For the federal Liberals, the drive for a new Charter of Rights and Freedoms, containing language guarantees for francophones, was to compensate for the indignities the French had suffered during the first hundred years of association in Canada and was to provide the basis for a renewed sense of partnership with the English-speaking peoples in the country. It offered Quebecers the modern liberal promise of guaranteed individual rights and freedoms throughout Canada in place of what federalists alleged to be the narrow separatist "delusions of communal nationalism" behind Quebec's territorial picket fence.

But the constitution was a necessarily prominent element in a wider federal-provincial contest of wills. As a symbol of values and a statement on the future relations of peoples in different parts of the Canadian federation, the constitution gradually came to preoccupy even the anglophone leaders of the federation, especially in the West. They saw in the constitution an opportunity to right the wrongs of the past and to restructure a newer, more just and more equal federation. On the one hand, this objective was seen to be furthered by reforming federal institutions, principally the Senate and the Supreme Court, so that they could better reflect the interests of the less populated areas of the federation in federal policy. On the other, many premiers came to see the constitution as a potential playing field for the direct expansion of provincial power and for the consequent reduction of federal powers now considered inappropriate or outdated. [1]

Observers of the Canadian constitutional process were constantly exposed to the themes of disgruntled regionalism or alternatively to dualism and the new conflicting aspirations of Quebec leaders during the constitutional talks over the 1970s and 1980s. These ideas about the nature of the Canadian federation and the need to change it through constitutional bargaining had become ever more pressing issues on the public agenda, especially prior to the Quebec referendum. For each government there was a conscious link between its philosophy of federalism and its constitutional agenda, just as there was an understandable preoccupation with the power and interests of a particular government and its constitutional program. In most cases, that linkage was quite obvious, especially where the governments were discussing the transfer of more power in a particular area — for example, family law, natural resources, trade and commerce or the fisheries — from one level of government to another. But in some cases, the governmental stake in constitutional reform proposals was more obscure. The federally inspired Canadian Charter of Rights and Freedoms might be seen as a case in point. Presented disinterestedly by Ottawa as a "people's" item that would not advance the powers of the federal government, its role in the government's overall philosophy of federalism and political program was much less evident.[2]

The federal constitutional program in 1980, it will be argued, in its determination to rebalance the federation contained in substance and in procedure quite a number of centralizing or unifying features, only some of which were finally acted upon in the constitutional settlement two years later. Moreover, the procedures that were rebuffed and the program elements that were dropped were generally those reflecting federal paternalism and central Canadian dominance, assumptions that, while relevant to the John A. Macdonald era, were no longer appropriate to the Canadian federation of the late twentieth century. In that respect, the Trudeau government's attempted resurrection of certain features of the older Macdonald tradition, most notably the primacy and adequacy of the national Parliament in the expression of the Canadian national interest in constitutional and other matters, was not in the end a successful counterweight in the government's program of restoring the balance of power in the federation. Its exclusion suggests the increasingly untenable nature of this model of federalism for the country.

On the other hand, the centralizing features of the federal proposals that were adopted in the form of the Charter of Rights and Freedoms were partially successful as counterweights only because of the popular and somewhat deceptive liberal ideology that sustained them. Unlike the explicit arguments for federal majoritarianism and parliamentary supremacy, this charter ideology as propounded by the federal government obscured rather than exposed the link to the question of the federal order of state and its institutions, while it made at least for a time a successful case for a "people's-based" nation-building instrument. Moreover, by entrenching minority language rights in the charter, this strategy had the potential of defusing or at least deflecting the country's oldest permanent conflict, namely, the French and English feud, away from the old government-to-government political arena of federalism (and away from separate state solutions like those of the PQ) toward a new nationally unified "neutral" judicial forum where citizens could directly challenge and seek redress from governments for infringements of these rights. This shift toward defending matters of overriding national significance through a federal judiciary armed with a national charter, rather than a federal Parliament armed with rusty imperial legal tools and old-fashioned moral superiority, was nothing short of a masterstroke, since by this means a new and politically acceptable way was found to preserve the centre against centrifugal pulls on the balance.

This constitutional analysis will be carried forward into the first years of the Mulroney government to show that the meaning of the 1982 constitutional revolution has now been finally understood and accepted by the federal Conservative party. This must be read as an astonishing and deeply ironical achievement. The adoption and consolidation of the reform elements of the Liberals' constitutional program — bilingualism, the Charter of Rights and Freedoms, even aboriginal rights — by the federal Conservatives suggest that this part of the Liberals' legacy will endure despite the real difficulties and initially heavy odds against it. The federal Conservatives' record and constitutional program also indicate that the earlier quasi-imperial elements of the Liberals' constitutional federalism — its unilateralism, its exclusive presumption to represent the national interest in defence of everything from the economic union to offshore development — have been not only scotched, but to some extent actually reversed. It is a curious paradox that in their straightforward pursuit of economic policy, notably free trade, the Conservatives may well achieve objectives that eluded the Trudeau government with its targeted constitutional program.

## The Defeat of Centralist Federalism

The part of the federal Liberals' constitutional program in 1980 that attempted to resurrect an older and more direct, if paternalistic, defence for the federal state emerged logically and yet paradoxically from the government's program to save federalism as a real balance-of-power system. If the latter were to be preserved, if Confederation were not to swing under current pressures entirely in the direction of "ten autonomous states," then the case for the unique and superior position of the federal order of government had to be made, if not indeed overstated. That nationalist undertaking was exactly what the Trudeau government did in the context of threats to Canada's existence, which they believed were at least as grave as those that originally beset Confederation itself. The theory they mounted, tagged by some scholars as "federal majoritarianism," was about as bold a restatement of the centralist assumptions of the bygone Macdonald era as has ever been propounded by a federal government in the twentieth century.[3] Trudeau gave succinct expression to that theory in a blunt and ringing declaration in the House of Commons on April 15, 1980:

> We are the only group of men and women in this country who can speak for every Canadian. We are the only group, the only assembly in this country, which can speak for the whole nation, which can express the national will and the national interest.[4]

While in a subsequent aside Trudeau acknowledged that in our federal system "the national government is [not] the sole voice" nor "the national Parliament the sole instrument of the national interest in every area," he maintained that the national government does, however, enjoy the final "right," indeed "obligation," to "uphold the national interest" against provinces "even in areas of provincial jurisdiction" whenever these powers are being "exercised in a way which [is] contrary to the national interest." That, he declared, is the reason

we find in the Constitution of Canada such things as the declaratory power, the reservation and disallowance powers, the spending power and the right to make orders in matters of education as provided by section 93, subsections (3) and (4).

I am not saying that these rights cannot be limited or bargained away. As a matter of fact, our government beginning in 1968 and 1969, proposed ways of limiting the spending power. Our government, as recently as at the federal-provincial conference in February of 1979, proposed ways of limiting the declaratory power. But what I am saying is that when there is a conflict of interest, not of laws which will be judged by the courts, the citizens must be convinced that there is a national government which will speak for the national interest and will ensure that it does prevail.[5]

It was because of that insistence on the primacy of the national community and of the supremacy of the federal Parliament as the ultimate expression of that national will that Richard Simeon called Trudeau a latter-day Sir John A. Macdonald.[6] Trudeau's defence of parliamentary supremacy as the fount of this authority contrasted sharply with the premiers' demand that the national will lay ultimately in the collective wills of the provinces and the federal government as expressed perhaps through First Ministers' Conferences and subsequent legislative actions by both orders of government.[7] While Trudeau acknowledged that the latter view "could be the essence of a federal state," he insisted that "it *has not* been the essence of the Canadian federal state" and questioned whether it "could be the essence of a parliamentary federal state."[8]

Trudeau's defence of federal parliamentary pre-eminence based on past practice and the legal underpinnings of a colonial era was hardly a persuasive answer to the contemporary state of affairs of the Canadian federation, nor was it in keeping with Trudeau's rational acceptance of the Canadian state's evolution away from Macdonald's centralized federalism in his writings from the 1950s and 1960s. It appeared here in this bald form only because it formed a crucial part of the defence Ottawa would require if it were to move a single step in its unilateral program of rebalancing the federation. In that respect, the upshot of this argument was hardly academic, since upon it would rest the legitimacy of the Trudeau government's plans for unilateral action over the constitution, energy policy and many other matters.

Hence, once again, after decades of grudging acknowledgment of the powerful place of the provinces in the federation short of wartime conditions, the idea was advanced that in fundamental conflicts with the provinces only the federal Parliament could truly speak for Canada, that only the Canadian Parliament could exercise moral leadership in the defence of the Canadian economic union or tame the selfish regional and provincial interests then appearing to threaten the integrity of the country. This notion carried credence only in the context of the federal fight against Quebec separatism and its milder manifestations in the truculent provincialism of several other provinces. But these were precisely the conditions for the rebirth of many of the centralist assumptions which up to that time had been gradually discarded or suppressed as outmoded and incompatible with the evolving federation of the twentieth century. For although there had been periods of strong federal power during this century, such as the post-1945 period of federal pre-eminence activated by a functional social consensus around applied Keynesianism and the welfare state, they had not been simple reversions to the older nineteenth-century theory of centralized federalism.

This return in the 1980s to a quasi-imperial tradition rooted in the Macdonald legacy of Canadian federalism was clearest in the Liberal government's extraordinary decision to seek a fundamental change in the nature of the Canadian constitution without the consent of the provinces. While the government argued defensively that this move toward patriation was a decision taken reluctantly only after more than half a century of futile efforts to obtain the agreement of the provinces on an amending formula in the face of the "trap of unanimity," it also staked out exceedingly bold legal and political claims against the very idea of a constitutional convention respecting provincial consent for changes to the constitution and in favour of the unilateral right of the federal Parliament to break any constitutional logjam with the provinces by going with a request to Westminster on its own.[9]

As Richard Simeon has noted, the defensive argument was somewhat "specious," since Canada was not suffering from constitutional paralysis, the modern round of constitutional talks went back only to the mid-Sixties, and the opposition to federal unilateralism consisted of a good deal more than one or two "recalcitrant premiers." The federal government had decided to include not only patriation and its own amending formula in its request to Westminster, but also an important and massive new addition to the Canadian constitution in the form of a Canadian Charter of Rights and Freedoms. The latter could scarcely be justified by pointing to a long history of failed negotiations with the provinces, nor to an election result, nor even to a mandate for entrenching bilingual and other charter rights from its win in the 1980 Quebec referendum; the case rested instead on the final right of Parliament alone to discern and express the national interest on this matter and to ensure that its constitutional will prevailed.

The procedure used entailed repeating "for one last time" the same humble request for the Parliament at Westminster to enact these constitutional measures for Canada and to have the Queen sign them into law. According to Edward McWhinney, that was in itself a very conservative and somewhat comical colonial exercise, hardly a new and stirring start to independent nationhood.[10] Instead of seeking a mandate from the Canadian people over the heads of "right-wing, obstructionist premiers" and then using it (popular sovereignty) as the source for a forthright declaration of political independence, Trudeau's government had taken an "ultra-positivistic" approach.[11] Under these circumstances, the government decided to use its exclusive power of drafting and forwarding constitutional resolutions to the Westminster Parliament as a unilateral instrument for a veritable "constitutional coup d'état."[12] That raised a whole thicket of ironies.

> We see [argued Simeon] the federal government seeking to achieve in Britain what it cannot achieve at home. There is a fine irony here: it is the very characteristic of our present constitution which Ottawa feels is so unconscionable which permits it to do what it is doing. For the government cannot win sufficient consent in Canada according to *any* of the formulae for amendment which have previously been proposed; nor can it even win consent by the very amendment procedure contained in the Resolution. Instead, it must by-pass the domestic process and ask Britain if we can be a colony one more time, asking Britain to change it before sending it back. I find it very strange that an action specifically prohibited by Section 91 (1) of the B.N.A. Act should be made by going to the U.K.[13]

However, having decided to go to Britain with no popular mandate from the regions of Canada and with only Ontario and New Brunswick in tow, the Trudeau government simply wrapped its actions in the language of parliamentary sovereignty and dared the Westminster Parliament to defy it. This attempted use of outdated colonial machinery to impose constitutional terms upon an unwilling Canadian community had disturbing parallels with the old paternalistic and heavy-handed practices of the nineteenth century; citizens of the country could still remember, for example, how a combination of federal and imperial power had originally worked to keep Nova Scotia and New Brunswick in Confederation and to carve out a federal hegemonic position over the territories of the new West. While the popular Charter of Rights and Freedoms enjoyed considerable national support and provided some cover for the federal government's planned use of the imperial machinery, polls indicated that a majority of Canadians objected to this procedure. They recognized, as indeed the Supreme Court later did in its September 1981 landmark decision on the patriation case, that such an action violated a constitutional convention regarding provincial consent and that Canada had long since moved on from the days of the nineteenth century when mere requests from Ottawa for substantive changes were sufficient to amend the Canadian constitution.

This policy venture was only the most dramatic illustration of federal unilateralism.[14] As subsequent chapters will show, the federal inclination to bypass the provinces and to govern the country increasingly from the centre was evident in a wide variety of other initiatives. At bottom these changes in direction pointed to a strategy of radical conservatism — an attempt to rearrange the balance of power toward the centre by reaching back to an earlier pattern of Canadian federalism for guidance and direction. While that strategy had the advantage of building from within the country's political culture and its own strong historical roots, it depended on a conception of the federal state that had become unrealistic. Provinces were now powerful, intergovernmental interdependence was unavoidable, foreign ownership had done much to erode the national dream of Canadian economic independence, and federal institutions and policies were regarded as so flawed that they no longer commanded national respect for their regional sensitivity and fairness. While the Trudeau government doubtless recognized the force of these countertrends and was aware that it could not simply resurrect the past — indeed, it did not wish merely to supplant provincialism with centralism — it was determined to borrow selectively from earlier periods of federal pre-eminence in its balance-of-power campaign. Often, as with its battle over fiscal federalism and social policy, the government's implicit reversionist strategy related more to the period of Canadian federalism following the Second World War than to the Macdonald regime. But it was all compositional variations on old thematic material, all decidedly déjà vu.

In the light of its apparent obsolescence, what is perhaps remarkable is the extent to which this federal approach was endorsed by a wide segment of the Canadian political community, including the national leadership of the NDP and the Conservative government of Ontario. Many of the centralizing unilateral federal initiatives — including the NEP and the constitutional program — were supported in procedure as well as in substance, particularly by anglophone party leaders and intellectuals from central Canada on both the left and the right. Most noteworthy is the strong and consistent support of the Ontario Conservative government; it joined forces with Ottawa in its plan to contain both Quebec separatism and western regionalism. Not surprisingly, many federal constitutional items and other policies appeared to reflect the status quo interests of Ontario at the expense of those forces seeking to reshape the country in their own interests. Central Canadian dominance was as prominent a feature of this brand of federalism as was its old-fashioned paternalism.

The same blend of elements could be seen in the federal case for defending the Canadian economic union against the alleged evils of economic provincialism.[15] Whereas John A. Macdonald was able to employ the imperial tools of reservation and disallowance against provincial measures that threatened the integrity of the national economy, these were no longer available as practical instruments of policy in the 1980s. Although the removal of these legal powers, now regarded by convention as inappropriate and inoperative, was vigorously advanced by provincial leaders during the constitutional talks, the federal government did not cede them. By 1980, the government had decided that unless the provinces gave ground over the Charter of Rights, these overriding federal legal powers would be retained and, moreover, that the exercise of the federal discretionary powers permitting intrusions into provincial jurisdiction — the spending power, the declaratory power, the emergency power — would not be checked by any prior need for securing some measure of provincial consent. On the contrary, in the absence of a true give-and-take settlement with the provinces, these centre-defending instruments were justified as part of a legal balance devised by the founding fathers to ensure, in the face of conflict, the upholding of the national interest.[16]

Indeed, the government sought more effective means for controlling economic provincialism in proposed constitutional measures, the net effect of which would expand direct federal jurisdiction and subject provincial actions that interfered with the economic union to judicial review. These proposals were contained in the government's demands for "powers over the economy" during the 1980 constitutional talks. In an exaggerated and one-sided attack on provincial restrictions and interference in the Canadian economic union, the government argued that only the federal order of government should be entrusted to defend the general national interest against these selfish, parochial and self-defeating measures. This could best be done by expanding federal powers over trade and commerce, by strengthening section 121 of the constitution to prohibit provincial nontariff barriers and, with respect to restrictive labour practices, by entrenching mobility rights for all Canadians in the new Charter of Rights and Freedoms. While this case was supported by a fairly simplistic free market rationale in a federal background paper written by A.E. Safarian, these extreme claims of damage to the union were not supported by later careful economic analysis.[17]

More disturbing was the political assumption that only provincial economic measures were seriously undermining the market efficiency of the Canadian economy and that similar federal restrictions would not be subject to judicial review. When the federal government tabled its draft proposals for the Canadian economic union, it became quickly evident that Parliament was to be largely exempt from the restrictions on the economic powers of governments whenever it acts in accordance "with the principle of equalization and economic development" or whenever the matter is declared to be "of overriding national interest." As Thomas Courchene has noted:

> Ottawa's view is that it should be allowed to do the very things that it desires to prevent the provinces from doing. One is left with the very distinct impression that provincial actions in the economic sphere almost by definition lead to the fragmentation of the economic union, whereas similar federal initatives, again almost by definition, are in the national interest.[18]

Such a self-serving view was hardly likely to convince the provinces during the constitutional talks or to justify the inclusion of this item in the government's unilateral initiative of 1980.[19] This strand of moral superiority and self-sufficiency in federal thinking carried over into much of the Trudeau government's economic policies, as we shall see in chapter 4. In view of the severe economic disparities in Canada and of widespread suspicion that federal policies under the guise of free market economics had long protected the interests of central Canada at the expense of the peripheries, it did not escape the attention of the western and eastern provinces that this federal constitutional initiative would most benefit Ontario. Once again, federal paternalism with a distinct central Canadian orientation was a noticeable part of Trudeau's constitutional program.

These patterns were also evident in the amending formula the Trudeau Liberals attempted to push through Westminster without the consent of the provinces. One feature of that formula suggested the superior federal role in initiating constitutional change by popular referenda rather than by some measure of intergovernmental consent. Although this part of the federal proposal appeared to enshrine democratic principles by allowing the people themselves to be the authors of constitutional amendments, there really was no way in which the mechanism could be used except by and with the consent of the federal Parliament. No provision was made for direct popular initiation of constitutional referenda (perhaps the ultimate logical instrument for a people actually exercising democratic control over a state's constitution, but probably for that very reason not yet accepted by any federal state, including Switzerland); nor was there provision for broader public participation in debating and approving amendments through constitutional conventions activated by subnational governments, an option already available to Americans under article V of their constitution. The provinces were given no means by which a given number of them could refer to the people constitutional proposals the federal Parliament was not prepared to consider. The assumption was that provincial government opposition might not truly reflect the opinions of the people on constitutional matters and, therefore, could hold back desirable change in the federation, whereas presumably the reverse could not reasonably be expected to happen. The federal Parliament would by definition reflect the public interest.

The centralist implications of this element of the federal amending proposal have been nicely highlighted by Alan Cairns:

> [The referendum mechanism] was potentially an immensely significant symbolic and practical redefinition of the constituent parts of the Canadian federal polity. It located ultimate sovereignty in an alliance between the federal government and national referendum electorates conceivably responding to amending proposals mainly of interest to the federal government and answering questions worded by federal officials. It was an incredibly ambitious attempt to strengthen the central government, elevate the status of the people as constitutional actors, and reduce provincial governments to the status of initial, but no longer final spokesmen for provincial interests. The fundamental thrust of the proposal was nation-building, if need be at the expense of provincial governments whose powers would henceforth be held on sufferance. The federal government, of course, preserved its own veto and had the exclusive power to activate the process, so there was no way in which it could be a loser.[20]

The proposal, drafted under the assumption that provincial electorates would be "more pliable ... in passing judgments on proposals from Ottawa for constitutional amendments" or certainly "less tenacious" than provincial legislators and officials, was calculated to favour federal interests.[21] That fact was clear in the exclusive federal control over the initiation process. While such a provision already applied in the Australian constitution, experts there have recognized it as an inequality "which is a little hard on the States if they want to get through an amendment which benefits them at the central legislature's expense."[22] The Australian experience has also shown that the referendum device is an exceedingly tempting means for the central government to aggrandize its power by putting up self-serving amendment proposals; Australians have traditionally rejected most of these overtures, usually aimed at expanding central powers over economic matters, but they did accept a massive transfer of jurisdiction over much of social policy in a 1946 amendment.[23] These results may suggest linkages between the expansion of federal power and anticipated relatively clear-cut benefits to citizens for a successful referendum outcome, just as the same mix was needed for the successful political launching of the nation-building Canadian Charter of Rights and Freedoms. Whatever the future results of referenda might have been in Canada — Trudeau perhaps tongue-in-cheek had bet the provinces would win more often, though the matter is one of conjecture — there was little doubt that an avenue was being opened up for circumventing provincial governments and for establishing new direct relationships between Ottawa and the Canadian people on fundamental matters of state.

A considerable central Canadian bias was also reflected in the general Victoria formula the Trudeau government had been advancing for over a decade.[24] This formula granted Quebec and Ontario in perpetuity power to veto all future constitutional changes. Other provinces that acquired at least 25 per cent of the Canadian population might later be added to this preferred club. These provinces would in this respect enjoy equivalent status to that of the national Parliament — that is, exercise the power to strike down single-handedly any amendment proposal. While such a formula ensured that Quebec as the principal focus of francophone power would enjoy a veto, it also enshrined provincial inequality and central Canadian legal domination of the federation, since only the populated heartland of the country could expect to achieve these levels of concentration in the near future. Moreover, this formula carried no special protections of unanimity on any sensitive areas of constitutional concern to the other provinces.

This amendment formula essentially carried forward the older regional logic of Canadian Confederation, enshrined, for example, in Senate representation. There the whole of the East and West of the country — each region consisting of four separate provinces — was put on a par with the single dominant provinces of Ontario and Quebec. This arrangement had not helped the second chamber reflect and defend regional concerns against "Empire Canada," but it did demonstrate rather graphically the lopsided nature of the Canadian federal union.

By the time of the 1981 constitutional negotiations, the opportunity to impose these constitutional principles onto the country had passed. In the final compromises of November, the federal amending proposal was sacrificed in favour of the provinces' preferred formula, while the battle against economic provincialism had shifted to other policy forums. The new general amending formula — Parliament plus seven provinces representing 50 per cent or more of the Canadian population — entrenched formal provincial equality as well as the "noxious" feature of opting out, while the referendum idea was simply dropped.[25] Even the inclusion of mobility rights in the charter was compromised so that preferential labour restrictions could apply in essentially have-not provinces where the level of employment was below that of the Canadian average.

All of these setbacks suggested that it was unlikely the Trudeau governemnt could quite so frontally turn back the clock, roll back provincial power and check the evolution of the Canadian federal system away from its centralized beginnings under John A. Macdonald. However, the Trudeau government's program for national unity and the defence of federalism was better advanced by the entrenchment of the Charter of Rights and Freedoms. This was the more important, subtle and popular element of its constitutional planning. Unlike the ill-fated reassertion of centralized federalism, this injection of liberal nationalism into a country hardly beginning to wake up from the conservatism of its colonial past was likely to be a lasting contribution to Canadian political culture, to federalism and to national unity.

## The Entrenchment of Nationalist Liberalism

It is remarkable though scarcely surprising that the actual French Canadian nationalist underpinnings of Canada's new charter have not received much commentary or notice, at least in English-speaking Canada. The charter itself has drawn enormous interest but more for its broad humanitarian appeal to "guaranteeing" rights in general than for the actual complex reasons for its placement in the constitution. It is especially sad to read those who explain the arrival of a new entrenched charter by pointing to the rise of modern liberalism and human rights advocates in English-speaking Canada. Though there were voices for the enactment of such a measure by progressives after the Second World War and though these demands found weak expression in the 1960 Diefenbaker government's Bill of Rights, there never was a sufficient consensus in English-speaking Canada for entrenchment of a rights charter. That is the reason why the Diefenbaker government had to content itself with a simple federal enactment applicable to itself rather than a constitutional measure binding on all the governments in the country. That is why, despite federal advocacy for such a measure over fifteen years, even fundamental human rights in the 1982 charter (as well as legal and equality rights) are still subject to legislative overrides.

Therefore, the meaning of the rights charter and certainly the reasons for its constitutional triumph in the 1982 settlement cannot be found in a sudden and inexplicable burst of liberal individualism in Canada. In that respect, the careful and useful retrospective study of the growth in a "rights consciousness" in Canada done by Cynthia Williams and Alan Cairns for the Macdonald Commission is instructive.[26] The study shows the gradual and painstaking emergence over several decades of a notion of individual rights inherent in Canadian citizenship as a result of many factors, including international law and the increasingly popular recognition of group rights after the 1960s; yet the study also makes patently clear that, despite these promising tendencies in Canadian political culture, the whole entrenchment enterprise would never have been successful without the decisive push for a charter by the federal government in the late 1960s. It was the central government in response to the threats of Quebec nationalism and separatism that pushed nation-building through a rights charter, and while the earlier work of broader acculturation and lobbying by civil rights groups helped prepare a more fertile ideological ground in Canada than would otherwise have been the case, the way was always fraught with division and controversy. American liberalism in the form of a constitutionally entrenched charter of rights faced many ideological enemies both on the left and the right in English-speaking Canada, while in Quebec during the 1960s and the 1970s, it was anything but a mainstream ideological preoccupation. Hence, since the charter though popular was not the product of some coherent national ground swell of the citizenry, federal advocates of the idea had to struggle vigorously to find a place for it within the still-dominant traditions of federalism and parliamentary government.

Furthermore, it is by no means clear how an admittedly growing sensitivity and interest in the question of rights must necessarily culminate in an entrenched charter, nor that this particular means of securing and advancing rights would flow from a modern sophisticated rights advocate. What tilted a more rights-conscious Canada in that direction? Why the extraordinary stress on group or minority rights that necessarily find their footing in constitutional entrenchment? It may well be that answers to these and other related questions can be best achieved, not through a broader study of the diffuse sources of thinking and influence around rights, especially in English-speaking Canada, but by direct examination of the actual politics and longer indigenous traditions upon which a determined and powerful federal francophone elite built its case for entrenchment. Looking from within that longer Quebec tradition seems a preferable route to understanding the new national foundation for "rights" and ultimately for accounting for the final emergence of the charter.

That perspective should be even more evident when the nature of the new constitutional rights in question are closely examined and when due regard is paid to the strategic role of the charter in the fight of the francophone federalists and their separatist enemies in Quebec. A substantial block of the most important rights in the charter — those put outside the scope of legislative infringement by the use of a notwithstanding clause — concern minority rights for francophones in anglophone Canada and for anglophones in an officially unilingual Quebec.[27] The defence of these collective rights of peoples is in some respects at odds with a purely individual defence of liberal freedoms, but the charter clearly gives these collective rights pride of place. In addition, declarations concerning the two official languages of the country and the exclusive rights belonging to the founding peoples find themselves curiously ensconced in an otherwise universalistic charter of individual liberal rights.

No doubt these inclusions would puzzle classical liberal theorists, indeed anyone unfamiliar with Canada's history, for these sections hint at a nationalist liberalism concerned primarily with the politics of linguistic accommodation in the country but which has somehow managed to make a plausible case of grafting itself onto a classical liberal rights charter. It was essentially in this fashion that the Trudeau government managed to entrench the political vision of Quebec's Henri Bourassa in the Canadian constitution and thus to close off for a time the alternative separatist outlet for Quebec nationalism. If this is the real meaning and genesis of Canada's charter, it must be seen as one of the world's strangest routes to liberal constitutionalism.

It is true, as Cairns has noted, that the Canadian political identity had been undergoing rapid change in the postwar period with the decline in the British connection and the power of the new American empire, the rise of French Canadian nationalism in the country, the rapid ethnic diversity of the population through immigration and the consequently painful struggle to reshape the meaning of Canadian political nationality.[28] The politics of dualism, multiculturalism, national self-determination for aboriginal peoples, and new rights for women all suggest that the old constitutional definitions of community in Canada were inadequate. It is also true, as noted earlier, that the rise of provincialism was forcing the Canadian government to seek better ways to defend the common purpose and integrity of the Canadian state. But it was the struggle against separatism that most threatened the federal government and preoccupied its attention. Indeed, the charter was actually drafted in the late 1960s when Quebec separatism was the only serious provincialist threat confronting Ottawa. And it was to the charter that federal leaders returned in the aftermath of the 1980 referendum, offering it to the people of Quebec as a plausible foundation for renewal of the federation, indeed as an alternative outlet for the expression of francophone nationalism.

Without this enormous political force behind it, the charter would never have seen the light of day during this century. It was by virtue of its role as a federal state measure to contain separatism that it was moved to the top of the government's constitutional priorities. Only later did public rights groups come to participate in the business of strengthening the rights provisions in the charter and of campaigning for it essentially on terms set by the federal government.[29] It was entirely instructive that with respect to the vigorous defence of the general human rights contained within the charter, it was always the public that prodded the federal government to close loopholes and strengthen wording so that general charter rights would receive more than cosmetic protection; but on language provisions the government had already staked out its program in forthright legal terms.[30] Similarly, when tradeoffs had to be made by the governments, it was always the language provisions on which the federal government would not budge. That was because these provisions enshrined the French Canadian nationalist vision and tradition that for almost a century had competed with separatism for the loyalty of the Quebec people.

This French Canadian nationalist foundation for the charter finds its roots far back in the history and political culture of Quebec. As A.I. Silver's splendid book *The French-Canadian Idea of Confederation* indicates, the Quebec-based vision of a country with a bilingual dual nationality only gradually emerged during the first thirty years of the Dominion, particularly in response to threats to francophones in western Canada. But by the 1890s the theory "of the perfect equality of the two races before the law" and the idea of constitutional guarantees for minority language and school rights and of the constitution as the source of a new harmony between the English and French within their common homeland had taken root.[31] Already it was challenging the older idea of Quebec as the sole homeland for the French Canadian nation, the logical intellectual antecedent for modern Quebec separatism. The new theory found its most consistent and dedicated champion in Henri Bourassa, and although Prime Minister Wilfrid Laurier failed miserably to give expression to it, the vision returned again in the 1960s in the recommendations of the Commission on Bilingualism and Biculturalism and later in Trudeau's constitutional charter between the two founding peoples.

It has been difficult for anglophones not steeped in that tradition to see the Canadian charter principally as the outcome of a long nationalist debate in Quebec and not so much as a simple export from the United States. Undoubtedly the latter American tradition has now been grafted onto the essentials of a bilingual vision of the country and was a necessary part of selling this whole strategy of nationhood to the Canadian people, especially in English-speaking Canada, but the centre and origins of this new constitutional edifice are uniquely Canadian. The powerful idea of the equal "rights" of the French and English languages in the life of the nation, of the "rights" belonging to the francophone and anglophone minorities in the country as a result of the Confederation bargain, was an antecedent of the nationalist liberalism that persisted in Quebec and coexisted uncomfortably and ambiguously with the idea of homeland Quebec. From the very beginning, the bilingual vision never entirely dislodged the idea of the special role of Quebec as the francophone centre in the country, but it sought to reach out from that centre first in an early and vain attempt to defend francophones from attacks elsewhere in the country and, later, in the face of an imminent threat of withdrawal from Canada by Quebec francophones, to reshape once again the linguistic partnership in the rest of the country. Here the liberal virtues of racial and linguistic equality, tolerance for differences, and the rolling back of past injustices to minorities were part of the Bourassa tradition Trudeau adopted. The emphasis on collective minority rights arises again here in the form of language and schooling rights, together with a national vision of a just and equal French-English partnership throughout Canada.

Another puzzle is resolved if this view of the charter's meaning is recognized. Why should an essentially conservative people, with little inclination to distrust governments on principle, have decided to bypass governments and entrust so many of its rights, especially language rights, to judges and not to politicians? This was the very debate around which the issue of the charter was fought, and the continued presence of the notwithstanding clause indicates that the federal government was only partially successful in making that transfer. Yet the decision to cede that power to the courts unequivocally in the case of language rights reflects once again this nationalist school in Quebec, which had learned through bitter historical experience that entrusting minority rights either to the goodwill of provincial governments or to federal remedial action was unacceptable. The politics of the late nineteenth century had taught Bourassa's successors the liberal lesson that reliance on any other mechanism short of constitutional guarantees was inadequate for a defence of fundamental rights.

Bourassa had purported to see a justification and guarantee of these rights, partly in a philosophical defence of language as a "divine right" within the Catholic faith, but more fundamentally on broad historical and constitutional grounds.[32] His philosophical defence was important because it ended up embedding language rights in a social context — in the individual's relation to church and community — and not as absolute individual natural rights. That meant that such rights were scarcely marked off as natural rights that individuals held as against society, but were "comprehensible only in relation to a group of ... human beings with whom the language is shared and from which personal and cultural identity is achieved."[33] It was therefore possible to claim language rights for a distinctive indigenous people with their own thriving identity while denying, for example, individual rights to education in the traditional language for immigrants and scattered communities.

When Bourassa was driven to defend his theory that French language rights were somehow legally "guaranteed" throughout the Dominion of Canada, he could not point to any explicit liberal rights charter for support nor did he appear to have any such conception in mind as a possible remedy for protection of francophone minorities at that time. Instead, he pointed to the British North America (BNA) Act (now known as the Constitution Act 1867) itself — particularly to section 93, which empowered the federal government to protect denominational schools from provincial infringement, and to section 133, proclaiming the equality of the French and English languages in the national Parliament and the Quebec legislature — and to provisions of the Manitoba Act of 1870, which proclaimed English and French as the official languages of that province, as evidence that both languages were to "have the right to co-exist everywhere that the Canadian people leads a public life: at church, at school, in Parliament, in court, and in all public services."[34] Such a claim was, strictly speaking, hardly sustained by these examples, but Bourassa was more interested in building his defence upon what he called the "spirit" of Confederation as a gentlemen's "double contract" between the two races of Canada, English and French, as well as between the union of British colonies. It was that moral bargain and not the legal niceties of the BNA Act that deserved to be respected if the Canadian experiment at union was to survive.

This constitutional defence was supported by appeals to history and to a sense of fair play from the majority anglophone populations in the other provinces. Had not French Canadians stood with their English-speaking neighbours in opposition to the Americans in the eighteenth and nineteenth centuries? Had they not steadfastly worked alongside the English in the building of the country they both now shared? From these common undertakings it appeared to Bourassa a matter of simple political justice to recognize "the duality of races, the duality of languages, guaranteed by the equality of rights."

It was only after the uselessness of these moral appeals had been amply demonstrated by political events, and after the manifest bankruptcy of the legal protections thought to be contained within the BNA Act, that ideological successors to Bourassa in Quebec, especially in the person of Pierre Elliott Trudeau, turned to an entrenched rights charter as a new vehicle for protection of these rights. But the earlier pan-Canadian liberal argument built around language rights was an indispensable antecedent to this development. Not only was Bourassa's view a logical foundation for the idea of a legally enforceable contract or "charter" providing equal rights for the two founding peoples, his was also an accurate and prophetic warning of the dangers that would be done to national unity by his contemporaries' expunging the rights of francophone minorities in the Canadian Northwest, Ontario and elsewhere. It required only the later rise of separatism in Quebec to revive his vision of Canada as a homeland for both French and English and to prepare the way for its enshrinement in an otherwise broad and universal charter.

The merger is not accomplished without producing a bundle of

>nies. The notion of a country putting in place a liberal charter
promises permitting legislative overrides for what are
described as fundamental freedoms (speech, conscience, assembly and
other "natural rights"), while denying such overrides for the "hybrid"
rights of language, speaks powerfully to the central purpose of the
charter as it was defined and defended by its chief constitutional
"author" and "advocate," the federal government of Canada under Justice Minister and, later, Prime Minister Trudeau. Moreover, the frequently advanced Liberal argument that the charter was essentially the nation's
answer to francophones who had voted against sovereignty-association
in the 1980 referendum was plausible only on a reading of the charter as
an expression of the new partnership between the French and English.
The fact that the federal government recognized that language rights
were hybrids — that is, as belonging not to individuals as permanent natural rights but to individuals strictly by virtue of their membership in
realistic minority communities — was clear in a number of revealing sections of the Charter of Rights and Freedoms.

First, rights to educational instruction in either of the country's official
languages under section 23 do not extend equally and by
natural right to all citizens of Canada. There is no freedom of choice for
the language of instruction, least of all for members of the majority linguistic communities. Instead, only individuals who are members of
minorities are granted these rights. Moreover, these rights continue only
so long as the social conditions permit the continued vitality of these minority communities. Subsection 3a permits the enjoyment of these rights
only "where numbers warrant" and withdraws them whenever the social
framework that had given them meaning disappears. In an even more
telling homage to Bourassa, section 59 does not extend to immigrants
rights to minority language education in the mother tongue of English in
Quebec unless that province later decides to extend such rights; on the
contrary, language rights at least in Quebec are to be granted only to
members of the indigenous minority communities, in striking contrast to
the universal guarantees of fundamental, legal and equality rights given
to "everyone" under the charter.

These exceptions were made in deference to the government of Quebec, which had refused its assent to the constitutional settlement and refused to expose the majority community to what it regarded as a potential threat of assimilation from immigration. This gesture demonstrates
how committed the charter founders were to protecting the collective
right of communities against undue claims for purely individual rights.
The same commitment can be read into the founders' acceptance of a
notwithstanding clause in the charter, a provision that would permit legislatures to override certain basic charter rights, presumably in the name
of the "collective good." That would turn out to be a highly

debatable compromise, particularly in the light of the Saskatchewan government's relatively breezy use of section 33 to exempt its public sector back-to-work legislation in 1986. All of these curious compromising features in Canada's Charter of Rights and Freedoms suggest, at least at the level of elites, the uneasy and half-hearted marriage of constitutional liberalism to the country's traditional political institutions and practices.

However, on the question of language rights for established minorities in Canada, uneasy or not, the charter meant a fundamental change in the nature of their institutional protection, and with it a change in the nature of Canadian federalism. If it is remembered that it was the old British imperial idea of the crown as the final guarantor and protector of minorities that had actually been built into the Confederation agreement and provided the rationale for the federal power of remedial action under section 93 and partially for disallowance and reservation of provincial legislation, it is apparent that the adoption of constitutional liberalism and judicial guardianship arose from the direct failure of this imperial theory. Even by the 1890s — at the level of politics — language, schools and religious questions were clearly recognized as too explosive for any notion of political guardianship to work; at the level of federalism, the imperialist theory was seen even then as increasingly out of whack with the evolution of the Canadian federation away from its initially centralized roots. For all of these reasons, the rise of a Quebec-based theory of the country, with a new dual nationality entrenched in the constitution, was the most important and powerful domestic anteced-ent for Canada's new liberal charter.

It was the Trudeau government, first through the Official Languages Act and later through constitutional entrenchment, that carried forward this new conception of Confederation into law. In one stroke it chal-lenged the sufficiency of parliamentary government for the defence of rights and relegated to the dustbin the clumsy federal government paternalism that was expected to compensate for provincial attacks on minority rights.[35] These actions did not conform very comfortably with much of the centralist federal theory on which the federal government was otherwise acting in the 1980s. The doctrine of federal majoritarianism, with its vigorous and relatively unqualified defence of the adequacy of the federal Parliament in matters of the national interest, hardly suited the rhetorical requirements of a charter advocate. Again and again Prime Minister Trudeau was forced to draw out the limitations of parliamentary institutions in the defence of the people's rights, while simultaneously advancing a forceful case for Parliament to speak and if necessary act alone on some of the most vital concerns of the nation, in-cluding unilateral patriation of the constitution.

Yet, these contradictory tensions aside, rights and national unity are still defended through central institutions. Francophone rights would not be shielded by an independent Quebec homeland, but by constitutional strengthening and extension. For the interpretation of these and other rights, as well as the application of social policy that would flow from this exercise, it was the centrally appointed members of the Supreme Court who would declare and enforce common values in the federation. It was assumed that the court, shielded by public acceptance of judicial neutrality and objectivity, could act as a real guardian of minorities against indifferent or unruly provincial or national publics and governments. This would be a new and more visible national institution with a mandate to protect the spirit of the linguistic accommodation in the constitution and, through that exercise, to convince minorities, especially francophones, that Canada could be a tolerant homeland for both founding peoples.

Although the Trudeau government had also sought to enshrine these values in a stirring new preamble to the constitution, this intention was left behind as part of the unfinished negotiating agenda from 1980. But the essentials of this part of the Quebec nationalist program were entrenched in the new constitutional rights charter. Meanwhile, in the wake of this settlement, of social and economic change in the province and of a severe worldwide recession, the forces of separatism began to weaken dramatically. In this way, it appeared that at least for a time the tradition of Henri Bourassa was overcoming that of Lionel Groulx and his separatist ideological descendants.

### Broader Centralizing Features of the Charter

The appropriation of a rights charter to defeat Quebec separatism and advance a different expression of francophone nationalism was obviously not without value in the Trudeau government's wider campaign against the excesses of provincialism. Despite the federal government's first insistence that a charter would not subtract power from legislatures at all, or if it did so, the subtraction would apply equally to federal and provincial levels of government, the provinces were always aware that the charter represented a much more serious threat. They fully recognized what later commentators have now acknowledged: on the level of symbolism, the charter was a potentially unifying force that must work against the logic of distinct provincial communities with their own rights, values and interests; on the level of policy, judicial review would promote centralization. Nor was Ottawa's relatively artificial exclusion of the judicial branch from the central insti-tutions of the federal order of government convincing.

Some scholars have made much of the symbolic role of an inspiring charter of rights for national pride, cohesion and self-consciousness. This assumption has sustained both outspoken critics and cautious defenders of the rights charter. Critics such as Edward McWhinney have charged that the federal government undermined the charter's symbolic value, in process, by failing to secure popular ratification of it in a referendum and, in product, by inferior and legalistic rhetoric. He claims, for example, that the Canadian closed-door negotiating route to the charter and its "heavy, wooden" style, "its technical lawyer's language" with "weasel-word exceptions" have prevented "the Canadian charter from achieving the inspiration and grandeur of the American or French charters."[36] On the other hand, there is a kind of charter mythology developing in the scholarly community, especially in the writings of Alan Cairns, which was carried forward into the Macdonald Commission. This school holds that a psychic and elemental rearrangment of constitutional norms has taken place in Canada as a result of the charter, a new collective sense of ourselves as a rights-bearing people. In effect, these advocates argue that there may well have been more "romance and poetry" as a result of the whole exercise than McWhinney imagined.[37]

Cairns speculates that the "long-run impact of this transformation of the *feeling side* of citizenship is potentially considerable. The language of rights is a Canadian language, not a provincial language. If the Charter takes root over time, the psyche of the citizenry will be progressively Canadianized."[38] The same idea was taken up later in studies for the Macdonald Commission, although with less colourful language and a more cautious prognosis. Still, the notion of a new collective Canadian sense of citizenship, presumably stimulated by the entrenchment of the charter as one pillar in the country's constitutional "triumvirate — parliamentary government, federalism and the Charter of Rights and Freedoms" — remained an abiding theme.[39]

It may well be that these arguments place too much weight on constitutionalism. McWhinney can easily be accused of confusing the importance of the language of the French and American charters with the momentous events undoubtedly associated with these documents. His complaint against the lack of poetry and excessive legal rhetoric in the Canadian constitution as compared with the American has been strongly challenged by Peter Russell, who has expressed serious doubts about building national unity merely through constitutional grandiloquence.[40]

Russell suggests that the precision of modern legal draftsmanship and the avoidance of high-flown poetic language in the Canadian and other modern charters may simply reflect the greater sophistication of peoples who since the eighteenth century have learned from bitter experience the limits and pitfalls of high-sounding universal declarations. This same modern sophistication may also reduce or challenge much of the puffery of the charter advocates. They have read back in a deductive rationalist fashion from a constitutional document and a highly uncertain process of its interpretation and application a psychic ground swell of support for the Canadian polity. Yet this is surely a premature and uncertain conclusion. Although constitutions can serve as powerful symbols, too little is known about how "the emotional chemistry of laws as political symbols operates, in precisely what kind of circumstances a particular set of symbols (for instance, a constitutional charter of rights) will have a particular effect (for instance, strengthening national unity)."[41] Without a better grip on these relationships and a better sense of exactly how the charter will be applied and interpreted by the Supreme Court in Canada, we run the risk that the symbol might turn out to be more a source of division or cynicism than of celebration.

The rationalist leap of faith in the unifying power of the charter is symptomatic of a widespread popular fallacy about the stabilizing capacities of constitutions. Too often constitutions are seen as the rational, unified expression of a people rather than the products of an accidental history often seized upon in politically hazardous times. The ritualistic exercise of declaring and entrenching fundamental values in a constitution is often mistaken for an historical shortcut, an easy way to leap over the existential difficulties of actually securing or living out these principles in practice. The American experience (and the French) suggests the flaws in these romantic notions: neither the American nor the French constitutional declarations of rights were initially the coherent expressions of a unified people, nor did they later serve to protect their countries from threats to national unity, including civil war.

The charter may ultimately serve Canadian national unity, but that will depend on how well or poorly these constitutional principles "take," on their link to the political culture and future political conditions of the Canadian people, as well as on the exigencies of judicial review. It is far from clear that the entrenchment of liberal ideology will effectively crystallize the country in this normative mould. Neither the displacement of conservatism and socialism nor that of other sources of political doctrine more sympathetic to regionalism or parliamentary government should be immediately anticipated. Even democratic theory itself can be set against charter ideology and make different claims on the loyalties of Canadian citizens.[42] As Charles Taylor's thoughtful essay indicates, it may well be that the entrenchment of a rights approach through judicial rather than political machinery may work against Canadians' continuing need to define themselves as a people through political action — in short, that "citizen dignity is closer to a participatory model than a rights model."[43]

The fact that the notwithstanding clause remains, that regional views are entrenched in the amending formula and that the regular political institutions of Canadian government are left untouched is testament to the continuing power of these traditions and to the incomplete nature of the liberal constitutional revolution attempted by the Trudeau government. It is therefore premature to speculate on the triumph of liberalism or the incipient rearrangement of psychic constitutional norms flowing from the 1982 settlement.[44]

Popular identification with the charter and with the notion of Canadians as a rights-bearing people will depend strongly on the performance of the Supreme Court as the agency responsible for the charter's interpretation and application. How does its record so far live up to expectations? After only a few years of charter litigation, those who had doubted that the Supreme Court would take a strong activist position have clearly been proven wrong: the court has taken up its new constitutional responsibility with unaccustomed vigour. In the first thirteen charter cases decided by the end of 1985, it rejected its earlier timid approach to the defence of rights under the statutory Canadian Bill of Rights and staked out an aggressive role for itself. In adopting an expansive rather than narrower legalistic approach to the charter, the court struck down portions of six statutes, granted wins to individual litigants in eight of the thirteen cases and even overruled three of its earlier decisions taken under the Canadian Bill of Rights. Most of the cases have concerned criminal law enforcement, where failures to observe procedural rights and safeguards (such as the right to be informed of the right to counsel upon arrest or detention, to be free from unreasonable search or seizure, or to avoid self-incrimination) have led to exclusions of evidence, dropped charges and acquittals, and/or the striking down of offending statutory sections. These results have increasingly shifted Canadian criminal law practice away from a "crime control" model where the emphasis is on effective law enforcement, toward the American model of "due process," which tilts toward the rights of the accused.[45]

These are likely to be highly valued decisions from the citizens' standpoint, but the matters become more contentious as cases shift onto broader social and political grounds. Not many of these have reached the Supreme Court, except for *Operation Dismantle*, the unsuccessful challenge to the cruise missile testing program as a violation of the rights to life and security of person under section 7. Lower court decisions on such matters as film censorship or Sunday-closing laws have been liberal in striking down unduly restrictive measures. However, on abortion challenges raised by both pro-life groups and their opponents, the courts have ducked controversy by declining to extend charter guarantees of life to unborn persons or of "liberty and security of person" to women claiming a right to abortion. Consequently, both camps are unhappy, but at least the courts have so far evaded a direct political storm by taking sides.

On substantive economic and political questions, the right-wing National Citizens' Coalition has funded and won two important cases, one in the Alberta Court of Queen's Bench striking down federal limitations on private political campaigning outside the intended limits of the Election Expenses Act, and another in the Ontario Court of Appeal removing the right of unions to use monies collected from any member for broad political purposes not approved by that member. The latter result, if confirmed by the Supreme Court, might well cripple the power of labour unions to protect the interests of their members in the broader political arena, while at the same time leaving business interests relatively free to carry on their usual lobbying and political work. These results indicated the influence well-heeled special interest groups could exercise over questions of broad public policy through charter litigation, and they were scarcely regarded by all Canadians as neutral or fair. In these kinds of cases the courts inevitably make enemies for themselves and for the charter. Controversial subjects like abortion, censorship, school prayers, compulsory retirement, labour rights, equality rights and affirmative action, all these, tackled in a zero-sum fashion, are likely to leave the courts politically in difficult if not no-win situations. While these issues may not endear the courts or the charter to large numbers of disgruntled electors, to the extent that these issues divert attention from the old regional and territorial divisions of Canadian politics, they may have a net positive affect on national unity.

Some of the issues concerning rights may turn out to be regionally sensitive, however, so that adopting a position may bring the courts into collision with governments and strong public opinion in particular parts of the country. It is easy to see how that could take place where the Supreme Court is required to protect linguistic minorities or the program of bilingualism in regions where these principles are not widely respected. Experience in the United States suggests that national policy-making by the court has often brought it into direct collision with state or regional interests — witness the long struggle with racial segregation directives against the State of Alabama and the like. In these encounters, judicial review can set off another round of states-rights rhetoric, this time against the "imperialism" of the federal judiciary. Already in the case of the *Quebec Association of Protestant School Boards et al.* v. *A.G. Quebec* (1982), sections of Bill 101 restricting access to English-language schools have been struck down by the Supreme Court as a violation of section 23 of the charter, a decision bitterly denounced by the Quebec government. In short, judicial review under the new Canadian charter may on some issues bring us back to the old territorial politics of federalism, although in a new guise.

This achievement by a federal institution of the power to supervise and strike down provincial laws and regulations, even to direct the provinces in policies that may be required to meet charter standards, appears remarkable. It stands in marked contrast to the provinces' outright rejection of federal majoritarianism and of the ambitious plan to expand the direct constitutional powers of the federal government. On those matters the provinces simply refused to accept this belated reassertion of the Macdonald tradition, even though bolstered by a plausible "people's" rhetoric. With the charter, however, the increased scope of federal power over the Canadian state was granted to a more "neutral" federal agency in return for the right to override its directives on certain rights in the charter for renewable periods of up to five years. Whether the notwith-standing clause will prove to be a serious miscalculation severely limiting charter rights remains debatable, but there can be little doubt that over the long run the establishment of central authority over the expansive field of rights has been secured.[46]

The centralization objective of the federal Liberals was considerably advanced in this form, although rejected in its outright government-to-government relationship. Although the Supreme Court is not simply an arm of the federal government and often rules against it in constitutional cases, especially in recent years, the court will now have a national mandate to assume in the new Charter of Rights and Freedoms.[47] This responsibility can only be discharged by declaring and defending the meaning of these national principles against all barriers and restrictions. That will convert the Supreme Court into "a kind of national Senate reviewing the reasonableness of provincial laws and policies."[48] This federally enforced judicial power will probably have a centralizing effect on the federation, project Ottawa much more forcefully into decisions concerning fundamental values, hitherto mostly the prerogative of provincial governments, and consequently extend and make more obvious the political and policymaking role of the courts.

Hence, the impact of the charter upon public opinion, and especially any positive contributions it might make to national unity, will depend heavily upon the exigencies of judicial review. That process has the potential to divide, to inflame, to anger, to disappoint Canadian citizens — conservatives, socialists, regionalists, Quebecers, even liberals — as well as to encourage them in the appreciation of their new national legacy of individual rights. Sometimes the conflicts will arise between minorities over civil rights issues, which are evenly spread across the country, sometimes between powerful interests and popular state laws and regulations, and sometimes between the federal enforcement of entrenched national principles and united blocs of regional resistance. These are a few of the possible alignments in constitutional court cases, and none of them suggest that the charter will always serve as an effective integrating force for nationhood.

Only the first class of conflicts may assist national unity — primarily by way of deflection. The skilful use of the charter by wealthy minorities to fight social legislation passed in duly elected legislatures is not likely to win over charter converts, particularly among those with a democratic cast of mind. Nor are politically inspired assaults on the social power of the working classes likely to prove an ideal consensual road to national unity. The National Citizens' Coalition's attempt to use the charter to reduce the political power of unions is just one example of how useful an instrument the charter may become to militant minorities with the financial means to go to court. Those without adequate financial resources to take the legal route to defend their interests will either find themselves literally outside the new policy forum or forced to plead for resources from the state. In September 1985 the federal government allocated $9 million over a five-year period to fund litigation under the equality rights, language rights and multiculturalism provisions of the charter, a fund to be administered by the Canadian Council on Social Development, but neither this fund nor the provision of legal aid really equalizes access to this important system of policymaking. As feminists' groups have rapidly learned from their own impressive activity in this area, all interest groups will have to use what political clout and financial resources they can muster to try to turn the charter and the legal system to their own advantage.

The heart of the charter, which the court must defend — the ideal of bilingualism and minority language rights — is just one Quebec dream of Confederation. Only recently enacted with lukewarm support from central Canada, it is especially vulnerable to attack from regions with little appreciation or regard for the French fact. The Manitoba backlash against bilingualism is perhaps an ugly spectre of things to come. This fight over the national integration of an essentially central Canadian vision of the country can easily lead to fierce legal skirmishes, with the Supreme Court exposed in some regions as a one-sided villain. These may be played out in relatively mean-spirited battles over whether the numbers of francophones in English-speaking Canada "warrant" the provision of French-language educational instruction. Already scholars are noting that future "acrimony will be most intense if shrinking numbers [of francophones in English-speaking Canada] induce future provincial governments to withdraw educational rights previously respected."[49] Even Quebec is not wholly won over to this conception of dualism and may revert to a barricade-like defence of its collective community against the future edicts of the Supreme Court.

All of this suggests that conflict will probably be a necessary part of the new program of judicial power and centralization introduced by the charter. Such conflict will likely predominate at least in the short term over the gradual process of national acculturation to the charter. And given the relative freedom of the Supreme Court to interpret the charter as it wishes, its relatively restricted sexual and class membership, and its often dubious qualifications for making policy through constitutional interpretation, the potential for citizen doubts about the wisdom of this direction of Canadian federalism is quite large. This will be especially so if the effect of the charter is, ironically, to restrict freedoms by limiting the powers of the state to block social threats to rights or by enhancing the power of well-financed elites to elude their social responsibilities. These are the classic dangers of a constitutional charter in liberal democracies, and they have always been present in American constitutional practice.

It seems wiser not to assume that the direction of Canadian judicial review will necessarily be toward a popular nation-building defence of citizen rights. Nor is it reasonable to assume that the charter will be held up as a kind of holy grail capturing the deepest loyalties of Canadians. With Canada's diversity and ideological complexity, that is an unrealistic expectation. What can be said with some assurance is that a new national institution with a centralist mandate has been created as part of the 1982 constitutional settlement and that this represents the only credible assertion of federal power tolerable to strong modern provincial governments exercising some lingering legislative overrides over it — hence, the federalist drift away from the political thinking of the Macdonald legacy and toward newer ways of preserving the centre. This shift in the political theory of federalism is already evident in the Mulroney program of constitutional federalism.

### The Conservatives and the Selective Consolidation of Liberal Constitutionalism

The arrival of the Mulroney government in September 1984 tended to reinforce the constitutional state of affairs already apparent in the latter Trudeau years. The new government recognized that the straightforward Liberal offensive in pursuit of a reinvigorated federal state had foundered on the rocks of provincial opposition, of resistance from the American multinationals and their government in Washington, and of massive economic recession. In criticizing that centralizing style of federalism in the election and especially in linking it to the severity of the recession in Canada, Mulroney exploited the opportunities offered by the failure of this Liberal strategy, promising a new climate of federal-provincial harmony. In fact, that federalism was an integral part of Mulroney's economic program of recovery in Canada.

On the one hand, this federalism took the form of a deliberate avoidance of constitutional politics, by now identified with all of the divisions and bitterness over the past decade or more. Attention was directed instead at economic renewal and at improving the functional relationships with the provinces. Thus, apart from a required constitutional conference on aboriginal rights in February 1985 and the initially unhurried task of bringing Quebec into the 1982 settlement, the government did not devote its energies in this direction. There was only one exception to this rule and that was the government's ill-tempered and hastily prepared resolution to restrict the powers of the Senate and thus put an end to what it regarded as Liberal obstructionism.[50] While the government had hoped for swift and effective action with the cooperation of the provinces in return for a promise to consider Senate reform within two years, that measure stalled primarily because of Quebec's blanket refusal to partici- pate in any resolutions as a continuing protest against the imposition of the new constitution and because of the arrival of a minority Liberal gov- ernment in Ontario. Without these provinces' support, there was not much likelihood of the resolution proceeding.

There was a provision in the new offshore agreement with Newfound- land to entrench the principles of the Atlantic Accord in the constitution provided the required number of provinces could agree (see chapter 3). That promise indicated a healthy confidence in the new government's style of cooperative federalism, but there did not appear to be any reason to expect speedy action. Still, the agreement conceded virtually all of the ground the Trudeau government had defended for over five years, and the constitutional promise was itself a significant development in Cana- dian federalism.[51]

As government leaders themselves recognized, the Newfoundland agreement and the Western Accord shortly afterward marked the formal end of federal state-building efforts at the expense of the provinces at least for the 1980s. There was no longer a strong federal push for the constitutional restriction of economic provincialism, although many pro- vincial nontariff barriers would be immediate targets of any free trade agreement Canada might sign with the United States. Since that kind of agreement was almost universally welcomed by the provincial govern- ments, perhaps in a blissfully unaware state of mind, it appeared that many of the federal Liberal objectives aimed at curtailing provincial re- straints on the economic union might be achieved by international nego- tiation rather than by an internal constitutional process. Thus, only the promise of access to the American market might persuade the provinces to free up their own economies. Such a posture would constitute about as complete a reversal of the logic of Macdonald's National Policy as could be imagined.

If the Conservatives' policy indicates retreat from the direct centraliz- ing measures of the Trudeau constitutional program, it also shows a re- markable accommodation to their federal rights strategy. Mulroney carried forward the same campaign for the entrenchment of aboriginal self-government in the constitution that had preoccupied Trudeau. Moreover, he encountered the same stubborn resistance to that policy, most notably from Alberta and British Columbia. With respect to the broader question of the Charter of Rights and Freedoms, the govern-

ment appeared to accommodate itself quite readily to the politics of constitutional liberalism, including continuing the practice of providing public money to rights groups for legal actions under the charter. There was
hardly a hint of the old Conservative anti-charter arguments about the
sanctity of parliamentary government, except peripherally vis-à-vis the
court fight against the auditor-general's right of access to cabinet documents. This was by any measure a remarkable and swift consolidation of
the successful parts of the Liberal constitutional legacy.

But the most dramatic and striking change in Conservative policy was
that party's unequivocal acceptance of the Liberal program of bilingualism under the direction of its new leader from Quebec, Brian Mulroney.
He staked out Trudeau's fight for the rights of linguistic minorities as his
own, fought off and faced down direct challenges to it by members of his
own party in Manitoba, and in the process made himself a much more
credible champion of francophone rights than Trudeau's Liberal successor, Prime Minister John Turner. During the 1984 summer election campaign, Turner fumbled badly, first by tossing responsibility for the issue
of minority rights back to the provinces and later by uttering equivocat-
ing statements about Quebec's Bill 101. He thus put himself on the
wrong side of the fence on the Liberals' most important constitutional
program, and the consequent loss of Liberal support in Quebec had
much to do with his massive election defeat on September 4, 1984.
Meanwhile, Mulroney had taken on the Trudeau heritage, grafted this
Quebec-based conception of Confederation onto his western-dominated
party, and sought to mollify the discontent of the enemies of bilingualism
in Quebec. He was as perfect a successor as Trudeau could have wished
for.

It now appears that the central aims of Liberal constitutional policy
over the past two decades are about as secured as can be expected.
Bourassa's vision of Confederation is now entrenched in the Canadian
constitution as part of a broader rights charter. This Quebec-driven
agenda is now firm policy for both of the major parties and is largely supported by the NDP. This represents not only quite a turnaround from the
longer history of these parties on the issue of linguistic minorities, but
also quite a reversal for parties that during the 1960s had flirted with national self-determination and the other Quebec-based notion of dualism.
Moreover, bilingualism is widely recognized as part of the new political
landscape of Canadian life — as seen in the remarkable expansion of
French immersion classes throughout Canada. This newly emerging elite
recognizes the new terms of partnership between the Frenchand English-speaking peoples and can be expected to defend it against unilingual
backlashes. So far has the politics of bilingualism come that ambitious
federal politicians now fear they may need more than mere linguistic fa-
cility to lead their parties in the future. The dismal results in Quebec of

anglophone leaders not culturally part of the French-speaking community but nonetheless relatively fluent in French — both Clark and Turner
— suggest that genuine biculturalism may also be a future requirement
of national leadership.[52]

While the Mulroney government may be able to do little about the
continuing assimilation of francophone minorities in English-speaking
Canada or the steady decline of the anglophone minority in Quebec over
the last decade, at least the principles and symbols of bilingualism are
firmly in place. And these are all the more necessary if the sociological
and political strength of minorities is in decline.[53] Meanwhile, separatism
in Quebec has probably been set back for at least a generation. The
strength of the strategy will ultimately be tested not only by the long-run
future of the linguistic minorities, but also by the ability of the judiciary
to compel national respect and observance of the spirit of this compromise. That will be a tall order for a new national institution in so divided
a country, but the future national unity of Canada may well depend upon
it.

Of course, the broader responsibility of the Mulroney government is
to effect a constitutional accommodation with Quebec so that it can be
brought into the 1982 constitutional accord. That would complete and
consolidate an historic settlement. This was the minimum that could be
expected from a prime minister promising reconciliation with Quebec,
and Mulroney accepted such a commitment for his first term in office.
That process began in earnest only after the December 1985 election of
the Bourassa government, when Intergovernmental Affairs Minister Gil
Rémillard officially kicked off negotiations in a speech on May 9, 1986, to
a select conference of officials and academics called to discuss the process of rapprochement. Such a sudden and public gesture signalled that
Quebec was ready to begin the process of negotiations and was anxious
both to receive concrete proposals from the federal government and to
test the opinion of other provincial governments. The Liberal Quebec
government's terms, long familiar from that party's earlier election campaign, were straightforward:

- the explicit recognition of Quebec as a distinct society;
- the guarantee of increased powers in immigration;
- the limitation of federal spending powers;
- the recognition of a veto right; and
- Quebec's participation in the nomination of judges to the Supreme
  Court.

This was an ambitious opener taken despite the concerns of other governments that intergovernmental discussions not be jeopardized by the
adoption of too public, too broad and too forced an agenda. Although

some were inclined to regard these as modest initial terms for negotiation (with even the federal Liberal leader John Turner ready to accept some of the demands, including the issue of recognizing Quebec as a distinct society), certain matters on the list were likely to be vexing and difficult, especially the claim to a veto power over constitutional amendments, which appeared to be a nonstarter. Canadians had learned by this time that constitutional renewal was an arduous and contentious enterprise at the best of times, and they had very little stomach for another round of constitutional discussions. It would thus be difficult for the Mulroney government to mount and sustain a policy of rapprochement with Quebec when public interest in and support for constitutional matters had so suddenly plummeted.

Negotiation for the initial constitutional entrenchment of the principle of aboriginal self-government followed by governmental commitment to give expression to that principle in subsequent talks with native peoples was also part of the unfinished constitutional business the Mulroney government was expected to push forward in this climate. As noted earlier, the first attempts to do so were unsuccessful, since the premiers of Alberta and British Columbia flatly refused to go along at the First Ministers' Conference in 1985 and native peoples were unhappy with a diluted provision developed to bring Saskatchewan and Nova Scotia on board that would have removed the constitutional requirement of governments to negotiate. Work was continuing, however, to see whether native groups and the required number of governments could be brought together on some constitutional provision perhaps by the spring of 1987.

The apparent failure of the "top-down" approach to negotiating aboriginal self-government had also moved a number of provinces toward a "bottom-up" approach, whereby negotiations would proceed on self-government agreements with local groups outside of the constitutional framework.[54] Whether that route would undermine or improve the effectiveness of the larger constitutional campaign remained in some doubt. Certainly the simultaneous pursuit of this twin-track process of bargaining indicated that there would at least be a better chance of some practical results from the whole undertaking, even if the eventual shape and impact of the outcome on the constitution was unclear.

Since the meaning of aboriginal self-government both for different native peoples and for governments is not without ambiguity — either with respect to the nature of the government (whether ethnic or public/territorial), or scope (whether local, regional or national), or powers (whether relatively autonomous or dependent) — the work is expected to be long and the results unpredictable and various.[55] The effects on federalism would very much depend on an answer to some of these fundamental questions, especially to the matter of powers. Does aboriginal self-government mean a mere delegation of quasi-municipal powers to native peoples or the establishment, in effect, of a third order of government? Roger Gibbins has written pessimistically about the compatibility of a full-blown model of aboriginal self-government and of the Canadian federal and parliamentary system. Many of the issues he raises have yet to be satisfactorily answered.[56] All of these conundrums implicit in the policy thrust of the earlier Trudeau government will challenge the Mulroney government, which opted for continuity in a federal "constitutional rights" approach to national unity and reconciliation.

Working out acceptable accommodations with native peoples and with the new government of Quebec, where substantial (or on one point even unanimous) provincial consent to important constitutional changes is required, will severely test the Mulroney government's rhetoric and performance with cooperative federalism. Although constitutional matters have certainly not been considered a central part of the Tory government's program — particularly in contrast to their high-profile launching of free trade talks with the United States — they still constitute a significant and ongoing element in the government's program on federalism. Indeed, working out an accord with Quebec will be one of the issues that will weigh in the electoral judgment of Quebecers in the next election.

The current constitutional agenda has, then, to a large extent been structured by past political events. These agenda items would, of course, have required some tidying up and action by whatever federal regime had taken office after the Trudeau years. None of them, however, are assignments easily discharged.

On balance, there remain continuities in the politics of constitutional change in Canada even if the unilateral and centralist elements of the earlier Trudeau program have largely been scrapped. That collapse of centralist constitutionalism was after all the price paid for getting a settlement in November 1981, although part of the agenda was carried forward in the later report of the Macdonald Commission in 1985 (see chapter 6). The enduring part of the Trudeau constitutional legacy has, however, taken hold successfully in the Charter of Rights and Freedoms, and that can be expected for better or worse to become part of the Canadian sense of nationhood. While the charter may not in itself be an inspiring shortcut to a new Canadian national identity, it certainly opens the door to fundamental changes in the idea of citizenship in this country, changes that may turn out to be much more in keeping with the kind of people we are or at least hope to become. Yet there is still a vast gulf between the constitutional principle, the rational image and the real world of Canadian politics; that truth contains both danger and promise for us. Nevertheless, it is a good sign and a nice paradox that the constitutional image has now been grasped even by the Conservative descendants of John A. Macdonald.

# CHAPTER III

# The Politics of Energy

Energy politics has been, next to the constitutional struggle, the most prominent element of federal-provincial conflict and collaboration during the 1980s. Indeed, during most of the previous decade it shared almost equal importance with the constitutional agenda and with the fight over Quebec separatism. That had not been the case in earlier periods, and it may not remain so significant a feature of federalism in the future. However, there can be no adequate grasp of the dynamics of recent Canadian federalism without a rather deep plunge into these political waters.

There are many reasons for this prominence of energy politics in the country, reasons that go to the very roots of international political economy as well as to Canada's historical and contemporary patterns of resource politics and power. Not only has the country been externally vulnerable to the incredible gyrations in supply and pricing in the world oil and gas market over the 1970s and 1980s, but these have in effect ricocheted back onto the Canadian federal structure, so that in a sense the country had to experience within itself, as well as outside in the world, all the well-known stresses and strains of succeeding energy crises. Just as with national actors in the international arena, the story of energy shortages, boycotts and dramatic price hikes forced both levels of government in Canada, as well as powerful domestic interest groups, to act decisively in the name of their own distinct and different interests and to react to the actions of others in the federation in a similar way. Conversely, with the later unexpected development of oil gluts and falling prices, both governments and private players in Canada had to scramble precariously for position.

Intergovernmental conflict over oil and gas, including questions of pricing, development and, not least, allocating resource revenues, was therefore a guaranteed outcome for Canada, particularly with extreme swings in commodity pricing and supply, and contributed in no small measure to the powerful collisions between sets of regional interests and those of the national government throughout most of the 1970s.

Moreover, because of the increasing governmental role in the energy sector, it was becoming an obvious centre for the conflict between regional aspirations and a nationalist economic platform, which included enlarging ownership of the economy by citizens, thought to be required to shore up the federal state. By the end of the 1970s, this battle had reached the point where the governmental players were ready to put their grand conflicting views of the country and the federation to the test. Energy then represented, practically and symbolically, just as high a ground for the playing out of state politics over western (and eastern) regionalism as the referendum and constitutional bargaining had for settling the Quebec separatist issue. The federal policy instrument for that political purpose was the National Energy Program unveiled by the Trudeau government on October 28, 1980, only weeks after the announcement of unilateral action on the constitution. It was a more complex, sweeping and breathtaking  policy initiative than any ever placed before Parliament. But its chief boldness arose from its awesome conformity to the government's federalism — the very picture of policy in the strategic service of state politics.

For if the object of the Trudeau government's constitutional strategy was to throw up guarantees and symbols against separatism and regionalism that would only subtly consolidate federal power, its National Energy Program was more directly and boldly centralist. Steeped in intoxicating nationalist rhetoric that challenged both foreign multinationals and "selfish" provincialism in the name of Canadian "patrimony," energy security and pricing fairness, the policy's primary purpose was the strengthening of the federal state. Just as it had done during the battle over the constitution, the government served up nationalism as a powerful doctrine for rebuilding federal power. Once again, the theory was advanced that the "people's" interests could only be furthered by promoting the Canadian state, by celebrating Canada as it might be expressed through federal instruments and agencies. Yet here federal nation-building could not be confined to an interstate struggle as was largely the case with the concurrent battle over the constitution.[1] When Ottawa chose to flex its muscles over energy, it was also taking on the multinationals on their own turf. The ensuing scrap left Canadian nationalist critics of traditional Liberal continentalism thunderstruck. Patriation of the economy was evidently to complement the drive to legal sovereignty.

With energy policy a vehicle for the "new federalism," Ottawa would now assert the primacy of the national interest over the direction of economic policy in energy matters and over economic rent from oil and gas against what it regarded as the lesser resource claims of the producing provinces. Moreover, at least in the sensitive area of national energy supply and development, the Canadian government declared that it could no longer operate comfortably with the existing high levels of foreign ownership in this sector. The NEP accordingly set a policy goal to "Canadianize" the oil and gas industry by 1990. These measures were, in short, not advanced as economic policy in the ordinary sense, nor were they the wild and random actions of a socialist-inclined government as feared by the free enterprise oilmen in Alberta's oilpatch. They were quite simply the rational and determined prosecution of federal state politics by policy means.

While federal-provincial conflicts over economic policy are hardly rare events in Canadian political history, the NEP represented the most comprehensive and sophisticated orchestration of policy in the name of centralized federalism that Canadians had ever seen. Yet the policy seemed to be aimed primarily at foreign interests in the energy sector in the higher name of the Canadian national interest. It was not difficult to see how this popular program of the federal Liberals suddenly made astonished converts out of even formerly disdainful critics like Mel Watkins or James Laxer. Yet as events would later show, neither the alluring image of nationalism nor the fighting posture against the multinationals was quite what it seemed.

If the Liberals tilted toward a centralist program of rebuilding federal power, the federal Conservatives appeared to have deserted John A. Macdonald's historical legacy in order to champion provincial rights and free enterprise. Of course, for any party shut out at the national level, the long march to power in Ottawa had to begin in sympathetic alliances with disgruntled elements out in the provinces. But, on the face of it, the party lineup in the early 1980s appeared to be a classic flip-flop on the historical position of the two major parties. James Laxer underlined this bizarre topsy-turvy polarization:

> The Progressive Conservatives, historically the party of state intervention and federal power, had become the party of free enterprise and decentralization. The Liberals, historically the party of regionalism and laissez-faire, had become the party of federal power and state intervention in the economy.[2]

Energy policy was an excellent area for the expression of the divergent interests and philosophies of federalism of the two major parties. The Conservatives went into the decade with an energy policy tilted much more sharply toward the interests of the producing provinces and the private sector. This was most graphically illustrated in the Clark period by the party's attempts to "privatize" Petro-Canada and to use a market-driven approach to energy pricing. It was reflected later in the Mulroney government's massive giveaways and policy gestures toward both the private sector and the producing provinces in the first year of the new government's mandate. The Conservatives' approach to energy policy was as fully charged with the politics of federalism as the Trudeau government's had been. Energy politics was for them an equally significant symbol of their brand of cooperative federalism, and they acted to put their stamp upon this sector as swiftly as the Trudeau government had. Their energy policy also signalled quite a different view of the role of the federal state in relation to foreign ownership than that of the Trudeau Liberals.

While there are some continuities in Canadian energy policy irrespective of these changes in federal regimes and there are dramatic differences in the nature of the international and national economic environment in energy between 1980 and 1985, these matters do not fully account for the particular policy directions taken by these governments. At best they provide an essential economic background that federal energy initiatives must take into account, a starting point from which different regimes work through intrastate conflict and accommodation. In this struggle, private interests will attach themselves to the level of government that appears best able to protect their interests.[3] It is only by wrestling with the politics of federalism that energy policy can be adequately grasped. This has never been more true than during the different energy crises of the 1970s and 1980s.

## Role of Energy as a Constituent of State Power

Although the Liberals' National Energy Program as a strategy of advancing state power may have been a delayed and unexpected development for Canadians, in world terms it was nothing new. For well over a decade sovereign states engaged in petroleum production had been attempting to wrest control away from a handful of giant oil companies to use in their own interests. The 1973 oil price explosion was in a sense a symbol of the success of this struggle, although the politics had worked themselves out a few years earlier with the achievement of stronger producer control over extraction and pricing. By 1973 the Arab states in OPEC, aware of the decline of American production, the end of oversupply in oil, and the greater dependence of the Western countries on petroleum to fuel their modern economies, were in a position to use oil as an economic and political weapon. Immediately prior to a meeting with the oil conglomerates called to demand a doubling of oil prices, the Arab-Israeli war broke out. It was not long before more price rises, production cuts and even embargoes on Israel's chief ally, the United States, were announced. The upshot of these developments was startling: a fourfold increase in the price of oil in a matter of three months.[4]

What followed was a spectacular transformation in the nature of global economic and political power. Old patterns between public and private sectors were revolutionized just as relations between and within nation-states underwent radical change. Oil-producing states (and oil-producing provinces within some states) suddenly discovered that energy now conferred upon its possessors more than its merely physical "energizing" properties. It offered a purer power potential — a vastly improved ability to influence national and international developments in their own interests, for as Anthony Sampson then observed, "the problem of the energy crisis is in the end a problem of political power. The two meanings of the word 'power' — the power of energy and the power of politics — are coming much closer together."[5]

While the fragile and fleeting nature of this power may not have been apparent at the time, there is no doubt that the transformation of oil into a relatively scarce, irreplaceable and expensive commodity controlled by a limited number of states did significantly alter the total balance of power between producing and consuming nations. Partly this was simply the consequence of reallocating huge financial resources. On the international level, for example, as a result of the 1973 oil crisis, the proportion of international reserves accruing to oil-producing countries increased almost threefold. From 1970 to 1980 their share rose from 6 to 21 per cent.[6] The same pattern is observable within a nation-state like Canada. From 1970 to 1979 the fiscal position of the three western producing provinces moved from a $67-million deficit to a massive $3.284-billion surplus.

## Table 3-1

## SURPLUSES AND DEFICITS OF FEDERAL AND PROVINCIAL/LOCAL GOVERNMENTS NATIONAL INCOME AND EXPENDITURE ACCOUNTS, 1970-79

| | $ Millions | | | % of GNP | | |
|---|---|---|---|---|---|---|
| Year | Federal | Sask. Alberta B.C. | Other Provs. | Federal | Sask. Alberta B.C. | Other Provs. |
| 1970 | 226 | -67 | -586 | .3 | -.1 | -.7 |
| 1975 | -3,805 | 377 | -2,624 | -2.3 | .2 | -1.6 |
| 1976 | -3,356 | 929 | -3,916 | -1.8 | .5 | -1.7 |
| 1977 | -7,693 | 1,784 | -2,355 | -3.7 | .8 | -1.1 |
| 1978 | -11,357 | 2,532 | -2,538 | -4.9 | 1.0 | -1. |
| 1979 | -9,169 | 3,284 | -2,551 | -3.5 | 1.3 | -1. |

Source: Canada, Department of Finance, *Economic Review: A Perspective on the Decade*, April 1980, Tables 11:1, 11:8.[7]

These figures also show that consuming areas paid out an ever greater share of their wealth to producing areas. This growing transfer of financial resources affected global and national distributions of power alike. Producing states or provinces enhanced their abilities to plan and direct their economies. They spoke with renewed political strength. Consuming nations and provinces conversely sought to reduce their dependency, to stem the outflow of capital and to restrain the ambitions of producers. Nor was this struggle merely state-to-state rivalry: private interests, deeply affected by oil pricing and supply, sought shelter from the state that could best defend their interests. They too stood to gain or lose enormously depending on whether energy was on the capital-generating or cost side of their ledgers. The fortunes of many private companies depended on changes in capitalism's balance of power and in private capital's relationship to the state. Perhaps nowhere are these complicated relationships more evident than in a federal oil-producing state like Canada.

The OPEC crisis produced here an exacerbation of regional discontents. There had always been regional conflicts over natural resource policy in Canada. Whether the resource was coal from Nova Scotia or oil and gas from western Canada, the interests of producers in the peripheries of the country tended to conflict with the interests of consumers in central Canada. Nor did the substance or style of resource politics change much over the years. Consumers and producers found themselves at opposite ends of a purely market relationship: producers tried to serve the national market at fairly competitive prices while consumers resisted whenever supplies could be more cheaply or easily acquired from the United States. These struggles have placed heavy strains upon Confederation. The oil crisis differed from all of the old disputes over resource policy only in the immense financial and political costs involved. These were sufficiently serious to present the Canadian union with a profound test of confidence.

The western provinces were naturally, as producers, interested in marketing their resources aggressively at a fair market price. In the pre-1973 period, that had been difficult for a variety of reasons. World oil prices were lower than those of Alberta, Canada's chief producer, and American demands were restrained by extensive domestic production. In order to protect the Canadian industry and to take advantage of cheaper international prices, the Canadian government in 1961 divided the country into two oil zones along the so-called Ottawa Valley Line.[8] The western zone was served by slightly more expensive Canadian crude by means of an interprovincial pipeline constructed in the 1950s; the eastern zone was supplied with cheaper imported oil. Energy supplies surplus to Canadian needs were exported to the United States in an unrestrained if not profligate manner throughout the 1960s.

While this policy left the country vulnerable to the vicissitudes of the international oil market and in particular to the giant oil conglomerates, there was then little fear over either disruptions in supply or exorbitant price-fixing. The Canadian government approached the energy question with the same blend of pragmatism and naivety it had always used in settling resource policy. Eschewing the traditional call for national self-sufficiency in fuels, it simply imposed an old saw-off between national priorities and market realities. Only with the success of the OPEC cartel in the 1970s did the wisdom of the policy come into question.

Since prices were low, there was relatively little economic rent over which governments could quarrel. In addition, the bias toward rewarding the private companies with the lion's share of rents contributed to modest revenues and lack of intergovernmental conflict. Since the national policy of exporting whatever the Americans might take suited the producing provinces and the companies alike, the status quo was, if not ideal, then at least acceptable to the players. The year 1973 changed all that.

Suddenly a host of urgent problems threatened to unhinge the old order. A fourfold increase in oil prices meant that the economic rent that could potentially be extracted from the sale of petroleum and petroleum products was awesome. The Alberta oil and gas industry, once a modest growth sector, turned out to be a "sleeper" with a multibillion-dollar potential. The political question of settling on who might share in the riches from the oil bonanza became a hotly contested issue between the industry and the two levels of government. Even more urgent was the question whether this potential profit-generating opportunity was to be allowed to take place at all. If international prices were to be adopted, it would be a wrenching and painful experience for consumers throughout Canada. Those consumers in central and eastern Canada without compensating economic benefits from the resource boom could be expected to complain loudly. With the weight of the Canadian population centred in central Canada, no government, least of all a minority government, could afford to ignore them.

To compound the difficulties, the oil companies now began to write down the size of Canada's oil supplies to suit their own economic interests. In a matter of a year Canada went from a land with petroleum so plentiful that it would, to quote Imperial Oil, be "sufficient for our requirements for several hundred years" to an energy-starved nation.[9] The oil price explosion also threatened to upset the federal government's balance sheet directly. Since the equalization program required the federal government to compensate for disparities in provincial revenue, the energy crisis forced Ottawa to transfer more dollars to other provinces to compensate for the new wealth building up in the West.[10] At the same time Ottawa was required to pick up the tab for higher-priced imported crude to serve the eastern oil zone created under the old oil policy.[11]

In short, if the interests of the oil players had been relatively amicably settled in the 1960s and 1950s, there was hardly a chance that they could now be similarly resolved. Government-to-government and government-to-industry conflict over pricing, production, export and economic rent was virtually guaranteed. Trudeau's minority government, in a move calculated both to calm consumers' anxieties and to restrain the interests of oil companies and producing provinces alike, decided to freeze the domestic price of oil at a level well below the international benchmark, to provide for a series of graduated increases in the price of oil, to use revenue generated from an export tax on oil sold to the United States at world levels to pay for the increased costs of importing oil into Canada's eastern oil zone and, finally, to set up a national oil company, Petro-Canada, to help the Canadian state combat the uncertainties over energy supplies in the national interest.[12] These measures enraged Alberta and the other producing provinces, since they denied them the opportunity to realize the market potential from their own resources while they offered other regions western resources at bargain basement prices; moreover, it appeared that the West was once again subsidizing central Canadian manufacturing without receiving any compensating advantages. What rankled even more was the apparently blatant discrimination in the unique tax treatment of western resources: western oil but not central Canadian electrical power would be subjected to federal export levies. Western premiers gave notice that they were now in no mood to bow to the economic and political domination of central Canada.

Yet even if the producing provinces were experiencing the restraining grip of the Canadian federal state, there was then no question that power relations were changing. Economic strength was shifting westward, and with it was going stronger political clout for the region. The Trudeau government could at best moderate the speed of the transformation. Meanwhile, since growing western power had an inverse impact on the federal government, it was now becoming clear to federal politicians and bureaucrats that the pendulum of power in the federal system was swinging even more dangerously toward rovincial capitals. As international oil prices continued to climb throughout the rest of the decade, provincial restlessness with federal restraints grew in almost exact proportion to mounting federal concern over provincial power.

The creation of Petro-Canada was a sign that the federal government was beginning to view the multinational companies that dominated Canada's oil industry as something less than reliable allies in a common nation-building exercise. In part this change in the political stature of the big oil companies was just a reflection of a worldwide public backlash and suspicion over price-gouging and obscene company profits.[13] But it also indicated that Ottawa was losing patience with the companies' manipulation of Canada's energy supply figures to suit their own economic interests; the time had passed when the nation could be held to ransom by information compiled and monopolized by the oil industry itself.[14] The Liberals could no longer accept a simple equation that what was best for the industry was also best for the nation. Of course, the industry in the rational pursuit of its own interests did not endear itself to Ottawa when it aligned itself with the producing provinces in a common demand for higher prices and more exports, when it interested itself in exploration and development on provincial lands and largely ignored federal interests in offshore and northern development, and when it remained indifferent to Ottawa's financial difficulties and hostile to a larger national share of the economic rents.

Nor was this all. In addition to threatening federal state interests directly, the big foreign oil companies now appeared to be threatening the balance of private economic power in Canada. With vastly increased profits, the energy companies were the fastest-growing sector in the Canadian economy. They were in a position to use retained earnings to expand into new areas of the Canadian economy, to buy out other enterprises and generally to consolidate their hold on the domestic economy.[15] Nothing could be better calculated to worry older established Canadian capital, especially manufacturing and other interests in central Canada. At the same time, Canadian capital was effectively shut out of the most important economic plays in the country.[16] All the studies on the baneful effects of foreign ownership generated for over a decade suggested to the federal government the danger of permitting further expansion of foreign multinationals; some critics even raised the spectre of deindustrialization in Ontario as part of the continuing challenge to the older innocent belief that foreign capital would automatically serve the national interest.[17] In short, pressures began to build up in Ottawa for a new assertion of federal authority against these threats of foreign capital.

In retrospect, these were all classic signs in international political economy of a widespread unrest evident in many countries over the patterns of dependency caused by state reliance on multinational oil companies. In an interesting study of the NEP as an example of an "obsolescing bargain" struck between a host country and the multinationals, Barbara Jenkins summarizes many of the conditions pushing countries like Canada toward increasing control over the multinationals:

> a shift in the host country's perception of the appropriateness of the returns to the companies relative to the risks; economic nationalists urging the government to stand up to foreign investors; the desire to exact greater financial gains from an increasingly profitable industry;

concern over economic dependence on a largely foreign-owned sector of the economy; and a change in government outlook from a laissez-faire attitude toward the industry to a more interventionist stance.[18]

With the arrival of the second worldwide oil price shock in 1979 and with Canada's continuing intense intergovernmental conflict over oil and gas, there was ample reason for Ottawa to be provoked into a serious reexamination not only of its energy policy but of Canada's entire political economy. There was no way in which Ottawa could isolate the effects of the international oil price spiral, nor therefore to separate its effects on interregional or intergovernmental relations. The politics of energy had become a comprehensive challenge with far-reaching effects on private and public power. So long as the interests of the foreign oil companies and those of the producing provinces appeared to threaten the vital institutional interests of the federal government and the economic and political territory of the federal Liberal party, there was no way a serious confrontation could long be postponed. All that was needed was the right combination of political circumstances — a so-called "window of opportunity" — for the appearance of a new national policy for Canada.

**The Emergence of the Policy**

It was essentially the 1979-80 election that laid down the political footings for a national energy program. Prime Minister Clark had in fact so politicized energy policy with his promise to privatize Petro-Canada that he virtually invited the Liberals to stake out a distinctive nationalist ground more in keeping with the known preferences of the Canadian people.[19] In addition, the scale of gasoline price increases contained in Finance Minister Crosbie's budget had helped bring the government down and had set the tone for the national election campaign that followed. Since Canadian consumers in every region of the country were directly and adversely affected by the Clark government's higher energy costs and since the proposed increases triggered an unprecedented display of regional bickering between consuming provinces in the East and producing provinces in the West, there was now no escape from the politics of oil.

For Liberal party strategists, armed with Goldfarb's readings of the pulse of the nation and aware that the battle would be won or lost in the heavily populated heartland of Ontario, an opportunity presented itself to regain power and to reassert national control over the power base of western regionalism. Clark's government had placed the Liberal party in the enviable position of defending its traditional electoral stronghold in central Canada by promising a "made-in-Canada" oil price structure while denouncing the Conservatives as dupes of selfish western interests. Although playing off the regions against one another in this manner was highly divisive, this had by now become almost a characteristic Liberal posture. For years the opposition parties had been tarred as more or less bumbling tools of Quebec separatism, ready to compromise the national interest for partisan advantage; it now required very little effort to brand them as sellouts to Premier Lougheed.[20] Adopting the high ground of the Canadian national interest, the Liberals in a speech by Trudeau in January 1980 promised:

- a "made-in-Canada" oil price
- energy security through accelerated domestic development and securing foreign supplies
- substitution of natural gas and other energy forms for oil
- strengthening and expanding Petro-Canada
- renewed emphasis on conservation and alternative energy
- ensuring Canadian ownership and control of the energy sector
- an economic plan to make energy the core of industrial and regional development.[21]

This move of the federal Liberals into a more substantive nationalist posture, especially their decision to expand Petro-Canada, should be seen against the general background of energy insecurity and the related threats oil power presented to the Canadian state. However, it should also be seen as the Liberals' response to the most blatant threats of the day, namely, Quebec separatism and the unbridled expression of regionalism elsewhere. Backing Petro-Canada, already widely popular in the country despite Clark's attacks on it, seemed, along with the other measures, an ideal way to inject some substance into the Liberal campaign against these forces.

Nor did Marc Lalonde, who as energy critic during the Liberal period in opposition masterminded the policy with the support of Trudeau, Allan MacEachen and some key insiders, worry about the required level of federal bureaucratic support for this initiative or about the expected private sector compliance with it. On the former issue, with senior officials from both Finance and Energy (the so-called ENFIN group, including Mickey Cohen, Ian Stewart, Ed Clark and George Tough, with Michael Pitfield and Bob Rabinovitch) later working together in support of different elements of the program, with direct input from Bill Hopper, the experienced head of Petro-Canada, and his vice-president, Joel Bell, there was little likelihood of serious bureaucratic resistance to the policy. Virtually all of these officials had a vested interest in Petro-Canada and in a strong federal presence in energy planning and management; virtually all joined Mickey Cohen in adopting a tougher approach to Alberta over economic rent and other matters — what has been called the "act first–

talk later approach."[22] Indeed, some of their members had already distinguished themselves, especially Ian Stewart, then deputy minister of Energy, Mines and Resources (EMR), by working fiercely from within the Clark government to prevent the dismantling of Petro-Canada by Conservative right-wingers like James Gillies, Clark's principal secretary.[23]

The Liberals also knew that there were powerful Canadian corporate interests — Power Corporation, Argus Corporation, etc. — wanting into the energy business, particularly since it offered the highest rates of return on investment and would continue to do so until 1982. If the barriers to the entry of Canadian capital could be lowered, these interests were expected to cooperate in the erection of a new national energy policy with explicit targets for Canadian ownership levels. In addition, there were some aggressive independent Canadian companies in the oil business that could be expected to line up behind the federal government's program if the policy structure and incentives were to be arranged in their favour. One such outstanding player was Jack Gallagher, president of Dome Petroleum, an experienced and aggressive risk-taker whose company had a special interest in the exploration and development of the federal lands in the high Arctic. Gallagher was a well-known nationalist with scant regard for the more cautious behaviour of the multinationals in Canada. He had lost little opportunity in informing the Canadian government and people about the vast potential petroleum reserves in the Canadian North and was actively pushing Ottawa toward their exploration and development.[24] Robert Blair, president of Nova, An Alberta Corporation, was also an active Canadian nationalist with interests in the energy business who, as co-chairman of the MegaProjects Task Force with Shirley Carr, then executive vice-president of the Canadian Labour Congress (CLC), was expected to look kindly on a major national initiative in energy linked to a national industrial strategy.[25]

Therefore, federal analysts assumed that in any federal venture Petro-Canada would not be the single flagship in a national program to expand the level of Canadian ownership in the industry. The government looked for support from Canadian business, including support from Canadian independent oil companies, and sought to draft the policy with their interests in mind. Even with an election mandate and a supportive bureaucracy and public opinion, the government knew it would require some support from the private sector in order to carry out the program, especially to face down the powerful set of interests adversely affected by the policy. On balance it seemed to be a manageable if tough venture, with clear payoffs for the strengthening of the federal state in the Canadian federation. The program therefore took its place alongside the government's unilateral constitutional initiative in the Liberals' inaugural parliamentary agenda of October 1980. The National Energy Program was in that respect a crucial part of the "line of policy" to be erected in defence of federalism. The year 1980 was to be a turning point for the ideological struggle with the provinces, for the politics of foreign ownership and for the state–private sector relationship.

### NEP: Nationalism, Regionalism and the Accommodation of Canadian Capital

The National Energy Program unveiled on October 28, 1980, stressed the national dimensions of the policy at the outset:

> This is a set of national decisions by the Government of Canada. The decisions relate to energy. They will impinge, however, on almost every sphere of Canadian activity, on the fortunes of every Canadian, and on the economic and social structure of the nation for years to come. They have major, positive implications for the federation itself.[26]

While no one was about to quarrel over the national significance of the energy initiative, there would be plenty of debate over its value and fairness. In that respect, this national policy was no more likely to reflect a genuine national consensus — to escape interregional rivalry — than had any fuel policy of the past. Indeed, probably no policy ever raised regional tensions to a more critical point than did the NEP, nor so seriously begged the question of its national claim to represent the interests of all Canadians. The Liberals' 1980 energy policy in several key areas reflected the sectional interests of central Canada and in particular the interests of established Canadian capital, and its political objective appeared to be aimed at undermining the economic foundations of regionalism in both the East and the West, while shoring up the Liberal party and its political base in central Canada. These biases, while understandable, do qualify if not vitiate much of the windy pan-Canadian rhetoric supporting the program.

The NEP's made-in-Canada blended price system merely reconfirmed the Trudeau government's commitment to domestic selling of western natural resources at prices well below world levels while shifting the cost of subsidizing imported oil for Canada's eastern zone onto consumers.[27] While the latter change unburdened the federal government of a heavy fiscal responsibility, it also amounted to an outrageous anomaly: the made-in-Canada price subsidized foreign countries for oil at market levels while Canada's producers were paid barely half as much.[28] Moreover, until a truly national transmission system in oil and gas was put into place, the NEP shut out eastern Canada from access to western resources and forced western producers to look to the United States for exporting their surplus. This dubious national policy was a logical outcome of earlier failures to develop a coherent countrywide fuel policy.

While the federal government made much of the "arbitrary and artificial" character of world oil prices, claiming that they did "not reflect conditions of competitive supply and demand, nor the costs of production in Canada or other countries," the argument was strained and misleading. As the country learned while riding both up and down the oil price spiral, commodity pricing is simply too volatile to respect rational considerations like production costs and the controlled release of supply is a commonplace practice in international marketing. As for the costs of production in Canada and elsewhere, there is little doubt that only the maintenance of relatively high international prices could make production ventures on the high seas or in oil sands projects economically viable. The federal government disclosed a better rationale for its policy when it claimed that oil pricing should reflect "Canadian realities" and be set to provide a "competitive advantage for Canadian industries."[29] In effect, these were code words for maintaining the old metropolitis-hinterland relationship between manufacturing interests in central Canada and the resource-rich areas in the East and West.

It was perhaps inevitable that a renewed national policy by a federal government dominated by Ontario and Quebec interests should have revived regional resentments over central Canadian domination of the federation. There was simply too blatant a connection between the return of the Liberals with powerful backing from Ontario voters and the promise of a cheap made-in-Canada oil price structure. After years of supporting central Canadian industry with resources at lower than market prices and with an onerous tariff structure that penalized consumers throughout Canada, it was hardly likely that producing provinces would look kindly on even more subsidies to Ontario.[30]

But the National Energy Program provided far more support for Canada's threatened industrial heartland than subsidized energy. It also directed the Foreign Investment Review Agency to block any attempts by foreign oil companies to take over Canadian enterprises, while at the same time it exposed foreign oil companies to massive takeover attempts by Canadian capital.[31] These parts of the program were accomplished by explicitly setting out the requirements of majority Canadian ownership and control in oil and gas by 1990, by rearranging the tax system so that depletion allowances for foreign-owned oil companies would be reduced and then eliminated while overly generous incentive grants would be provided to companies meeting Canadian ownership and control requirements, and by curtailing the share of economic rents to be enjoyed by the foreign oil companies. These policies had the immediate desired effect, as they depressed the market value of these securities and prompted a spate of takeovers of foreign firms so extensive that the value of the Canadian dollar was threatened.[32] Canadian ownership levels rose appreciably, as did Canadian corporate debt. Dome Petroleum was only the most spectacular example of Canadian companies that followed the government's advice even at the risk of assuming a massive debt load.

This national program won substantial support, especially from the Canadian left, which applauded Canadianization while it largely ignored the NEP's interregional effects.[33] Once again a decisive state initiative that, like the constitutional action over human rights, dealt with nation-building on the grand scale was widely endorsed without much questioning of its centralizing character. For many Canadian nationalists it was enough that something was being done to resist Canada's global economic dependency; the older question of the justice of Canada's metropolitis-hinterland relationship would just have to wait for, in Mel Watkin's words, "a promised industrial strategy as the essential second leg of a full national economic policy."[34] Then the political resolution to Canada's unequal economic union might be found. Canada's hinterland regions found this advice intolerable, not least because it repeated the same assurances they had heard before and deferred an essential question in any truly national policy to some later undetermined future.

Such a centralizing program did not involve much rethinking of traditional Canadian national policy. It was a nationalism for the most part consistent with the vision of the country held by John A. Macdonald in his first National Policy, hardly more than a variation on the old theme of dominant sectional protectionism. Although there were some new and distinct program elements added in this "Third National Policy" — notably "Canadianization" ownership concerns and objectives — there remained, despite the promise of a special Western Development Fund, a disquieting continuation of earlier patterns of federal paternalism and centre-periphery relationships. But perhaps in the foreign-dominated economy of the 1980s, and in a politically lopsided and deeply divided federation, going back to the roots of Macdonald's centralized economic nationalism seemed radical enough.

### Nationalism and the Politics of Sharing

The other essential part of the Liberals' political program in energy was to ensure that the federal government received a much larger share of oil and gas revenues. The costs of maintaining national responsibilities appeared to have been growing relentlessly even while provincial governments seemed by comparison financially comfortable. Indeed, a government like Peter Lougheed's of Alberta was seen to be literally awash with petro-dollars. Ottawa, burdened with a growing deficit and ongoing responsibilities for equalization payments and for health, postsecondary education and other state support measures, was determined to improve on its mere 12 per cent take of this vast source of revenue. As the NEP declared, with the initiation of new taxes on oil and gas, the federal government intended to move its share of the total revenues from oil and gas production to 24 per cent by 1983 primarily at the expense of the industry's share of the total pie.[35]

In Alberta this could only be interpreted as a virtual declaration of war: an assault on the rights of provincial ownership over natural resources. As Peter Lougheed put it in a television address on October 30, 1980, the federal government's energy plan was like "having strangers take over the living room."[36] He retaliated by announcing a series of planned production cuts, the net effect of which would deprive Canadians of 180,000 barrels of oil per day by the end of September 1981 unless an agreement satisfactory to the Alberta government was worked out beforehand. Lougheed was careful to promise to reverse these cuts in the event of any real shortage of fuel supply in Canada (and thus to deprive the federal government of a ground upon which it might exercise its emergency powers to step into the situation); the production cuts forced Canadians to pay higher prices to make up for the shortfall.[37] In addition, the Alberta government withheld its approval of the Alsands and Cold Lake projects and initiated a legal challenge to Ottawa's gas tax as a federal encroachment upon provincial crown property. This fierce showdown between Alberta and the federal government continued for almost a year until immense pressures from industry and the public forced them to settle their differences. A new energy pact was signed on September 1, 1981, an agreement that saw Alberta sanction the new federal share of revenues largely in return for a higher projected price structure for oil and gas and for a federal withdrawal from its natural gas exports tax.[38] In fact, the new agreement left the federal share of projected revenues only six percentage points behind the share of the producing provinces who owned the resources in question.[39]

Even the arrival of a worldwide recession, with falling oil prices, did not initially upset the new federal share of economic rent. Thus, while the 1982 *Update* on energy policy published by Ottawa confirmed that governmental revenues were not nearly as great as had been anticipated and that the industry's share of the economic rent during these hard times had returned to virtually the same level enjoyed in 1980, the federal government maintained its augmented share of petroleum revenues. As Table 3-2 indicates, two years after the introduction of the NEP and after a massive recession, the industry's share had hardly changed, while the increased federal revenue take was being covered entirely by forgone provincial revenue.[40] The producing provinces' share of the economic rent had dropped from just under a half of the total to less than a third.[41]

The clash of national and regional arguments over energy policy raised once again the debates over the nature of the federal state Canada was to become and over the question of fair treatment of regions of the country. Some of the arguments flowed out of differing interpretations of the constitution, some from differing readings of Canadian history and

# Table 3-2

## REVENUE SHARES OF INDUSTRY AND GOVERNMENTS
### (in percentages)

|           | 1979 | 1980 | 1981 | 1982 |
|-----------|------|------|------|------|
| Industry  | 41.2 | 45.4 | 39.7 | 40.3 |
| Provinces | 45.7 | 42.4 | 37.3 | 32.3 |
| Ottawa    | 13.1 | 12.2 | 23.0 | 27.4 |
| Total     | 100  | 100  | 100  | 100  |

Source: Petroleum Industry Monitoring Survey (Ottawa: Supply and Services Canada, 1981 and 1982.)

policy. But behind the analysis and rhetoric lay vested economic and political interests seeking either to advance or defend their positions in a basic restructuring of power in the country. Although state initiatives in energy placed the intergovernmental struggle directly into Canada's political economy in a way the constitutional struggle had not done, the salient issue of centralization or decentralization of the federal state remained a central concern. Unfortunately, the energy question did not highlight this federal question with anything like the clarity of the constitutional struggle. Perhaps for that reason the political odds tended initially to be in Ottawa's favour.

Ottawa's case rested on essentially two grounds: first, that the Canadian people had virtually paid for the development and expansion of the oil industry over many years with generous tax incentives and therefore had earned a right to draw benefits; and second, that the overwhelming concentration of production in Alberta was causing dangerously large interregional transfers of wealth. Ottawa purported to find the share of provincial revenue from petroleum unacceptable and the fiscal position of Alberta especially anomalous:

> At present, provincial governments receive more than three quarters of the oil and gas production revenues accruing to governments. Alberta, with 10% of Canada's population, receives over 80% of the petroleum revenues gained by provinces.[42]

The first argument was marshalled against both the industry and the producing provinces even though the industry had clearly been the actual recipient of the federal largesse. The producing provinces had at best an indirect benefit from federal tax support of a national petroleum industry dominated by foreign multinationals. Indeed, while profits from operations under Ottawa's generous tax regime had continued to flow into foreign company coffers throughout the 1950s and 1960s, royalties to the producing provinces had never been especially large.[43] It was ostensibly in deference to these facts that the federal revenue share was projected to be drawn primarily from industry's share of revenue and not from that of the provinces under the original 1980 program. As indicated above, however, by 1982, industry was not repaying these benefits by sharing its revenue with the Canadian people; the producing provinces were.

The second argument centring out Alberta as an unconscionably rich province smacked of the kind of electoral game that the Liberals had played in the 1980 campaign, especially in Ontario. The federal government had rarely before been seen to be as vigorous in the denunciation of regional economic disparity as it chose to be now with the bloc of petroleum-rich provinces. Nor had it ever taken so aggressive a position on the taxation of other natural resources or energy sources, such as electricity exports to the United States from Quebec and Ontario. The special attention drawn to share of national population appeared to reveal the critical issue for Ottawa. Excess wealth might be allowed to build up in provinces with substantial shares of the national population, but not in the underpopulated peripheries of the country. If the latter should happen, there would be a requirement to share the wealth with the majority of the Canadian people outside. This was splendid logic for a majoritarian government in Ottawa that drew most of its electoral strength from central Canada where coincidentally the majority of the Canadian people lived. Its logic appeared less than reasonable elsewhere.

It was difficult to believe in the authenticity of a national energy program developed by a government with negligible representation from western Canada and without serious input from the producing provinces. Neither the federal claim that it spoke for the "higher" national interest nor the pious talk of fairness and sharing helped very much. Regionalism in national policy remained as active and as predictable a force in Canadian politics as ever. The arguments were standard fare in national fuel policy, even if the conflict over the distribution of costs and benefits was fiercer than ever.

The constitution provided very little guidance for the revenue dispute. Although for the purpose of raising revenue and controlling activities on public lands the provinces were given exclusive ownership rights over natural resources under section 109 of the Constitution Act 1867 (the three prairie provinces not receiving those rights until the Constitution

Act 1930), the federal government was given unlimited powers of taxation. Other constitutional sections presented a see-saw of competing grounds for both provincial and federal regulation of natural resource subjects.[44] The provinces' rights to regulate property and civil rights, particularly their rights to regulate natural resources, competed directly with federal powers to regulate trade and commerce, especially interprovincial and international trade. (The new resource provisions under section 92A added later as part of the 1981 constitutional settlement — namely, the right of provinces to apply indirect taxes on natural resources and to make laws in relation to interprovincial trade in natural resources subject to certain limits and qualifications — might at first glance appear to clarify these issues and stabilize the constitutional see-saw, but that is not the case. Federal paramountcy and many federal constitutional instruments, including those mentioned above, remain undiminished.)[45] To compound the difficulties, there was no consistent policy of federal regulation of natural resources, including the taxation of resources, by which the fairness of energy policy could be judged.

Under these circumstances, although the federal government was for a time successful in securing a greater share of revenues from petroleum production in Canada, it did so only at the price of exacerbating the negative impact of regionalism upon national unity. While strong support for some of the nationalist elements of the program was forthcoming from all Canadians, in particular the Canadian left, there was still some disquieting evidence of concern over the policy's effects on Canadian federalism. Mel Watkins was only one of many analysts who was rueful over the unfinished regional agenda.[46] Indeed, there remained other concerns. The policy might have the effect of weakening native peoples' rights, and there were doubts raised about the contribution such a vast bureaucratic, indeed Bonapartist, venture might make to Canadian life.[47] So long as Canada remained an unequal union, it was not realistic for the Liberals to look for a chorus of congratulations over its new national policy.

## State-building or Nation-building?

Throughout the publications of the federal government, including the 1980 NEP document itself, ran a curiously engaging argument; this argument promoted the easy, not to say seductive, identification of "Canada" or "all Canadians" with the interests of the federal government. On the one hand, this took the form of a simple equation of the interests of Canadians in sharing in the country's oil wealth with having "more companies that are owned by all Canadians — more companies like Petro-Canada."[48] In this way the virtues of public enterprise were ingeniously conflated with the Canadian national interest. On the other, the interests of all Canadians were said to be crucially tied up with the federal government's state plans of expansion such as its fiscal assault on Alberta's position or its grandiose ventures for Arctic and offshore development.

This was an easy argument for federal politicians who had already declared that only the government and Parliament of Canada were the true voice of the Canadian people. It had also become a rhetorical device used in the constitutional struggle, as noted in the previous chapter. But the appealing symmetry of the argument only served to mislead and befuddle Canadians. Although in a sense actions or policies profiting the government of Canada might indirectly enhance the position of the Canadian people too, such as the diverting of income from foreign hands into Ottawa's, it is by no means true that whatever enhances Ottawa's interests also serves Canada's or the Canadian people's interest. The fallacy of the argument is immediately grasped if one reflects on the antithetical relations of the taxpayer (the Canadian citizen) and the tax collector (the federal government) or if one looks beyond the question of federal governmental interest to the issue of the public good. It is even more problematic when the federal nature of the Canadian state is taken into account: only the totality of governmental power arranged in artful balance under the Canadian constitution might arguably be said to "represent" Canada.

But the reductionist equation of the Canadian with the federal interest served as a plausible foundation for "national" energy policies aimed at rearranging the country's balance of power in Ottawa's favour. The centralist thrust can be seen in the massive shift of attention from oil and gas exploration and development on provincial lands in the West to the "Canada Lands," the federally controlled areas under the seas in the Arctic and on the East Coast. Declaring these to be lands "owned" by all Canadians, the federal government invited citizens to accept its ambitious and highly expensive program of exploration and development as a national priority.[49] While promising to "be very demanding in its assessment of export proposals" in order to assure sufficient future domestic supplies of energy, Ottawa approved increasing sales of cheaper western supplies to the United States and at the same time exhorted Canadian taxpayers to bear much higher costs for developing Arctic and offshore resources to improve "Canada's oil supply-demand balance."[50] On the face of it this was a rather curious nationalist logic.

To achieve the intended redirection of effort toward exploration of the riskier and more expensive oil fields under federal control and to ensure that the federal government benefited substantially from development of these reserves, Ottawa laid in place a new regulatory framework. The new regime required:

- stiffer work requirements from those companies holding exploration permits on federal lands,
- tax incentives to Canadian-owned and controlled companies to drill on federal lands,
- so-called "back-in rights" amounting to a 25% Crown interest in every productive venture on Canada Lands,
- a minimum 50% Canadian ownership level for a company producing on Canada Lands,
- commitments to use Canadian goods and services in oil and gas production on Canada Lands,
- more economic rent for federal coffers.[51]

These measures indicated that Ottawa was determined to recover much of the power it had lost to the energy-rich producing provinces over the 1970s, while at the same time strengthening its ability to act as a truly national government in economic development. In addition, revenues flowing from petroleum production on federal lands could be expected to shore up the dismal fiscal condition of the federal state and allow it to carry out its national responsibility of redistributing wealth, including equalization payments to the poorer provinces. In short, if control over energy was now recognized as a much more important constituent element in a state's power and a vital foundation for a national industrial strategy, Ottawa was not about to bow out of the energy game.

Under the high world-price scenario prevailing in 1980, the Canada Lands could best be seen as a counterweight to Alberta's vast oil and gas reserves, an Ottawa-controlled vehicle for propelling the federal state into a powerful if not predominant role in energy in this country. The NEP made clear that Ottawa intended to make the fullest possible use of its new role as an energy actor. On the fiscal side, provisions were put in place for the government to draw substantial royalties from new production on its lands; state petroleum actors like Petro-Canada would be given preferential and highly visible roles in Canada's energy future and thus convince Canadians of the vital stake they had in their national government's role in economic development. But perhaps as important as the development of a petroleum industry in Canada's frontier zones was the fact that control over the larger question of industrial strategy would shift dramatically toward a strengthened Ottawa. Federal energy documents showed that the development of the Liberals' national policy on energy was expected to have a dramatic effect on the shaping of a national industrial strategy where Ottawa and not the provinces would play the predominant role in the economic development of the regions.

To accomplish this reinvigoration of the federal state would require the redeployment of capital from the provinces' petroleum strongholds largely in the West to the preferred federal zones. Even though drilling there was a vastly more expensive and risky operation than on provincial lands, especially risky in the light of falling world prices for petroleum, Ottawa was determined to establish a policy structure that would focus attention on its own lands. Indeed, by taking a larger share of petroleum revenues from the West and then disbursing it through the Petroleum Incentive Program (PIP) grants to Canadian-owned companies doing exploration on its own lands, the government of Canada attempted to finance the riskier frontier developments with capital wrested from its energy competitors, the foreign companies and the producing provinces.

It was because of these rather elaborately laid plans for defending the federal state that Ottawa proved so intransigent on the question of ceding jurisdiction for the offshore to coastal provinces. This question, together with the issue of a Canadian Charter of Rights and Freedoms, was the central stumbling block in the summer constitutional discussions of 1980. After the discovery of the vast Hibernia oil field off the coast of Newfoundland in 1979, Ottawa and the coastal provinces were becoming more and more aware of the vast economic potential these reserves represented and were digging in with their respective constitutional claims to jurisdiction. The dispute finally went to the Court of Appeal of Newfoundland, which ruled on February 17, 1983, that rights to explore and exploit the coastal seabed rested exclusively with the federal government. The Supreme Court of Canada considered the same question in a reference case referred to it by Ottawa. In March 1984 the national government again won the court battle. So confident was the Justice Department of the legal result that several months prior to the expected court ruling it had authorized Petro-Canada to begin drilling in a field that was adjacent to Hibernia without a licence from the province of Newfoundland.

The offshore dispute was probably the most bitterly fought contest between a have-not province and the federal government. Newfoundland's premier, Brian Peckford, was certainly as aggressive a fighter for provincial rights as any that might have faced Ottawa in the past, and he was also passionately committed to defending the Newfoundland way of life from an unduly hasty plunge into offshore development. He insisted on a fair division of revenue with Ottawa and wanted at least an equal say on decisions affecting the pace and nature of offshore development. This was not merely a spinoff from Peckford's philosophy of federalism. At issue was a whole nexus of functional and sensitive concerns for Newfoundland: how to ensure that development would proceed with a minimum of social problems and disruption to community life; how to foster stronger local control to overcome patterns of dependency; how to maximize employment and local business development; how to protect the traditional industries, especially the fishery, from the effects of oil development; and so on.[52] From Prime Minister Trudeau's perspective, where Peckford's program was not dismissed as a mere grab for money and power, it was treated as a reincarnation of separatism dressed up in phony regional garb; having spent his professional political career battling insularity and chauvinistic nationalism in Quebec, Trudeau was not about to leave the field to an upstart regional nationalist.[53]

While certain principles of energy policy — pricing, energy security and supply, the role of Petro-Canada and the offshore question — had all appeared as election issues in 1979-80, the debate was anything but clear and complete. Neither the nature, nor the costs nor the adequacy of this brand of state nationalism was adequately recognized. Instead, it was the Clark government that from the outset was placed on the defensive. If a more thorough challenge to Liberal policy had been offered, many issues, including the enormous transportation difficulties in bringing Canadian frontier sources to market, would have been quickly exposed. Even later the NEP was strangely silent on the matter, though this would have to be a critical part of any serious development of the Canada Lands. If this debate on transportation had gone further, it would have become increasingly clear that Canadian production of frontier sites could only be economical if the costs for transporting these supplies to market were underwritten by further extensive sales of Canadian energy to the American market. Ironically then, the same dependence on continental energy arrangements would be necessary to make Canadian frontier development viable. As John McDougall has so ably demonstrated, a national energy policy would then be mired in the same patterns of dependency that have afflicted Canada in the past.[54]

Many other critical questions would undoubtedly be raised if a "national" energy program were politically required to measure up to a national constituency rather than to serve as an exercise in centralized federal state-building. As Bruce Doern has argued, the Liberals in 1980 were as much a regional party as were the Conservatives and the New Democrats, and their anti-provincialism did not really amount to a credible national program.[55] Regional costs and benefits would have to be spelled out more closely rather than disguised in majoritarian rhetoric. Although the 1980 election had virtually endorsed the idea of expanding Petro-Canada, the nature and mix of private and public enterprise in oil and gas would also have been a hotly contested issue in a genuine national energy debate. The performance and accountability of crown corporations, together with their claims to be "people's instruments" rather than remote statist organizations, might have been elements in that debate; so too would have been the claims of entrepreneurs like Jack Gallagher of Dome Petroleum who advanced their corporate interests as legitimate national objectives. The point is, of course, that the federal Liberals' rhetoric and program did not have to stand up to that kind of debate.

Perhaps because the politics of energy quickly became a structured contest between "Canada" and the selfish demands of regionalism in East and West, Liberal unilateralism was initially more successful here than over the constitutional issue. In part this was because Ottawa was proceeding from a more secure constitutional footing and in part because the federal government was repeating the old political logic of sectionalism long associated with national fuel policy in Canada.[56] Most important of all, the power of Canadian nationalism proved to be an enormously potent weapon, sustaining the Trudeau government's economic and political goals even during a difficult period.

On the other hand, what was less evident at the time was how readily the multinational oil companies as the declared targets of the NEP adapted to this new national policy and managed to work profitably from within it. Although the new system of land tenure and exploration incentives seemed ostensibly to work against them, the companies lost little time in devising means of getting around it. First the multinationals discovered that after using additional tax write-offs, they could bring their net cost of exploration to 33 cents per dollar of expenditure compared to 20 cents for companies with a high Canadian ownership rate.[57] Access to the more heavily subsidized rate for "Canadianized" companies was, moreover, easily secured: by farming out the exploration work to a Canadian partner in return for a 50 per cent interest in the lands being drilled, the multinational received a free ride on its exploration program in exchange for the 50 per cent cut for the Canadian company. Meanwhile, the taxpayer picked up most of the bill through PIP grants to the Canadian company. "When you cut right through it, it is really not a bad deal for the multinational," declared a key federal official.[58] Judging by the marked shift in exploration expenditures on Canada Lands — from 60 per cent by foreign-owned companies prior to the NEP to 73 per cent by Canadian companies under the PIP grant system in 1984 — the arrangement did prove an attractive one.[59]

The foreign oil companies, supported by most Canadian independents, joined forces with the producing provinces to bring direct and massive pressure on Ottawa to change course. President Reagan's administration was also drawn into this triangular lobby. Some elements of the policy were softened or modified as a result of these pressures, including easing the provisions on Canada's back-in rights on offshore production, improving the share of company revenues, and backing off on the export tax on natural gas; but the lobbying was unable to secure its primary aim of dismantling the NEP.[60] The federal Liberals were for a time able to ride out the storm, reaching out over the heads of the pre-

premiers and the multinationals to see some of the goals of the NEP supported by the Canadian people.

However, the close alliance of most Canadian oil companies and the multinationals against the NEP proved to be an embarrassing and unexpected development for the federal government, especially since planners had so carefully arranged the policy framework to be in the joint interests of Canadian companies and the federal state. As Barbara Jenkins noted in her extensive study of both federal officials and leaders in the industry, this part of the political plan backfired, as the deeper interests of capital coalesced against both nationalism and state regulation:

> Government officials were "shocked" and "disappointed" at the reaction of Canadian companies to the NEP. They had expected a reaction from the MNCs [the multinationals] involved, for the NEP's PIP grants clearly discriminated against them. But why were the Canadian oil companies so angered by a policy from which they clearly stood to benefit? Government officials claim they made a fundamental error in judgment in regard to the Canadian companies. As one official phrased it, they underestimated the degree to which the Canadian companies considered themselves to be "Capitalists," not "Canadians." As one government official marvelled: "In the weeks following NEP's introduction, there was a unanimous negative reaction by Canadian companies. NEP was intended to be the greatest thing since sliced bread for Canadian companies in the oil and gas sector, it wasn't a socialist document.... We underestimated the affinities — intellectual, ideological, and commercial — between foreign companies and Canadian companies, particularly the ideological factors."[61]

However, in the broader court of public opinion, nationalism was enthusiastically received. The identification with Petro-Canada as a national symbol of Canadians' participation in their own economic future was successfully achieved; its share of petroleum sales continued to rise throughout the recessionary period when the market share of other companies was shrinking.[62] In addition, the broader Canadianization objective of the program whereby more foreign companies would be acquired by Canadian-owned public and private interests continued to be realized, with most of the increase in Canadian ownership levels accomplished in 1981 and 1982 at what turned out to be excessive costs. In that exercise, not only Dome Petroleum and Petro-Canada got behind the Canadianization drive, but also the province of Ontario with its ill-fated purchase of 25 per cent of U.S.-owned Suncor in October 1981.[63] "In the four years after the introduction of the N.E.P.," noted Pratt, "Canadian ownership of upstream production revenues increased from about 28 per cent to 40 per cent. Measured as a percentage of all petrol-eum-related revenues, i.e. upstream plus downstream, Canadian owner-ship rose to about 47 per cent following the complex takeover of Gulf Canada by the Olympia and York group and Petro-Canada in 1985."[64] None of this progress, however, changed the fact that the foreign-owned companies continued to dominate the industry and were now generally better positioned than many heavily indebted Canadian-owned com-panies to weather any prolonged down cycle in world oil prices.

Yet the evidence still suggests that in many respects both the formal goal of Canadianization and the revenue-enhancing objectives of the NEP appeared to have been secured under the Liberals in spite of mas-sive opposition from powerful interests. In retrospect, it is surprising that the government's centralizing strategy over energy was initially as suc-cessful as it was. Canadians did respond, for example, to the nationalist rhetoric as the policymakers had hoped they would. The enlargement of Dome Petroleum and the creation of its subsidiary, Dome Canada, was widely supported by Canadian investors, just as the expansion of the public sector in the form of Petro-Canada was by the general public. The nationalist dimensions of the policy had also quite overshadowed the left's doubts over the program's broad social and political implications.[65] For many on the left, Canadian nationalism and political centralism had become but two inseparable strands in a necessary plan to defend Cana-da. By an extraordinary twist of fate, their project to repatriate the Cana-dian economy had converged with the Trudeau government's plan to re-build federal state power.[66]

Thus, for a time even the Trudeau government's intended political plan to isolate the federal Conservatives under Joe Clark as the only right-wing champions of decentralized federalism was successful. The Clark Conservatives' federalism had become enmeshed with some right-wing elements in their program, such as the party's hostility to public corporations and its defence of "free enterprise," its general attack on the costs of the public sector, or its links with the provinces' attack on medicare. This association of the political right with decentralized federalism was the intended counterpoise to the Trudeau government's position on federalism, a political realignment that pitted the right against a centre-left coalition.[67] In this exercise the NEP was just as criti-cal as the unilateral constitutional initiative had been in setting up this polarization of parties whereby "provincialists" could be isolated as ob-stacles to nation-building.

Nonetheless, Ottawa's state-building exercise strained federalism and brought on an unprecedented display of regional resentment in the form of western legal actions, project and production cutbacks and a fierce and successful Ottawa-bashing election in Peckford's Newfoundland.[68] These were conditions that enormously encouraged the Conservatives' alliance-building with disgruntled elements in the provinces and that gradually made their promise of cooperative federalism appear more attractive to the Canadian public. But it was the unexpected onset of falling oil prices and worldwide recession that really upset the political and economic calculations of the Liberal policy and prepared the way for a reversal of this carefully orchestrated defence of the federal state.

### The Erosion of the NEP's Market Underpinnings

While the NEP was built upon a consensual view about the continuing upward direction of world oil prices in an OPEC-controlled system, in fact market forces were increasingly rendering that portrait obsolete. The rapid rise in prices over the 1970s had spawned extensive new production by non-OPEC players (for example, Great Britain in the North Sea and expensive extractive processes for recovering oil from difficult terrain, including Canada's tarsands in northern Alberta) and had boosted the fortunes of other energy industries, such as coal and the newer alternatives in nuclear power, solar energy and so on. It had also driven consumers throughout the world into a variety of conservation measures designed to reduce their dependency on imported oil. None of this worked toward the long-term interests and stability of the oil cartel. In addition, after the 1979 oil price shock, the new prominence of spot trading, the dissolution of term contracts, and the trading of oil on the futures market undercut the ability of OPEC (or of anyone else) to control supply and therefore to manage prices.[69] OPEC's share of the world oil market was steadily falling, supplies were plentiful, and demand, especially during the recession early in the decade, was falling. OPEC production quotas, designed to maintain world price levels, were becoming less and less effective instruments of control even under ideal conditions, but with frequent quota violations of OPEC members and the aggressive inroads into the world market by non-OPEC members, only the forbearance of Saudi Arabia kept any semblance of order in the market. However, Saudi Arabia, in pursuing this course of self-abnegation, had by 1985 fallen to fifth place among world producers — behind the Soviet Union, the United States, Britain and Mexico. How long it would tolerate that state of affairs remained an open question, but the outlook appeared precarious.

In any case, since world price increases did not materialize in the 1980s as conventional wisdom had earlier assumed, the federal government was forced to take a much smaller revenue share than expected. Prices fell so sharply that oil sands plants scheduled for completion in Alberta were halted and interest in the development of Arctic and offshore reserves abated. Scheduled price increases were postponed as the domestic price moved up to and exceeded the federal government's 75 per cent ceiling set under the program. In such tough times, both the federal and provincial governments had to cede a larger share of economic rent to the oil industry through reduced royalties and taxes so that the companies' proportion of total revenue returned to pre-1980 levels.[70]

> The upshot of these concessions and the declining prices [argued Pratt] is that the oil industry in 1984 received 55 per cent of total upstream (production) revenues, while the provincial share dropped from 46 per cent of such revenues in 1979 to 27 per cent in 1984. The Lougheed government admitted that the average royalty on a barrel of "old" conventional oil had by 1985 fallen to 24 per cent, which was little more than it was in 1971 when Lougheed took power. Helliwell et al., in a recent analysis of the N.E.P. and falling oil prices, conclude "that by far the largest part of the direct revenue losses have accrued to governments. The combined effect of the energy agreements and the subsequent policy adjustments, including the 1983 amendments, has been to put the producing industry in almost exactly the same position that it would have had under the higher prices forecast in the original 1981 energy agreement."[71]

Lower prices even threatened the success of the government's conservation efforts by taking away much of the economic incentive to conserve energy supplies. All of these consequences showed how vulnerable Canada's national policy was to international developments and how innocent had been the assumptions of apparently endless price increases for petroleum.

The recession, together with backtracking under lobbying pressures from the United States and oil-producing interests in Canada, had also undermined the industrial part of the Liberals' national strategy. The higher energy package agreed to with Alberta in September 1981 undercut the expected industrial advantages for central Canadian manufacturing even though prices were still well under world levels. Declining productivity, bankruptcies, company losses or sharply reduced profit levels for Canadian manufacturing continued throughout the recessionary period of the early 1980s. On the governmental level, the difficulty could be read symbolically in the mushrooming federal deficit.[72] These were not appropriate conditions for a continuation of the strong federal state-building efforts of 1980.

Indeed, the NEP and other forms of state interventionism became identified with the recession itself or were blamed as the chief causes for the particular severity of the recession in Canada. While some in the industry were later ready to admit that falling oil prices and worldwide recession were among the primary reasons for a falloff in the industry in the early 1980s, the NEP remained a convenient straw man for this downturn in the industry and they made the most political mileage they could of it.[73] Under these circumstances, the fortunes of the Conservative party as the chief critic of the energy program rose dramatically. As the Liberals struggled to change gears in an altered political climate, it was already clear in Finance Minister Lalonde's later budgets that the period of Liberal economic leadership and government interventionism had come to an abrupt halt. The initiative for continuing economic growth and planning was being returned to the private sector.

Fear over the future of the Canadian economy had undermined the politics of nationalism and federal-provincial conflict. This was just as true for the embattled PQ government in Quebec or for provincialist premiers like Peter Lougheed as it was for the Trudeau regime that had fought them so vigorously. The sudden retirement of all of these leaders — René Lévesque, Lougheed and Trudeau — by the mid-1980s indicated that federal politics in Canada was undergoing a new dynamic system change. Perhaps nothing illustrated that better than the September 1984 election of the Conservatives under Brian Mulroney and the return to the politics of cooperative federalism. As expected, energy policy would be one of the earliest and most revealing indicators of the new federal-provincial climate.

### Energy Policy under Cooperative Federalism

The Mulroney approach to federalism was an expected sequel to the bitter confrontation politics of the later Trudeau years. The Conservatives placed reconciliation with the provinces, together with economic renewal, among their highest priorities in office. These aims reflected what the polls showed as a new national consensus on these matters. These goals were also in keeping with the interests of their political allies in the provinces, most of whom enjoyed the same party label.

However, the pursuit of federal-provincial peace was possible only because so many of the festering issues that had divided the country over the previous twenty years had now been settled or at least postponed to a much later time. Most of the head-to-head fury over the issue of Quebec independence had worked itself out in the 1980 referendum and in the constitutional bargaining thereafter. This issue had constituted the raison d'être of the Trudeau and Lévesque regimes, and with the federal victory, both leaders retired quickly from the political limelight. The taming of the PQ, begun first by Lévesque and continuing under Pierre Marc Johnson, represented a bitter acknowledgment by that party of Quebecers' commitment to federalism and an agreement to put the issue of independence on ice for the time being.

Worldwide recession and shifts in the global economy and oil market also made their initial contribution to the new politics of cooperative federalism. Apart from the sobering effect of recession on politicians at both levels of government, many of the old economic stakes in intergovernmental rivalry were immediately reduced. Perhaps nothing illustrated that fact so nicely as did gradually falling oil prices. This had a marked depressing effect on the former blustering provincialism of the three western provinces, just as it cooled federal envy and interest in the natural resource rents in oil and gas. Moreover, Ontario was no longer carrying on its rearguard action against market pricing for these resources. Indeed, as the natural gas agreement with the producing provinces in October 1985 indicated, Ontario was much more inclined to push for rapid deregulation of pricing to take advantage of falling values, while Alberta producers were suddenly converted into temporary advocates of regulation.

Nevertheless, this continuing jockeying between consuming and producing provinces on the "down" price escalator was still a good deal less strident than on the "up." Without the intense economic heat from escalating world prices, the level of friction in federal-provincial politics over oil was bound to drop no matter who was in power in Ottawa. But this state of affairs, which the federal Tories enjoyed for approximately their first eighteen months in office, depended on a happy convergence of factors and most importantly on the maintenance of reasonably stable oil prices. As soon as Saudi Arabia dashed those prospects early in 1986 by sharply forcing down prices below $10 (U.S.) a barrel in order to recover its share in the world oil market, regional tensions and intergovernmental conflict in Canada reappeared. Yet even under these circumstances, this change did not produce a total zero-sum game between consuming and producing provinces: all governments were now worried about how to prevent a precipitous drop in oil and gas prices from casting overboard the whole policy structures and investment projects in energy that had been worked out over the years of rising petroleum prices.

Moreover, the western provinces had won many of their constitutional objectives in the compromise that led to patriation of the Canadian constitution. Alberta's amending formula providing for no vetoes for Ontario and Quebec was now enshrined in Canadian law, and Saskatchewan's concerns for stronger provincial control over natural resources had also been recognized in the final package. While these measures did not come without concessions, it was still true that the western provinces shared a spot in the winning circle with the federal government and its allies in the constitutional battle.

Perhaps most significantly, after the departure from power of Prime Minister Trudeau, with his political theory of federalism and his notions of applying counterweights to provincial power, there was an opportunity for the expression of a different philosophy of federalism responsive to a new set of interests and concerns shared by both levels of government in Canada.

All of these conditions permitted Mulroney to give shape to his idea of cooperative federalism and to fit it into its appropriate place in a program of economic renewal. While it is doubtful that Mulroney ever had as intellectually coherent and self-conscious a political theory of federalism as did Trudeau, his vision played an important practical part in the government's new program of economic renewal. And it was the latter concern, the preoccupation with economic growth and survival, that now pre-empted the political stage.

It was in the field of energy policy that the Mulroney government made its ideas about the mutually supporting goals of cooperative federalism and economic renewal most clear. It did so with dramatic new initiatives that reversed the direction of federal-provincial politics in this sector, diminished intergovernmental rivalry and competition, and cleared the way for private sector reinvestment. These policies were the Atlantic Accord with Newfoundland in February 1985, the Western Accord with the three western provinces in March, and the natural gas agreement in October of the same year. Each of these measures reflected the private sector's impatience with federal-provincial obstacles to economic development and the Tory government's sense that no federal concessions were too great to see these obstacles removed and the economy started again. At bottom they rested on a belief in the ultimate compatibility of federal and provincial objectives if these were pursued with mutual goodwill and along mutually profitable functional relationships.

The Atlantic Accord represented a stark contrast with the Trudeau government's posture on the offshore issue and dramatically illustrated how far federal-provincial relations had changed. This historic accord, which granted Newfoundland an owner's right to draw royalties from the exploitation of the vast petroleum wealth lying off its shores, has to be seen as the apogee of Mulroney's cooperative federalism. Despite a unanimous decision from the Supreme Court in March 1984 awarding Ottawa the exclusive right to exploit and develop the offshore, the Mulroney government less than a year later granted to Newfoundland equal management powers, a decisive say on the mode of development on the offshore, and all rights to apply royalties and taxes "as if these resources were on land, within the province." This was an astonishing victory, even more surprising since one of its provisions, namely the question of Newfoundland receiving all royalties even after it had ceased to be a "have-not" province, went considerably beyond Peckford's own bottom line on that subject in a national tour in May 1984.[74]

This stunning political result flowed out of an earlier understanding reached between then opposition leader Brian Mulroney and Premier

Peckford and spelled out by letter on June 14, 1984. In it were contained all of the essential principles of the later Atlantic Accord, including recognition of the right of Newfoundland and Labrador to be the principal beneficiary of the wealth of oil and gas off its shores, equality of both governments in the management of the resources, and the guarantee of mutual consent prior to any changes to the agreement. While these terms were less than those offered by the earlier Progressive Conservative government of Joe Clark, which had flatly proposed to transfer "ownership of the mineral resources of the continental margin" to Newfoundland, they were about as far as any federal party could have gone after the 1984 Supreme Court decision, which after all had granted Ottawa exclusive legislative jurisdiction (the right to "explore and exploit"), not ownership, over the continental shelf. Moreover, the provision in the accord that permits the federal government, in the event of intergovernmental disagreement, to overrule Newfoundland on fundamental decisions affecting the pace of development whenever "national self-sufficiency and security of supply" are not reached (and the converse when these conditions are met) merely incorporated principles Peckford himself acknowledged in May 1984. Thus, while the terms of the accord, when judged against earlier offers or Newfoundland's own demands in the late 1970s and early 1980s, may appear modest, they were what the Newfoundland government itself recognized as the best and most realistic deal that could be struck after the high court decisions in St. John's and Ottawa.

The Newfoundland government itself acknowledged that over the years it had shifted its negotiating position from a claim to outright provincial ownership, to one of joint ownership, and finally to simple joint control and mutual sharing. Indeed, the only significant advance in the accord from what Newfoundland had earlier come to regard as its bottom-line realistic target was the complete and unrestricted ability of Newfoundland to apply royalties and taxes, while federal revenues (excluding those arising indirectly through Petro-Canada profits) were restricted to those taxes that normally pertained on provincially owned petroleum resources elsewhere in Canada. That was nonetheless a substantial achievement, even if the costs of development and prevailing world prices indicated that whenever offshore development actually proceeded, Newfoundland royalties would likely have to be set at modest levels for a considerable period of time.

The federal position under Prime Minister Trudeau had also shifted over the years from a simple federal claim to pre-eminence toward accepting, as in the Nova Scotia agreement of 1982, a distinct (if minority) provincial representation over management decisions and the principle of full provincial receipt of revenues until coastal provinces had reached "have" status, with a gradually reduced share thereafter. As noted earlier, the Trudeau government had come to see control over energy projects and revenues as an important dimension of intergovernmental politics and power in the federation and, for that reason, it was loathe to concede this theatre of operations to the provinces. Yet Newfoundland clearly was not prepared to sign a deal along the lines of the Nova Scotia agreement, since that would provide inadequate protection and compensation to the province; without a settlement, there could be no development of Hibernia.

It was in the face of this impasse, and because of their earlier commitments as a party and their promise to restore cooperative federalism while getting Canada's economy moving again, that the federal Conservatives decided to strike a generous deal very much on Peckford's latest terms. Accordingly, joint management of the resource was to be effected through a Canada-Newfoundland Offshore Petroleum Board whose neutral chairman would preside over an equal number of members appointed by the federal and provincial governments. Ottawa would retain the exclusive right to set Canadianization policy and its own taxes, while Newfoundland alone would set the royalty regime. On fundamental decisions affecting the nature, pace and mode of development, the board's decisions would be subject to approval by the respective governments, with Canada enjoying paramountcy in the event of intergovernmental conflict when national self-sufficiency is not met, and Newfoundland when a state of national self-sufficiency and security of supply is met. In a press conference on the occasion of the signing of the agreement, it was a proud Premier Peckford who ticked off these key items and others of interest:

- There will not be a dollar for dollar loss of equalization payments as a result of offshore revenues. There will be a very gradual and generous (for Newfoundland) phase out of equalization payments which allows this province to catch up socially and economically to the rest of Canada.
- The laws and regulations pertaining to the agreement cannot be changed without mutual consent.
- The Government of Canada agrees to put the Agreement into the Constitution of Canada if the required number of provinces agree.
- Newfoundland's social legislation will apply.
- The Agreement covers the petroleum resources of the whole continental margin, approximately 700,000 square miles.
- Preference will be given for local labour and local goods and services.
- Research and development and education and training provisions for Newfoundland will be a part of development plans submitted by companies.
- A development fund of $300 million [75 per cent funded by the fed-

eral government] will be established immediately.
- The offices of the Management Board will be in Newfoundland, relevant federal government departments will establish offices in Newfoundland, and all geophysical, geochemical, and geological information will henceforth be located in Newfoundland.[75]

No such package could have been won from the previous Canadian government, but with intergovernmental agreement, it seemed that development might finally proceed. While worries over the impact of an offshore boom on the Newfoundland economy and society continued, the exploitation of such a potentially huge energy reservoir appeared to offer the only hope of economic salvation for the most economically depressed province in the country; every Newfoundland politician was therefore anxious to see this resource potential used to wipe away the unemployment, social problems and indignity that came with being the poorest of the have-not provinces. That bleak legacy contributed in no small way to the acceptance by Ottawa (and by other premiers, including William Davis of Ontario) of these generous terms over the offshore.

One analyst has sought to place the Atlantic Accord at midpoint of a centralization-regionalization scale of outcomes, suggesting that it should be regarded as a "middle-ground compromise between extreme regionalism or provincialism on the one hand and extreme centralism or federalism on the other." As Figure 3-1 indicates, "Newfoundland has not achieved the level of provincial control enjoyed by Alberta over its land-based resources, but it has done much better than northern Scotland and notably better than Nova Scotia."[76] Similar results appear in a more detailed treatment in Table 3-3, on page 104, which compares the Atlantic Accord with the 1982 Nova Scotia agreement and the Newfoundland Regulations of 1977, which laid out the province's ideal policy outcome. A like judgment, namely, that the accord represented a reasonable compromise between the extremes of provincialism and centralism, was fairly common in press and academic commentary.

While there has been some disappointment among Newfoundlanders that the earlier commitment to provincial state participation in the oil industry (by taking an undivided 40 per cent interest in every lease) had been overlooked in the accord and that the province's guarantee of priority of supply of industrial feedstock and of provincial control over education and training might be called into question, on the whole it has been recognized as an incredibly good deal. Newfoundland enjoys the right to choose the mode of development or production system, subject only to a federal veto if that system "unreasonably delays the attainment of self-sufficiency and security of supply." Once Canada has achieved both of the latter conditions, Newfoundland would enjoy paramountcy over virtually all fundamental decisions on offshore development.

**Figure 3-1**

**CONTIMUUM OF JURISDICTIONAL CONTROL BY DEGREE OF CENTRALIZATION-REGIONALIZATION**

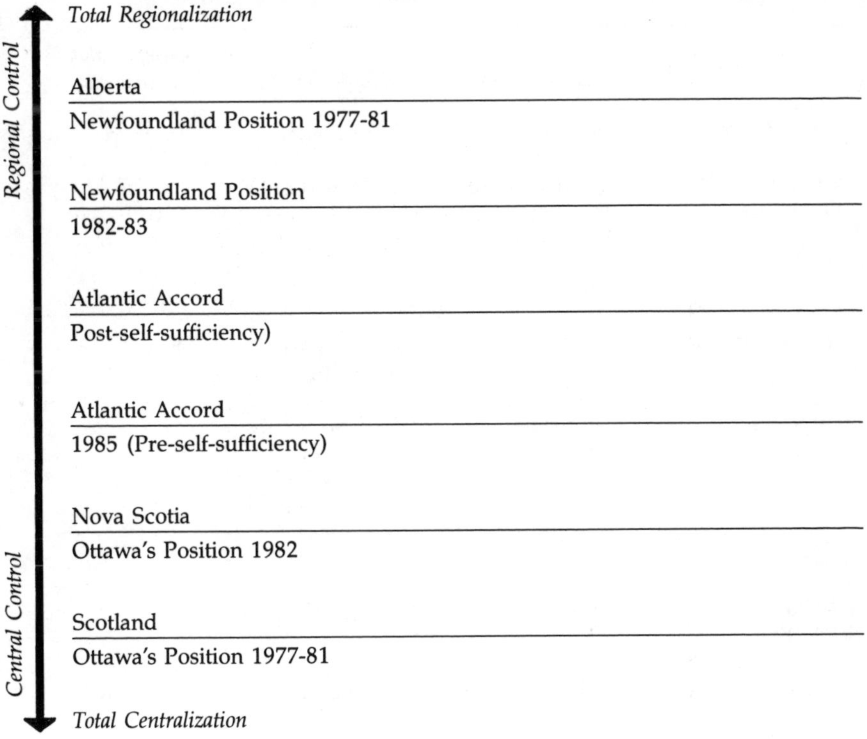
Total Regionalization
Regional Control
Alberta
Newfoundland Position 1977-81
Newfoundland Position
1982-83
Atlantic Accord
Post-self-sufficiency)
Atlantic Accord
1985 (Pre-self-sufficiency)
Nova Scotia
Ottawa's Position 1982
Scotland
Ottawa's Position 1977-81
Central Control
Total Centralization

Source: J.D. House, *The Challenge of Oil: Newfoundland's Quest for Controlled Development* (St. John's: Institute of Social and Economic Research, Memorial University of Newfoundland, 1985), Figure P1, p. 305.

In the event of disagreement, the accord makes provision for an independent arbitration panel that would take on the thankless task of determining under what circumstances one or the other of the two governments could exercise paramountcy in disputes over fundamental decisions. The decision of the panel would be binding on both governments, thus leaving the final determination of the national interest on such fundamental matters in the hands of appointed officials. This was a considerable departure from the traditional principle that, in the last instance, governments should be empowered to overrule administrative agencies such as the National Energy Board on such questions.

Since the accord appeared to settle the intergovernmental bickering

## Table 3-3

## THE ATLANTIC ACCORD COMPARED WITH THE NOVA SCOTIA AND THE NEWFOUNDLAND AND LABRADOR PETROLEUM REGULATIONS 1977

|  | Atlantic Accord | N.S. Agreement | Newfoundland Regulations |
|---|---|---|---|
| MANAGEMENT | Joint (Equal) | Joint (Federal) | Provincial |
| MODE/PACE OF EXP. & DEV. | I. Federal (Prov.) (pre-self-suffic.) II. Provincial (Fed.) post-self-suffic.) | Federal (Prov.) | Provincial |
| PROVINCIAL PARTICIPATION | 12.5% (?) | 12.5% (gas) 6.25% (oil) | 40% |
| REVENUES | As if land-based | I.N.S — weak N.S. fiscal capacity II. Can. — strong N.S. fiscal capacity | As if land-based |
| SECURITY OF SUPPLY | Eastern Can. | Eastern Can. | Newfoundland |
| PRICING | Federal (Prov.) | Federal. (Prov.) | Fed/Prov. |
| DEVELOPMENT FUND | $225 federal grant | $200 federal loan | |
| LOCAL BENEFITS | Nfld. first | N.S. first | Nfld. first |
| R & D | Federal | Fed/Prov. | Provincial |
| EQUALIZATION PAYMENTS | Offset payments | ? | |

Source: House, *The Challenge of Oil,* 310.

and gave a green light to development of the Hibernia site in a tough period of economic difficulty, the nation was hardly in the mood to weigh the long-term costs and benefits very carefully. Certainly, from the perspective of those living in have-not provinces, the generous deal with Newfoundland signalled a serious federal concern with finally improving the economic bargain of Confederation in their favour. The agreement was held up in that respect as a model of sensitive federalism, of federal flexibility in the national interest. Most particularly, it illustrated, as then energy minister Pat Carney put it, that the old notion that only Ottawa could "identify and contribute toward the national interest" was dead. Pursuing the national interest was "not the sole prerogative of the federal government," but was a goal to which Canadians from all regions could be just as committed as any "politicians in Ottawa."[77] This was a vintage expression of the new theory of cooperative federalism, a belief in the mutuality of interest of provincial and federal governments and communities.

While this doctrine may have been intended to throw a mantle of harmony and cooperation over intergovernmental relations and over serious divisions in the Canadian political community, it could not disguise the fact that peace was being purchased with massive federal concessions. The rhetoric about granting equality of treatment to all petroleum-producing regions, whether on land or offshore, ignored the fact that the offshore petroleum field was not Newfoundland's territory; it disguised the fact that Ottawa was deliberately rejecting any role as a potential recipient of energy royalties on these Canada Lands. Henceforth, the Canada Lands, or at least those parts immediately adjacent to coastal provinces, would be, in management terms, a federal-provincial resource zone and, in fiscal terms, lands whose oil and gas resources were to be treated "as if they were on land, within the province." Although the agreement was technically confined to Newfoundland, its provisions would later extend to other provinces. Indeed, Mulroney lost little time in notifying other interested parties, such as Nova Scotia, that these terms would be extended to them, and a new Canada–Nova Scotia offshore agreement was signed in August 1986. Until the development of provincial status for the territories in the Canadian North, that still left Ottawa with firm control over the Beaufort Sea and presumably with a strong stake in Petro-Canada, though the latter was clouded by the announced plans to privatize the company. However, the policy direction and the broad devolution of power was clear enough.

This shift toward cooperation with the provinces by making concessions over resource rents and management powers was accomplished more easily in the mid-1980s — in a period of declining oil prices, reduced state involvement, and changed priorities — than was possible five years earlier. Concern had shifted from the earlier preoccupation with "dividing the pie" among the regions of Canada, toward "increasing the pie" — stimulating economic growth and employment — across all regions.[78] In addition, the legitimate provincial claims for a strong measure of control over the nature and pace of offshore development were too compelling for the federal government to overlook. In that respect, the attempt to factor in these claims to power and control through a complicated system of shared control, with "an elaborate scheme of trumping powers, with the upper hand shifting from one level of government to another depending on the subject matter of the decision, the timing of the decision, and external factors," was considered inspired by constitutional specialist John Whyte:

> The embellishment in the Atlantic Accord of paramount authority moving between the two governments is inspired. It reflects the reality that consensus is more likely achieved in the context of complex countervailing forces. It also reflects the desirability that neither level of government have overriding authority in respect of all disputes. Finally, it reflects the fact that different conditions make it appropriate for different levels of government to have the final say.[79]

Yet, whatever the regulatory ingenuity of the accord, it cannot be said to help resolve the long-standing difficulty about intergovernmental sharing of resource rents, which became exceedingly inflamed during the oil price explosion of the 1970s. Although the federal government will continue to be expected to finance offshore exploration through tax breaks and incentives, and to fund 75 per cent of the special development fund to help Newfoundland provide infrastructure and other support for this undertaking, these costs are not at all balanced against what can confidently be expected to be the rather slim federal fiscal share through corporate income tax of future economic rent. While Petro-Canada profits will provide a substantial indirect payment, the system of revenue division over resources either here or elsewhere in Canada is anything but rational and satisfactory.

As Jean-Paul Lacasse has noted, there remains a continuing need to sort out a general agreement on resources revenue sharing, especially during the relative lull provided by lower international oil prices. Failure to address that issue was a critical part of the federal-provincial conflict during the 1970s, which ultimately led to the NEP. Resolution of the revenue-sharing issue would provide the essential basis for rationalization and simplicity, and for federal-provincial peace.[80] Any such agreement would have to encompass all significant resources, and it might or might not be tied to a horizontal equalization scheme of distributing a portion of resource rents from have to have-not provinces.[81] If any of these ideas of sharing and evenhandedness were better advanced and understood in the federation, the federal decision in the accord to remove any capping on Newfoundland's royalties (or those of other coastal provinces enjoying the same deal) would be far less troublesome.

In a critical overview of the revenue side of the Atlantic Accord, Peter

Cumming has argued that this agreement may contribute substantially toward interprovincial inequalities and to future federal-provincial discord. He points out that

> if there are further significant offshore discoveries, and if there are further world price increases due to OPEC, both of which are quite possible in the long term, then Newfoundland could quite possibly have the highest per capita fiscal capacity in the nation. Newfoundland might well be 10 to 20 times wealthier than say, Prince Edward Island, New Brunswick, or Manitoba. In contrast to our history since Confederation, which has seen the reduction of regional disparities in fiscal capacity, the Atlantic Accord may well create growing regional disparities. Newfoundland is not obliged to share its rising wealth with the rest of Canada; and to get even a part of it, a federal government would be forced to repeat the federal-provincial conflicts seen in Alberta and the western producing provinces over the past decade.[82]

It is also worth noting that Newfoundland (and Nova Scotia, which has taken up the accord's provisions) has also won a substantial exemption from the normal reduction of equalization payments as a result of the receipt of offshore revenues for a period of twelve years, a position that accrues to no other province suddenly in receipt of additional revenues. This can only complicate the abnormalities and difficulties under the equalization formula, by providing yet further ad hoc departures from its logic and rationale while failing to provide a resolution over the sharing of resource rents even in relation to the equalization program itself. Cumming was inclined to dismiss "the short-term glow of co-operative federalism" prompted by the accord and to argue that the "truth, in the long term, is that the offshore settlement represents a new, potentially centrifugal force for Canada as a nation."[83]

In light of the Mulroney government's concerns over the weak fiscal position of the federal government and especially over the size of the federal deficit, the revenue provisions in the accord seem curious. While a settlement did offer the opportunity for the energy industry to start moving again, with the promise of new jobs and higher federal taxes, the accord represented a serious fiscal liability for the future. Furthermore, the government landed itself in exactly the same dilemma with the Western Accord, which it signed with the three western producing provinces only a month later on March 27, 1985. Once again, the pattern of the new form of cooperative federalism was clear and the price for federal-provincial peace was a repudiation of most of the potentially lucrative federal fiscal measures contained within the NEP. While these actions did not help with the battle over the federal deficit, they certainly

did win the Conservative government a high, though temporary, measure of provincial goodwill.

The so-called Western Accord contained Ottawa's promise to remove
a long list of federal taxes in the oil and gas field. Some of these, such as
the elimination of the Oil Import Compensation Charge and the Petroleum Compensation Charge, were necessary tax changes flowing from
the government's decision to deregulate crude oil prices by June 1, 1985.
But others, such as the promise to remove all export charges on oil and
petroleum products and, most notably, to remove in planned stages the
Petroleum and Gas Revenue Tax (PGRT), were aimed at mollifying the
anger over the NEP of both the producers and the producing provinces.
The Conservatives had adopted the producers' objection to a federal tax
on revenue, agreeing that taxes should only be levied on profits; similarly, they had accepted the long-standing arguments of Alberta and other
producing provinces about the unfairness of federal export levies on oil
and gas.[84]

With the producing provinces agreeing to let the cash from these federal tax measures flow through to the industry, an enormous boost was
given to oil company profits at the expense of the federal treasury. Moreover, the government retained only the threat of "monitoring"
reinvestment as a thin reed with which to enforce the "jobs for tax
abatement deal" it had made with the oil industry. The companies
expected to receive even more benefit with the relaxing of oil export
restrictions and the dismantling of the made-in-Canada pricing structure
in favour of the world oil price. Those companies holding "old oil" —
discovered before 1974 — previously pegged at $29.75 per barrel, would
especially profit with the immediate rise in price to $38.00; such
companies included the foreign multinationals, notably Texaco Canada,
which ironically had previously done so little indigenous research and
exploration. These measures, added to the earlier governmental concessions to the oil companies, were clear indications of the extent to which
the foreign multinationals were being welcomed back by governments at
both levels.

The PGRT was entirely removed for all new production of oil and natural gas after April 1, 1985, while a gradual program to phase out the tax
on prior production was announced. The tax, with an approximate annual value then of $2.4 billion to Revenue Canada, was to be reduced at
an estimated total revenue loss of over $10 billion by 1990. Table 3-4
shows how drastically the accord was to affect the total of federal oil and
gas revenues. Finance Minister Wilson had to hunt elsewhere for equivalent revenues, and the deficit-fighting capacity of the federal government
was eroded. The same study also estimated that even after revenue gains
from other sectors from the economic stimulus of the accord were fac-
tored in, they were not enough to compensate for lost energy

# Table 3-4

## ESTIMATED REVENUE IMPACTS OF THE ACCORD
### ($ billions)

| | 1985 | 1986 | 1987 | 1988 | 1989 | 1990 | 1985-90 |
|---|---|---|---|---|---|---|---|
| *Federal* | | | | | | | |
| PGRT | *** | -0.6 | -1.3 | -1.9 | -3.0 | -3.5 | -10.4 |
| IORT | - | - | - | - | - | - | - |
| NGGLT | - | - | - | - | - | - | - |
| Export tax | -0.2 | -0.3 | -0.4 | -0.5 | -0.5 | -0.5 | -2.4 |
| COSC | -0.4 | -0.9 | -0.9 | -0.9 | -1.0 | -1.0 | -5.1 |
| Income Tax | 0.1 | 0.3 | 0.4 | 0.4 | 0.4 | 0.3 | 1.8 |
| PIPS[1] | | 0.8 | 0.8 | 0.8 | 0.9 | 0.9 | 4.2 |
| Total | -0.5 | -0.7 | -1.4 | -2.1 | -3.2 | -3.8 | -11.9 |
| *Provincial* | | | | | | | |
| Royalties | 0.2 | 0.7 | 0.8 | 0.8 | 0.8 | 0.7 | 4.0 |
| Export tax | -0.2 | -0.3 | -0.4 | -0.5 | -0.5 | -0.5 | -2.4 |
| Income tax | *** | 0.1 | 0.1 | 0.1 | 0.1 | 0.1 | 0.5 |
| Total | 0.1 | 0.5 | 0.5 | 0.4 | 0.4 | 0.3 | 2.2 |
| *Industry* | | | | | | | |
| Gross revenues | 0.4 | 1.8 | 2.1 | 2.4 | 2.5 | 2.5 | 11.7 |
| After tax | 0.2 | 1.2 | 2.0 | 2.7 | 3.7 | 4.0 | 13.9 |
| *Energy Investment* (1971) | | | | | | | |
| Nonresidential | *** | 0.1 | 0.2 | 0.3 | 0.5 | 0.5 | 1.6 |
| M & E | *** | *** | 0.1 | 0.1 | 0.1 | 0.1 | 0.4 |

[1] Estimates of the revenue impacts of the phase out of the PIP are taken from 1985 budget documents.

Source: Mary E. MacGregor, "Macroeconomic Impacts of the Western Accord," *Western Economic Review* 4, no. 3 (Fall 1985): Table 3.

revenues. The 1990 federal deficit was estimated to be $3.9 billion higher than it would otherwise have been.[85]

Clause 7 in part III of the agreement indicated that the government of Canada would no longer discriminate through future tax-based incentives to the oil and gas industry either with respect to the ownership level of the company or the location of its exploration and production. While Petro-Canada remained as a potential instrument, this provision in effect gutted the whole policy thrust of the NEP, which had been designed to advance both Canadianization of the oil and gas industry and federal government interests in development of its own lands in the Arctic and high seas. Although the NEP had used PIP grants to achieve both policy goals, the western agreement also announced the end of this program in 1986. As many commentators had noted, the PIP had turned out to be a boondoggle that foreign ompanies learned to get around with farm-ins with Canadian companies, that had rewarded drilling dry holes equally as well as successful exploration, and that had produced very little in the way of new finds for the more than $8 billion taxpayers had invested in the program.

The replacement regime, announced on the fifth and final anniversary of the NEP in late October 1985, was a tax-based system that offered a 25 per cent tax credit on wells costing more than $5 million and a credit against royalties for those costing less. This ystem offered far less incentive for exploration, particularly in the expensive frontier areas, while it tended to reward those companies with an already healthy cash flow (chiefly the multinationals) and to discourage smaller, cash-poor Canadian companies.[86] This was a policy result that Bruce Doern and Glen Toner had speculated would not likely occur as a result of the new power of the Canadian companies under the NEP.[87] It appeared that only the continuing provision that producing wells have at least half Canadian ownership would carry forward some of the policy objectives of the NEP.

The third leg of the government's policy, announced in late October 1985, essentially completed the Conservative government's transition to a market-driven approach in energy by providing for a phased-in deregulation of the domestic natural gas market by November 1986. This also meant the removal of the earlier formula whereby export prices could not fall below the Toronto floor price for gas, and the substitution of a newer rule that pegged export prices to the United States to that of the nearest Canadian export point. Hence, Ontarians and others could be paying more for Canadian natural gas than would Americans, a fact that predictably caused some unease in the new minority Liberal government of David Peterson. This was, however, a policy development very much in line, on the one hand, with the new framework of Conservative policy and, on the other, with market realities south of the border. Prices for natural gas were dropping like a stone in a highly unstable market in the United States, and Canada was in effect forced to adapt.[88] Lower prices were an obvious outcome, and that was a welcome and effective weapon with which to challenge the Peterson government with Ontario consumers, but at the same time it meant that producers in western Canada would face considerable difficulty in staying afloat.

With the signing of the earlier offshore agreement with Newfoundland, it was evident that Ottawa no longer regarded the offshore as a distinct federal zone that it might use to counterbalance the power of the producing provinces. There was therefore little purpose in playing federal-provincial politics with the incentives structure for the oil and gas industries. Energy Minister Carney recognized that there would likely no longer be a "stampede into frontier areas." The Conservatives, how-ever, hoped for continuing "steady activity" and offered the companies, in lieu of the lucrative PIP grants, the withdrawal of the hated back-in provision that had permitted the federal government in partnership with Newfoundland and Nova Scotia to buy retroactively a 25 per cent stake in any successful oil and gas find. Moreover, the Conservatives reneged on an earlier election promise by refusing to introduce a "Canadian share" provision to replace the deleted back-in clause. These measures represented an unqualified victory for the multinationals and the Amer-ican government, which had carried on so vigorous a campaign for the removal of these Canadian policies.

While the policy goal of Canadianization remained as a general target for the Conservative government, one considerably advanced by the 1985 purchase of Gulf Canada by the Reichmanns and the expansion of Petro-Canada through its subsequent purchase of Gulf's western assets, it was no longer linked to a drive to rebuild federal power. Although the federal government authorized Petro-Canada to purchase the Gulf assets and gave an advance tax ruling that saved the companies in the deal hun-dreds of millions of dollars at taxpayers' expense, this did not indicate that the government was continuing the Liberals' earlier policy of Canadianization through the expansion of public sector control and ownership. The refusal to inject further government equity, together with the removal of the back-in share in the government's new offshore policy, showed that there would no longer be special rewards for government-owned corporations like Petro-Canada. Indeed, following the Reichmann deal, Petro-Canada was regarded as a much more attrac-tive prospect for private investors, and rumours persisted, subsequently confirmed by Carney, that the privatization of Petro-Canada would be the necessary price to show that, appearances notwithstanding, the Con-servative program of Canadianization bore very little resemblance to the earlier program of the Trudeau government.[89]

At the time of the signing of the Western Accord, Carney joked with her provincial counterparts that the NEP was now gutted. By late Octo-ber 1985, with the announcement of the new natural gas policy and the removal of the back-in provision on the offshore and of the PIP system of exploratory incentives, that judgment could hardly be denied. Announc-ing that the "final nails have been driven into the coffin of the National Energy Program," the Conservatives had carried out their threat to dis-mantle the centrepiece of the Liberals' new nationalism.[90] Although Doern and Toner suggest the continuation of some NEP objectives and the permanent alteration the policy made to the Canadian energy scene, there is little doubt that the central political objectives of the policy have now been exposed and rejected.[91] Neither the federal drive against the provinces nor the multinationals in the industry had proved successful. Five years is hardly a long life for so massive a policy venture, but all indications, even those from new Liberal leader John Turner, pointed to the fact that Ottawa had finally turned its back on federal state-building in economic policy — probably for a long time.

Hence, the Western Accord marks a retreat of federal fiscal interests in the energy field, a reversal of the older policy of slanting federal energy policy toward Ottawa's own narrower state interests, and a joint intergovernmental decision to return oil and gas to the more or less normal operation of the marketplace. These were all powerful policy signals of the passing of the energy crisis of the 1970s, of falling world oil prices, of oil gluts, of OPEC's declining power as a cartel, of lessened governmental concern with world prices and supply, and therefore of the reduced role of the state in this field either as regulator, operator or rentier. The declining interest in control and regulation could be seen in another remarkable provision of the Western Accord: the decision to permit short-term exports of crude oil and petroleum products of whatever volume without the prior approval of the National Energy Board. All of these measures indicated how far the politics of oil had changed. Just as in the pre-1970 period in Canada, such conditions permitted a much less strident expression of Canadian federalism than was possible during the energy crises of the 1970s.

The reduced state role can also be seen in Alberta's own measures following the Western Accord, the so-called second shoe of the federal-provincial energy agreement. On June 24, 1985, Alberta announced a series of measures that would augment producers' incomes by approximately $400 million at the expense of the provincial treasury. Marginal royalties rates on both old and new oil and natural gas were reduced, along with increased royalty tax credits and royalty tax holidays; provincial incentives programs designed to counteract the effects of federal incentives under the NEP were to be phased out in line with the removal of discriminatory federal incentives. These and other moves by the producing provinces showed that they too were moving back from their relatively aggressive state postures of the 1970s.

Thus, the changed world situation in energy did permit the governments of the country a much cooler period within which to scale down their stakes in this sector and to resolve the divergent intergovernmental interests of consuming and producing provinces. But this does not explain the unusually severe nature of the federal Conservatives' attempted disentanglement from this sector. Although a reluctant Ottawa will continue to be an indispensable backer of oil exploration and will still be subject to pressure from oil companies to bankroll various initiatives, it has signalled its desire to play a much reduced role in the field.[92] Such a posture is in keeping with the government's preference for private sector economic leadership and its idle wish for reduced state involvement in the economy, but it is even more the political outcome of the National Energy Program in federal-provincial relations. The net effect of that doomed venture has been to set back the federal role in this sector for years to come.

Doern and Toner, for example, argue that the loss of the PGRT will, if replacement revenue is not forthcoming, reduce the ability of the Mulroney Conservatives to keep their commitments to Newfoundland for offshore development or to other regional economic development projects, or to continue to encourage Canadian oil companies with tax benefits even approaching the value of the old PIP grants.[93] With the announcement of the new natural gas pricing agreement, containing the new meagre system of tax incentives, that danger has already arrived, together with the old pre-NEP fiscal advantages for multinational oil companies. These changes, when coupled with deregulation and falling prices, have left small Canadian companies highly vulnerable to takeover bids by the multinationals. They must now "fight for survival or be bought out."[94] These are not encouraging signs for the future of the Canadian economy or the Canadian state.

However, it is clear that Petro-Canada as the biggest oil retailer in the country following its 1985 purchase of the western assets of Gulf Canada is not about to fade from the Canadian energy scene. It will remain as a lasting consequence of the Trudeau government's initiatives, although its ability to pursue its distinct public mandate may be severely undermined if the company is forced to undergo substantial privatization by selling shares to the private sector. That may be the future of the publicly owned company in this period of Conservative governments driven by the free enterprise rhetoric of private capital. Moreover, with the exception of debt-ridden Dome Petroleum, at least the strengthened Canadian majors, now including the financially powerful Reichmann interests, will probably ensure that Canadian interests in oil and gas will survive the NEP and its aftermath in a stronger position than their predecessors.

### How Far Can Oil Prices Fall? The Fate of the Tory Energy Strategy

As we have seen, the success of Tory policy with energy and with cooperative federalism depends upon the continuing compatibility of and mutuality of benefits and interests for both industry and governments from a market-driven rather than state-driven approach to these questions. What harmony exists between Ottawa and the provinces derives in large part from the fact that most governments now share similar assumptions. As Roy Romanow in a perceptive overview in 1985 noted:

> Both orders of governments in Canada today appear to hold similar views of how natural resources management should be used as a policy instrument. Both seem to believe that natural resources policy should not be driven by specific, activist government objectives, but rather should be basically shaped and directed by market forces. Neither level is placing great demands on the resource sector as a policy tool, except perhaps under the Atlantic Accord. In these circumstances, conflict over natural resources management in a federal state is obviously much more tractable.[95]

Tory policy does, however, rest at bottom on the expectation of substantial payoffs from this approach, particularly in the form of new jobs, investment and regional harmony. Energy Minister Carney made it abundantly clear that the government expected to activate stalled projects and bring on all kinds of new supplies — in oil, electricity, gas — by reducing taxes, regulations and intervention so that energy can once again become an "engine of growth."[96]

There is a startling degree of optimism in much of this thinking, which is in turn built upon a consensus of opinion fostered by the oil industry in its lobbying of the Conservative party after 1983. That consensus rested essentially on the assumption of short-term price stability in the oil market, followed by price increases for oil by the early 1990s, and of stronger American energy supply requirements, particularly in natural gas, by the late 1980s. By the spring of 1986 that consensus was already being severely tested by the spectacular drop in international oil prices, by Saudi Arabia's determined effort to restore its share of the oil market even if at lower prices, and by the chaos in the continental natural gas market. As G. Campbell Watkins had noted as early as 1985, the prevailing consensus sustaining Tory policy might turn out to be just as wrong as the consensus that had undergirded the NEP.[97]

In any event, these developments, if they persisted for very long, threatened to unhinge not only the economic dimensions of federal Tory energy policy but also the promise of intergovernmental peace and harmony. Within weeks of the fall in international prices, companies were cutting back their exploration budgets, laying off personnel and asking for more and more governmental aid in an attempt to ride out this "down" side of the energy crisis. Alberta and Saskatchewan responded nervously with further cuts in royalties and taxes, while simultaneously demanding more help from Ottawa in the form of a swifter removal of the PGRT and assistance in keeping the oil sands and other projects going when prices were rendering them temporarily uneconomic. Talk of hefty federal loan guarantees to induce the companies to get Hibernia under way was also heard, while an outlay of $200 million up front as part of a new offshore package with Nova Scotia was announced in late August 1986. These reports raised even more concern and resentment in the Alberta oilpatch.

Consumers in central and eastern Canada were urged not to seek short-term gains, but to take a longer-term view of protecting the domestic oil industry. Some company presidents, such as Robert Blair, were already calling for floor price supports in May 1986. These and other belated calls for price protection and intervention in the market place went very much against the prevailing Conservative policy at both levels of government so recently enshrined in interprovincial agreements, and represented an embarrassing ideological contradiction. But virtually all Albertans were calling for recognition by the country of the national dimensions of the industry and of the need for consumers to repay the producing provinces for sacrifices made during the years when a made-in-Canada price structure had been in place. It was clear from the nature of these pleas, however reasonable, that power was already slipping away from the hands of producers and producing provinces and toward consumers, manufacturers and the provinces representing them.

Meanwhile, there was scarcely a welcoming response from these consumers, at least in the first stages of the crisis, as they demanded that the benefits of falling oil prices flow to them, while the federal government tried to put the best face it could on this unexpected turn of events by arguing that lower prices ultimately benefited the national economy. Although the Ontario government later began to express concern as the long-term prospect of this downturn in the energy industry began to sink in, it could hardly ignore the interests of consumers in the province. Nor could federal Tories remain unmoved by central Canadian interests, particularly as they began to gear up in the latter half of their mandate for the next federal election. The Alberta government took an increasingly dim view of the adequacy of national responses to the crisis, as was glaringly revealed in Premier Getty's open denunciation of the federal Tories in August 1986 for their failure to remove the PGRT at once and in his warning about renewed western separatism. This was a distressingly familiar pattern in Canadian federalism and did not bode well for the Mulroney government's plans for cooperative federalism and interregional harmony. Even with the announcement of the prompt removal of the PGRT on September 8, 1986, there was little rejoicing, since low oil prices, compounded by depressed agricultural markets, were severely hurting the region. Ultimately, it remained to be seen how unkindly the market might challenge the underlying assumptions of Tory economic policy and federalism.

## Conclusion

On a broader plane, this chapter suggests that the mercantilist philosophy that had sustained the Canadian state's relation to the politics of oil during the 1970s and that was carried through in the NEP, is no longer a viable option for Canada in the new international climate. Oil has ceased to be a threatened commodity of strategic national importance and its value as a source of governmental revenue is at least in the short run very much less significant than it was in the previous decade. Petroleum, accordingly, is being returned to the normal operation of the market and increasingly placed outside the active administration and regulation of the state. This international system change has forced Canada to move away from administered pricing both in Canada and in exports to the United States, where intense competitive market pressures have played havoc with Canada's administered export prices for oil and gas.

This is the fundamental background against which the shift in federal energy policy toward deregulation should be understood. Although the Western Accord contains an "Ontario clause" permitting the federal government to intervene to prevent exports of Canadian oil and gas in the event of shortages or to limit prices if there is a return to spiralling international prices, a comfortable supply-side faith about energy and its beneficial role in the future Canadian economy and state underlies current Conservative policy. The willingness of the government to pursue simultaneously development of any or all energy projects promising more jobs for Canadians (only recently tempered by the startling fall in international oil prices), its liberality with exports of scarce Canadian natural resources such as light crude to the United States, and its pursuit of free trade all point to the triumph of laissez-faire economics and continentalism over the mercantilism of the recent past. They also point to a federalism with markedly less punch for governments at both levels in the federation.

In addition, the energy agreements of the Conservative government show that the role of the Canadian state has in relative terms declined more sharply. This is most striking in some of the terms of the Newfoundland-Canada agreement, although it is present too in the Western Accord. The forces of economic regionalism, though weakened by the current fall in commodity prices, have not been turned back as a result of the Trudeau initiatives of the 1980s, but may have made some substantial progress against the idea of centralized economic direction of the economy by Ottawa. Mulroney's cooperative federalism appears to recognize that fact by increasingly rationalizing the provinces' role in national decision-making and the economy. These trends are already apparent in Canadian federalism vis-à-vis trade policy as we will see in the next chapter.

CHAPTER IV

# Economic Policy*

The debate over the National Energy Program (NEP) had already exposed the close connection between federal state-building and this particular area of economic policymaking. As G. Bruce Doern and Glen Toner argue, the politics of federalism so infused and informed the policy that it would be naive to look for its logic purely in the economic imperatives of the energy industry itself.[1] The same might be said of Ottawa's larger economic development strategies under both the Trudeau and Mulroney governments, and especially of the various plans for economic renewal advanced in the 1980s. While these initiatives were strongly influenced by international and domestic economic conditions, it would be foolhardy to presume that the politics of federalism would play anything but a strong and indispensable role in them.

Trudeau's philosophy of preserving appropriate counterweights or pendulum balance between the different orders of government had convinced him in 1980 that he must act decisively to restore the balance of power in Canadian federalism. He and his Liberal colleagues had done so with unusual determination and vigour on the constitution and on energy policy. However, new national economic challenges also required Ottawa to help the country adapt to changes in the international economy and to reshape and restructure the economic foundations of the country. In that respect, the federal government was able to point to international economic trends dangerous to Canada's long-run interests, just as it had with the oil crisis, to justify both a more vigorous economic role for the federal government and renewed restraints upon economic province-building.

On one level, this move toward strengthened federal leadership over the economy might be read as merely part of a normal interventionist pattern that had been gradually developing in Canada and other countries as a result of increased vulnerability in an interdependent world

---

*This chapter was prepared with Scott Sinclair.

market. This "emergent statism," where government itself increasingly took on the role of entrepreneur, merchant banker and trader in a precarious international economic environment, appeared to some analysts to be well under way, long before 1980, at both levels of government in Canada.[2] But Canada's particular mode of integration into the international political economy contributed to serious internal problems of economic imbalance calling for correction and restructuring.

Due to the weakness of its manufacturing, Canada found itself disadvantaged in the most dynamic sector of world trade, that of industrial goods. Despite rates of economic growth only half those of the previous decade, international trade among advanced capitalist nations was increasing, with manufactured goods accounting for the largest component in unit value and quantity.[3] However, Canada's competitive position was slipping, a trend already indicated by its declining share of world trade. But the dramatic rise in the value of oil and gas following the second oil shock in 1979 appeared to provide, in the view of Liberal policymakers, an opportunity to use Canada's traditional strength in natural resources to improve upon its sagging competitive position in industrial goods.[4] If, for example, a larger share of resource rents could be garnered by Ottawa and directed to industrial restructuring or if more of the spinoffs from energy megaprojects could be captured by Canadian manufacturing firms that were potentially competitive in the international market, these anomalies might be corrected.

Not incidentally, such a program of economic renewal, a so-called "second shoe" partly modelled after the strongly interventionist NEP regulatory regime, dictated a strengthened role for the federal government. Concern over the economy and over Canada's shrinking share of world trade would, if taken up, provide the kind of policy challenge that could make Ottawa a more relevant and important order of government for all Canadians. Over the 1970s, however, the federal government had been quite unclear on how it wished to address this economic issue: whether to pursue a strategy of increasing trade liberalization (with consequent forced restructuring by market forces) or a more interventionist and nationalist posture with restructuring to some extent planned and controlled from within an industrial strategy. Its policies tilted at times in both directions and were therefore a veritable see-saw of conflicting and confusing purposes.[5] By 1980, the Trudeau Liberals appeared to have opted for the latter strategy largely, as will be argued, for their own political reasons; certainly, no new economic consensus drew the federal government in this policy direction.

Therefore, despite more than a decade of hesitant and cool response to the very idea of a national industrial strategy, Trudeau adopted in the 1980 election campaign virtually as "nationalist" a position on this topic as he had on energy and the constitution. Moreover, to the surprise of cynics, the Liberals' Throne Speech went on to promise a beefed-up Foreign Investment Review Agency and more aggressive federal industrial policy. The appointment of Herb Gray, regarded as the most hard-line nationalist in the cabinet, to head the key ministry of Industry, Trade and Commerce confirmed the message that the federal state was now ready to play a more active role in Canadianizing and restructuring the economy. Such a program provided both political visibility and relevance for the federal state and comprised an important element in the restraint of economic province-building.

The federal drive to strengthen the national economy had a decidedly centralist bent. As early as the summer of 1980, during the constitutional talks with the provinces, Ottawa unveiled a new constitutional agenda item intended to strengthen its powers to protect the domestic economy from provincial restrictions and infringements. In a lengthy attack on the damaging effects of provincial economic development policies on the economy, Ottawa sought constitutional instruments to curtail these practices and thus, indirectly, to tame the ambitions of the provinces. These initiatives were followed up by an array of policy decisions in the general area of economic development, the net effects of which were to circumvent, contain or undermine the provinces in their previous economic roles and/or to give Ottawa itself a more forceful and direct role in the economy. Taken together, these proposed measures were developed in order to breathe new life and purpose into a federal state that had grown weary of deferring to "province-building."

While the Mulroney government did not take power until well after the onset of the 1982 recession and after the fiscal position of the federal government had eroded significantly, it too faced a similarly daunting economic challenge. Here, however, the federal state lurched toward the ideological option already being championed by certain premiers, by business and bureaucratic interests, by conservative forces in Britain and the United States, and most forcefully by the Macdonald Royal Commission.[6] In an apparent break with traditional Canadian conservatism from the days of John A. Macdonald, Mulroney turned to those who preached the older nineteenth-century "liberal" virtues of "free trade," reduced state involvement, and sober fiscal policy to fight unemployment, rising national debt and industrial malaise.[7] These postures suited a more modest definition of the role of the Canadian state in the economy and a more complacent attitude toward American ownership and power in the country.[8] After all of the intergovernmental conflict over the centralizing character of the Trudeau government's economic federalism, this Tory program of economic renewal, linked explicitly and in seeming complementary fashion to a new heralded era of "cooperative federalism," purported to provide a way out of old economic and political impasses.

In deference to the traditional pattern of major party politics in the

Canadian federal state, the Mulroney Conservatives had planned their return to power in Ottawa by championing the interests of the provinces and of disaffected private sector interests against the ruling Liberals. Their arguments against the Trudeau Liberals as insensitive centralists sounded remarkably similar to the rhetoric of their nineteenth-century partisan opponents shut out by what then seemed like an unending Conservative dynasty during the 1880s and 1890s. Indeed, in a delicious ironical twist, the Mulroney Conservatives made off with much of the Liberals' historical legacy: not only the old electoral championing of provincialism, but also that party's long-standing but deadly flirtation with freer trade and market competition over government protectionism. In a curious way, Canadians were able to experience once again in the 1980s how partisan interests would play havoc with the traditional policies and principles of the major parties.

Thus, if economic difficulties in the 1980s make it clear that changes are needed in Canada, they do not by any means create a similar demand for a particular pattern of federalism or for a particular kind of political economy. While stronger federal economic leadership may be required to offer some vision of the economic future of the country and a strategy of how to get there, the role of politics and philosophy is still critical. In that respect, Canada's economic crisis, apparent by the mid-1970s and more pressing after the onset of the recession of 1982, would place severe demands upon any national government and test its understanding of the principles and practices of economic policymaking in a federal state. For our purposes, the economic pressures serve as an ideal background against which to measure the different policy responses of the Trudeau and Mulroney governments.

### Federalism and Economic Development

While the question of economic development in any modern liberal democratic state will naturally set off both ideological argument over the appropriate role of the state in the economy and political controversy (if not scandal) around particular patterns of government-industry relations, in a country like Canada there will also be the politics of federalism to consider. Here the state structure allows the possibility that both levels of government may act in relation to economic development and stir up the usual mix of political controversy which that will entail. Private interests may seek to lobby either or both levels of government in the pursuit of their own interests. This makes for a complicated government-business playing field as well as for an increased likelihood of federal-provincial conflict. These intricate sets of relations have characterized Canadian federalism virtually from the time of Confederation.[9]

From the strict perspective of intergovernmental relationships, there is wide latitude for philosophical disagreement about the role to be played by each level of government in relation to economic development. The constitution provides very little guidance on the appropriate balance of responsibilities and, in this respect, might be looked upon as a power reservoir for the different policy goals of provincial and federal politicians rather than an authoritative guide for distributing economic responsibilities. Moreover, apart from being the subject of pushing and jostling from private interests, economic development, it need hardly be stressed, is a perfectly acceptable springboard for the ambitious play of provincial and federal bureaucrats and politicians.

All of this suggests that there have been and will continue to be powerful pressures for government involvement in economic development in Canada — involvements that will necessarily generate federal-provincial conflict. But even if this were not true, the case for heavy government involvement in development from the earliest days has long been accepted by Canadians. Despite recent revisionist work charging that the National Policy was both premature and inefficient especially in overinvestment in railways, that legacy has not been dislodged.[10] During either the mercantilism of the colonial period or the later British imperial adoption of so-called laissez-faire economics, Canada's development was fostered only with special government support and protection. Some of these state measures included outright gifts of crown land to promote settlement and resource development, special charters providing for private monopoly control of certain staples trade, and expensive public works. With the advent of Confederation, the role and importance of government did not diminish. Both federal and provincial governments were involved almost from the beginning in building the economy and, during the process, rewarding their friends and allies in the private sector. Despite the windy and misleading claims of free enterprise advocates, the state was a director partner in Canadian economic development from the earliest colonial days.

With the founding of Canada and the ushering in of the country's first National Policy under John A. Macdonald, for example, it was the Canadian state with its plans for a national transcontinental railway system, protective tariff, and western expansionism that set out the ambitious program of nation-building. The Conservative political alliance between the federal state and prominent business interests in central Canada was in that respect a sort of model of federally inspired and federally led development for the country which thereafter appealed to nationalists of a centralist frame of mind. Although this pattern of development left the government wide open to scandals and charges of favouritism, with the significant state role in the building of the country's economy, any government might naturally come to see the political advantages, if not always the pitfalls, of this pattern of economic development.

It cannot be said that the provinces were slow in seeing the advantages this economic leadership offered. Nor were the more powerful provinces content with the distinctly junior status John A. Macdonald's economic plans had assigned to them. Undeterred by Macdonald's economic centralism and by his government's frequent imperial use of disallowance against them, provincial governments, especially in Ontario, began to build up their own private clientele of interests and to establish their own plans for natural resource development, hydroelectric projects and so on. The fight for a provincial economic role against federal paternalism was perhaps most bitterly depicted in the struggle of the western provinces for control of their public lands. All of these were early signs of the frequently competitive struggle in economic development between national and provincial levels of government, now regarded as a more or less normal feature of Canadian political life.

It is easy to exaggerate the activities and achievements of the provinces in this area during this early period and especially easy to generalize upon these competitive dynamics for other provinces in the federation. But there can be little doubt that federal-provincial conflict over economic development began very early and did not merely emerge on the scene with the arrival of truculent provincialists from the East and West in the 1970s. Even before the First World War the language of federal-provincial conflict in this area shows an uncanny similarity to the rhetoric generated by modern contests of this kind. Those who wished to defend the pre-eminent role of the federal Parliament, for example, would stress its unique right and responsibility to speak for economic development in the name of all Canadians, while those who wished to advance provincial objectives would marshal the appropriate provincialist rhetoric and milk it for all it was worth. Each government would seek to tap popular sympathies and mobilize private interests behind its economic objectives and its own vested theory of the federal state.

These are the historical dynamics of federalism and economic development. They are, however, neither uniform nor constant. The relative level of conflict in this area will vary from time to time, not least according to the generally accepted levels of government involvement in the economy. But, within this restraint, the pendulum of power as reflected in economic development may shift from one order of government to another at different times in the federation. In fact, students of federalism have been inclined to use the criterion of economic leadership and power as a significant measure of the shifting balance of power in a federal union.

For example, when the economy is being shaped by an aggressive federal strategy, such as Macdonald's National Policy following Confederation or the so-called Second National Policy following the Second World War, analysts argue that the pendulum of power in the federation shifts markedly toward Ottawa and away from the provincial capitals. However, when federal leadership is challenged by aggressive provincial-business development strategies, such as those used for forest, mineral and hydroelectric development projects in the 1920s and earlier, or for oil and gas development in the 1970s, the reverse is said to occur. The shifts in Canada's political economy — the relative price and importance of different kinds of staples at particular points of time, the changing international political economy and the relative policy priorities of governments — can help explain the alternating cycles of intergovernmental dominance and acquiescence in the federal state.[11]

The Rowell-Sirois report, for example, completed in the late 1930s, was following this idea when it linked economic leadership roles for the federal and provincial states with federal and provincial power during the first seventy years of the federal union; not surprisingly, it found a congruence between general dominance (or weakness) of a particular order of government and the relative economic leadership (or followership) it provides at one period of time. The same pattern of congruence, often supported with reinforcing statistical evidence from governmental shares of tax revenues and expenditures, shows up in most commentators' discussions on federalism, although the theory upon which they are based is rarely set out explicitly.[12]

Whatever the merits of this law of federal power dynamics, there can be no question that the arrival of the positive state in modern liberal democratic societies has accelerated the scope and importance of the traditional Canadian state activity in economic development. Big government — whether measured by the levels of tax, public employment, crown corporations or the regulatory control of the economy — has increased the political stakes in economic policymaking at both levels in the federal system.

The effects of these developments on the federal system are as unpleasant as they are predictable. If, as Alan Cairns has argued, successful economic leadership can give one level of government "unchallenged priority in the political system," when both the provinces and Ottawa compete more actively for that distinction, "an increased incidence of federal-provincial conflict" can quickly develop.[13] In 1978 this was yet "another crisis of Canadian federalism" to be added to the country's other dismal assortment of woes. It seemed indeed a characteristic of modern state actors at federal and provincial levels, whether in the bureaucracy or in the political executive, to seek to expand their power wherever possible. This addictive condition was said to drive modern state leaders so furiously that when they met, like Adam Smith's narrow-spirited businessmen, their ambitions soon drove them to "conspire against the public."[14]

This is a colourful if somewhat overdrawn argument that scarcely fits contemporary times. But over much of the 1970s and early 1980s it was easier to speculate about such power dynamics in the federal system. That period witnessed the coming apart of the post–Second World War consensus on which national economic policy (and federal hegemony) was based. Coming at a time when the country was also wrestling with separatist forces in Quebec and regional alienation in the East and West, these developments added yet more heat to federal-provincial controversies. It is in that context that the Trudeau government's economic federalism should be judged and the post-confrontation Mulroney regime understood.

### Economic Decline and the Failure of National Policy

Although it was not until after the successful fighting of the Quebec referendum in 1980 that the Trudeau government began to apply in a clear and concerted way its centralist federalism in economic policy, there were many earlier indications that national economic policy ought to reflect the government's federal philosophy and interests. There was the aggressive expansion of federal support for Canadian companies at home and abroad, especially where such expenditures would counteract the work of Quebec and the other provinces in the same area.[15] There were special programs that required and promoted linguistic accommodation in the private sector on hiring policies, product labelling and so on. There was the creation of Petro-Canada as a national player in the sensitive energy field, the Canada Development Corporation (CDC) to foster Canadian ownership of more sectors of the economy, and FIRA to screen and supervise additional foreign investment in the country. There was Ottawa's decision to control oil prices against the market and producing provinces alike, to join private companies in court battles aimed at limiting the natural resource powers of the provinces, and later in 1976 to impose wage and price controls. None of these reflected a government in any way afraid of exercising its economic powers.

Perhaps most revealing of the use of economic policy for the rational pursuit of federal purposes, however, was the experience with regional economic development. After years of Conservative and Liberal ad hoc attempts at promoting economic development in the poorer provinces and regimes, the Trudeau government broadened federal development policy with the Department of Regional Economic Expansion (DREE) in 1969. Here the earlier objectives of reducing regional disparities were expanded to include not only stricter federal control over planning objectives, administrative efficiency and programs, but a closer fit with preferred federal political goals. Higher federal visibility in the provinces, the counteracting of economic provincialism and the gradual development of a direct relationship between Ottawa and recipients of federal services in the provinces were to be encouraged.[16] These changes undercut the earlier patterns of coordination and cooperation through provincial governments and unilaterally asserted instead the priority of federal goals and processes. Although these strongly centralist measures were later relaxed in 1973 following the near defeat of the Trudeau government in 1972, the same spirit returned in the post-1980 period.

Several underlying economic factors prepared the way for a far more vigorous assertion of federal power over the economy in the 1980s. Chief among them were Canada's apparent economic decline as a trading nation, an alarming drop in Canadian productivity, unimpressive levels of research and development, technological dependence, and continuing high levels of foreign ownership in the Canadian economy. These were all the dubious fruits of the original National Policy, which had essentially created Canada's model of import substitution industrialization, and especially of the many later decades of Liberal policy that had sought to power Canada's branch-plant economy with massive injections of foreign capital.[17] Over the years, several government reports had questioned this economic legacy of foreign ownership, although by the end of the 1970s there appeared to be some evidence of lessened foreign control, along with signs of increased Canadian concentration of ownership and a contrasting multinationalization of Canadian industry.[18]

At the same time, however, Canadian dependence on export markets left the economy vulnerable to the effects of the extended recession of the early 1970s and to the protective measures taken by American and other major trading partners. While, on the one hand, countries were negotiating General Agreement on Tariffs and Trade (GATT) provisions that significantly reduced tariff barriers, on the other, the very same signatories to that agreement were turning increasingly to nontariff barriers to protect their own producers in world markets characterized by increasing competition and surplus productive capacity.[19] The old tariff instruments of the National Policy were becoming irrelevant in this new context. Moreover, the rise of the newly industrializing countries in the Pacific Rim and the international competition among the established industrial nations with internal markets of at least 100 million people represented serious challenges to Canada's conventional economic strategy and possible threats to the nation's future standard of living. Meanwhile Canada's economic reliance upon the United States as a market for its goods and services grew steadily throughout the 1970s and 1980s despite the Trudeau government's efforts to expand and diversify trade with other countries.

To compound these difficulties, the economic theory upon which federal economic leadership had been based since the Second World War was increasingly under attack. Keynesian economic theory appeared to be beaten and discredited by the rise of stagflation; the ability of governments to manage and direct the economy in an efficient upward direction came more and more into question. With the breakdown in this consensus and the grim record of rising unemployment, inflation and national debt, the provinces began to challenge the federal government's authority and ability to manage the economy, and pointed to their own rival economic theories, initiatives and experiments as models for national development.

While the industrialized centre of the country worried about its future position in a more competitive international economy, the peripheries clamoured for better treatment under national policies for their natural resources — especially oil and gas — and for a serious attempt to redistribute secondary manufacturing across the country. In Quebec the use of the state for building up francophone power in the economy was proceeding swiftly, and many other provinces were also employing state corporations to serve a variety of public policy objectives. Indeed, this province-building drive had now moved most provinces into creating a host of nontariff barriers, including restrictive trade and employment practices, subsidies, procurement policies and the like, which were alleged to have damaged the economic union.[20]

These economic difficulties suggested the need for a dramatic new direction for the federal government in relation to the Canadian economy, while the political conflict with the provinces over economic development had to be faced. Naturally there were advocates aplenty offering up economic and political prescriptions for the nation's ills.[21] Virtually all of these plans presupposed assumptions about the appropriate roles for provincial and federal governments in relation to the economy. No plan purporting to address the problems of the country could ignore federal-provincial tension and discord in this area.

The direction chosen by the federal Liberals under Pierre Elliott Trudeau was already clear. The National Energy Program and the unilateral constitutional initiatives indicated that the Liberals had decided the time had come to confront and turn back provincialism wherever it might present itself. During the constitutional talks in the summer of 1980, Ottawa had unveiled a new constitutional item "to secure the economic union in the Constitution." Building on the Safarian study commissioned by them, the Liberals demanded that the economic union be strengthened by extending section 121 to provide for the prohibition of nontariff barriers, by expanding the trade and commerce powers of Parliament, and by entrenching mobility rights for all Canadians in the new Charter of Rights. These claims were justified by a deceptively simple economic analysis that condemned virtually any restriction on the "efficient" allocation of factors of production.[22] Despite the fact that Ottawa was itself most responsible for interregional distortions, the government attempted to argue in classical liberal fashion that anything less than a "free" economic union (that is, no provincially created barriers) would seriously distort and harm the Canadian economy.

This was curious rhetoric indeed from a government that had so bluntly expressed reservations about the beneficent operation of a market economy.[23] It was even more ironical in the light of the highly interventionist National Energy Program being prepared for release that fall. Despite the fact that the government was also planning to move away from economic liberalism toward a modestly dirigiste direction in industrial policy, as a means to beat back provincially inspired economic measures, it proved to be too enticing a doctrine.

Neither the provinces nor the general public were nearly so alarmed about these provincial economic restrictions, nor at that time were they so caught up in laissez-faire liberalism. They were familiar with many such deviations from the pure operation of a market economy in the name of the public good, some of these restrictions put in place by Parliament itself. Nor was the argument that only Parliament could legitimately decide where the public good demands some derogations from the economic union likely to be satisfying. Not only was such a doctrine an affront to many Canadians' understanding of federalism, but the government's case for Parliament "representing" the country did not even stand up to the most elementary examination. Electorally, the governing Liberals were virtually without representation from western Canada, while the opposition Tories and NDP were almost bereft of representation from Quebec. How then could the Liberals claim to be answerable and sensitive to all Canadians in the development of national policy? Unless electoral conditions changed or federal institutions were to be reformed to make them more sensitive to regional interests, there was always the option of pushing through regionally biased policy with electoral impunity.

This attempt to monopolize economic policymaking for Parliament through the constitutional process was defensible only on an exaggerated reading of the effects of provincial restrictions. Since no abstract economic equilibrium analysis could claim to produce an optimal division of constitutional powers over the economy, reliance was put on the "distortions" that the offending provincial economic measures were having on the economy. But these are notoriously difficult to define, let alone to measure. Those econometricians who have hazarded estimates put the total impact of combined federal and provincial restrictive measures at only 1 per cent of gross national product for goods and less than .05 per cent each for capital and labour.[24] For these reasons, it is wise to assume that the exaggerated urgency of the federal case better reflected its political concern over the growing economic clout of the provinces than it did the results of sober economic analysis.

With the federal government shielding many of its prerogatives from the proposed language of the revised section 121, it was clear that the target was provincial governments. As chapter 2 on the constitution indicated, not much came of these constitutional initiatives. Only a much fettered mobility clause found its way into the final constitutional accord in 1982. The matter was, however, passed on to yet another forum for reflection and continuing action when the Trudeau government created the Macdonald Commission. Its recommendations to strengthen section 121 to include services, to expand federal powers over trade and commerce, to develop a code of economic conduct, and to monitor provincial economic measures continue, in effect, the ongoing constitutional campaign against economic provincialism begun by Prime Minister Trudeau.[25]

### Industrial Policy and the Defence of the Federal State

Federal-provincial politics over economic development were apparent too in the energy battle that was being waged in 1980-81. In monetary policy the two orders of government were also frequently at loggerheads, with the Trudeau government resisting provincial demands to lower interest rates and let the value of the Canadian dollar fall. But it was in industrial policy that the Trudeau government found policy options especially congenial to its plan and vision for the Canadian state.

The debate over industrial policy had in fact been going on for some time during the 1970s in government bureaucracies, research institutes and the universities. As the position of the economy worsened under the shocks of the energy crisis, inflation and high interest rates, public interest was increasingly focused on how to reorient Canadian economic policy in the light of the new international challenges and the internal problems of the Canadian economy. By the mid-1970s two elite schools of thought had developed with alternative economic diagnoses and prescriptions. While on one level this debate merely appeared to be a highly technical argument among specialists, it was in fact loaded with powerful political overtones and implications. Not least of these was the often implicit philosophy and politics of federalism carried by each side of the debate.

One side of this debate, the advocates of "technological sovereignty," looked to the federal government to develop a new National Policy that would defend the economic integrity of Canada by a closer monitoring and reduction of foreign ownership in the economy and by active encouragement of rationalization of Canadian companies into world-class enterprises able to compete in international markets.[26] This school, whose chief champion in the federal establishment was the Science Council of Canada, attributed most of the country's economic difficulties — low productivity, declining trade, low levels of research and technological innovation, inappropriate economies of scale — to foreign ownership and the truncated branch-plant economy it had spawned. It aimed to rectify this latent flaw in Canada's original National Policy by new state policies to develop indigenous technology and research capability, to exact performance requirements from foreign multinationals and to tailor public procurement policies in favour of Canadian firms and technology.

Such an approach had much to recommend it from the vantage point of those interested in shoring up the federal state. While Ottawa had after the mid-1970s largely abandoned even the pretence of an independent monetary policy and increasingly assumed a modest and less confident use of the tools of macroeconomic management, the technological sovereignty option at least permitted a vigorous federal role in promoting selected firms or sectors. Technological research and innovation, supported by federal policy, appeared as the key to capturing a greater portion of increasingly competitive world markets and to rejuvenating Canadian manufacturing.[27] Hence, while it would hardly restore Ottawa to the indisputable position of national economic leadership it had enjoyed during wartime emergencies or in the earlier Macdonald era, industrial policy presented an alluring opportunity for the federal government, just as it had with the NEP, to wrap its economic program in powerful pan-Canadian rhetoric.

Yet the federal government had even less experience with a microeconomic approach than had the provinces. Indeed, there was little reason to insist that federal bureaucrats could target potential industrial winners more effectively than their provincial counterparts, who after all were arguably more attuned to local conditions and needs. At the very least, cooperation in identifying and responding to specific opportunities and coordination in areas such as procurement seemed indispensable.[28] With Ottawa's adoption in the 1970s of conservative monetary policies largely responsive to U.S. conditions and its retreat from Keynesian demand management, it was unlikely that it could, by occupying the disputed ground of microeconomic industrial policy, recover an authority equivalent to that which it had earlier exercised.

Moreover, there were other problems: the government was itself badly divided over the wisdom of such a strategy; there were powerful enemies of the strategy at home and abroad; and there was a natural liberal ambiguity about adopting so statist a role in the economy.

Ottawa had made a number of tentative uncoordinated steps in the direction of an industrial policy over the previous decade. As early as 1972, then minister of industry Jean-Luc Pepin and officials of his department had raised the notion of an industrial strategy, but the idea was greeted with considerable scepticism in the private sector and in the more conservative echelons of the federal civil service. The Department of Finance in particular had been a powerful opponent of it. After 1973 the idea seemed to have disappeared from official policy pronouncements, though it continued to receive ongoing study and credence by the Science Council of Canada. It was not until the election campaign of 1980 that some of the ideas of the technological sovereignty school began to make their way into the speeches and campaign promises of then opposition leader Trudeau. In a campaign targeted at critical seats in southern Ontario, the Liberals promised lower energy prices and industrial renewal, while the Clark government, ignored by Premier Davis and Ontario's Big Blue Machine, found itself cast as the tool of western regional interests. Challenging the Tories' plan to dismantle Petro-Canada and privatize many state enterprises, the Liberals reached out to claim some of the planks of the technological sovereignty school:

- performance reviews of large foreign companies;
- provision for publicizing proposed takeovers of Canadian companies by foreign enterprises and government financing for Canadian counteroffers;
- strengthening of FIRA;
- policies for the encouragement of more domestic research and technological innovation; and
- the use of procurement policies to stimulate demand for Canadian technology, products and firms.

Coupled with the election promises on energy policy, including the expansion of Petro-Canada and the use of energy as a vehicle for Canadian industrial renewal, these commitments indicated the beginnings of a reinvigorated National Policy with distinctly centralist overtones.

As Stephen Clarkson has indicated, this new Liberal nationalism was primarily an anti-provincialist campaign, although it could only be mounted because of the rise of a more "nationalist" class of capitalists eager to profit from it.[29] This was exactly the combination of interests from which the government expected support in the battle over the NEP. The publication of the Blair-Carr report indicated that a potential nationalist alliance between indigenous Canadian entrepreneurs and labour might be struck that would support Canadianization of the economy under federal leadership.[30]

However, in the face of determined American opposition to its National Energy Program and a full-fledged fight with most of the provinces both over the NEP and its unilateral constitutional measures, the Trudeau government, while largely holding the line on these policy initiatives, quickly backed off from its plans for a national industrial strategy. Herb Gray's brief to the cabinet, which had called for stricter performance reviews of foreign-owned firms by a strengthened FIRA, was shelved, while the government, on American insistence, sought a ruling on its performance requirements of multinationals under GATT.

The decision confirmed Canada's right to screen foreign direct investment and require commitments respecting exports from foreign investors, but it struck down provisions requiring purchase of Canadian products instead of imports as a violation of GATT's article 3 on "national treatment." With that loss, much of the policy force that remained behind the industrial strategy option evaporated.

In March 1981, however, the government, in a face-saving white paper accompanying the budget, announced a new megaprojects strategy. This was, in effect, a revival of the old staples-centric approach, backward linked to exportable high-tech, with the kicker being oil and gas. The government identified $440 billion of investment in future resource projects in the North, the eastern offshore and the West, offering, in turn, plenty of potential for stimulating manufacturing and resource technology contracts in central Canada.[31] It was a precarious gamble, built on the same innocent assumptions about the rosy future for commodity prices that was propping up the NEP. With the collapse of those premises in the subsequent recession, much of the political steam that had been built up for an innovative national economic policy under Ottawa's direction had been spent. It was not long before plaintive calls went out to Washington for talks on sectoral free trade. Clearly these overtures, together with other accommodating policy signals, indicated that economic nationalism was already being given a quiet burial scarcely more than halfway through the Liberals' mandate.

With the disarray caused by falling commodity prices, the only tangible remnant of the mooted industrial policy package was the extensive reorganization of the federal cabinet and bureaucracy. This restructuring was intended, among other things, to rationalize federal conception and delivery of regional development projects in the context of the government's wider rebalancing program. After almost a decade of experiment with a decentralized federal Department of Regional Economic Expansion with authority to negotiate general development agreements (GDAs) with the provinces, the program was now in considerable difficulty. On the one hand, there remained elements in the federal bureaucracy, especially in the powerful line departments of Finance and Industry, sceptical of DREE's attempts to lure industry to the backwaters; on the other, the industrial strategy debate had exposed threats to the industrial heartland of central Canada from international competition, growing trade dependence on the U.S., and especially from American protectionism. Not only was central Canada increasingly being redefined as a potentially disadvantaged region in need of renewal, with federal money flowing disproportionately to cities with already established industry under the 1981 Industrial and Labour Adjustment Program (ILAP) and the Industrial and Regional Development Program (IRDP), but regional subsidies were themselves seen as potential targets of

American countervail. These conditions called into question regional development incentives and their role in the government's broader economic policy.

Moreover, with the GDA approach to economic development, too much resistance had developed to DREE's freedom from central office control and especially to the indirect political credit it provided provincial governments. Henceforth, this failure to conform to the new centralist policy of circumventing provincial governments would be corrected.[32] The new minister, Pierre de Bané, was determined to bring economic development policy into line with the government's wider political program of centralist federalism. Beginning with the renegotiation of the P.E.I. Comprehensive Development Plan in 1981 and in later negotiations of subsidiary agreements with other provinces, de Bané promoted federal visibility, implemented direct delivery of federal programs, and shifted federal funding away from provincially delivered programs.[33] With the political payoffs implicit in this new approach, cabinet even approved a 25 per cent budget increase for regional development in the 1981-82 fiscal year, a temporary and short-lived improvement over declining spending in per capita constant dollars for regional economic development from the mid-1970s on.[34]

Yet even these political reworkings of DREE's delivery mechanisms could not spare the department in the subsequent 1982 reorganization. It was abolished, and regional development, now ostensibly a common concern in all economic decision-making, was to be coordinated by a new central agency, the Ministry of State for Economic and Regional Development (MSERD). There was now no longer any single federal agency solely responsible for regional economic development. GDAs would be gradually phased out in favour of economic and regional development agreements (ERDAs) that would restore central political control of projects and enhance federal delivery and visibility.

After considerable grumbling, most provinces managed to accommodate themselves to this new regime and to sign new ERDAs. Quebec, however, had profound objections to them. Partly as a consequence of this and of the continuing federal-separatist feud, the province found itself the subject of extraordinary actions by the federal government in this field. In unprecedented unilateral actions, for example, the federal government announced two major regional development projects for Quebec without the consent of the government of that province: a $224-million project for the Gaspé and Lower St. Lawrence region in May 1983 and a further $108-million Quebec economic development program in June 1984. Complaining of the difficulties of securing provincial agreement with the Parti Québécois government, Finance Minister Marc Lalonde and Minister of Economic and Regional Development Donald Johnston attempted to win the constituents' favour by literally going over the heads of the provincial leaders to the people themselves. This was entirely in keeping with the new policy of unilateral defence of the federal state.[35]

Other examples of unilateral federal policy initiatives, including an attempt to circumvent provincial governments by providing grants directly to municipalities in the provinces, continued to illustrate the consistency of the federal objectives and strategy. In 1981 Ottawa repudiated its earlier policy of sending such monies through provincial governments on the understanding that priorities would be cooperatively set by provinces and municipalities and acknowledgment of federal financial support would be given. Instead it began to issue direct grants to municipalities under its own job creation program of June 1983. Although all provinces condemned this intrusion into their constitutional responsibilities, Quebec went further with legislation to penalize municipalities that received federal funds without provincial approval. Ultimately, Ottawa was forced to sign an accord with Quebec restoring the principle of funding through provincial governments.

The federal program to check economic provincialism was also carried forward with Bill S-31 in 1982. In this case the matter concerned the attempted blocking of provincial ownership in interprovincial transportation enterprises. Quebec's Caisse de Dépôt et de Placement, a Quebec crown corporation with up to $5 billion of pension and other income for equity investments in Canadian and foreign companies and under board orders to "direct its resources increasingly toward Quebec's economic development," had purchased almost 10 per cent of the shares of Canadian Pacific (CP) and was seeking representation on its board. With a generous guideline permitting purchase of up to 30 per cent of any single corporation's equity, the Caisse had already achieved effective control of Provigo Inc. and, with the help of another Quebec crown corporation, the Société Général de Financement (SGF), had the same hold on Domtar Inc.[36]

In a forthright counter to Quebec's move on Canadian Pacific, Ottawa struck back with a general bill to restrict provincial ownership to 10 per cent of the voting shares in any transportation company operating across provincial or national boundaries. While serving as a warning about the potential dangers of "balkanizing" provincial interventions on the national transportation system and common market, this anti-provincialist move also had the effect of protecting CP management and thus of cementing this federal-corporate alliance. Although the federal government had already had legislation in place to restrict or control provincial ownership in the airlines, banks and broadcasting sectors, the provinces were not about to have their investment operations and influence further restricted. Immediately British Columbia, Alberta, Saskatchewan, Ontario and Newfoundland joined in the battle. But only fierce opposition from within the Quebec caucus and business community managed to turn Ottawa around on the issue. In a scathing review of the whole policy venture, Alan Tupper concluded that "Bill S-31 combines bad politics and half-baked economics."[37]

It would be foolish, however, to pretend that the entry of provincial government investment vehicles and holding companies did not raise serious implications for the Canadian economic union and for intergovernmental relationships. In a study done for the Macdonald Commission, Huffman, Langford and Neilson warn that the examples of the Caisse operations and of a more activist direction promised by the Alberta Heritage Savings Trust Fund suggest that "the capacity for provincial influence, sometimes direction, over significant market decisions must be more fully appreciated as a new element in federal-provincial relations and in the evolving nature of the economic union." They argue that, since the Caisse example "gives rise to the prospect that the extensive commingling of public and private ownerships in large corporations may create a supra-constitutional form of state capitalism" and "strain relations between the host governments and the private sector," either there must be more investment sensitivity and self-restraint by governments or "comprehensive ownership limitations on *both* levels of government" may become necessary in future.[38]

The latter contention (namely, that if a policy of restraint on government investment levels in private companies were to be applied, Ottawa itself ought to be so contrained) was in fact a prominent part of business arguments to the federal government over Bill S-31. It was, however, the view of the federal government that, by virtue of their limiting territorial and sectional interests, only the provinces were in need of restraint in the national interest. Parliament would, by definition, be the logical expression of the Canadian national interest, since only it could truly claim to represent the views and interests of all Canadians. To restrict its freedom to express that national will would therefore be an absurd self-abnegation. That argument conveniently overlooked all the well-known limitations of Parliament as a genuine forum for expressing the national will, just as it overlooked the fact that Canada is also a federal country.

All of these coordinated federal state-building initiatives in the economic area do not appear, on balance, to have been successful in turning back provincial power. Most of them have already been jettisoned by a new federal government more sensitive to provincial rights and powers. But even before the September 1984 electoral victory of the Conservatives under Brian Mulroney, the provinces had managed to fight back successfully in a number of these areas — from the constitutional battle over the economic union to Bill S-31 and municipal funding. Indeed, one of the most striking aspects of the initiation of federal unilateralism was that it provoked what Ken McRoberts has called "double unilateralism," where federal actions merely met countervailing measures adopted by the provinces.[39] The process was in many respects self-defeating.

One of the most serious consequences of this political warring between the two orders of government is a decline in policy effectiveness in tackling problems. Not only can politically inspired unilateralism send the governments off in costly and inefficient duplication or contradiction of each other, it can materially injure the public interest groups caught in the government crossfire. A good example of the latter would be the Quebec municipalities' loss of significant federal funding during the period of intergovernmental feuding in this area.[40] It has in fact been characteristic of many groups outside of the arcane federal-provincial power dynamics to complain bitterly over the effects of these disputes on their own operations. As noted in chapter 3 on energy and will be seen in chapter 5 on fiscal federalism and social policy, when intergovernmental collaboration breaks down and the politics of double unilateralism begins to unfold, it is the public itself that suffers the ill effects in a myriad of direct and indirect ways.

One long-term consequence of these federal-provincial wars, especially where they involve massive uprooting of earlier bureaucratic arrangements and practices such as those operating under the old GDA agreements under DREE, is that functioning patterns of trust and cooperation between federal and provincial officials are simply destroyed. Since regional economic development necessarily requires intergovernmental collaboration, whatever the "high" politics of federalism, these patterns will somehow have to be developed under whatever kind of bureaucratic regime. As J. Stefan Dupré has argued, it would be far better to perfect and improve those working relationships to achieve additional objectives than it would be to pull them down and start again.[41] The tragedy is that the high politics of executive federalism does not often lay much stress on these mundane matters.

This gives credence to Donald Smiley's contention that the development of executive federalism and the enlargement of intergovernmental relations bureaus has in fact undermined the effectiveness of Canadian federalism. While it has undoubtedly contributed to more conflict, it is difficult to isolate this element as a predominant cause. McRoberts, for example, attributes a good deal of this destructive pattern of federal-provincial relations to the working through of the federalist-separatist feud in Quebec — a struggle that coloured almost every aspect of intergovernmental relations prior to the establishment of the new Canadian constitution and for some time afterward. Whatever the ultimate cause, there is little doubt that the pursuit of high politics can play havoc with functional concerns in a variety of policy areas.

Perhaps the most ironical consequence of implementing this brand of unilateral centralist federalism is that it paves the way for the triumph of its ideological opponents. Just as the vigorous assertion of central power by the government of John A. Macdonald ultimately prepared the way for a more provincialist Liberal coalition under Laurier in 1896, the pursuit of Trudeau's federalism literally called forth its political counterpart in the Mulroney Tories. Nor do the parallels between the nineteenth-century period and the twentieth end here. Both of these highly centralist programs were advanced during periods of relative economic decline, a fact that limited their success and hastened their demise. How the pendulum of power might have swung in the Canadian federal state had circumstances been otherwise is an intriguing question.

It is not difficult, however, to see how the Trudeau government's pursuit of the politics of federalism in economic development led to internal ideological contradictions that may have cost it dearly. On the one hand, the government followed a fairly rigorous and unrelenting free enterprise line of argument against provinces during the constitutional struggle over the economic union (while quietly inserting in draft provisions a federal right to intervene); on the other, it tried to defend both the National Energy Program and its planned but ill-fated industrial strategy with interventionist language appropriate to a dirigiste state. No doubt it is convenient to have frequent wardrobe changes in political attire for all those special moments when federal interests may require them, but these were intolerably muddled signals for the same government to be sending out to the Canadian people at the same time. In view of the fact that the Liberals were confronting a rising movement toward conservative values and laissez-faire rhetoric throughout the English-speaking world (perhaps best manifested in the persons of Prime Minister Thatcher and President Reagan), it was doubtless foolhardy to have adopted such language to fight off the provinces. As they quickly discovered, the strategy boomeranged when business increasingly demanded the same self-restraining ordinances from Ottawa as Ottawa had demanded of the provinces. Moreover, free enterprise rhetoric only served to strengthen the case of the federal government's opponents both at home and abroad.

In fact, the Tories rode to power in 1984 on a political program attacking the centralist federalism of the Liberals and their inept economic interventionism. By that time the combination of the recession, falling oil and gas prices, and public exhaustion with federal-provincial warring, especially over the economy, had deprived the Liberals of the broad nationalist coalition that had won them the 1980 election. These developments had already become clear by the middle of Trudeau's period in office, and the Liberals sought unsuccessfully to adapt to this changed environment. After scarcely more than a year into the Mulroney government's mandate, Canadian politics would show how drastically matters had changed. With Quebec separatism in retreat and the forces of regionalism quieter, the old days of federal defensive expansionism were over. The issue of Canadian economic renewal had moved in to occupy centre stage.

### The Mulroney Gamble on Free Trade and Cooperative Federalism

The election campaign in the summer of 1984 already confirmed a shift away from the unprecedented federal-provincial confrontation generated in Prime Minister Trudeau's last years in power. All parties, even the Liberals under the new prime minister, John Turner, appeared to be falling over themselves with offers of goodwill to the provinces. The Mulroney Conservatives, with PC allies entrenched at the provincial level in most provinces, distinguished themselves over the others in this respect. In the aftermath of so much federal and provincial conflict, it was a natural electoral response, especially since the condition of the economy had worsened over those years.

The change might just as easily be accounted for, however, by the fact that the politics of federal centralism had run its course and could no longer draw upon political challenges and resources to sustain it. Not only had the primary object of federal concern been mollified by the turning back of Quebec separatism and the entrenchment of official bilingualism, but severe recession had reduced the pools of support for nationalist economic ventures and policies.[42] In that respect, the National Energy Program could be read as a lingering pathetic metaphor for this dilemma as it teetered uncertainly in the face of a new conservative anti-statist political climate and falling energy prices.

The new approach to economic development adopted by Prime Minister Mulroney's government drew immediate and superficially appealing conclusions from this changed environment. Instead of the recent practice of seeking to circumvent the power of the provinces in national economic policymaking, the new government took the opposite tack of welcoming the provinces as legitimate players — indeed "partners" — in the economic life of the country. Hardly seven months into office, Prime Minister Mulroney had met the provinces in two full-scale conferences, each of which was designed to underline the new federal approach of working with the provinces to resolve the nation's economic problems.[43] These were followed up by a full-scale conference with business, labour and other important interest groups on the future direction of federal policy.

There had always been at least two federal options in dealing with the rising power and importance of the provinces as players in the Canadian economic union: one, to fight that development by seeking to constrain if not turn back its growth; the other, to rationalize the provinces' new status in a formal way and to bring provincial governments into closer and cooperative relations with the federal government. Neither option was without its risks, although initially cooperative federalism looked like an easier policy to sell.

The problem was that the new rhetoric of consultation and co-operation with provincial governments could only be sustained in the long run with tangible actions by the federal government to remove outstanding regional irritants. There was, of course, a price for cooperation, a price that would in the end spell the diminution of federal power and authority, so vigorously and recently pursued by the Trudeau government acting on the other option. This pattern, already evident in federal concessions in the energy field, was the ironic consequence of the Trudeau government's efforts to rebuild federal power in relation to economic matters at the expense of the provinces. In most respects, its successor merely cancelled these policy efforts and began to move federal-provincial economic relations in the opposite direction.

There were at least two factors behind these new federal moves. One was Mulroney's earnest desire to get the economy moving again. The removal of the irritants to expansion of the oil and gas sector was considered vital to the Conservatives' economic program of jobs and prosperity. For that reason Energy Minister Carney was given clearance to strike a deal with the provinces that would put an end to federal-provincial bickering in the area and establish stronger market incentives for investment in oil and gas. The movement to world pricing for oil and gas was a clear indication that the Conservatives were abandoning the old Liberal policy of maintaining a made-in-Canada pricing structure in favour of a market-driven approach. While this position assuaged provincial concerns, only a year later falling international prices for oil and gas began to call that decision into question (especially for the producing provinces) and reopened the old interregional politics around administered pricing.

Behind these changes, in turn, were the altered power positions in Ottawa of the province of Ontario and the producing provinces. Under Prime Minister Trudeau, there was a fairly consistent regional bias in policy toward Ontario and Quebec, which explained Premier Davis's steadfast support for the Liberals despite the blandishments of party labels. Mulroney's first cabinet indicated that western power had arrived in Ottawa; many of the senior ministers in the powerful Policy and Priorities Committee were western members with backgrounds in business. Meanwhile Ontario was undergoing a leadership change, fol-lowed by an electoral campaign in May 1985 that saw the venerable Tory hold on the province loosened and the arrival of a minority Liberal gov-ernment. These developments weakened Ontario's influence in the na-tional capital.

Prime Minister Mulroney confessed as much when in September 1985 he admitted that western power had arrived in Ottawa and that it was now time for those interests to make a reasonable accommodation with Quebec.[44] Although the Conservatives had a large number of representatives from Quebec in their caucus, because of the long Conservative hold on the West and the relatively recent inroads in Quebec, there were virtually no senior Quebec ministers to help balance the experience and power of the Conservative ministers from the West, the Maritimes and Ontario. These realities played their part in the priority given to a Western Accord and a settlement with Newfoundland. In fact, these policies were already largely developed by the Conservatives while in opposition, and they reflected the electoral and experiential weight of gravity in the party at the time.

Perhaps for the same reason there was considerably more enthusiasm in the party for a market-oriented approach to public policy and far less enthusiasm for the interventionism and rational state planning that had come to characterize Trudeau's regime. As commentators have noted before, the inclination to use the state to restrain and supervise a market economy was far more readily accepted by the francophone intellectual elite that came of age in Quebec in the 1960s than it was elsewhere in the country, and that fondness for the dirigiste state carried over into federal and Quebec politics over the next two decades.[45] The Conservatives, with strong support in the West and substantially more business representation than the Liberals, pointed the Canadian state in an opposite direction.

The trend was already clear during the brief tenure of Prime Minister Joe Clark. Despite the widespread popularity of Petro-Canada, the party planned to "privatize" the company to suit its own ideological predilections.[46] That venture ended in disaster. The Mulroney government shortly after winning power also made it clear that the role of government had to be reduced and that a useful avenue to this end would be to sell off several crown corporations to the private sector. Accordingly, under the enthusiastic direction of Industry Minister Sinclair Stevens, plans were announced to put Canadair and de Havilland on the block, along with Eldorado Nuclear Ltd., Teleglobe and several others. Although these companies were already targeted for ultimate sale by the Liberals as early as 1982, the new minister appeared to be in undue haste to be rid of them. On December 4, 1985, the government announced the sale of de Havilland to Boeing Corporation, a giant American multinational, for the paltry sum of $155 million.[47] This action, taken after the expenditure of almost $750 million on the company in recent years by Canadian taxpayers,[48] demonstrated the alacrity with which the government wished to unload crown corporations. In addition, the government moved swiftly to divest itself of its holdings in the Canada Development Investment Corporation (CDIC), an agency the Trudeau government had created to rejuvenate temporary corporate losers and to advance Canadian ownership of the economy.[49] These moves were all in keeping with the pervasive motto of "less government" so popular in the United States and Britain, and despite occasional lapses in practice, they came to characterize the first years of power of the Mulroney government.[50]

The same attitutes made their way into regional economic development. The Mulroney government quickly moved this policy area away from its earlier centralist mould and back into a comfortable fit with co-operative federalism. There were no development programs announced over the heads of the premiers, nor any circumventing of provincial governments. Indeed, the government joined with the provinces in an historic declaration enshrining the principles of regional economic development and of federal-provincial cooperation in an intergovernmental position paper in June 1985.[51] That document can be seen as the strongest intergovernmental statement on the goals and permanence of this feature of Canadian federalism. It supplements the commitments to reducing regional disparities under section 36 of the Canadian Charter of Rights and Freedoms and institutionalizes the intergovernmental nature of this area of policy. The position paper is remarkable for its candid admission of the failure of earlier national policy to take account of its unfair and unequal impact on the regions, of the importance of national transportation policy to regional development, and of the need for public sector activity in have-not regions where the private sector is weak. Presumably, the claims of regional economic development are henceforth to be taken into account in all pertinent national policy, including fiscal and monetary policy, investment policy, industrial and transportation policy, and trade policy. Such general talk was no realistic substitute for clear federal targets and an effective department to implement them, but with the promise of intergovernmental coordination and consultation, the provinces at least had a springboard upon which to launch claims for a stronger say in federal policy.

Despite the extensive verbiage, there was a marked shift toward a more "realistic" market approach to regional development that would stress rigorous selectivity, comparative regional advantage, productivity and the removal of interprovincial barriers to trade. In this way an uneasy attempt was made to carry forward old arguments over the integrity of the national economic union to regional development and to paper over the unequalizing effects of a capitalist market economy with lofty rhetoric. None of this convinced experienced specialists like Donald Savoie who worried about the effects of this shift in priorities, especially on regional economies, like those in the Maritimes, lacking strong private sectors.[52] Balancing regional development with a market approach was a precarious undertaking, more so during a period of severe governmental financial constraint. Regional development had already become a prime target for federal cutbacks in the battle over the bulging federal deficit. These policy decisions reflected some impatience with the unsuccessful attempts at government-induced development, a feeling that the same level of program expenditures could no longer be maintained with rising federal debt, and a wish to remove these distortions and inefficiencies in the market.

Some of these sentiments were expressed in the Macdonald Commission report. Although it continued to endorse the idea of regional development as part of the "Confederation bargain," the programs were nonetheless not expected to interfere with market efficiency and rationality. The commission recommended that for provinces to receive regional grants they must sign a Code of Economic Conduct eschewing provincial protectionism, while federal subsidies and grants to generate jobs and to encourage firms to locate in have-not areas would be scrapped or largely hived off to the provinces. Similarly, the federal government was to cease its regionally differentiated programs of unemployment insurance and tax credits to help support have-not areas. Instead these monies would be spent on improving productivity and efficient labour skills. Other sections of the report suggested grants to individuals to encourage mobility from have-not to have areas as a more rational approach to this problem.

The lowered priority for regional economic development was reflected in the Conservative estimates for this item. While the Liberals were projecting a 14.8 per cent envelope expenditure for economic development (including energy) as a percentage of total outlays in 1985-86, the Conservatives were projecting only 12.3 per cent.[53] This reflected cuts in economic development, including energy expenditures, which the Conservatives had announced in the November 1984 statement. This contrasted sharply with an increase in the percentage of social spending by the Tory government as a result of its backing away from the muddled debate over universality at the end of 1984. While the Conservative budget of May 1985 marked the resumption of cuts in social spending to curb the deficit, the lower priority of regional economic development remained. In fact, it is the biggest loser in government expenditure projections, falling dramatically in both absolute dollar terms and as a percentage of total program expenditures.[54]

In marked contrast to these continuing governmental restraints on program expenditure, the budget provided for substantial and preferential tax savings for private capital. These "back-door" indirect tax expenditures amounted to $425 million in 1986-87 and $745 million the next year, versus $213 million and $295 million for direct expenditures over the same years.[55] One of these new tax expenditures provided by the 1985 budget was the removal of capital gains tax on the first half-million dollars of net capital gains. These giveaways moved the government far away from the Carter Commission rationale for a more equitable tax treatment on all income whatever its source but were justified as an incentive for wealth enhancement and national economic recovery through private sector investment. Although nothing in this budget package ensured that capital eligible for this tax break must be in Canadian enterprise, it was the government's hope that business would take the opportunity to begin a national economic recovery. It was made clear that only with an acceptance of this challenge could business fight off a return to government interventionism.

The Mulroney government adapted to the demands of most provinces, to new pressures from business and to their own sense of economic policy when a relaxation of controls over foreign ownership was introduced. This new direction was indicated in the so-called defanging of FIRA. Although FIRA had never amounted to a serious threat to the interests of foreign capital and was a mild agency by world standards, there was a persistent perception outside (and later inside) the country that the agency was a serious roadblock to foreign capital.[56] As the economy became more severely battered by the recession, both FIRA and the NEP took the symbolic brunt from interests unhappy with the Trudeau pattern of federalism. Gutting both became key elements of the Conservative election campaign and important symbols of the welcoming of foreign capital into Canada.

Announcing in the House of Commons on December 7 that Canada was "now open for business," Industry Minister Sinclair Stevens proposed in Bill C-15 the replacement of the Foreign Investment Review Agency with the more innocuous-sounding Investment Canada. The powers of the new agency were entirely in keeping with its bland title. Instead of exercising control over all takeovers and new foreign investments as was the case with FIRA, the new agency was shut out of screening all new investment except that "related to Canada's cultural heritage or national identity." New foreign investment not touched by the exception would then enter Canada without any restriction. In addition, Investment Canada's screening of takeovers was restricted to companies with more than $5 million of assets unless, again, they fell within the culturally sensitive area raised above. Indirect takeovers — whereby one multinational company with Canadian subsidiaries is sold to another foreign company — would only be screened if the assets exceeded $50 million unless they too concerned sensitive cultural industries. The latter rules removed virtually 90 per cent of the screening of proposals formerly done by FIRA and the cabinet, although the asset rule allowed the agency to retain 90 per cent of former screening in dollar terms.

In addition, the test the agency used to approve foreign investments was weakened from the earlier evidence of "significant benefit" to Canada to a more modest "net benefit." This simply required the foreign investor to show that benefits outweighed costs prior to winning agency approval, a much milder — almost arithmetical — proposition. Investment Canada was further instructed to "promote" foreign investment and not merely to "screen" it. Relaxing the definition of what constitutes a "foreign investor" under the act while setting tight timetables for any screening decisions, Stevens's welcoming doormat was clearly being put out for all to see.

While all of these measures were hardly likely to mollify long-standing critics of foreign direct investment in Canada, the ill effects from these new relaxed screening rules can easily be exaggerated. FIRA had always approved in excess of 90 per cent of applications, most foreign direct investment concerning modernization of existing facilities in Canada had always been unreviewable and remained so under the new law, and the portion of total annual investment in Canada that remained reviewable was far less than 1 per cent.[57] In that sense the bill might be seen as an exercise in symbolic politics for external consumption with little real departure from earlier practice. But it is hardly an unimportant symbol for those who had been critical of the silent surrender of Canadian economic independence for at least two decades.

One of the most remarkable results of the new policy was the escalation of pressure by American interests for the removal of any restrictions on culturally sensitive industries, such as publishing, in Canada. By November 1985 it was apparent that Gulf and Western Industries of New York would adopt a "scorched earth" response if Canada did not allow it to complete its indirect purchase of the book publisher Prentice-Hall Canada.[58] Threats were being received that unless Canada ceded its controls on foreign publishing in the country, the upcoming free trade talks would be in jeopardy, as would Canada's new image as a friendly place in which to invest. All this suggested that the interests of foreign capital had not been satisfied with the massive Conservative reversal of policy but would go on to demand more and more politically damaging concessions from the Mulroney government. This was among the first tests of the new government's innocent assumptions about the compatibility of increased foreign investment and the maintenance of national sovereignty.

Unlike the advocates of technological sovereignty, the Mulroney government did not accept the idea that the high degree of foreign ownership of the economy was at the root of Canada's economic

difficulties. Indeed, his government welcomed more foreign investment as a spur to the Canadian economy and adopted the most pro-
American foreign policy position of any Canadian government since
the days of Louis St. Laurent in the 1950s. As Stephen Clarkson has put
it: "Now under [Mulroney's] management, the Canadian Government
has reverted to the historically more comfortable if less dignified posture of continental dependence as the first principle governing its international relations."[59] By the mid-1980s these were the logical counterparts to Trudeau's brand of centralist federalism, which had become
associated with anti-American as well as anti-provincialist sentiment.
The Mulroney campaign had criticized these features of Trudeau's
federalism, especially as they applied to economic policy; it promised
instead to befriend America and the provinces in a new program of
economic renewal. A foundation was being laid for yet another historical flirtation with free trade.

## The Lure of Free Trade

In fact, free trade as the key to overcoming Canada's economic malaise
had been the chief bold policy alternative to the technological sovereignty school in economic strategy debates in government, research institutes, the universities and the private sector for many years.[60] Although
business and labour were slower to join this debate and did not take an
active part until after recession dust had settled on the Trudeau government's great nationalist initiatives in the energy field, by the time of the
Macdonald Commission enquiry, they were throwing themselves vigorously into the industrial policy debate. The hearings showed that business, with some qualifiers and exceptions, was generally supporting the
free trade option, while labour was not. This return of class politics over
the issue of protection was in that sense a remarkable rerun (albeit with
business switching sides) of the great recurring political debates from the
1870s until our own time.[61]

In an essay on this subject for the Macdonald Commission, J.L.
Granatstein has given the idea of free trade with the United States almost
equal prominence in the life of this country with the racial and linguistic
conflicts between the French and English. It has appeared 'under various
names — reciprocity, commercial union, unrestricted reciprocity, limited
customs union, or sectoral free trade ... for almost a century and a half,
creating its own myths and tempting our political leaders or frightening
them. This issue will not disappear."[62] Confederation itself arose in part
as a reaction to the economic threat of losing access to the American market with the abrogation of the reciprocity treaty by the United States in
1866. John A. Macdonald's National Policy for Canada emerged in the
late 1870s chiefly because of Canadians' continuing failure to reopen that
market. Ironically Macdonald even justified the National Policy — "clos-

ing our doors and cutting them [Americans] out of our markets" — as principally an effective bargaining device for getting the Americans to pry "open theirs to us."[63] While the National Policy turned out to be a permanent and satisfactory arrangement for the Conservative party, providing as it did for hefty federal revenue under the tariff and a politically profitable alliance with manufacturing interests in central Canada, it did not entirely close off the chronic and cyclical attractions of the idea.

During bad economic times, at the end of boom periods or in conditions of great uncertainty — in 1891, 1911, 1935, 1938, 1947-48 and the mid-1980s — the idea of free trade has re-emerged as a kind of national panacea for the country's ills. In the 1880s, both major parties found the idea irresistible, with the Liberals declaring themselves officially for unrestricted reciprocity and then campaigning on that platform in 1891, and the Conservatives rejecting it in the name of Britain and Empire only after their secret overtures to Washington respecting a reciprocity agreement were once again rebuffed. In that respect, the Canadian colonial fling with economic dependency did not end with the hysterical outrage over British "abandonment" of Canada with the repeal of the Corn Laws in 1846 or the later rejection by the Americans in 1866, but was carried forward as a perennial if often unconscious element in the nation's thinking.

Despite frequently rude international setbacks and a very rocky domestic record around the politics of free trade, the major parties have returned to it, addict-like, with more or less regularity and trepidation. The Liberals found themselves burned over the issue in 1891 and again in the 1911 election campaign. Established manufacturing interests in central Canada had then found a curious mixture of British imperialism and Canadian patriotism, a powerful ideological potion with which to put away free trade advocates. The memory of that sorry debacle had so unnerved Prime Minister King that, even with the substance of a secret trade deal in hand with a popular and powerful U.S. following the Second World War and after almost a decade of profitable tariff-reduction programs with the Americans, he flatly scuttled the customs union project in 1948.[64] "Selling out to the Yanks" was not a campaign slogan he wanted hung once again around Liberal necks.

Perhaps for that reason, when the issue returned again amidst the general wreckage of national economic policies following the massive 1982 recession, the idea emerged as a cautious sectoral approach by a somewhat crestfallen Liberal regime and not as a bold new initiative.[65] That program, however, was a nonstarter so far as the Americans were concerned and failed to attract broad Canadian support. The idea of seeking a comprehensive trade agreement did not begin to seize the imagination of the public in anything like its older forms until it was first floated and then pushed aggressively by the Macdonald Commission in the mid-

1980s. The commission, in fact, did not begin to promote this view until private interests, alarmed over threats of American protectionism, began to clamour for it.[66] Even then, however, when the Conservative government gingerly picked up the free trade mandate in 1985, it preferred to describe its position by the more innocuous term of "trade enhancement" and not the old hex, free trade.

This historic Tory adoption of what was popularly considered traditional Liberal policy would be surprising if there had not always been this allure of free trade for every governing federal party during periods of economic difficulty. In any case, what made the ideological conversion easier and much less dangerous was the knowledge that business in central Canada was for the first time apparently supporting free trade and openly rejecting the older Macdonald protectionist policies. Calls for access to the American market, for increased competition and for world product mandates for Canadian companies were coming from none other than the Canadian Manufacturers' Association, the Canadian Chamber of Commerce, the Canadian Federation of Independent Business, business institutes and think-tanks, the new confident world-class Canadian enterprises such as Northern Telecom and of course from the powerful Business Council on National Issues.[67] That made it possible for the Conservatives to consolidate an extraordinary alliance between the traditional free trade supporters in natural resource industries in the West and East with the industrial interests in Ontario and Quebec. Since free trade was also clearly the majority option among provincial leaders, especially prior to the election of Liberal governments in Ontario and Quebec, moving on free trade seemed an ideal way to mesh national economic policy and cooperative federalism.

It appeared that the old coalition that had sustained protectionism and the National Policy for virtually a century was becoming unglued. Several factors contributed to this development and to the impetus for a new continentalist policy. On the one hand, the multilateral dismantling of tariffs under GATT was already proceeding swiftly by the 1980s and upsetting the old protectionist logic of Canadian economic policy; on the other, as a result of the premium on the U.S. dollar, Canadian dependence on American markets had grown dramatically and these markets were being increasingly threatened by a wave of U.S. protectionist sentiment. Canadian exports to the U.S., which, for example, constituted 65.2 per cent of exports in 1975, amounted to 75.6 per cent by 1984. In that respect, as Robert Young has argued, more and more Canadian companies, including even the "smaller, more protectionist and nationalist elements of Canadian business," were joining the big firms in an interest in continentalism. On a broader plane, recent changes in the structure of

Canadian capital have also added to the logic for a continentalist approach:

- Rising Canadianization over the 1970s had ironically left Canadian business "more open to the threat of protectionism" and reduced the influence of American multinationals in combating or moderating American protectionist measures directed against Canada.
- The success in increased Canadian penetration of the American market, especially by a group of internationally competitive Canadian multinationals, dictated a much larger North American playing field for these leading business enterprises.
- The growing concentration of ownership of Canadian business permits losses from adjustment to free trade in one subsidiary to be balanced by gains in another, and there is thus "less pressure for protection arising from isolated companies threatened with terminal losses."[68]

All of these were signs that business might no longer need the protective state assumed under the old National Policy, and its ambitions could not be comfortably contained within the old economic framework. Briefs to the Macdonald Commission indicated that scores of companies increasingly identified themselves as international players seeking secure access to a world-scale trading bloc and the ability to plan continental rationalization of their operations. Hence, with this shift of interests, the anti–free trade coalition was much weaker in Ontario and Quebec than it once was; only labour, fearful of the dislocations and job losses that would ensue from this policy change, presented a relatively cohesive bloc of opposition. Public opinion polls indicated a favourable attitude toward freer trade, although on this issue it was admittedly a potentially volatile and uneasy state of opinion.

Since the regions of the country, especially western Canada, were now far less homogeneous than they once were, it was unlikely that free trade would provoke the same old regional divisions; the western economy had become so diversified that it could speak on economic issues with far less clarity and unity than it once did. The change could be read in the complicated politics over the Trudeau government's abrogation of the Crow's Nest Pass Agreement in 1983 where a great deal of intraregional conflict in the West muted the expected effects of regional resistance to these changes.[69] Similarly, if free trade discussions ultimately had the effect of opening access to the U.S. market but only at the expense of a U.S. demand for restrictions on the power of agricultural marketing boards, the position of the West could be expected to be a much less "unified" interest or regional posture than in the past. With a changing demography, economy, elite and political system in this and other parts of Canada, the politics around free trade increasingly revolved around class rather than regional cleavages.

There appeared to be other advantages to taking up the old if dangerous issue of free trade with the United States. The nervous Conservative embrace of free trade, tentatively expressed in the so-called Shamrock Summit between Prime Minister Mulroney and President Reagan at Quebec City in March 1985, had the advantage of confirming and consolidating the recent marked shift in Canadian policy toward the United States. This overture was in itself a powerful symbol of the new preoccupations of the Canadian state and of the change in the prevailing vision of federalism. Therefore, unlike the humiliating experience the U.S. suffered in 1981 when it openly called for a North American common market with Canada and Mexico, only to find these countries snubbing the invitation, the United States discovered both Canada and Mexico much more willing and compliant partners after their economies had taken a beating in a subsequent worldwide recession and a fallout in commodity prices. The Mulroney regime was well disposed to reinforce its other policy signals to the U.S. and the world investment community that Canada was really turning away from economic nationalism and toward a market-driven open-door policy.

The free trade horizon was not, however, altogether clear and beckoning. Despite business enthusiasm, American interest, majority provincial support and compliant public opinion, Ottawa still had to contend with the encroachment of dark and rumbling clouds of opposition. The most menacing of these centred on the governments of the most industrialized and populated provinces. The Conservative governments of William Davis and Frank Miller and especially the subsequent minority Liberal government of David Peterson, dependent as it was on support from the NDP, were considerably more cautious about the effects of free trade in Ontario, while a similar spirit of caution appeared to have enveloped Quebec's government under Robert Bourassa after the 1985 election. While it was difficult for these governments to take a strident position against free trade, particularly in the face of strong support from powerful interests within the province, they insisted that the case for such an historic move must be more than "the leap of faith" advocated by Royal Commission Chairman Donald Macdonald or by the neoclassical sermons of academic economists. The Peterson government distributed its own studies that contested the abstract free trade arguments and the tired incantations of economic theory concerning comparative advantage — not only did these studies show a job loss estimate in Ontario much higher than that presumed by free trade advocates, but also a capital flight of American subsidiaries from Canada once the tariff and nontariff barriers were brought down.[70] Premier Peterson insisted that the logic and evidence for any Canadian move in this direction be sound, and he demanded, with considerable support from the other premiers, that the provinces must have a direct say in the instruction to Canada's negotiators respecting any international economic agreement with the U.S. and an ultimate veto over any package Canada might bring back from the bargaining table.

The latter arguments suggested that, whatever the underlying socioeconomic changes in the regions and the shifting loyalties of interest groups to national economic policy, there would continue to be plenty of scope for intergovernmental conflict over this issue. In that respect, in the November 1985 First Ministers' Conference, it was striking how premiers who strongly endorsed free trade for Canada nonetheless joined with opponents like Peterson so long as he was able to confine the issue to a vigorous defence of provincial rights in national economic policymaking and did not focus on the substantive merits of the policy itself. Ontario's decision to stress the building of a reliable information base for intergovernmental discussions on free trade and to beat the drums of provincial power to frustrate a too hasty Ottawa–western Canadian policy alliance over free trade was a shrewd counterattack. So too was its speedy attempt, after the long PQ interlude, to re-establish ties with the new Liberal government of Robert Bourassa in December 1985 and hence to attempt to put in place once again the traditional central Canadian axis of power in the federation. None of these gestures were particularly good omens for the ruling Conservatives in Ottawa, but they did indicate how rapidly Ontario could shift gears from a "nation-defending" posture in its earlier support for the Trudeau government's attack on provincialism to a "province-defending" strategy once the Mulroney government appeared to be taking a course that might threaten its interests.

None of this intergovernmental manoeuvring escaped the notice of business and other free trade advocates, some of whom in central Canada ironically took up the old hinterland argument formerly used by disgruntled regionalists against establishment interests in Ontario and lobbed it into the court at Queen's Park. One such belated defence of western and eastern interests has come from free-trader John Crispo, who has attacked Ontario's exploitative, "selfish, and short-sighted position," and warned of the East and West pulling out and joining "the United States, lock, stock and barrel" unless "narrow-minded nationalists with their Queen's Park allies" are not stopped from wrapping their interests so "deceptively in a Canadian flag."[71] This appropriation of regionalist rhetoric by advocates of central Canadian business interests now shedding protectionism for continentalism is a bizarre turn of events, just as is the ironic attack on the Ontario government's caution over free trade. Such arguments suggest how readily the politics and ideology of federalism can be used in the free trade debate even within a single province.

The divisions over free trade, including intergovernmental friction, ought not to obscure what is from the point of view of federalism, and especially of the federal-provincial balance of power, the more important issue: the remarkable unanimity of provincial interests in securing a place for themselves in international economic negotiation and national economic planning. That objective, after all, had been a long-standing preoccupation of provincial governments throughout the previous fifteen years and one the Trudeau government had just as firmly resisted. Having opted for free trade as a broad national economic strategy after the failure of Trudeau's nationalist economic measures in the early 1980s, the Mulroney government was driven by constitutional necessity, if not indeed by inclination, to bring the provinces on board as virtually co-equal partners in this exercise. The constitutional imperative arose from two unavoidable realities: first, no Canada-U.S. agreement purporting to touch nontariff barriers could avoid encroaching upon provincial turf and policies; and second, Ottawa lacked the constitutional authority to enforce any such international agreement when the legislative subject matter lay within provincial jurisdiction.

As a result of a ruling over the Labour Conventions Case by the Judicial Committee of the Privy Council in Britain in 1937, the courts appear to have qualified Ottawa's right to implement treaties when the subject matter falls within provincial jurisdiction. Such a view is in marked contrast to the generous and expansive interpretation of federal treaty-implementing powers in other federal states like Australia and the United States. Although it is possible that a future court decision might broaden federal authority over trade and commerce to permit the encompassing of intraprovincial trade matters under a broad free trade agreement with the United States — especially where distinctions between intraprovincial and international trade can be shown to be unrealistic and unworkable — and thus sustain such an undertaking on other grounds, the treaty-implementation power does not in itself offer much encouragement.[72] In fact, the confinement and subjection of the federal treaty-making authority to the division of legislative powers has since the 1930s forced Ottawa either to avoid international agreements when these fall in provincial jurisdiction or to seek provincial cooperation for developing and implementing such treaty matters.

On a broader plane, this constitutional and political development has served as a logical footing for many of the later claims of the provinces to certain "rights" to international representation in their fields of legal competence. This intergovernmental struggle over the international field was most pronounced in the Ottawa-Quebec feuds after the emergence of the Quiet Revolution in 1960, and became intimately tied up with

Quebecers' broader political drive for recognition as a distinct national state or quasi-state identity. While Ottawa retained the field of foreign policy and the exclusive right to represent Canada abroad, it faced a bitter and serious battle of diplomacy and legitimacy, especially in the 1960s when France under President Charles de Gaulle supported Quebec separatism. Although the urgency of that issue tended to decline somewhat during the later 1970s and 1980s as Ottawa gradually secured France's official neutrality on Canada's internal politics, there remained a strong federal concern, heightened by these developments, to restrict the claims of the provinces to international recognition. Only after the defeat of Quebec separatism and the election of the federal Tories to power in 1984 was that tradition relaxed, to permit the premiers of Quebec and New Brunswick to be represented under reasonably generous federal rules and control in the conference of *la francophonie* (roughly the French-speaking equivalent to the Commonwealth) in Paris in February 1986. That decision ended in disaster as newly elected Quebec premier Robert Bourassa peremptorily broke the accord with Ottawa and proposed without notice an aid program for Africa. Not only was the proposal not raised with Ottawa beforehand, it was also outside Quebec's competence and concerned the use of European, not Quebec, funds. Bourassa had successfully grandstanded for the benefit of local consumption at home, while the prime minister of Canada was reduced to uttering cries of betrayal and to displaying his wounded pride. This sorry episode underlined how precarious and difficult it would be for the Tories to extend the logic of cooperative federalism to the international arena.

Yet in a sense that was precisely the dilemma in which the free trade overture placed Ottawa. Lacking constitutional authority to act on its own, the federal government was virtually forced into rationalizing and legitimizing the role of the provinces in the negotiations. The Macdonald Commission had in fact recommended that course of action as the most likely route for success, with the understanding that, in the longer term, the provinces agree to be bound by a new constitutional procedure that would validate sections of the treaty imposing provincial obligations whenever two-thirds of provincial legislatures, representing at least half of Canada's population, passed resolutions in support of the treaty. Hence, the same level of federal-provincial consensus required of Canada's general amending formula (with, however, no right to opt out) would be extended to provincial obligations under the treaty. Since provinces held such immense power to reverse the trade agreement with the United States, it seemed only prudent to involve them in the negotiating process so that there would be a much higher chance that the treaty could be implemented. But once this compromise was proposed, it was only to be expected that there would be an elaborate intergovernmental dance over the precise meaning of this relationship. In short, the perennial conflict over the place and power of Ottawa and the provinces would once again be thrown up before the nation.

The first round in this conflict took place at the annual First Ministers' Conference in Halifax at the end of November 1985. There Premier Peterson tabled a proposal that called for review and approval by first ministers of the recommendation for exploratory discussions; that required the chief federal negotiator in the upcoming talks with the United States, Simon Reisman, to take his instructions from a federal-provincial committee of ministers, not from the prime minister or the federal cabinet; and that ensured regular reporting to both orders of government, provincial representation on the negotiation team and final approval or rejection of the trade agreement by first ministers. That would in effect transfer authority from the federal cabinet to the first ministers as the real source of power in treaty negotiation as well as implementation, a development the courts had certainly not pronounced on, but which appeared to follow as a matter of practice from the limitations put on the federal power of treaty implementation. As Peterson triumphantly remarked: "The bottom line is that the negotiator will [this time] receive his instructions from the first ministers. That means 11 partners in policy formation." The same point was put, in graphic if jumbled metaphors, by Premier Grant Devine of Saskatchewan when he claimed that "the first ministers will act like a board of directors, operating on a consensus basis. We're the quarterback."[73]

Mulroney promised "consultation" with the provinces and agreed with the "principle of full provincial participation" but had little more to say to clarify the matter. That left both sides claiming victory, with federal officials attempting to limit and contain the meaning of these enticing expressions. The matter was finally left for the parties to establish common goals and come up with an acceptable mechanism for provincial participation over the next ninety days. In the end, the provinces did not succeed in winning "seats at the table," although they were given assurances of consultation and regular monitoring of the process of negotiations every three months by the first ministers. Clearly the old federal claim to an exclusive role in defining the national interest in trade and economic matters and then simply projecting it onto the international scene was no longer tenable. There is little doubt, therefore, that the collaborative model of Canadian federalism got a considerable boost from the Mulroney government's free trade initiative. This was a far cry from the rehabilitated nationalist rhetoric that flourished under Prime Minister Trudeau only a few years earlier, just as it was an apparently blatant turnabout for Ontario from its earlier position on limiting provincial power over the economy.

In some respects, with the rise of free trade under Mulroney's brand of federalism, Ontario had virtually replaced Alberta and even Quebec as the chief defender of provincial power. Alberta was, for example, reluctant to push provincial claims too far on the free trade talks and offered only muted resistance to the unilateral federal cutbacks on the level of assistance to provinces for social programs under health and postsecondary education, also reaffirmed in the November First Ministers' Conference. It refused to support a Manitoba resolution denouncing Ottawa for these cutbacks. An explanation tor this lies partly in the sympathetic partisan alignments between Ottawa and Edmonton and in the Mulroney government's then generous concessions to Alberta's interests in the energy field. But the essential reason was that, despite the alluring echo of Ontario's new provincialist rhetoric, Mulroney's free trade option seemed a golden opportunity to challenge at its very roots the old structural patterns of dominance in the Canadian economy that had worked themselves out over the first hundred years of the National Policy. That suddenly converted Alberta into an ally of Ottawa, while it simultaneously strained relations between Queen's Park and the national government.

Therefore, although the provincial players may have changed chairs, their fundamental interests had not. If Ontario could build a provincial coalition strong enough to ensure the protection of its vital interests, it would not implacably fight free trade discussions with the U.S. As Peterson had earlier acknowledged, he was not enthusiastic over free trade, but he didn't "have the power to stop [the talks]" so his best option was "to get in and shape the decisions."[74] In fact, the free trade initiative had already been sold by the Macdonald Commission as "the most significant and long-term" step toward "the strengthening of national unity and the removal of ... regional alienation in Canada's political history." Its "healing effect" would arise from its banishing of the perception that "the manufacturing and industrial economy of central Canada" is maintained at the expense of the primary producers especially in the East and West.[75] This language was an open advertisement by the commission for the proposed end of any status quo hegemonic position for the province of Ontario in its economic relations with other regions of Canada even if justified in terms of self-serving patriotism. It was also a blunt statement that there was nothing sacred about the pattern of East-West trade as a support for Canadian political unity and that regions should now permit trade to follow its own "natural" market linkages. While this may have sounded like economic liberation for the people in the peripheries, it was like waving a red flag before status quo Ontario.

Of course, free trade advocates could not understand this position in the light of what they believed would be the proportionately higher returns to Ontario from the expected economic growth and restructuring following a Canada-U.S. agreement. What they failed to recognize was that Ontario was also most at risk, particularly in the impact of job losses and economic dislocations, from any such agreement. Ontario was also considerably more sensitive to the impact such an agreement might have on the behaviour of branch plants of American multinational companies operating in the province. While the scale of sunken costs in these enterprises suggested that no mass exodus should necessarily be anticipated, the Ontario government worried about important segments of that market either closing up shop or, more probably, converting their Canadian operations into a mere sales and distribution network. If, as Abraham Rotstein has warned, "warehousing [may] replace manufacturing," the province would be facing severe difficulties at precisely the point when the range of the government's policy instruments to deal with them would be explicitly constrained by international agreement.[76] Ontario could, in short, least afford to be cavalier about the balance sheet of costs and benefits.

In fact, if either of the above scenarios takes place as a result of free trade — that is, a serious economic decline in central Canadian manufacturing and employment prospects with or without greater benefits for the peripheries or, as one analyst has argued, an Ontario growth in real per capita income up to twice as large as that experienced by the peripheral provinces[77] — regional tensions are scarcely likely to be submerged as promised by the Macdonald Commission. As Charles Pentland has argued, much of the integration argument assumes the stabilization and reduction of regional tensions through more wealth and raised standards of living, but what if regional tensions have their roots in other sources that are "exacerbated" by integration? "A possible increase in regional disparities, the emergence of stronger provincial or regional ties to the American economy, the continued rise of provincial or regional political identities and, conceivably a general sense of growing alienation on the part of Canadians from a federal government preoccupied with the technocratic politics of North American integration — these considerations need to be balanced against the notion of free trade and prosperity as a domestic panacea."[78]

Certainly it would be questionable how far the old political bargain over balancing market efficiency in Canada with programs of regional redistribution could long survive a free trade environment. Free trade would push efficiency much more dramatically and would begin to undermine the logic of regional economic development programs in the country. As trade and money flows follow their natural market course with no substantial recirculation of regional investment monies back into the country, Ontario would probably cease its political support for such programs.[79]

Apart from these imponderables, the free trade policy had also to contend with a powerful and potentially explosive range of objections coming from economic and cultural nationalists and from people concerned with the democratic and policy implications of any such international agreement. The nationalist threat could be read in the rise of a broad grassroots movement concerned with what it believed was a sellout of Canada to American interests. The leadership of this movement, entitled the Council of Canadians, came from Marion Dewar, the mayor of Ottawa, and Mel Hurtig, one of the former founders of the Committee for an Independent Canada, which had been active in the 1970s, but this time the movement appeared to have broadened its membership and concerns to encompass not only economic nationalists but also unions and the cultural and artistic communities. However, whether this nationalist coalition could really offer a genuine alternative nationalist program, sensitive to regional concerns and transcending the old centralist bias in left and liberal nationalist programs of the past, remained very much in question. Nonetheless it went into operation even before the Mulroney government's announcement of free trade talks and began to mount an impressive national media blitz and mobilization effort against the government's program. Other long-standing nationalist critics, such as Mel Watkins and Abraham Rotstein, joined in the fray, as did leaders of cultural interest groups and women's associations, such as the National Action Committee on the Status of Women. As the Canadian government passively awaited American response to its invitation for talks, the forces of opposition seized the initiative and from the start placed the government on the defensive.

Once again, although this time with new voices and new interests, free trade was said to threaten Canadian sovereignty and the future of an independent Canadian nation. While the old imperial ingredients had blissfully fallen out of the anti–free trade rhetoric, new and more compelling arguments were raised about the hidden costs of a Canada-U.S. agreement. Critics pointed out that tariff barriers were coming down in any case as a result of the liberalization of trade under GATT and would stand at 5 per cent or less for 96 per cent of our industrial exports by 1987, that the Canadian economy had not yet received much of a boost from the substantial tariff reductions with the United States already in place, and that the move toward restricting nontariff barriers would merely shackle both levels of the Canadian state from exercising any lingering policy instruments on behalf of the Canadian people. In short, in order to arrive at what the Americans would regard as "fair trade" and "a level playing field," virtually all of the usual state instruments used around the world for industrial policy — subsidies (often so expansively defined they could encompass a country's pillars of social policy), procurement, tax policy, legislated exclusionary rules to protect domestic interests from outside competition, regional development grants, cultural development grants and policies, and even an independent currency exchange policy — would likely have to be foresworn or at least sharply limited. But the pressures would not only be external: Canadian governments could also find themselves caught in "policy pincers" with Canadian companies also demanding "harmonization" with U.S. social policy standards in order to avoid being placed "at a competitive disadvantage."[80] This hamstringing of policy would come, moreover, at precisely the point when economic stress would be most severe as a result of dislocations arising from trade liberalization, severe industrial competition from NICs, the transfer of American production abroad and growing difficulties in the American position in world trade. After reviewing these dangerous simultaneous trends, Rotstein acidly concluded:

> It is not clear what remains of the economic prerogatives of a self-respecting nation state....Try to think of a set of policies which would involve: no subsidies, no "voluntary quotas," no production quotas where they may touch U.S. firms or their subsidiaries abroad, no manipulation of the exchange rate, and "harmonized" tax rates and monetary policy. This is nothing less than a formula for turning the Canadian economy into a paraplegic.[81]

While the Macdonald Commission had blandly hoped that most of these essential policy instruments of Canadian nationhood could be exempted from the scope of a treaty with the United States — indeed, even excluded from the discussions at the outset — these optimistic views were not reflected in American sentiments, which pushed for a comprehensive market arrangement without restrictions on pro-American defence contracts or the use of countervail and anti-dumping duties against treaty partners. Even the recent U.S.-Israeli treaty still permitted, at the insistence of Congress, the operation of countervail and anti-dumping provisions. Further, the American government chose to slap the Canadian shakes and shingles industry with a 35 per cent duty when talks on free trade had barely begun in May 1986 without acknowledging any unfair trade practice (an action that prompted Canadian retaliatory action), and there were continuing threats that American protectionist attacks would extend to the entire Canadian softwood lumber industry. Nor did the American government appear to take kindly to early Canadian attempts to take some policy areas — for example, the "sacred" elements of Canadian nationhood, including regional development, social and cultural programs and the Auto Pact — off the negotiating table. These objections came as early as two days after the Mulroney invitation was received in Washington, and U.S. chief negotiator Peter Murphy later continued to insist that the Auto Pact and Canadian social programs were on the table. Meanwhile, the Prentice-Hall acquisition by

Gulf and Western was accepted by the Mulroney government even though it contradicted the government's earlier attempt to shield Canadian cultural industries from the economic logic of continentalism.[82] The attempt to isolate Canadian cultural sovereignty as a legitimate protected sector in the national interest was clearly not understood or supported by American policymakers. None of these were auspicious beginnings to the historic free trade discussions.

On the broader democratic front, the limitations a free trade agreement covering nontariff barriers appeared to place upon governments in both countries could only be exceedingly worrisome. Canadians had long heard complaints about the anti-democratic nature of executive federalism in Canada whereby the normal political operation of legislatures, interest groups, and publics was increasingly being circumvented — indeed being presented with virtual *fait accomplis* — by secret deal-making of executive political and bureaucratic leaders at both levels of government. This anti-democratic drift would be rapidly escalated by this venture into international bargaining. Not only would the bargaining process be shielded from legislative and public control, but the known effect of a deal over nontariff barriers with the United States would later constrain democratically elected legislatures at both levels from acting on behalf of their own domestic political interests and forces. In that sense, the initiative on free trade underlined the dramatic shift of power away from democratic state politics and toward market-driven forces.

As if this constellation of forces and concerns against free trade were not enough, the federal government learned very early on that even its strongest supporters for free trade, the Canadian business community, were hardly interested in a straight-up free trade deal as the Americans would understand it. No sooner had the Macdonald Commission manifesto preaching the virtues of modified laissez-faire been promulgated than prominent business leaders began changing the menu by ordering " 'assured access' including autopact style Canadian production guarantees in some sectors in return for cross-border rationalization." What business seemed to want, according to Giles Gherson's account of a key business conference following the issuance of the Macdonald Commission report, was a North American trade bloc that would give Canadian companies full access to the U.S. market, with special adjustment-related advantages guaranteeing full security for Canadian companies, while the Americans as the dominant partner played tough with international trade competitors.[83] In a line of argument closer to the nationalist than the laissez-faire economists, William Blundell, chairman of Canadian General Electric, declared that "in any trade treaty, you don't want to blow the small Canadian manufacturers and branch-plants right out of the water and reward those who will simply import products. The arrangement has to be managed so that those who have invested here over the years are rewarded.... Major Canadian companies aren't going to support any trade deal unless they're certain they're going to come out on top." Similarly Dudley Allan, president of Control Data Canada, argued for guaranteed access to the U.S. defence budget and, in effect, for a sort of continental Fortress America in the face of competition from Japan and other competitors.

This kind of argument of course made the Macdonald Commission's old-fashioned rhetoric about stimulating growth through free market competition sound like arid academic nonsense, but it was doubtless closer to the real nature and interests of the business community's original advocacy of the idea. It was not long before the business community was disclaiming free trade and arguing for enhanced trade, or some other vague, more innocuous-sounding tag. This kind of program would appear to conform much more closely to Premier Peterson's minimum practical test for a successful free trade package, but it is nonetheless remarkably out of touch with political realities in the United States and the world. Such a program would likely find itself mauled between an angry protectionist Congress and a righteous free trade administration under President Reagan, while on the international level it would raise the ire of North America's powerful trading partners.[84]

With the business community firmly entrenched in the policy process on the sectoral committees and on an International Trade Advisory Committee chaired by Walter Light, former head of Northern Telecom, which reports directly to Trade Ambassador Simon Reisman, these negotiating objectives may carry more weight than the free trade rhetoric of the Macdonald Commission. Drawing on its own experience, earlier sectoral studies, continuing work with sectoral trade committees, and especially the summer 1985 negotiations with sectors and firms, this group, assured Chairman Light, "will be heard" on what the industry requires and what it can afford to pay in negotiation. As then trade minister James Kelleher admitted, "they have a lot of leverage over us, Light will drive us, and we will have to account to ITAC, whatever we do."[85] While such information will be vital to the negotiations, it would nonetheless appear that the long-standing complaints of democrats over the domination of the public agenda through secret bargaining by politicians and bureaucrats under executive federalism must now perforce be extended to the formalized, powerful and confidential role of the nation's business elite.[86] Is it any surprise that labour and a whole range of public interest groups seemed restless with the unfolding politics over free trade?

There was, however, no turning back from the extraordinary political fallout from free trade. The die was cast when the Mulroney government made the historic September 26 announcement in the Commons that

Canada wished to negotiate with the United States "the broadest possible package of mutually beneficial reductions in tariff and non-tariff barriers between our two countries."[87] With that decision, Ottawa cut its ties with caution-counselling Ontario under the Liberal Peterson government and bowed to the new coalition of interests, that new federal-provincial-business axis of power, on which Mulroney's federalism was based.

The effect of the free trade proposal on the balance of power between the provinces and the federal government and on the state–private sector relationship will be taken up later in the conclusion, but it did appear from a variety of perspectives that the federal government was entering dangerous and difficult political terrain. Juggling the domestic political demands, exorcising the free trade ghosts against nationalist critics, bargaining for Canadian interests against formidable American pressures, placating the relentless power demands of the provinces and of business in the negotiating process, calming international concerns over North American protectionism, while simultaneously attempting to fight deficits and win the next election, scarcely represented an attractive prospect for any group of politicians, least of all ones with little political experience in office. Signs of stumbling were apparent very early. The nationalists had pre-empted the government and begun to define much of the terms of the public debate to the dismay of free trade supporters; the United States was irritated with Canadian defensiveness before the talks even began, while it simultaneously sought to protect its own industries; and the provinces, under the leadership of Premier Peterson, appeared to have wrung very significant concessions from the federal government in international negotiation and national economic policy. It was understandable that Prime Minister Mulroney would have turned to Pat Carney, his earlier formidable and successful minister of energy, to take up this demanding assignment as the new trade minister in the cabinet shuffle of June 1986.

As a result of earlier court decisions, any free trade deal would depend on provincial compliance at least for those parts of the agreement that trenched on provincial jurisdiction. That constitutional trump card seemed to make for a far more powerful play for provincial claims on the substance of Canada's international and national economic policy than would any direct provincial claims advanced in the past. But there was an offsetting irony in this "victory." The pursuit of free trade appeared to have more serious long-term consequences for limiting provincial economic power than would have any of Prime Minister Trudeau's past challenges to the provinces in the economic field. Many of the special nontariff barriers to which Americans objected were provincially created restrictions raised in order to give residents of each province special trade and employment protection. Free trade could well take direct aim at Quebec's preferential labour policies on government-backed construction, at provincial subsidies for preferred businesses or industries, at procurement policies and the like. In fact, many of the favoured policy instruments for economic province-building could well be targets in free trade negotiations. As the Macdonald Commission well understood, free trade carried strong implications for a decline in governmental activity in the economy, and with it, a corresponding decline in provincial power to restrict or limit the normal operation of a market economy. That matter, and the related issue of the exacerbation of regional economic disparities, did not yet appear to have curbed the initial enthusiasm of those provinces supporting free trade and may not have been fully pondered by them.[88]

The latter argument, however, also has profound implications for the scope of any nation-building efforts in the economic area. The logic of releasing market power from governmental restraint so that comparative advantage and maximum competitiveness and efficiency may be allowed to operate also applies to the federal level of government in both countries. Free trade spells a diminution of governmental power in general and a reassertion of private sector power in shaping the future of both countries, even if, as Bruce Doern has argued, there is still paradoxically an ongoing need for a strong state role to help identify winners and losers under free trade and to prepare an adjustment policy for declining industries.[89] With Canada's economy by far the smaller and weaker of the two, under this scheme it is easy to see how perilously positioned Canada's interests would be. It is perhaps for that reason that the Trudeau government headed in the other direction, toward a modest defence of economic sovereignty under a reinvigorated federal state. But by the mid-1980s, as both polls and the profusion of testimony to the commission by elites throughout the country indicated, that option appeared to have run its course and no longer had a viable political base on which to operate.

## Conclusion

It was the Macdonald Commission that gave official blessing to the new economic direction for the federal state. It summed up the conventional establishment wisdom of "a more market-oriented industrial policy" when it deplored Canada's earlier undue reliance upon dirigiste approaches that "relied on intervention too often, too extensively, and in too *ad hoc* a fashion."[90] In a candid admission that the usefulness and economic wisdom of an approach similar to the country's first National Policy was very much in doubt, the commission also argued that Canada's federal system was inappropriate for a federally led highly interventionist industrial strategy.[91] This was in keeping with much of the research advice to the commission, but it clashed sharply with the views of other scholars on industrial strategy and economic federalism, including those of Michael Jenkin.[92] As he had argued, the challenge was not to beg off from "biting the industrial policy bullet" but rather to develop a workable federal industrial policy with much more regional sensitivity than ever before, with specific and targeted objectives for the provinces and regions, with a strong federal institutional framework and with genuine intergovernmental participation and support. Short of that activist role, the federal government's role would "be doomed to irrelevance."[93]

No doubt the Trudeau government's example suggested the limits of a unilateral, federally imposed industrial strategy, especially if it were only partially thought out, incomplete and subject to constant political revision. It certainly suggested the limits of an industrial strategy primarily motivated by a drive for federal power rather than for broader economic rationality and political evenhandedness. The tragedy is that the Trudeau government, operating from its own political concerns for federalism, had employed an economic approach not for its own sake and not in its own terms. The consequence was a tarnishing and undermining of the approach itself, for after the Trudeau interventionist measures of the 1980s, dirigisme took on a bad name. Although the unexpected arrival of a worldwide recession did much to discredit whatever interventionism was then being employed, the approach could not become disentangled from the political centralism that had been the prime reason for its use. After that and all the federal-provincial discord it generated, the temptation was very strong for elites and the public to give up on a government role in the economy at both levels in the federal state and to return to a purely market approach. That was part of the political meaning behind the move to free trade.

It may be that something of these dynamics played against the Macdonald Conservatives too with their centralist economic program during a period of worldwide recession in the nineteenth century. Free trade for the Liberals seemed then a dramatic alternative strategic approach to the economy. Certainly that period had shown how difficult it would be to mount a national economic program within a centralist federal framework. With the subsequent growth of provincial economic power, the odds on repeating such a program successfully in the 1980s are a good deal slimmer. It may also be that the prospects for navigating a free trade agreement with the United States are hardly encouraging either.

For the historian the greatest irony of the story may be the remarkable play of musical chairs between the two major parties. The great Liberal train robbery that made off with the Macdonald tradition in the late twentieth century is only matched by the twentieth-century Conservative marriage to nineteenth-century liberalism. Perhaps this only illustrates how little historical consistency matters in party policy when the issue is the winning and shaping of power in a federal state where the weight of competitive provincial influence is always present.

# CHAPTER V

# Fiscal Federalism and Social Policy

If there is one area where some pretence to measuring the state of the power positions of the respective orders of government can be made and where those positions can be most readily altered by Ottawa in the name of "rebalancing" the federation, that is surely in the field of intergovernmental finance. Unlike the general policy fields discussed earlier, the financial relations of the governments lend themselves rather easily to quantitative measurement and it is therefore tempting to treat the results, especially the respective share of revenues and expenditures of federal versus provincial governments, as a kind of "power ledger," as a more or less authoritative statement on the state of balance in the federation. Such a rough but descriptive art has been common practice among analysts of federalism for some years, and the Trudeau government wasted no time in drawing upon this tradition to make its case against the rising tide of provincialism in the Canadian federation. Moreover, apart from their convenience as a diagnostic and descriptive tool, financial relations data are also highly responsive to change by unilateral federal action.

What made this an even more attractive theatre of action for the Trudeau Liberals was that this field, normally of interest only to "the rare but hardly endangered species, the treasury tax planner," contained within it social programs of such concern to the Canadian people that they could be expected to move behind a federal anti-provincialist rebalancing campaign that seemingly defended them.[1] At the heart of federal-provincial financial relationships developed over the previous four decades lay a corpus of jointly funded social programs, many of which, though highly popular with the Canadian people, were increasingly threatened or eroded by governmental underfunding and/ or by provincially created administrative barriers. Accessibility to the health care system was one obvious area of concern with the rise of extra-billing of patients by doctors over and above the publicly funded fee schedule, and of hospital charges and user fees. These issues were said to be directly linked to provincial failure to observe the conditions set out by Ottawa on the founding of medicare and hospital insurance decades earlier, and they provided an exceedingly attractive and popular platform for reasserting federal power over the provinces in the Canada Health Act of 1984. The claim of provincial default and underfunding extended to other programs as well, including postsecondary education. These arguments were used both as a justification for expanding federal supervision of the provinces in the whole field of jointly funded programs and for holding provinces to public account for their spending decisions. This part of the federal program was pursued early in the Trudeau government's mandate and continued as a preoccupation virtually until the announcement, on February 29, 1984, of the prime minister's retirement.

Once again, the political ground chosen for the federal rebalancing program with the provinces was as carefully considered and as powerful as it had been earlier with economic nationalism, energy policy or the Charter of Rights. A deliberate attempt was made to link up with public interest groups to defend the integrity of national social policies against provincial infringements and to present the federal government as a champion of the fundamental interests of all Canadians. This centre-defending strategy offered political visibility for the national government and presented an attractive case for the larger and enduring stake that all citizens had in the federation despite the transitory appeals of regionalism or separatism.

Since most of the social policies in question lay ostensibly in provincial jurisdiction, this might at first appear to be a curious ground upon which to construct a federal state-building program. However, Ottawa had already built up a strong and indeed pre-eminent claim on social policy over the previous four decades, in part through constitutional amendments such as those that transferred jurisdiction over unemployment insurance and pensions to Ottawa, but more often by using its financial clout to induce provinces into national programs in these areas, thus indirectly circumventing the legislative division of powers (or presumed "watertight compartments") of the Canadian constitution. In that respect, the federal government's taxing and spending capacities again proved to be exceedingly important instruments of power in Canadian federalism.

Though fiscal specialists had never developed what might be called a political theory of finance (a comprehensible picture of how the distribution and exercise of money in a federal state precisely affects the balance of power between central and provincial governments), they had long recognized that the national government exercised leverage over the federation by virtue of its wide capacities to tax and spend. Some distinguished specialists had argued that the political power flowing through intergovernmental financial arrangements was so great that it could easily effect a *de facto* reworking of the constitution and therefore of the federal-provincial balance.[2] Reworking these relations was therefore a natural route for the Trudeau government to have taken, and one that promised rather quick political dividends for their efforts.

### Political Power and Intergovernmental Finance

Intergovernmental financial relations had from Confederation always been tied up with the issue of political power and the appropriate uses to which it might be put. That was clear at the outset when the relative levels of government power, which flowed from the initial division of spending responsibilities and taxing authority under the constitution, were considered. It was said, for example, that Canada's constitution revealed its highly centralized form in part because of the assignment of unlimited taxing authority (and of all provincial debt) to Ottawa. This federal power to raise money by "any mode or system of taxation" contrasted sharply with what for the time appeared to be the highly restricted provincial power of direct taxation within the province. The tariff had always been the essential source of revenue in the colonial system, while direct taxation was so hated and so little used at the time of Confederation that it constituted less than 20 per cent of government revenue in 1866.[3] As the Rowell-Sirois report had noted, this arrangement of taxing authority reflected the founding fathers' assumptions about the expensive and important undertakings of the federal government as compared with the relatively meagre list of provincial responsibilities. At that time the nation-building program of railways, canals and frontier settlement was expected to consume the largest part of government revenue and draw to the federal state the powerful economic interests of the country. In short, the provision of unrestricted taxing power formed an essential part of the superior political position of the federal government.

If this were not a telling enough indicator of the relationship of centralized power and finance, the system of statutory subsidies that was put in place to supplement provincial revenues derived largely from fees and receipts from natural resources was even more so. At the very outset of Confederation, the founding fathers left the provinces financially dependent upon Ottawa for support of their responsibilities. These subsidies amounted to 80 or 90 per cent of revenues in Nova Scotia and New Brunswick, and between half and two-thirds in Ontario and Quebec.[4] This indignity was worsened by the fact that the subsidies were expected to be fixed as a "full and final" settlement of financial obligations to the provinces. Such a posture was highly unrealistic and merely resulted in repeated provincial demands for better financial terms from Ottawa and, as time went on, in more aggressive provincial pursuit of tax sources, especially the income tax. Hence, acrimony over fiscal matters was one of the earliest forms of federal-provincial conflict in Canada, giving rise to the first Interprovincial Conference in Quebec in the mid-1880s and the first Federal-Provincial Conference to revise financial terms in 1906.

The system of subsidies violated one of the central tenets of classical federalism, namely, that each level of government ought to be able to tax in order to draw revenue sufficient to meet its own constitutional responsibilities without dependence upon another order of government. The division of taxing authority under the Canadian constitution was never arranged to give effect to classical federalism in any case, but rather to arm the federal Parliament with most of the instruments of power. By the turn of the century as a result of court judgments, party politics and socioeconomic change, that construction of the federal state was giving way to a more classical model of federalism where provinces assumed a stronger position in the country. With rapid urbanization, costly provincial expenditures on schools, roads and economic development strained the old formula for financing governmental operations in Confederation and called into question the logic of a fiscal system created for another time and other purposes. This problem became ever more acute as the constitutional responsibilities of the provinces — especially social welfare programs, education, natural resource development, the building of telephone and hydroelectric systems — grew more important and more costly, while federal spending (except during wartime) assumed less importance.

The provinces tried quite early to correct their financial and political dependency, chiefly by exploiting the field of direct taxation (as generously defined by the courts) through the initiation of personal and corporate income taxes and succession duties. As a result of these and other initiatives, provinces collectively reduced their dependence on federal grants from 50 per cent of provincial revenues in 1880 to 26 per cent by 1910.[5] The financial pressures of the First World War, however, quickly drove the federal government to institute personal and corporate income taxes of its own and thus to establish for the first time joint occupancy of these tax fields, although even by the early 1920s tariff and excise duties still constituted approximately 90 per cent of federal revenues.[6] The provinces continued to finance their ambitious programs of expenditure on highways and other expensive undertakings during the 1920s chiefly by adding consumption taxes on alcohol and gasoline to their repertoire of revenue-raising instruments. By 1930, federal grants amounted to no more than 10 per cent of provincial revenue, while the provincial-local share of government revenues was double that of the federal order of government.

The onset of the Great Depression and the Second World War indicated both how vulnerable the provinces' sources of tax revenues really were, with some provinces, especially in the West, teetering on bankruptcy during the 1930s, and how swiftly the federal order of government could reassume the lion's share of revenues and expenditure responsibilities under a different set of political circumstances. The exigencies of depression and war, followed by the adoption of Keynesian economic policies and the welfare state after the war, brought the federal government into a strong and dominant position over most of the major tax sources. Indeed, Ottawa had persuaded the provinces in 1941, under the so-called Tax Rental Agreement, to permit it to take over the exclusive right to levy personal and corporate income taxes in return for guaranteed payments of equivalent value to the provinces for the vacating of these fields. These arrangements were renewed after the war and continued until 1962, with only Quebec remaining a firm holdout against this centralization of intergovernmental finance. In short, as the tables on pages 168 and 169 indicate, the federation had seen extensive shifts in the fiscal fortunes of both orders of governments over the years, changes that hinted at variations in the distributions of political power over time.

Apart from demonstrating the shifting and dynamic nature of the governments' pattern of fiscal relations, Table 5-1 also indicates how permanent has been the provinces' dependence on federal grants for the discharging of their constitutional responsibilities, even after the provinces became free to set their own levels of direct taxation with the expiry of the Tax Rental Agreement in 1962. Vertical imbalance, indicating a mismatch between expenditure responsibilities and the revenues of the two orders of government, has remained a feature of Canadian fiscal federalism. Moreover, as Robin Boadway has argued, this imbalance is now not so much due to exogenous factors as to a deliberate federal policy to set its level of tax room in the modern co-occupied tax fields at a point where continued provincial dependence on federal grants is unavoidable. Many of these modern grants, unlike the unconditional statutory subsidies provided to the provinces at Confederation, carry strings-attached conditions providing Ottawa with leverage over spending and other policy decisions of the provinces. In principle, the federal government always had a "feasible policy option ... to transfer tax room to the provinces rather than to transfer funds through grants," and hence to reduce the dependency of the provincial order of government, but for a variety of reasons, that political choice was not made.[7] Although a rational and plausible defence for such practices can be mounted, such as the need to promote efficient and equitable provincial spending in programs with high extraprovincial "spillover" effects, a continuing vertical imbalance, more or less unilaterally and artificially induced, scarcely contributes to federal-provincial harmony.[8]

The fiscal system is also plagued with horizontal imbalances, namely, sharp gaps in the revenue-generating capacity of the different provinces. As a result of the development of distinct regional economies and of

## Table 5-1

### FEDERAL AND PROVINCIAL-LOCAL SHARES OF TOTAL GOVERNMENT REVENUES
*(percentages)*

| | From Own Sources | | After Fed. Grants Are Deducted from Fed. Revenues and Considered Revenues of the Prov. Local Sector | |
|---|---|---|---|---|
| Year | Federal | Prov. Local[b] | Federal | Prov. Local[b] |
| 1926 | 44.9 | 55.1 | 43.1 | 56.9 |
| 1930 | 33.4 | 66.6 | 30.5 | 69.5 |
| 1940 | 54.5 | 45.5 | 50.2 | 49.8 |
| 1945[a] | 71.4 | 28.5 | 69.2 | 30.8 |
| 1950[a] | 64.1 | 35.9 | 59.8 | 40.3 |
| 1955[a] | 63.6 | 36.4 | 61.1 | 38.9 |
| 1960[a] | 58.2 | 41.8 | 51.6 | 48.4 |
| 1965 | 54.5 | 45.6 | 45.9 | 54.1 |
| 1970 | 50.9 | 49.1 | 39.8 | 60.3 |
| 1975 | 51.8 | 48.2 | 39.2 | 60.8 |
| 1980 | 46.6 | 53.3 | 34.7 | 65.4 |

[a]Tax rental payments are assumed to be provincial revenue from own sources and have been deducted from federal revenues.
[b]Municipal or local revenues are treated as provincial revenues because municipal or local governments are "creatures" of provincial governments and cannot be considered an independent order of government.

Source: Department of Finance, *Economic Review*, April 1981.

growing economic disparities under the National Policy, these divisions between "haves" and "have-nots" complicated federal-provincial and interprovincial relationships. With some provinces virtually bankrupt in the Great Depression, scholars began to wonder whether it was not at least an implied principle of Confederation that governments have the

# Table 5-2

## GOVERNMENT EXPENDITURES IN MILLIONS AND AS A PERCENT OF TOTAL GOVERNMENT EXPENDITURES

| Year | Federal | | Provincial-Local | | Total |
|------|---------|------|------------------|------|-------|
| | $M | % | $M | % | $M |
| 1926 | 306 | 37.8 | 504 | 62.2 | 810 |
| 1943 | 4,264 | 85.0 | 758 | 15.0 | 5,022 |
| 1955 | 4,356 | 58.1 | 3,142 | 41.9 | 7,498 |
| 1960 | 5,752 | 50.5 | 5,628 | 49.5 | 11,380 |
| 1965 | 7,120 | 43.0 | 9,434 | 57.0 | 16,554 |
| 1970 | 11,865 | 38.3 | 19,149 | 61.7 | 31,014 |
| 1975 | 27,838 | 41.2 | 39,673 | 58.8 | 67,511 |
| 1980 | 47,945 | 40.6 | 70,117 | 59.4 | 118,062 |

Source: *The National Finances*, 1981-82. Intergovernmental grants are credited to receiving level of government and hospital expenditures have been added to provincial share. CPP and QPP expenditures are excluded from table.

requisite financial means to carry out their obligations under the constitution. That was a principle very much at issue during the proceedings of the Rowell-Sirois Commission at the end of the 1930s, and it underlay its recommendation to provide adjustment grants for the fiscally disadvantaged provinces. Equalizing provincial revenue, in the language of section 36 of the 1982 constitutional settlement, "to ensure that provincial governments have sufficient revenues to provide reasonably comparable levels of public services at reasonably comparable levels of taxation," appeared to be only one of many modifications the Canadian fiscal system required.

Resolving such financial anomalies cannot be regarded as simply a functional problem, divorced from the wider question of the axis of power in the federation. These problems could be tackled in different ways, with different kinds of outcomes and implications. Horizontal imbalance could be corrected, for example, interprovincially by a mechanism that would distribute revenues from have to have-not provinces, such as that used in West Germany, or federally by a redistribution of revenue through the general tax system.[9] The first would expose the transfers as a direct cost to the richer provinces and would enshrine the interprovincial nature of the national program; the second would give the federal Parliament a special political role as a champion of the fiscal interests of the have-not provinces and presumably a role in refereeing disagreements among the provinces. Canada opted for the latter alternative, first implicitly as part of the tax rental system begun in the Second World War and then in a direct unconditional manner in 1957.[10] But the point is that, apart from the functional concerns for efficiency and equity in any program, equalization schemes can generate radically different political outcomes.

Once that course had been taken, however, it was clear that any sharp increases in intergovernmental fiscal disparity, especially if caused by provincial revenue increases drawn from sources not much tapped by federal taxation, would lead to profound intergovernmental conflict. With the energy crisis in 1973, that political escalation took place. In terms of horizontal imbalance, the rapidly growing fiscal resources of the oil-producing provinces widened the gap between provinces, while simultaneously putting heavier financial pressure upon Ottawa to meet its equalization bill. As the earlier chapter on energy policy indicated, there was no significant compensating access to these revenues by the national government. Ottawa responded to these pressures by limiting the "count" of natural resources in the equalization formula in 1974 and again in 1977, and when those reductions were not sufficient to keep Ontario from becoming a recipient of equalization payments, it amended the rules to exclude payments to any province with per capita personal income higher than the national average. These distortions in the equalization formula, equally as arbitrary as the later offset provisions respecting equalization payments for coastal provinces that might receive royalties under the Atlantic Accord, were only part of the long-term risks and consequences of assuming this political mantle.

Similarly, vertical imbalances between expenditures and revenues could be remedied directly either by simply transferring the expensive provincial burdens to the fiscally stronger federal order of government by constitutional amendment, or by formally granting the provinces through a negotiated agreement guaranteed tax room in most of the major joint fields of taxation within a system of equalization between have and have-not provinces. Each of these proposals carry radically different consequences for the balance of power between the provincial and federal governments. While the first option of transferring provincial jurisdiction has in fact been used in two highly expensive social welfare areas, namely, unemployment insurance in 1940 and old age pensions in 1951 and 1964, the federal government has shown little interest in negotiating a formal limitation of its taxing capacity to correct this artificial vertical imbalance with the provinces. Of course, Ottawa has, especially since the mid-1960s, offered tax abatement (providing room by moving back its level of tax or "tax points" in favour of the provinces) either as an alternative to provincial participation in certain national shared-cost programs or as part of a total package of fiscal transfers over established programs such as under the Established Programs Financing (EPF) Act in 1977, but the broad issue of ceding its policy leverage over the provinces through a formal and comprehensive concession of tax room or through the offer of exclusive tax sources has not been taken up.

Instead, the politics over vertical imbalance has frequently been worked out in a more indirect and ad hoc fashion, and almost invariably in ways that appeared politically attractive to the national government. The constitutional instrument chosen in effect to redress the expenditures-revenue mismatch with the provinces was the broad federal spending power, which essentially permitted Ottawa to make grants to the provinces (or to anyone else) for such purposes as it saw fit to support. Where such grants were earmarked to redress horizontal imbalances, such as with the equalization program, or were deliberately transferred to the payee without conditions, there appeared to be no major intrusion into areas of provincial decision-making. However, often such grants were conditional in nature and were offered to the provinces only for certain purposes and sometimes only if they agreed to meet specified criteria, such as the maintenance of national standards or other requirements in the program area. Ottawa adopted exactly that route, especially after the Second World War, to create or fund most of the important national social programs, including welfare assistance, medicare, hospital insurance, and assistance to postsecondary education. This use of the federal spending power was a novel way of tackling fundamental problems, but one that provided the federal government an easy passage into provincial areas of jurisdiction, a ready national constituency of interests, and increased political leverage.[11] It was on this issue that much of the heat of federal-provincial conflict was centred during the 1950s and 1960s, especially in Quebec, which sought, often successfully, to opt out of many of these centralizing initiatives in provincial areas of jurisdiction.[12]

Despite all of the political controversy over this use of the federal spending power, governments have proved to be exceedingly reluctant to test in the courts the constitutionality of federal conditional grants to the provinces. The spending power, nowhere explicit in the Constitution Act, appeared to flow from the federal power to tax (s. 91, head 3), to legislate in relation to "public property" (s. 91, 1A) and to appropriate federal funds (s. 106). But how far does this grant of power authorize payments, together with the dictating of terms for receipt of such payments, to governments for constitutional matters outside federal jurisdiction?

The matter has never been squarely put to the judiciary, although general restrictions were imposed upon the federal spending power by Lord Atkin of the Judicial Committee of the Privy Council in Britain in the *Unemployment Insurance Reference* case of 1937.[13] There the federal spending power was not seen as an adequate support for an insurance program that trenched upon provincial jurisdiction, and there appeared to be clear limits to the interference with provincial subject matters that might be permitted by any taxing and disbursement scheme. That same view, namely, that the federal spending power ought to be confined to objects within federal legislative competence, was also ironically enough the conclusion of Pierre Elliott Trudeau as constitutional scholar rather than as federal politician. However, as E.A. Driedger has argued, a grant of money by the government of Canada is not a "law" in relation to "public property," but merely a "gift," a sovereign prerogative to dispose of public property in whatever ways the government sees fit.[14] Moreover, from a legal point of view, there is no compulsory imposition of an obligation upon the provinces entailed with federal grants, but only a "voluntary" (albeit politically irresistible) acceptance of terms freely entered into by the province.[15]

Whatever the ultimate legal status of these arguments, there was no question that this exercise of the spending power provided Ottawa with an enormously important and potentially intrusive political weapon. But the subsequent turmoil over federal invasion of the provincial legislative domain through conditional grants had by the late 1960s moved the federal government away from this instrument of power, not least because it appeared to be pushing Quebec into a "special status" by virtue of its having opted out of most of the national shared-cost social programs. The federal government, now led by a francophone prime minister who had criticized the abuses of the federal spending power in the 1950s, even proposed during constitutional discussions in 1969-70 that there be constitutional limits on the use of the spending power.[16] No action was taken on the constitution, however, although there was later a marked federal shift away from shared-cost programs toward block-funding of social programs with the 1977 EPF Act. By then the mounting costs for the federally constructed welfare state were beginning to drive Ottawa toward applying brakes on such uncontrolled expenditures by removing any automatic linkage between federal and provincial spending.[17] Yet only a few years later, the federal political reliance upon the spending power and upon the conditional nature of federal grants to the provinces had returned with a vengeance.

Early indications that fiscal federalism would be drawn into the ambit of the Trudeau government's rebalancing program came with growing federal complaints about the shifting fiscal balance of power in the federation. In many publications and pronouncements, the government declared that the federal share of spending in relation to that of the provinces had fallen precipitously and that its proportion of total taxes paid by Canadians pointed in a similar direction. It leapt quickly from these observations to claim a similar congruent decentralization of power in the federation. Again and again the fiscal "evidence" of decentralization was used to bolster a federal claim that the pendulum of power had swung too far toward the provinces and the balance of power needed to be restored. Moreover, the government claimed a vertical fiscal imbalance when Finance Minister MacEachen attempted to link the growing federal deficit to the cost of providing transfers to the provinces and indicated that there would have to be cuts in these transfers to correct this imbalance. At the same time, federal complaints about provincial abuse of the EPF arrangements became more loud and insistent. These were all signs that the Trudeau government's program of restoring the balance by reasserting federal power was now reaching out to encompass fiscal matters.

Thus, it was toward the fiscally sensitive area of social policy, where the federal government had already developed a strong presence in spite of constitutional niceties, that another prong of the Liberals' centralist program was directed. This campaign took a variety of forms: unilateral changes to the EPF arrangements, tightening of the fiscal support to the provinces, politicization of provincial underfunding of social programs, a vigorous reassertion of the "national standards" test expected of provinces under the shared-cost programs in support of medicare and hospital insurance, and unrelenting pressure for an acknowledged federal role in the field of higher education. For the first time in the history of fiscal arrangements, the federal government opened up this area of intergovernmental activity to public comment and scrutiny by sending out a parliamentary task force under Herb Breau to provide a platform for all sorts of groups to complain about underfunding of social programs arising from these flawed intergovernmental fiscal arrangements. Citizens were encouraged to examine the extent of provincial commitment to these programs and the advisability of direct federal delivery of some of them. Interest group leaders, in their customary lobbying of federal politicians, were none too subtly pressured into taking a position on the intergovernmental fiscal disputes and into spelling out their views on the federal role and responsibility in their field, on pain of seeing yet further federal cutbacks. It was not a time for national interest groups to sit comfortably on the fence, and many complained about the damage done to their operations by being caught in this competitive cycle of intergovernmental warfare.

Meanwhile, the growing federal deficit, while also contributing its share of responsibility for some of these initiatives, offered an ideal backdrop for this federal "get tough" policy. It appeared to justify the severity of the federal approach to fiscal matters in 1982 and deflected attention away from the larger political program of centralization.[18] Provinces whose sources of federal funding were cut, denounced the federal government for merely transferring its deficit onto themselves. Nor did they accept the federal arguments about a fiscal imbalance or about their responsibility to share in shouldering the burden of the national debt. The 1982 fiscal negotiations were by far the most contentious on record. In the end they were simply bypassed, and new fiscal arrangements were imposed on the provinces unilaterally. Moreover, although the new arrangements were to cover the next five-year period, they were left open to changes by the federal government at any time prior to the expiry of the agreements. While these decisions could in part be superficially justified by the politics of restraint, there was far too broad a political pattern to the range of initiatives for that view to prevail.[19]

In this strategic area, the federal government was proceeding from a position of considerable strength. Unlike the unilateral ventures into the constitutional area and the provincially dominated field of energy, there was little the provinces could do about a federal government determined to act unilaterally with respect to its own fiscal priorities. While a convention had begun to develop that the provinces would "negotiate" with the federal government over fiscal matters through a complex set of intergovernmental machinery culminating in an agreement among first ministers, there was no federal legal or even compelling moral obligation to follow that course. Moreover, although the field of social policy that was in dispute lay under provincial jurisdiction, the federal government had, except in Quebec, already established a pre-eminent national position in social policy over the previous four decades by the use of conditional grants, and that position was still largely intact despite the rising power of the provinces over the previous two decades. That social legacy enjoyed widespread national support. The federal government felt quite strong enough to challenge the provinces in a direct showdown over provincial erosion of these systems and to focus public displeasure on them.

Under those circumstances, it was axiomatic that much of the intended fiscal agenda would be successfully pushed forward. The cuts were effected, and interest groups were more critical of provincial underfunding and more willing to rationalize the national government's role in these fields. Meanwhile, the cuts, compounded by recession, contributed substantially to the severity of provincial restraint measures, adopted in Quebec and elsewhere, that undermined support for provincial regimes. Most important of all, the political appeal around defending the medicare and hospital insurance systems was so overwhelming that the Trudeau government even won all-party support in the House of Commons for its powerful attack on the provinces through the Canada Health Act of 1984.

The arrival of the Mulroney government promising federal-provincial peace in September 1984 indicated, however, that there was a longer-term electoral price to be paid by the Liberals for having adopted so contentious a posture toward the provinces. But with growing national debt, not even the cooperative federalism of the federal Tories could blunt the bitter politics of fiscal federalism. After a short year of respite, the federal move to cut transfers to the provinces continued even before the expiry date of 1987. Moreover, the government was increasingly faced with unsatisfactory arrangements with the provinces over EPF, problems unlikely to go away. Provincial bitterness over the Mulroney government's decision to cut the level of increase in transfer payments for health and higher education was already bringing the honeymoon period of federal-provincial relations to an end, as the November 1985 First Ministers' Conference in Halifax indicated. Not even the Tory record of concessions to the provinces on energy and other matters could compensate for this worsening of fiscal federalism. This was perhaps testament enough to the powerful role of finance in shaping federal-provincial relationships.

### Finance and Power: From Conditional Grants to Block-Funding

The expansion and centralization of federal power in the aftermath of the Second World War was achieved, as we have seen, chiefly through the ambitious use of that government's fiscal capacity sustained by an overarching social consensus. The need for the construction of the modern social welfare state and for applied Keynesianism in economic policy gave the federal government the authority to continue the centralization begun during the war.[20] Not much of this was accomplished through formal constitutional amendment, except for the unemployment insurance and old age pension programs. Nonetheless, it amounted to a *de facto* transformation of the constitution, an indirect transfer of power accomplished through new intergovernmental fiscal arrangements.

There was, for example, the 1941 Tax Rental Agreement that permitted the federal government a monopoly on the application of income and corporation taxes in return for guaranteed federal transfers to the provinces. In this way a centralized and uniform system of income taxation was substituted for the earlier tax jungle of the 1930s.[21] The subsequent decisions following the war to extend these arrangements partly in the name of modern economic management theory allowed the federal government an undeniable primacy in these matters. By the 1960s, with Quebec going its own way and other provinces pressing for the right to apply their own levels of taxation, the system was somewhat decentralized in the 1962 Tax Collection Agreement, which permitted provinces the right to set their own rates within a single harmonized tax framework while Ottawa moved back its level of taxation in these fields and picked up the cost of tax collection. However, provinces had to accept the federal definition of the tax base and their rates of income tax were set as a percentage of federal tax; hence, their revenues were automatically subject to change whenever Ottawa unilaterally altered its own tax policy. Moreover, the level of federal tax in the co-occupied income tax field was still set high enough to permit the federal government to continue its grants to the provinces for programs in provincial areas of jurisdiction, thus perpetuating provincial dependency. Indeed, Ottawa subsequently applied the finishing touches to the federal construction of the modern positive state with the introduction of medicare in the late 1960s under explicit national program requirements, while postsecondary educational support was extended far beyond the earlier postwar program for veterans and the subsequent modest per capita grants in support of universities.

The instrument for much of this federal expansion of power was the conditional grant. In effect, it was a grant of money, offered to the provinces only for certain purposes and often only after provincial acceptance of certain federal stipulations, for programs principally or exclusively in provincial areas of jurisdiction. These were usually shared-cost programs, often funded on a 50-50 basis. These "50-cent dollars" were hard for provinces to refuse, even though they carried with them federal encroachment upon provincial turf. Once the provinces had entered into them, they were politically locked in, since it was virtually impossible to withdraw from these popular programs. Provinces, especially those with modest fiscal resources, were also finding that by virtue of these arrangements, their own spending priorities were being increasingly dictated by federal action. As provincial power grew during the 1960s, particularly in response to the crisis in Quebec, these concerns were carrying more and more weight in the national capital.

In addition, there were in-built limits to this strategy, one of the most obvious being the fiscal capacity of the respective governments to carry the mounting costs for these programs. Expenditures on health and education grew at astonishing rates throughout the 1960s until the mid-1970s, far outstripping expenditure increases in other areas. In fact, this period of general untrammelled government spending seemed to indicate that the fiscal system was getting "out of control"; hence, at least in the view of some analysts, the shift to block-funding could best be seen as the result of "fiscal eggs laid between 1965 and 1975 [coming home] to roost as full-grown, angry chickens."[22] The ground was being prepared for fiscal restraint and the later contraction of services. As Premier Robarts had worried at the time of Ontario's forced entry into the medicare program in 1968, this political scenario would leave the provinces in an even more severe position as the federal government sought to curtail its level of support for these programs. By the late 1960s there were already signs that Ottawa wished to contain the uncontrolled and unlimited demands the 50-50 shared-cost programs put on the federal treasury. By then, the attractions of driving federal power with generous financial lubricants was being called into question.

The government offered to withdraw from the shared-cost arrangements in 1973 in return for fixed financial transfers to the provinces, but to worried provinces, that seemed to suggest the federal abandonment they had long feared once the going got rough. Ceilings were nonetheless imposed, first on federal transfers in support of postsecondary education in 1972 and then on medicare in 1975. At that point the attractions of block-funding to both parties were becoming more apparent. By disentangling federal payments from provincial levels of expenditure, the federal government could get a better grip on the growth of its own expenditures in support of these programs, while provinces would presumably be free to control their own expenditures and effect economies in the nature and administration of the programs. Moreover, unconditional grants did not raise all of the old objections concerning federal intrusiveness into the provincial domain. The stage was set for fiscal decentralization under the 1977 Established Programs Financing Act.

Under the new scheme, the federal government offered the provinces both cash and tax points equal in value to federal per capita program contributions in the base year of 1975-76. The transfers were to be escalated each year according to a moving average of GNP growth over the most recent three-year period. The act also provided for a continuation of a modified version of the revenue guarantee first introduced in 1972 to compensate provinces for temporary losses of revenue due to federal tax reform.[23] This was not legally tied to the programs in question, although its presence in the EPF legislation and the fact that it was rolled into federal program cheques going to the provinces made for considerable later doubt and confusion on that score. Although the federal government for its own budgetary purposes split the total tranfer into a 32 per cent component for postsecondary education and a 68 per cent component for health, there was no requirement that provinces observe this breakdown or even that provincial spending on these programs match the level of federal increase each year.

The new plan, the provincial governments felt, improved efficiency in these social programs, since they would no longer lose federal funds for achieving program savings. It also provided a fairer method of ensuring equality in per capita terms on the amounts the provinces received under the program. There was an offsetting provision "for continuing federal participation with the provinces in the consideration and development of policies of national significance in the fields of health and post-secondary education." The federal government in particular looked forward to a role in the interprovincial Council of Ministers of Education and to a place in any talks on system rationalization. Finally, the new act provided for fiscal stability by building the arrangements into a five-year cycle. These arrangements could not be modified in such a way as to reduce provincial entitlements without mutual consent prior to March 31, 1982, and could not be terminated without three years notice.

The new system the Trudeau government adopted was ushered in by a sweet and enthusiastic chorus of government leaders singing the praises of cooperative federalism. That was unusual enough, but hardly three years later the system was being just as firmly denounced by the new post-referendum majority Liberal government as a splendid test case of the evils of provincialism and of the pitfalls of cooperative federalism. Predictably, the government pointed to what it regarded as reduced provincial spending on these programs while its relative share of funding had continued to grow. That assessment was of course rejected by the provinces, and even the Economic Council of Canada (ECC) did not find the level of provincial spending restraints either unusual or excessive.[24] The federal government also began to attack what it viewed as provincial violations of the program conditions for the national health system and the "diversion" of federal funds from the health system. The latter argument was rejected by Justice Hall in his August 1980 report, although the former argument concerning provincial acceptance of hospital user fees and extra-billing by doctors came under considerable criticism.[25] Finally, the government of Canada began to link the EPF transfers to what it called a "fiscal imbalance" in the federation and to a dangerous trend toward provincialization of the Canadian state.

### Unilateralism in Fiscal and Social Policy

These arguments prepared the way for the Trudeau government's plans to reverse growing provincial power and the alleged drift toward fiscal decentralization. Those aims were clear in the fall 1980 budget, which announced Ottawa's intention to cut back federal transfers to the provinces. Yet since fiscal negotiations had normally been conducted between officials and ministers of the respective governments, a living model of the executive federalism the federal government now felt had worked to the advantage of the provinces, the government knew that it would have to find new ways of reworking the process if changes were to be made. In the end, it decided to delay negotiations with the provinces, to join the political chorus of complaints about government underfunding and/or erosion of social programs and to fix the blame for that largely on provincial governments, and to bring into the political equation the full weight of interest groups affected by intergovernmental fiscal negotiations. In many respects, the political strategy was based on the approach used for the attempted unilateral amendment of the constitution.

Just as the federal government cultivated the goodwill of human rights groups by opening up the constitutional process to public participation through submissions to the joint House-Senate Committee, it supported the creation of the first Parliamentary Task Force on Federal-Provincial Fiscal Arrangements to act as "a federal magnet for interest groups dissatisfied with provincial spending and policies in health care and postsecondary education."[26] Although there was a strong *prima facie* case for improving public input into these crucial negotiations, the government attempted to use the committee in part as a vehicle for its own case against the provinces. Throughout its public hearings, the committee, under the chairmanship of Herb Breau, heard complaints from interest groups about provincial underfunding and abuse of social programs, as well as repeated expressions of support for a strong federal presence in these policy areas. There was, of course, no way in which such a political process would question the constitutional propriety of this use of the federal spending power, nor question the fiscal capacity of the governments.[27] The process was designed to put the provinces on the defensive, to demonstrate the impressive political coalition of interests supporting federal involvement in social policy, to prepare the way for demanding more financial accountability of the provinces and to reassert federal power and visibility.

As with the public participation exercise over the constitution, there were, of course, limits to the extent to which the government could control the committee and make it serve its purposes.[28] The Breau Committee did not, for example, accept the need for cutbacks in transfer payments to the provinces, nor did it buy the federal contentions that provinces were diverting federal funds, that cooperative federalism was not working and ought to be scrapped or that the national deficit problem was inextricably linked to the cost of transfer payments. With impressive public backing, it did, however, strongly endorse the continued federal presence in social policy and demanded stricter accountability of the federal government to Parliament for the use made of federal transfers and a stronger federal monitoring and enforcement of program conditions, especially in health care. Moreover, while it did not argue for stricter program conditions in the field of postsecondary education, it did criticize the failure of the provinces to involve the federal government in intergovernmental discussions in that field as promised in the 1977 fiscal agreements, and it called for urgent future collaboration on that subject.

In terms of the federal government's priorities, that was not an unhappy outcome from this first quasi-controlled public experiment in the politics of fiscal federalism. The process had shouldered up its determination to move away from the looser, decentralized block-funding arrangments of 1977 and to reassert federal leadership in social policy. As with public participation in the constitutional process, the government had brought on board a powerful array of groups anxious to protect their own interests, if necessary by acquiescence to a remarkable display of federal power in the Canadian state. In the constitutional initiative, the object was to secure public support for the unilateral constitutional initiative through the entrenchment of a popular Charter of Rights and Freedoms; on the fiscal front, the object was, as Rod Dobell has put it, to work upon "the desire of provincially based interest groups operating in areas falling within provincial jurisdiction to appeal to the federal government for action [standards, criteria, rules, whatever] to offset the impact of provincial government spending [and legislative] priorities."[29]

By the time that the Breau Committee had reported in August 1981, there was precious little time left for the usual intergovernmental negotiations prior to the March 1982 target date for renewal of the fiscal arrangements. In this way the federal government left the provinces with little chance to react to its ideas on a variety of fiscal matters. Moreover, the government responded quite selectively to the committee recommendations, implementing those that suited its program and ignoring others. The proposals to change the formula for determining equalization payments and to restrict increases in its rate of growth to the GNP, for example, were submitted only five months prior to the expiry of the existing legislation and did not follow the committee's recommendation to maintain the general nature and support of the equalization program. Similarly, Ottawa's plan to remove the revenue guarantee contained within the 1977 arrangements, taken in express defiance of the recommendation of the Breau Committee to roll it into program expenditures under EPF, was simply announced, with little opportunity for the provinces to use the machinery of multilateral negotiation to fight effectively against these initiatives. Faced with unanimous provincial opposition to these changes, the federal government, after making some adjustments to its proposal on equalization, proceeded unilaterally with the April 1982 enactment of Bill C-97.[30]

A year later the government in Bill C-150 (later renumbered C-12 and passed in early 1984 in the new parliamentary session) adopted the Breau Committee's recommendation to separate federal transfers for health and postsecondary education, while it rejected the committee's argument for continuing funding increases along the lines of the earlier EPF formula. The formal separation of the program components marked a retreat from the principles of block-funding, and the first stage of federal demands for accountability for federal expenditures in these new "targeted" programs. That objective was powerfully advanced in an amendment to Bill C-12 put forward by Flora MacDonald: it called for a Commons committee study of an annual report by the minister on the achievement of "national purposes" in postsecondary education. On the funding side, instead of the customary federal increases, the federal government added to its earlier cuts in equalization by applying its inflation-fighting 6 and 5 per cent limits upon federal payments in support of the postsecondary education program. These actions, too, were unilaterally taken, and they indicated that the provinces could expect no predictability in federal transfers but would have to live from year to year with the uncertain prospect of yet more federal cutbacks.[31]

It appeared that the role of the Finance Department had been usurped by the larger political program of the later Trudeau years and by the horizontal grip of central agencies responsible for carrying out that mandate. The significance of Bill C-12 was that it politicized this area of fiscal federalism more directly than any disputes had done in the past and opened up the prospect of yet further federal encroachment upon these policy areas. As Dobell has pointed out, the bill with no guarantee of federal funding for postsecondary education beyond 1984 "opens the door for the introduction of conditions designed to promote the achievement of 'national' (federal) objectives or standards in postsecondary education," while the capping presages a possible later linking of "federal increases to a matching of provincial increases."[32]

The culmination of the Trudeau government's program of rebuilding federal power in fiscal and social policy was, however, Bill C-3, the Canada Health Act, introduced into Parliament on December 12, 1983. This "other shoe in negotiations concerning established programs financing" was aimed at recovering power lost under the block-funding system and at monitoring and enforcing federal terms on these shared-cost programs.[33] Indeed, the whole question of the penalties for provincial violation of the general federal conditions on hospital insurance and medicare set out in the 1960s — comprehensiveness, universality, portability and accessibility — had lain as a vague and dormant issue during the previous fifteen years of growing government expenditure. Now, as accusations concerning provincial restrictions on accessibility in the form of user fees and extra-billing by doctors began to build during a period of financial restraint, the meaning of these conditions acquired a new saliency. They would be the instrument by which the federal government would assert its national responsibility to defend the health system against yet another exposed flaw in right-wing provincialism. This was playing politics with a vengeance.

The Health Services Review under Justice Hall in 1980, which cited extra-billing practices and hospital user fees as threats to the national health system and recommended their abolition, was a necessary prelude to this new assertion of federal power. In addition, the parliamentary task force under Herb Breau in 1981 reaffirmed this reading of the matter, while it also provided yet another forum within which citizens could express their fears over the perceived erosion of medicare and of the principles upon which it was based. Indeed, a variety of public interest groups, especially the new health reform groups and coalitions, nurses organizations, consumer associations and the like, took advantage of this opportunity to voice the public's concerns over declining accessibility with considerable success. This was an essential element in the preparing and shaping of public opinion for some kind of remedial federal action.

The fact that this movement was proceeding at precisely the same time that Ottawa was also unleashing its constitutional and energy policies did not incline provincial politicians and officials to consider as dispassionately as they might otherwise have done the recommendations of the Hall or Breau reports. On the contrary, they were rather more encouraged to view these issues in broader political terms, especially in the framework of intergovernmental relations. This spillover was a natural enough consequence and may have in fact encouraged provinces to accelerate the conflict with Ottawa by proposing to extend the impugned practices in the face of federal threats. For example, at the beginning of 1983, only British Columbia had a general system of user charges both for hospital accommodation and outpatient, emergency and minor daycare surgical services, while Newfoundland had only ward charges and Alberta a small hospital admission charge. In March 1983 Alberta, citing rising costs, inadequate federal financial support and the need for some deterrence against abuses, announced a new program of hospital user fees and later a crackdown on those who were in arrears on their medical premiums; that action was followed quickly by New Brunswick's announcement of its new system of user fees effective in July of that year. These actions drew the expected fire from Health Minister Monique Bégin and tended to confirm federal worries about the potential dangers if these practices were not finally checked. Such skirmishes over social policy only tended to reinforce the already highly conflictual patterns of federal-provincial relations at this time, especially those between Ottawa and Edmonton.

Given the state of Canadian public opinion, which had become aroused over these issues and was overwhelmingly inclined to the federal view of the matter, there was an obvious incentive for Ottawa to act. Since polls had long indicated that the provinces had already been receiving most of the political credit for the health programs over the years, while Ottawa was mostly taking the flak as the taxing authority with no visibility, this seemed an ideal way in which to correct those misperceptions and establish the federal government in the eyes of citizens as a defender of the national integrity of the health system.[34] Furthermore, there was in this policy field, as there had been in the constitutional initiative, a variety of public groups ready to come on board the federal centralizing train provided that the integrity of the health system was the ostensible destination.

Given its broad political dimension and importance, the question of securing provincial compliance with banning these practices in this joint field through a new legislative enactment was taken up both by the Department of Health and Welfare under its aggressive minister Monique Bégin and by the new horizontal Ministry of State for Social Development under Jake Austin.[35] They jointly developed, under the Canada Health Act, the federal "penalties approach," which would be used to counteract what were regarded as provincial threats to the health system. Lacking constitutional authority to outlaw these practices directly, the federal government resorted to an indirect ban by using the spending power to punish provinces that permitted these offending practices. Extra-billing and the charging of user fees were expressly declared to be inconsistent with the principles of accessibility and universality upon which medicare was founded, and the provinces permitting these practices would find federal payments reduced by an amount corresponding to the income generated by these practices. These funds would be held for up to a three-year period and would be returned to provinces that subsequently banned these practices prior to the April 1987 deadline. Moreover, in keeping with the recommendations of both the Hall and Breau reports, any province that did not permit extra-billing was urged to negotiate with the medical profession within the province on matters of compensation and to accept the use of conciliation or binding arbitration to settle disputes relating to compensation. Failure to "provide for reasonable compensation" could lead to federal cutbacks in transfers "by an amount that the Governor in Council considers to be appropriate, having regard to the gravity of the default."[36]

While earlier enactments had always permitted the federal government to hold back all payments to provinces for violations of the terms of the shared-cost medicare programs, the new provisions of the Canada Health Act were much more effective and subtle, since they provided a realistic graduated approach to cutbacks and, hence, to the enforcement of federal conditions. The three-year time limit for recovering withheld funds, together with the pressure of public opinion, also acted to encourage delinquent provinces to move toward banning these practices relatively quickly.[37] Moreover, while Ottawa had always been able to shape the nature of the medicare system by deciding which medical services to fund prior to EPF block-funding arrangements, the new approach gave it a much higher political profile, not least with the public health interest groups that were clamouring for action.

Although this latter-day politics over conditional grants was merely part and parcel of the larger Trudeau political program carried over into social policy, it was also a logical outcome of a fiscal crisis some critics thought was beginning to threaten the whole welfare state created by the Liberals after the Second World War. Provinces, for example, argued that the rise of extra-billing and user fees was a direct outcome of inadequate federal funding and that the mounting costs of the health system made it imperative that more cost-saving measures be adopted and that alternative cheaper modes of care based on preventive and rehabilitative practices rather than curative approaches be devised. Since federal funding only covered more costly curative health services, there was virtually no incentive under the shared-cost arrangements for a more balanced and cost-efficient system of health care. The underfunding argument was rejected by the federal government, but there was little doubt that after the passage of the Canada Health Act the provinces were expected to cope with rising costs with inadequate federal grants and reduced access to other financial sources. While the threat of reduced accessibility to health care from the trend toward user fees and extra-billing was checked by the new act, the federal response was scarcely an adequate answer to the long-run problems of the health care system.[38]

It was this drift toward uniformity, toward prescribing provincial codes of conduct in social policy, and away from experimentation with alternative systems of health care within a decentralized fiscal system to which many critics objected.[39] However, the act was undeniably successful as a political venture for the federal Liberals. They garnered all-party support in the Commons for the measure and enjoyed widespread popularity for their defence of the integrity of the health care system. Moreover, they managed to move further away from the politics of block-funding, to impose stricter federal conditions on this shared-cost program, and thus to tilt the federation in a more centralized direction. Even accountability and greater federal visibility were achieved by the requirement for more information from the provinces on the operation of the medicare program (though the regulations for providing and disclosing financial information are still lax) and the provision under section 13 that federal contributions to medicare be given "appropriate recognition."

### Federalism and the Politics of Higher Education

All of these belated assertions of federal power respecting jointly funded programs under provincial jurisdiction naturally carried over into postsecondary education. This field had already had a strong federal presence for well over three decades and, like health, was entangled in the intergovernmental politics over EPF. Moreover, charges of provincial underfunding and of resistance to federal involvement as promised under the 1977 EPF arrangements were even more bitter here than in the health field. Meanwhile, the subject area was rapidly assuming more and more importance to the federal government both for its obvious role in economic renewal and for its powerful social and cultural place in nation-building.

Federal entry into the highly sensitive field of education, entrusted to the constitutional care of the provinces under section 93 subject only to special guarantees and federal protection for denominational schools, was first accomplished in a gradual and often uncontentious way, usually justified on the grounds that certain aspects of education related directly to other federal responsibilities such as national defence, the promotion of the national economy or the development of agriculture. Military academies and schools for the children of the armed forces fell easily into the first category, while federal programs for technical and vocational education and for agricultural instruction fitted neatly into the second and third.[40] In addition, a federal presence in the promoting of research, especially of a scientific nature, began as early as 1916 with the founding of the National Research Council. These activities, funded entirely by Ottawa, were accepted by the provinces as plausible federal ventures in areas related to special national interests; they did not appear to threaten the provinces' primary constitutional responsibilities for education. They did, however, open up a line of argument and a range of precedents for later federal movement into the field.

Apart from participating in a joint venture with the provinces to support student aid in 1939, the federal government did not move outside this general range of activities until after the Second World War. At that time, however, there existed a combination of circumstances that would escalate federal participation dramatically. One of the most significant of these was the pressing need to deal with the massive numbers of veterans returning from service; they made an uncontestable claim upon federal resources to help support their re-entry into normal civilian life, including the provision of higher educational opportunities. Ottawa responded with financial grants both to students and to the universities until the veterans' educational programs had been phased out by 1951.

This financial support was vital to the expansion of the university system in the postwar years and brought universities into direct contact with the federal government just as had federal contacts with universities for required research during the wartime years. Hence, as the federal program of university support through veterans' allowances began to wind down and the prospects of severe financial contraction of the postsecondary educational system loomed before them, the universities became vociferous advocates of federal involvement in higher education. Ottawa responded with a program of direct cash grants to universities to replace its earlier financial support through the veterans' program. In this way, a developing client-patron relationship was established between the federal government and institutions of higher learning in the provinces. This federal encroachment upon the constitutional jurisdiction of the provinces so offended the Quebec government that a year after the introduction of the program, it forbade the universities in the province to accept the federal funds.[41]

The association of the national government with the financing of universities was now well established, although it did not match provincial levels of funding throughout the 1950s and 1960s.[42] The rhetoric used to justify federal involvement — namely, the national dimension of higher education and its relationship to economic growth and technological development — continued to be mounted by university leaders, government consultants and federal representatives. Although increasing federal sensitivity to incursions into provincial jurisdictions led the federal government in 1967-68 away from direct funding of the universities and toward financial arrangements through provincial governments, at no time did Ottawa's financial commitment to higher education do anything but expand.

The postwar years, in marked contrast to the interwar period, were in fact characterized by a sharp predominance of federal over provincial power. It was Ottawa that was now expected to maintain economic prosperity, contain unemployment, provide an effective and modern social security system, resist the increasingly powerful threats of Americanization of the country and promote national unity. Most of these new challenges suggested special educational responsibilities Ottawa now reached out to assume. On the economic front, the federal government expanded its programs for vocational and manpower training by offering federal dollars to move the provinces swiftly into vocational education at the secondary school level and later into community college development. It expanded its work in the field of student aid with the passing of the Canada Student Loans Plan in 1964. On the cultural front, it accepted many of the recommendations of the Massey Royal Commission on National Development in the Arts, Letters, and Sciences; the creation of the Canada Council in 1957 moved the federal government into much more direct involvement with university research in the humanities and social sciences and with the promotion of a national arts community. To counteract the threat of rising Quebec nationalism during the 1960s, Ottawa launched a policy of official bilingualism and began to mount an extensive array of programs in second-language training. With each national responsibility and with each crisis, the federal role in education deepened as did the scale of its financial commitment.

It was the selective and generally defensible nature of federal involvement in the field that made possible this expanding federal presence in education, but there is little doubt that the ground was being prepared for a strong if discrete federal claim to the area in the future. Nor is there much doubt that federal funding for educational initiatives had a distorting effect on the priorities of provincial governments; in fact, it was partly in deference to these concerns that federal funding for education later became more and more untied. All that was needed in order to strain this complicated set of intergovernmental arrangements was the heightening of federal-provincial political conflict: exactly the kind of confrontation that developed between Ottawa and the provinces throughout the 1970s.

With the coming to power of a separatist government in Quebec, together with rising regional power in the West, Ottawa's concerns for a stronger national voice in education grew considerably. After the Quebec referendum, one of the more pressing issues for the Canadian educational system was, in the words of Francis Fox, secretary of state and minister of communications in 1981, "to enhance the sense of belonging to Canada."[43] Declaring education to be "the lifeblood of the country," the vital human link tying the country together, Fox officially reasserted the growing federal interest in education and national unity.[44] In fact, that matter had already been evident over the previous decade with the variety of federal policy instruments that had been used to promote Canadian national self-consciousness and knowledge: the directives to the federal research councils, especially the Social Sciences and Humanities Research Council of Canada, to promote Canadian studies as a national priority; the measures taken to promote Canadians on university teaching faculties; and the support for Canadianization of the educational curriculum.[45] The Symons report, the expansion of Canadian studies programs, the federally backed immersion and bilingual programs, and many other policy ventures in the universities were all played out against this rising nationalist trend in educational matters. This movement "of self-conscious nationalism," complained Desmond Morton, had converted "Canadian universities into institutions of national consciousness-raising," required "to perform the almost mystic function of "Canadianization."[46]

Certainly in Quebec it was hardly likely that this nationalist drive in education, under federal leadership, would do anything other than conflict with the priorities of the PQ overnment — or, for that matter, any other province-centred educational program. Education was also caught in an intergovernmental crossfire over its role in economic development, where both governments wished to see postsecondary education linked to their own respective programs for training and development.[47] As Canada's economic difficulties deepened in the late 1970s and in the recessionary period of the 1980s, there was increasing pressure, especially from the business community, for better federal-provincial collaboration in this field. These concerns found their way into the proceedings and report of the Macdonald Royal Commission, as did the complaints of the affected interest groups in the postsecondary education community. However, it was unlikely, in the face of continued underfunding by the provinces under EPF, the growing dependence of the universities on the provinces and the policy standoff between the governments concerning any agreed federal role in intergovernmental deliberations over higher education, that these functional concerns would obstruct the Trudeau government's plans for a restoration of federal power in this area.

As noted earlier, the Breau Committee wrote part of the federal script with its arguments for improved accountability of the provinces for federal transfers in support of higher education and for a clearer delineation of federal objectives upon which these payments were being made. These were rapidly adopted as federal negotiating demands with the provinces. On the other hand, the government turned down the committee's recommendation for continuation of federal funding, including the revenue guarantee built into the EPF legislation, and instead terminated the revenue guarantee entirely and later applied fiscal constraints to the postsecondary education transfers by fixing its 6 and 5 per cent guidelines upon these transfers. Almost at the eleventh hour, on February 4, 1982, after preliminary skirmishes with the provinces at the ministerial level, Prime Minister Trudeau set out the requirements the provinces must observe if they expected any continuation of the EPF arrangements through to 1983-84. These included demands for provincial expenditures on postsecondary education to rise "in each of the next two fiscal years at a rate at least equal to the rate of increase of EPF cash and tax transfers" and for provincial governments to undertake "to discuss with the Secretary of State mechanisms by which the achievement of the major national objectives with respect to the overall support of post-secondary education may be assured with a view to defining these objectives in federal legislation governing EPF post-secondary transfers." These federal objectives included:

(a) Mobility — no discrimination or preference for students or faculty on the basis of province of origin;

(b) Accessibility — the assurance of reasonable access to postsecondary education and adult training programs for all qualified Canadians;

(c) Accountability — the provision of adequate information on the post-secondary education programs, to enable Parliament to assess the efficacy of its funding programs and for national and international planning;

(d) Co-operative planning — agreement to joint federal and provincial planning for the implementation of means to achieve national objectives in post-secondary education and training;

(e) Language — agreement to provide full opportunity for the people of Canada to increase their knowledge of Canada's official languages through formal learning and for members of minority official language groups to receive post-secondary education in their own language.[48]

All of these moves indicated that the federal government wished to attach the same policy of national legislated conditions to the transfer of federal funds in support of higher education that had always applied to health. This was a considerable and specific escalation of federal requirements beyond those in all previous arrangements, since it required not only the agreed outline of national objectives in federal legislation, but also provincial undertakings regarding appropriate mechanisms to ensure the achievement of these objectives. Moreover, the federal funding proposal required a return to a linkage between federal funding increases and provincial expenditures in support of postsecondary education. Needless to say, these demands were not taken up and the funding cuts followed.[49]

The provinces, in turn, generally passed these cuts in the level of federal increase on to the institutions. Indeed, in some provinces, such as British Columbia where the politics of restraint were being waged with unrelenting ferocity, the institutions first received no increases at all and then began to suffer actual cuts from earlier levels of funding. Coming on top of a long period of reduced government expenditures for postsecondary education, these and other cuts were having serious negative consequences on the quality of programs, personnel, libraries and physical plant. Universities, increasingly conscious of their dependency on governmental support for maintenance of the system (student fees and corporate sector revenue having dropped dangerously below the proportion of total university revenue they had occupied before 1945), had never been more vulnerable to direct control by the state.[50] In the last analysis, the cuts, federal-provincial acrimony and the long-term political threats from government financing were beginning to bring home to the higher education community the price to be paid for their dependence on intergovernmental transfer arrangements, and they provoked in turn a search by these interest groups for ways of accommodating the governments and stabilizing their own threatened field of operations.

The new direction could be seen, for example, in the position of the Canadian Association of University Teachers (CAUT) when in May 1984 the council of the CAUT, even with the consent of FAPUQ, its Quebec wing, approved a draft national postsecondary education financing act.[51]

The CAUT draft act, while reaffirming the principle of provincial constitutional jurisdiction over higher education, largely accepted the need for national legislated standards under which federal payments for postsecondary education would be made. It also accepted the arguments for provincial accountability to Parliament for the provision of financial information, for improved parliamentary mechanisms for reporting and debating on postsecondary education transfers and objectives, and for cooperative intergovernmental arrangements in the field. These measures, subsequently supported by the Canadian Federation of Students, showed that interest groups, after years of plaintive neutrality, had begun to move much closer to the federal agenda. However, on the funding question, in a direct rebuff of the punitive approach used in the Canada Health Act, the CAUT draft bill eschewed financial penalties for violation of program standards and instead provided financial incentives to encourage higher levels of provincial expenditure. This plan, aimed at securing the financial and other interests of members of this policy constituency, indicated how far the intergovernmental wrangle over financing was pushing injured groups into seeking remedies.

It seemed that the details of intergovernmental fiscal matters could no longer be treated as the exclusive preserve of finance officials and their ministerial superiors. Public interest groups were becoming more and more aware of the wider political stake they had in these fiscal negotiations. That process had already begun with the first opening up of the fiscal subject matter by the Breau Committee in 1981, and it continued with the later public meetings of the Macdonald Commission. Now it appeared that such groups were using these vehicles not only for expressing their discontent over underfunding and intergovernmental bickering, but also as a platform for proposing the reworking of the patterns of intergovernmental interaction.

The interest groups preferred to patch up the EPF fiscal arrangements rather than face other more radical proposals then being considered by the federal government. These included the possible reduction or withdrawal of federal funds to the provinces in support of higher education and their redeployment in alternative directions more in keeping with federal goals. These alternatives included redirecting the funds toward meeting the indirect costs of university research, toward the creation of distinct federal research institutes, toward training and employment programs or toward a voucher system of payments directly to students. All of these alternatives raised the prospect of even more intergovernmental conflict and considerable uncertainty about the impact of these changes upon the colleges and universities.

Although the announced retirement of Prime Minister Trudeau on February 29, 1984, put all of these options in abeyance, it was clear that the festering difficulties around postsecondary education were unlikely to go away no matter who might assume power in Ottawa. It was reported by Richard Gwyn that Trudeau had decided to go ahead with a student voucher system if he were to remain and be returned to power. In that way, the old direct client-patron patterns of federal support between individuals, educational institutions and the federal state, such as that used with the veterans program prior to 1951, would be restored. Provinces would be more or less circumvented and would lose much of their administrative and financial clout over institutions of higher education. While the institutions would still remain the constitutional charges of the provinces, spending patterns would be arranged to check and counterbalance that constitutional power. Thus, the political strength flowing from the ingenious use of the federal spending power would again demonstrate itself.

As it turned out, the Mulroney government assumed power in September of that year without a clear sense of how it wished to deal with these problems. While it had uttered the expected promises of improved funding which opposition parties are prone to, its brand of cooperative federalism did not seem to mesh well with any of the contending proposals for correcting the flaws in the fiscal arrangements. Certainly in the field of health, despite its earlier adherence to the Canada Health Act, it had argued that the fundamental problem was not one of intergovernmental arrangements but of underfunding. Commitments were made during the election campaign to increase transfers for health, and assurances were also given about improved funding for postsecondary education and research. While the application of yet more financial lubricant to the system made for a temporarily smooth ride with the provinces and the interest groups, it did not sit well with the Tories' promised program of fiscal restraint to fight the rising federal deficit, nor was it likely to provide realistic answers to the intractable politics of fiscal federalism. The new government's only consolation for this absence of policy was the promise of two impending federal reports on the subject, one by retired mandarin Professor A.W. Johnson on postsecondary education and the other by the Macdonald Commission on the whole fiscal framework and the economy. These would provide policy and ideas against which the Mulroney government's federalism might be measured.

### Fiscal Restraint with Cooperative Federalism?

The Conservatives under Brian Mulroney had hardly begun their trek toward cooperative federalism in fiscal matters before the Trudeau government presented them with a dubious Christmas present in the Canada Health Act of December 1983. That measure was carefully calculated to force the Conservatives either to side with their friends in the provinces in opposition to the application of federal financial penalties for provincial violations of the medicare system or to desert the provinces in order to court public opinion, overwhelmingly in favour of the bill. To the astonishment of the Trudeau government, Mulroney astutely chose the latter course and managed to convince both his caucus and provincial allies of its cruel but necessary logic. The Conservatives recognized that, while they enjoyed massive support for their presumed competence in economic matters, polls indicated they were most vulnerable with voters on their perceived insensitivity to social policy. It was this weakness the Liberals wished to exploit in a future campaign, but the electoral trap did not snare its intended victim.

However, it had to be admitted that adherence to the Canada Health Act with its federally enforced code of social conduct on the provinces was a curious beginning for a political party championing cooperative federalism. Although provincial leaders anticipated assistance from the Tories if elected to counterbalance the effects of these cuts, the anomaly remained as the opening shot in a difficult period for social programs under the politics of fiscal restraint. With the costs of carrying the national debt rising in a disturbing exponential pattern, it was becoming clear that the old financial lubricants that had smoothed out potential intergovernmental disputes would no longer be as readily available. In short, the peace of cooperative federalism, sustained by disbursements from a healthy federal treasury, might no longer be purchasable. This danger was certainly heightened by the other policy ventures undertaken by the Mulroney government in the name of cooperative federalism and economic renewal. Fiscal pressures arising from the withdrawal of the Petroleum and Gas Revenue Tax (a decision taken even before the spectacular fall in world oil prices) and the retreat from offshore royalties under the Atlantic Accord, both calculated to win favour with the producing provinces and the oil industry, were certainly going to make it much harder for Ottawa to sustain its level of transfers in support of social programs and equalization. That fact was recognized by the Mulroney government and became part of its attempted cost-benefit tradeoff with the provinces. But such a strategy was scarcely a firm and reliable foundation for intergovernmental harmony.

During the first year-length honeymoon period in office, the government postponed dealing with these unpleasant matters. It agreed to abide by the existing EPF agreement, including the normal escalator provision on increases in federal transfers to the provinces, for the 1985-86 fiscal year. This exemption of federal transfers to the provinces from the deficit-fighting program of the new government was all the more noticeable in view of the wide-ranging cuts made in many other federal program expenditures. Both the November statement of program cuts by Finance Minister Wilson, the December row over the principle of universality in social programs, the May 1985 budget carrying a curious bundle of expenditure restraints and tax increases along with removal of the capital gains tax on sums below half a million dollars, and the later spectacular and successful public campaign to defeat the partial deindexation of old age pensions were all signs of the new government's vain and often bungled attempts at getting a grip on the federal deficit. While these belt-tightening battles were going on, the government was pursuing its program of reconciliation with the provinces and the oil industry at the long-term expense of the federal treasury. Naturally, Energy Minister Pat Carney received public accolades for her generous overtures to a new spirit of cooperative federalism, while the finance minister was left to ponder the grim fiscal implications of these policies.[52] This was a short-run policy that could not long be sustained. It would soon be the turn of the provinces to share the burden of the national debt, although after the energy agreements most of the cuts (apart from reduced federal support of energy exploration and regional development) would be felt in federal transfers in support of health and higher education.

Before the end of 1985, at the first ministers' meeting at Halifax in November and at the meeting of finance ministers the following month, the provinces learned that the federal government was not about to budge from its intention to cut the level of increase of transfers under EPF even before the expiration of the five-year fiscal arrangements in 1987. This about-face was justified on the grounds of restraint and of the need for the provinces to share in shouldering the cost of national deficit-fighting. The federal plan was to cut more than $6 billion off the level of federal increases for health and higher education through to 1990-91. The anticipated savings in transfers in 1990-91 alone were expected to be approximately $2 billion. The finance minister indicated that the new escalator would not follow the inflation rate but would be a rate equivalent to the growth in the GNP minus 2 per cent.[53] Meanwhile, program expenditures in these fields were rising well above the inflation rate.

If the government had anticipated receiving either from the Johnson report or the Macdonald Commission remedies to the problems of EPF, especially to those in postsecondary education, that were also compatible with their rather exotic hybrid commitment to fiscal restraint and their loosely defined brand of cooperative federalism, they would certainly have been disappointed. While both of these reports grappled with the serious flaws in these arrangements, neither could offer recommendations that did not in one way or another involve the federal government in collisions with the provinces.

The Johnson report recommended among other things that the federal government continue its support for postsecondary education at a rate consistent with the GNP and population increase, but that there be a direct linkage of federal increase (up to that maximum) with the actual increase of provincial expenditures for that purpose in each province. That would provide an incentive but not an obligation for the provinces to increase their contributions to postsecondary education at the GNP rate. This recommendation sought to remedy the declining share of provincial financial support for higher education, which had developed as a gaping flaw in the unconditional grant arrangements during the EPF period, while not interfering as directly in the policies and priorities of provincial governments as the earlier pre-1977 matching system of conditional grants would have done. However, the report argued that if the national purposes for the program and the political commitment to maintain it were to continue, these federal transfers must be clearly designated for the program to which they apply.

It appeared that there was very little recognition by the provinces of the dangers and vulnerability of the existing unconditional fiscal system in a climate of restraint, and therefore little evidence of provincial willingness to change the status quo. Instead, the provinces attacked the credibility of the Johnson report on technical and moral grounds and largely missed opportunities to seek an accommodation over outstanding grievances. As for the Mulroney government, its pursuit of national reconciliation with the provinces ruled out any thoughts of a row over higher education. There was no strong leadership from the secretary of state to undertake this kind of reform initiative, nor was the Finance Department interested, since it was more preoccupied with trimming expenditures wherever possible. In short, there was no federal will to act. The result was predictable. As the November First Ministers' Conference indicated, federal transfers for this purpose would become entirely subject to the usual politics of deficit-cutting with no special federal political stake (apart from indirect impacts on the economy) in the program outcomes. By eschewing negotiation, the governments had tacitly agreed to the continued drift of underfunding, to pushing aside the unresolved conflict and to a continued lack of rational focus in these arrangements.

If the federal government appeared to find the Johnson report proposals too contentious for its political tastes, there was even less likelihood that it would pick up the more radical centralizing proposals of the Macdonald Commission on this subject. The commission actually recommended Trudeau's former scheme of a student voucher system as an alternative way of delivering the cash component of federal transfers for postsecondary education. The rationale supporting this proposition spoke of "overcoming inertia" and of "creating a more competitive, dynamic, and diversified" educational system. In short, the market-driven ideology behind so many of the commission's recommendations was carried over into these fiscal arrangements. While it said nothing about the political centralization that would flow from this advice and made all of the required bows to provincial constitutional authority in the field, the commission was attempting to move federal arrangements back to a universal equivalent of the postwar direct payments to veterans. Ottawa's direct links to individual Canadians would then be enhanced, while provincial governments would be simply circumvented.

While the commission's rhetoric concerning the power of the market as an effective regulator and stimulant even in the postsecondary educational system was likely to be received with some sympathy by the Mulroney Conservatives, the centralist assumptions also underlying the proposal flew in the face of the government's program of cooperative federalism and national reconciliation. The scheme did, however, contain a hidden political agenda: if undertaken, it would help secure federal payments to this sector much more effectively than would transfers to governments. Direct federal grants to individuals for educational purposes would be politically difficult to withdraw during periods of restraint. The voucher system could be a kind of insurance policy against fiscal attacks by government deficit-cutters. However, since the proposal would be regarded as dangerous and destabilizing by the educational institutions and as intrusive and offensive by the provincial governments, this was a merely abstract argument unlikely to be tested in Canada. While the commission chairman later modestly characterized the recommendation as a "shaking of the tree" to bring the players toward negotiation, there was little sign that it was having any such effect.

## Conclusion

It would not be until the spring of 1987 that Canadians would finally learn whether the problems around EPF arrangements would be tackled at all, but the omens were not promising. There was far too little federal or provincial interest in disturbing these arrangements to make an early settlement likely. However, there remained the continuing federal requirement to report to Parliament on the national objectives and financing of postsecondary education and the persistent pressure of the interest groups who did want a settlement of the outstanding intergovernmental irritants. Moreover, the governments would be subjected to yet more heat from interest groups in health, postsecondary education, and their allies in the social envelope from the coming cuts. These political interventions by the interest groups could be expected to exacerbate federal-provincial relations both by encouraging the tendency of each level of government to blame the other for the underfunding problems and by pressuring Ottawa to impose codes against provincial cost-cutting practices.

Doctors were meanwhile continuing their court challenge of the Canada Health Act while most of the provinces were acknowledging the obvious and beginning to legislate against extra-billing and user fees. The politics around that issue, including the federal threats of financial penalties for provinces that permitted those practices and the pressure of the April 1987 time limit for recovering withheld funds, had moved many provinces into compliance. The minority Liberal government of Ontario, for example, having agreed to end extra-billing as part of its accord with the provincial NDP and not wishing to be outflanked by that party on so popular an issue, proceeded to ban extra-billing in June 1986, even in the face of a messy political showdown with the Ontario Medical Association (OMA). The result was a strike by many doctors, including the closure of some emergency wards, a serious breakdown in the government-OMA relationship and a massive loss of face for the medical profession. Any long-term damaging side effects from the dispute were, however, largely borne by the provincial government, while the federal Parliament remained relatively insulated from the heat of a political battle it had helped to structure two years earlier with the passage of the Canada Health Act. While the federal legislation did not dictate the Ontario legislative model used for banning extra-billing or control the negotiation process, it had established the primary lines of combat between the government and medical practitioners in that province, and by using the spending power to apply financial and political pressure on so popular an issue, it had pushed Ontario and other provinces into taking action. For example, Nova Scotia had not even waited until federal penalties could be brought into effect before it banned extra-billing on June 11, 1984. It did so by requiring doctors, whether inside or outside the provincial health plan, not to charge above the plan rates, a model later copied by Ontario.

The fact that the political repercussions would be so unequally and inversely correlated with the constitutional right was a disturbing feature of this whole exercise. Ottawa rather painlessly made itself a political champion over certain aspects of health delivery (a provincial jurisdiction) for Canadian citizens, while the provinces carried the political risk when the time came to enforce the new federal conditions on doctors in the provinces. No matter how one views the issue of extra-billing, that fact has to be seen as a troubling paradox. That the political consequences could be passed down so neatly, indeed perversely meted out against the order of government that actually held the constitutional right and responsibilities in the area, only underlined the clever politics but dubious constitutional morality surrounding this use of the federal spending power.

But the politics around the issue were not over. These spilled out from the political arena and, after the passage of the Ontario legislation, moved into judicial forums. The court actions taken against both the Canada Health Act and the Ontario legislation by the Canadian Medical Association promised to carry on the issue, with potentially important legal ramifications and consequences for the Canadian federation.[54] On the one hand, the challenge to these enactments raised by sections 7 and 15 of the Canadian Charter of Rights and Freedoms provided the Supreme

Court with an opportunity to expand its own policymaking role, especially by passing on the question of an alleged "freedom of contract" or a professional right to carry out a professional practice without unreasonable governmental interference as part of the guarantee of "liberty" and "security of the person" under section 7 (with concomitant guarantees of "equality before the law" under section 15). This line of argument, buttressed by a number of recent promising court judgments, ensured that the Supreme Court would be called upon to decide whether section 7 contains "economic rights" similar to those that arise from the "due process" clause of the American constitution. That prospect, which seemed so unlikely after the Canadian decision to exclude a right to property (and to avoid the language of "due process" and to use the more procedural term "fundamental justice") in the charter, now seemed "a real possibility."[55] If that argument were to be accepted and the enactments banning extra-billing struck down, many other laws designed to protect the public interest but that also impinge on freedom of contract (such as workers' compensation, minimum wage laws, etc.) would be subject to attack.

Ironically, one of the constitutional arguments being levelled against the Canada Health Act struck directly at the validity of the federal spending power and, therefore, promised to give the courts a chance to review that matter after decades of debate over its propriety. Hence, the legal and political dynamics around the appropriate use of federal fiscal capacities had now come full circle. It was penalized interest groups, not provincial governments, who were claiming that Ottawa had exceeded its powers. While most constitutional experts raised doubts about this kind of challenge, the courts could hardly have more telling illustrations of federal intrusion into provincial jurisdiction through the spending power than in the toughly worded explicit conditionality set out in the Canada Health Act and in the subsequent Ontario measure that purported to meet those terms. In a detailed review of the spending power as it relates to the Canada Health Act, one student has raised serious questions about the conventional legal wisdom on this matter by bluntly asking:

- whether the courts will really be persuaded that Ottawa is merely acting like a "private philanthropist" here and the provinces "freely accepting" these terms;
- whether the test of constitutionality (or the "pith and substance") of the matter will not extend beyond the mere grant of money but also to the legislated conditions which are inseparable from it; and
- whether therefore the real intended goals, "the reasonably expected and known impact of these conditions," will not form part of the constitutional characterization of the enactment.

> After examining all of these points [he concludes], a court would sit back and ask "On balance, what is this statute really about?" Their concern would be to get at the heart of the Act. An objective reading of the Act as a whole suggests that the pith and substance of the *Canada Health Act* is the administration of health care and not merely the making of a conditional grant for health care purposes. Because the Act seemingly has the effect of redefining provincial systems of health care, it would appear to be *ultra vires* the federal government.[56]

Whether the courts decide to go behind the apparent face of this measure as a mere grant of money offered by Ottawa and freely accepted by the provinces and to ask more probing questions about the true nature of the legislative subject matter (its goal, effects, pre-eminent aspect) remains to be seen. But there can be little doubt that after decades of contentious political debate, the scope and limits of the federal spending power will finally be tested in the Supreme Court of Canada.

In retrospect, it is astonishing how the use of the federal spending power and the structure of intergovernmental fiscal arrangements have permitted this new and now disturbingly dissonant pattern of Canadian federalism to develop. The federal-provincial conflict over higher education and health in the 1980s, complete with its associated interest group activity, would have been inconceivable without the gradual buildup of federal financing of these systems over the previous three decades. As we have seen, during those years, a stronger federal claim to equality if not pre-eminence in these fields was being carefully established with the advancement of every federal dollar for that purpose, just as patterns of financial dependency on those federal dollars were also being laid in the health and postsecondary education constituencies. These developments were clearly extraconstitutional and unanticipated by the formal division of powers between the governments.

While the federal control behind the flow of these dollars was somewhat disguised throughout the period of province-building in the 1960s and 1970s ushered in first by Quebec's Quiet Revolution and later by the West's "petroleum revolution," the arrival in 1980 of an aggressive majoritarian government in Ottawa was all that was needed to make that federal power apparent. Once the Trudeau government began to exercise the political capital that had been built up from its extensive financing of social measures, it was clear to all how dramatically the pendulum of power in Canadian federalism could shift to Ottawa in social policy.

This underlines Thomas Courchene's remark that changes in fiscal relations can bring about *de facto* amendments of the Canadian constitution with more regularity and more force than any cumbersome formal amending procedure would ever be likely to do.[57] Moreover, since these arrangements are much more subject to the pressures of day-to-day political life, including lobbying by private interests at both levels in the federation, the reshaping of the distribution of power in the federation in this form can be a political exercise in which citizens themselves become directly involved. That is part of the meaning of this remarkably powerful element in the reshaping of the Canadian federation: at one level, the adaptability and flexibility of this instrument for public policy and the redefining of the federation; at another, the threat it presents to intergovernmental peace and the faithful pursuit of the spirit as well as the letter of the constitution.

The Breau Committee had something of this in mind when it reminded Canadians that the shifting fiscal patterns in the federation are in one sense just metaphors for a larger political struggle for power and policy. It would be appropriate to give the committee the last word:

> The exercise of political power has driven the structure of the Canadian federation through dramatic swings over the course of a century, and presumably will continue to do so. None of these shifts came easily or without controversy.
>
> This history teaches above all that fiscal federalism in general, and revenue-sharing in particular cannot be approached with fixed standards or a purely analytical eye. Tables depicting revenue shares are in fact describing the successive outcomes of a perpetual contest between political forces searching for the revenues vital to accomplishing their political goals for Canada. These contests certainly reflect economic determinants, but they also reflect distinct views of the country and its needs at a given time — and they reflect the distinct personalities and accidents of history that shape the development of any nation.[58]

# CHAPTER VI

# Public Policy in the 1980s

Rarely has Canadian federalism changed so quickly and dramatically as it has during this decade. While it was once possible to write year after year about a recognizable set of national concerns and related policy issues in modern Canadian federalism spanning at least two decades (earlier called the "holy trinity" of Quebec nationalism and separatism, western and later eastern regionalism, and American foreign ownership), these have now moved sharply from centre stage within the span of a few years, and a new set of concerns is arising, if somewhat indistinctly, to take their place. Of course, in a broad sense the perennial trinity of dualism, regionalism and Canada-U.S. relations has never really been far from Canadian preoccupations, and the last of these three elements, this time in a renewed attempt at securing a free trade agreement with the United States, now stands prominently on our national agenda. But even here, the nature and character of Canada's relationship with the United States seems to have shifted from the defensive nationalism of the last quarter century toward a warmer period of economic and military integration.

This alteration in national preoccupations could be read in government and business lamentations over the health of the country's economy at home and its competitiveness abroad, and in the apparently shrinking capacity of the state to meet the multifarious demands placed upon it by modern society. Dour reflections on the fiscal or legitimation crisis of the state began to spread from their earlier theoretical containment, largely within the political left and right, and to challenge the centre. Increasingly, the postwar liberal legacy built around Keynesian economics, social ameliorization under the welfare state and a benign international economic order under Western control came under attack.

The signs could be read earlier in the Trudeau government's repeated struggles with stagflation in the 1970s followed by serious recession in the early 1980s, in the inflationary energy price shocks of the 1970s and the beginnings of a reverse trend a decade later, in the severe attempts to keep a lid on wages and growing government expenditures, and in the repeated warnings concerning Canada's declining productivity in an increasingly harsh and competitive world. Expansion of the welfare state had virtually come to a halt in the late 1960s with the introduction of medicare — the last of the great postwar social measures. Although there were benefit improvements, especially in social assistance and unemployment insurance, in the early 1970s, by mid-decade liberalism seemed to have reached the end of its expansive phase and to be now more preoccupied with retaining and paying for what had been built up over the previous three decades.

The approaching Quebec referendum and the subsequent vigorous intergovernmental conflict over the constitution, the National Energy Program and all of the other policy matters provided for a time a partial shield against the arrival of this neoconservative politics of scarcity — postponing in particular the subsequent attack upon competitive federalism and the liberal state at both levels of government. But by 1982-83, with world recession sending the Canadian ship of state floundering in a sea of red ink, fear over mounting deficits provided neoconservative critics with new grounds to attack expensive social programs and allegedly bloated inefficient government. While dissenting voices pointed to the large cyclical component of the deficit and the enormous tax expenditures deliberately forgone to private capital, they made relatively little headway against the new orthodoxy.[1] Therefore, anxiety over the public debt, and the conservative ideology built around it, increasingly dominated the political agenda, and governments were forced to put aside their competitive versions of nationalism and state expansionism and to work on economic renewal and deficit reduction.

The major parties, now under the new leadership of then prime minister John Turner and Brian Mulroney, from similar backgrounds in the corporate business world, gave prominence to these themes in the 1984 federal election. Both responded to widely felt public attitudes by preaching the need for reconciliation with the provinces and to defend the social safety net, but both also took aim at "big government" with programs to eliminate duplication of services and the size of the public service. Moreover, only pressures from organized women's groups succeeded in driving either of the two major parties toward further liberalism with promises of legislation on equal pay for work of equal value. International trends and domestic settlements over language and energy politics, combined with the sorry state of the country's finances, had now virtually pushed out the old stirring campaign themes around Quebec, Canadian nationalism or the Ontario-West energy feud.

While the public as a whole remained committed to the social programs created over the previous decades, though critical of abuses, and did not regard the deficit as an immediate threatening problem, business elites were pressing hard for sacrifices in federal social expenditures as

part of the necessary price for bringing down the deficit. British Columbia, under Bill Bennett's Social Credit government, was meanwhile well
along in its program of reducing the size of the state and of limiting expenditures, especially on social programs, while most other provincial
governments, including Quebec's under the newly elected Bourassa Liberals, were beginning to reduce services and sell off certain crown corporations acquired during the earlier spree of state expansionism. In Quebec this program was even being tagged as a new nationalist venture,
though this time tilted toward the new francophone business elite rather
than toward the middle class of francophone state office-holders of the
1960s and 1970s.

On the other hand, the retention of power by the NDP in the Manitoba
election of February 1986, the unexpected strength of the Alberta NDP
in the provincial election in May of the same year and the formidable
challenge to the Divine government in Saskatchewan by the same party
under Allan Blakeney seemed to indicate that the Canadian people were
scarcely joining with any enthusiasm the conservative tide sweeping
countries like the United States and Britain. In fact, the defeat of the Ontario Conservatives under a right-of-centre leader like Frank Miller and
the installation of a new minority Liberal government under David Peterson in May 1985 indicated that Canadians were continuing to opt for
centre-to-progressive government. The Peterson government, with NDP
support, was pushing forward with legislation on equality rights for
women, the banning of extra-billing, and stronger environmental legislation with considerable public backing in spite of strong opposition from
doctors, business and other injured interest groups. There was therefore
considerable political uncertainty about the long-term direction of Canadian politics.

These ambiguities were reflected at the federal level. On the one hand,
the Conservatives under Brian Mulroney had been accused, particularly
by their own tough-minded supporters, of holding to a business-as-usual
attitude toward popular social programs during the election and in the
subsequent parliamentary battle over universality in December 1985,
while, at the same time, following the new conservative political menu of
privatization, leaner government and deficit-cutting. This precarious balance threatened to come unstuck in the November 1984 financial statement by Michael Wilson, was reaffirmed in the heat of the universality
debate and was only marginally challenged in the subsequent budgets of
May 1985 and February 1986. The bitter fight over the government's
plan to restrict indexation of old age pensions in the May 1985 budget
had in fact led to a full-scale government retreat on that issue and served
as an enduring warning of the dangers of tampering with social policy.
Therefore, while the program of downsizing government and privatizing
federal crown corporations was continuing and the deficit was being

attacked by a combination of chopping government expenditures and hiking taxes, the crucial issue of tackling the question of the affordability and restructuring of social and income security programs in tighter times kept being put off for study and for later action.

While temporizing on this front, there was nevertheless plenty of evidence of a neoconservative approach to recharging the economy in the government's broad inducements to private capital investment through the tax system, in the reduction in the role of the state and public investment in the economy, in relaxation of foreign ownership controls and in the promotion of free markets and enhanced continental trade. In this confused political climate, it was unclear just how far the general rise of neoconservatism in the English-speaking world would impinge on Canada, its public policy and its pattern of federal-provincial relations. That was the fundamental question mark that hung over the mixed record and confusing signals of the Mulroney government as late as two years into its mandate.

Though the present and future appeared shrouded in mystery, the extent of change could be gauged somewhat from looking at the preoccupations, achievements and failures of the last Liberal government under Pierre Elliott Trudeau. Though close in time, that period seemed already to be moving unduly rapidly into mere historical memory as both the script and the cast of political characters changed. Along with the departure of Pierre Trudeau, René Lévesque, Peter Lougheed, Bill Davis, Bill Bennett and so many of the others who had dominated the political stage also went their unusually successful projection of the direct concerns of federalism and statehood in national politics. In fact, it was the persistence and consequence of that old struggle, first in the Quebec referendum and then in a bold series of subsequent policy initiatives by the federal government both before and even after the onset of worldwide recession in the early 1980s, that gave meaning to the whole period. No equivalent phase in Canadian history has ever been so dominated by intergovernmental rivalry, by competing theories of state and citizenship and by the struggle to define and give expression to Canadian federalism.

### Federalism and the Politics of Balance

The philosophy and politics of this struggle is so comprehensive and difficult that it is easy to lose one's way. Not only were there important shades of difference in outlook, objectives and interests among provincial leaders allegedly championing some common kind of decentralized federal state for Canada (there is need for a separate book on that subject alone), but, even if looked at from the federal perspective alone, there were many complex elements and apparent contradictions in its program. There was first the central and decidedly ambiguous program of advancing the position of francophones in Canada through the entrenchment of new rights in the charter, while simultaneously retarding an alternate expression of francophone nationalism that logically culminated in an independent Quebec state. Hence, one saw the bitter federal campaign against nationalist theory defined in exclusively ethnic or linguistic terms and the equally vigorous case for political nationalism in the defence of Canada. The latter was in the last analysis the chief theoretical foundation for virtually all of the startling policy initiatives undertaken by the Trudeau government in the 1980s.

There was the free market rhetoric used by the government to contain and circumscribe provincial power that appeared to threaten the economic union of Canada, and the equally vigorous nationalist and protectionist rhetoric used to shield federal measures restricting the market in energy and elsewhere or to protect Canada from free market "threats" emanating from the United States. There was the unbridled defence of parliamentary sovereignty in unilaterally changing and then bringing home the constitution and proclaiming, again unilaterally, a new national policy over energy resources. There was the equally withering indictment of parliamentary institutions in the defence of human rights or, in its proposals for Senate or House reform, of the Parliament of Canada's admitted weakness in adequately representing the regions in the Senate or in the elected government of the day. There was the championing of the rules of constitutionalism between governments in Canada and of the role of the Supreme Court in umpiring the relations of citizens to governments under the new charter, and at the same time an apparently deliberate policy through prompt pre-emptive action to escape that court's judgment on its Britain-bound unilateral constitutional package. The list can go on and on.

Perhaps most confusing of all was the Trudeau government's steadfast refusal in all of the policy areas we have touched on to acknowledge that it was pursuing a course of marshalling power in Ottawa in deference to its own centralizing philosophy for the Canadian federal state, and its insistence that it was merely "rebalancing" the federation. Here Canadians were invited to entertain the notion that Ottawa was simply operating as the dispassionate "balancer" of an imbalanced or deranged order of relations between the governments of Canada and that it was ultimately the last focus for the defence of the "common good" amidst selfish centrifugal forces. This decision to defend federalism as a real system of balanced powers was an extraordinary philosophical underpinning for a centralist program of policy. In that respect, it departed sharply from the old justifications for a strong federal power under John A. Macdonald or from the functional case for federal pre-eminence during wartime or in the postwar construction of the Keynesian welfare state. In fact, this campaign reminded Canadians not so much of the question of centralization versus decentralization as preferred arrangements of power under a federal state — that had already been endlessly debated in politics and academic literature for decades — but of the essential liberal premise of effective counterbalancing powers that must undergird any truly federal state.

The question remained, however: was this ideology of federalism mere smoke screen as the provincialists suspected or was it really an operative framework for federal policy in those years? Analysts of balance-of-power theory in international politics had long ago warned that states espousing the doctrine of "balance" were rarely concerned with a genuine equilibrium of power in the international system but were more commonly interested in a "strong balance" or "favourable balance" leaving a wide margin of advantage to themselves.[2] Balance-of-power rhetoric could thus simply be decoded either as a description of or a prescription for a particular distribution of power in the world and not at all a preference for equilibrium. Who after all would genuinely prefer equilibrium with the attendant risks and threat of immobility to a "slight" disequilibrium in one's favour? Further, since playing a balance-of-power policy on the international front, as Britain was alleged to have done for four hundred years to check dominant powers on the continent of Europe, entailed the presence of a presumed neutral "balancer" ready to apply its weight against whichever state was threatening the balance, how could this image apply to domestic politics within a single federal state, especially when the central government as the self-declared balancer was itself the chief contestant on one side of the binary division of sovereignty? These ought to have been prickly issues for any self-confessed liberal policy of applying counterweights to provincial power and of restoring the balance in the Canadian federal state, but they do not appear to have given Ottawa much pause.

There were other problems to consider with the ideology of federalism as balance. Apart from the dilemma over who was to measure and enforce the balance, by what standards could it be measured? That had been no simple task for specialists in the balance of power in international politics, but at least they had a firmer grip on the elements of power to be set on the scales for measurement — armed forces, alliances, resources and territories, perhaps even political will — than could a domestic statesman purporting to measure the federal-provincial balance of power in a country. As noted, the federal government in the pursuit of its program of balance had already become actively involved in trying to track and measure the distribution of power in the Canadian federation by a number of relatively crude indictors. There was its attempt to use the complicated patterns in intergovernmental finance as a rough but reliable "proxy" for the question of the larger distribution of power in the country. In that process both domestic indicators and international comparisons were drawn into the power-measuring net. With the calculations completed to its satisfaction, it was not long before the federal government claimed an imbalance of power in the federation on that basis. Canada had been "proved" to be the most decentralized federation in the world. Of course, the illustrations proved nothing of the sort, and the whole exercise was instead summarily and scathingly dismissed by finance specialists like Richard Bird.[3] After a careful review of the difficulties of measuring so nebulous a concept as centralization, of interpreting it and of comparing it across countries, he bluntly declared that

> there is no necessary correlation between whatever is measured by the indexes that can be constructed and the real degree of centralization of political power.
>
> Each index simply measures the degree of centralization of some particular indicator (or perhaps indicators, if it is a composite index) and no more. No index can truly measure the degree of effective centralization of decision-making power, and there is no point in pretending that it does.

Bird went on to argue that even if it would be "fairly safe" to say that most indicators suggested that Canada's public finances "had become more decentralized in recent years," the data would say "nothing about whether the present degree of decentralization (whatever it is, and however measured) is too great or too little." In short, he concluded drily, "playing with such numbers is not a very useful way to approach Canada's current political problems."[4]

Yet a policy of preserving the balance, if it is to be something more than a mere rhetorical cover for a program of state-building at either level of the federation, required this kind of knowledge. Only with reasonably reliable indicators of the shifting distribution of power in the federation could a politics of balance work with any credibility within the country. In that sense, too, the business of measuring the ingredients of power, of placing them on the scales and drawing conclusions from them, was more vexing and politically difficult domestically than it was in the foreign policy of nation-states, which, where balance politics even required a public justification, simply entailed measuring the power of other countries and selling the case to one's own population. However, having chosen that ideological ground for its campaign of federalism, the Trudeau government was virtually forced to go on and extend the argument to show other indicators of declining federal power in critical areas in modern society, including economic development, energy and social development.

When the balance-measuring exercise moved off public finance data, it became no easier to track the distribution of power and make a case for a rebalancing effort. What was to be the definition for "decentralization" against which a countervailing line of policy must be deployed? How was it to be measured and a trend established? Since the exercise compelled a more or less arbitrary selection of policy indicators, which unlike the public finance data could not be easily aggregated into neat if not exactly compelling indexes, the centre-building argument depended in the end on pointing fingers at provincial policy intrusions against the economic union (that is, the market); at provincial investment and ownership instruments, including the bulging Alberta Heritage Fund; at provincial misuse of regional economic development; at provincial diversion of funds from nationally established social programs under health and education; and so on. This was not a particularly helpful beginning. Many of these areas, as noted earlier, were upon close examination actually complicated fields of intergovernmental activity where it is difficult to draw one-sided reductionist conclusions about the inordinate "power" of one level of government, about zero-sum solutions, about apportioning blame or about fixing the exclusive and appropriate balance of government activities and functions. In short, this policy involvement and intermeshing of the provincial and federal governments merely reflected what was then a worldwide trend toward increasing state activity and regulation, and the old-fashioned notion of federalism as the maintenance of some discrete and appropriate balance of power between the orders of government simply fails to take account of that fact or to provide realistic answers to it.

Just as the finance data could be turned around by the use of other indicators, the debate over power in policy could just as easily be turned against Ottawa as for it. Claude Morin had argued much earlier that Canada had been centralizing the true levers of political power for almost a century.[5] The spending power had, for example, proved to be an exceedingly powerful policy instrument for centralization in the Canadian federation over a whole host of subject areas, from social policy to regional economic development. Indeed, policy developments in the latter area had in Prince Edward Island justified a virtual federal veto over most areas of policy under provincial jurisdiction under the terms of the Comprehensive Development Plan of 1969-84. Considerable power and intrusion in other provinces, though less formally exercised, has been acknowledged by experts on regional economic development. Federal policies concerning unemployment insurance, transportation policy, taxation and monetary policy, inflation, interprovincial and international regulations over natural resources, export promotion and controls, and a host of other matters could also easily be shown to intrude on provincial priorities and concerns, to frustrate the efforts of provinces to maximize economic growth within their own jurisdiction, and to tilt the real arc of policy toward the centre. These arguments must be counterbalanced against federal claims over excess provincial power. In the end, there is simply no way in which to collate, discriminate and weigh the opposing trends and to settle authoritatively the overall direction and balance of power of the federation in public policy.

But leaving aside the problems over the measurement of the configuration of power in the federation, how would any presumed empirical results help answer the essential question of what role the respective governments ought to play in the life of the nation? It was easy enough for any federalist to say, as federal ministers were repeatedly inclined to do in the early 1980s, that there must be room for *both* orders of government if the country is not to move either toward breakup or simple national unification. But that hardly illuminated the real meaning of the federal program of rebalancing the federation. What was this ideology pointing to?

Preston King has provided some theoretical assistance with his work on federalism as ideology and especially his brief venture into the political theory of balance in federalist thought.[6] He has shown that the theory of federalism is but "one sub-set" of liberal pluralism, with close affinities to doctrines such as the separation of powers and a system of checks and balances, providing "unity in diversity" within a territorial state. It is also, however, an ideology that has produced from its beginning deep fissures between those who tilt toward the "unity" side of that equation and those who tilt in the other direction toward "freedom" and "diversity." A third option, an ideology of balance wedded closely to constitutionalism and to a contractual understanding of federalism as a pact, "promotes neither liberty nor authority, neither centralism nor decentralism, but both conjointly." The difficulty is that in practice such a policy does not lend itself "to an ethical or ideological notion which is altogether perspicuous....Balance [may be] merely a metaphor for 'right' or 'just'; accordingly, any unequal or imbalanced relationship (especially of power) can be referred to as 'balanced,' as long as we approve of it." This conclusion shows how vapid and perilously self-serving the ideology of balance can be. Moreover, if the idea of applying counterweights in a federation to secure balance is taken seriously, it can only lead to "immobilism," whereas any decisive or passionate course of action in politics must "display imbalance [or] disequilibrium." In the end, to avoid "the swamp of anarchism" that would follow from the notion of balance as pure equilibrium or the constant warfare entailed in implementing the moral imperative of checking power with power, even the theorists of balance in the federation are finally driven to accept the notion of some "preponderant power" in the system.[7]

This is a suggestive treatment for highlighting the dilemmas and even the evolution of Pierre Elliott Trudeau's thinking on federalism. There can be no doubt about Trudeau's indebtedness to liberal theory and especially to the ideas of checks and balances, of counterweights to power and of a relatively strict constitutionalism for the protection of federalism, freedom and individuality. These ideas were so powerful that in the 1950s they forced him to side with his political enemy Duplessis in opposition to federal financial support of universities, a matter otherwise dear to his heart, merely because the initiative offended his strong sense of constitutionalism and of the federal-provincial balance. Elsewhere he had argued that the passivity of the Quebec state at that time had encouraged these and other kinds of incursions and that the best defence for a functioning federal state was the vigorous exercise of the power conferred upon both levels of government by the constitution. That would produce the "creative tension" of opposing systems of power, as well as valuable outlets through federalism for social and political experimentation.

The same constitutionalism had inspired Trudeau soon after taking office to propose limits upon the use of the federal spending power, once again as a reasonable check upon a device by which the federal order of government might otherwise threaten the balance. Reasons of constitutionalism conjoined with financial prudence also led him later, in the absence of constitutional limits to the spending power, to back away from conditional grants and to deliver more and more tax resources to the provinces in an untied form. Yet the "immobility" over changing the constitution, which, in the absence of an amending formula, seemed to flow from past experience with a course of strict constitutionalism, together with increasingly grave threats to national unity from the mid-1970s on, drove Trudeau to question the adequacy of this model of federalism.

In 1980, with the government having so recently faced down a powerful separatist threat in Quebec, it still received very little sign of a spirit of give-and-take in the constitutional negotiations with the provinces, and it confronted what it regarded as dangerous and growing threats from the oil-producing provinces. Under these circumstances, the government could not simply settle for the politics of mere balance as equilibrium — though much of its centralizing policy program was carried out and defended in those terms — and it was finally driven to insist that there had to be a "preponderant power" at the centre in the event of fundamental conflict in the Canadian state: hence, on the defensive side, the need for holding on to federal discretionary instruments like disallowance or the unrestricted spending power, which earlier were to be ceded as incompatible with the federal-provincial balance, and, on the active side, unilateralism and the politics of imbalance, of breaking the logjam over the constitution if necessary by transgressing constitutional convention if not law. Ottawa argued again and again that, in the last instance, the centre had to be stronger than the pull of regionalism or separatism, that the legal and political instruments at the centre had to be strong enough to ensure that the national will in fact prevailed in a conflict of interests (not laws) with the provinces. This was the ultimate and ironical end to a policy of federalism as balance that Trudeau had tried to bring to Canadian politics.

## Nationalism in the Service of the Federal State

The Trudeau government recognized that to pursue a program of policy that would effectively act as a counterweight to decentralizing trends over the previous two decades would require a compelling force to support it. It was acknowledged that if speeches supporting centralizing measures were to remain fixed on the need for a balance of countervailing powers in the federation, they would likely draw about the same enthusiasm from the Canadian people as lectures on celestial mechanics. As Trudeau had long recognized, the Canadian people would require at least an equivalent, if not emotionally more powerful, collective vision in support of the federal state to one the provinces might put up for separatism or regionalism. The natural doctrine for this purpose was nationalism, which if carefully managed and defined could both counter the alienation and anger on which separatism and regionalism fed and provide a compelling case for the federal state as the logical expression of that nationalism. The strategy was, as we have seen in chapter 1, clearly anticipated in Trudeau's writings in the early 1960s along with the related notion that the whole ambit of public policy could be orchestrated and made subordinate to it.

Promoting federalism by selling Canadian nationalism had already been deployed successfully in the propaganda war on sovereignty-association in Quebec, especially by Jean Chrétien on the referendum campaign trail and by the prime minister at a couple of critical junctures in that debate. What was needed after the successful outcome was some fleshing out of that emotional vision with policies that would have powerful appeal throughout the country. This line of policy in defence of national unity included essential elements that had been part of Trudeau's formula for defending Canadian federalism for decades — an entrenched Charter of Rights containing language and minority educational guarantees, increased Canadian ownership of resources and industry, state protection of the national economy and national culture, and so on. This state-initiated and state-centred program of nationalism in the fields of human rights, energy policy and economic development has been traced in earlier chapters, along with its major successes and failures as it ran up against worldwide recession.

This program, though presented as an integral and cohesive vision on behalf of "Canada," can be seen on analysis to comprise a number of quite distinct strands or elements that need not have gone together or, indeed, even have been included in every nationalist's lexicon. For example, since the Trudeau program of nationalism was being ostensibly projected forward merely as part of a larger campaign of defending federalism against separatist ideology and against provincialist threats to the intergovernmental balance of power, it mixed, in a curious instrumental fashion, universal nationalist emblems and goals with its own narrower anti-provincialist program. Hence, in energy policy, the nationalist dimensions of the program extended not only to increased Canadian ownership in the industry as a matter of policy, but also (and much more arguably) to increased federal state ownership through Petro-Canada, to new federal revenue from oil and gas ultimately at the expense of provincial governments and to increased exports from conventional sources to pay for expensive tax grants to develop the so-called Canada Lands at the expense of cheaper exploratory work in the western sedimentary basin. In these and other ways, the state-building features of the program began to shape and define more and more of the "national" content.

Similarly, in the constitutional and economic development field, many of the centralizing features of the federal program could only with the greatest difficulty be construed as national requirements, unless one was inclined to accept the simple proposition that what was best for the national government or Parliament (or national market) was also best for the nation. In what sense would the removal or restriction of provincial powers over the economy really address a nationalist rather than merely federal concern? Was the nation really won over to laissez-faire, especially insofar as it curtailed only provincial power? Would hamstringing provincial economic power necessarily lead to greater national unity through improved economic growth, to fairness in federal economic policy or, more tellingly, to interregional equity and the end of the long bitterness over metropolitan-hinterland relationships in the country?

The same scrutiny and scepticism are needed with many of the other nationalist claims in this federal state-building program, whether the issue be exclusive federal control over constitutional referenda, the national fight over hospital fees and extra-billing (while Ottawa simultaneously cut the level of federal support of health under EPF) and so on. In short, once nationalism was put into merely utilitarian service in this kind of program, the politics of federalism began to overawe the national agenda and to expose its essential competitive state-based character. Yet given the enormously powerful nationalist rhetoric linking the people of Canada willy-nilly to the federal order of government, and the desirability of the policy results in the form of the charter, the National Energy

Program or the Canada Health Act to a host of public interest groups and allies, it was a remarkably effective strategy — even for as sophisticated and modern a public as Canada's.

Virtually all analysts who have examined the unleashing of these initiatives over the constitution, social policy, fiscal federalism and energy have commented on the federal state's relatively successful use and incorporation of public interest groups and others in the private sector in this "nationalist" campaign. The charter drew the enthusiastic support of civil libertarians, women's groups, and other progressive reform elements — almost none of whom in their representations and activities spent much time even thinking through its implications for the federal state. The charter was in itself sufficiently attractive as a policy vehicle to consume their attention, and all "enemies" of it, such as most provincial governments, were by definition placed on the wrong side of public opinion on the issue. That point was driven home again and again by the federal Liberals. Similarly, the Breau Committee on social policy and fiscal federalism was supported by public interest groups critical of underfunding and of extra-billing by doctors. So too with the friends of the NEP, both capitalist enthusiasts like Dome Petroleum and assorted left-leaning nationalist thinkers, who were drawn inexorably into this state-building program because some of its features appeared to satisfy their long-standing goals or interests.

This opening up of federal-provincial politics was in many respects a welcome and long-overdue development, since it had the effect of exposing the politics of executive federalism to public scrutiny, criticism and sometimes even correction. During the constitutional battle, for example, only the active involvement of public interest groups in the work of the joint parliamentary committee succeeded in strengthening the rights provisions in the charter, and later, only vigorous public pressure upon provincial governments succeeded in reversing some of the negotiating work of the November 1981 First Ministers' Conference by restoring aboriginal rights in the charter and restricting the scope of the notwithstanding clause over sexual equality. However, these encouraging signs of the power of public participation and of broader democratic influence against executive government were still warmly supported by the federal government as part of its broad planned objective of aligning itself with public opinion and pitting the provinces against it, and it is doubtful whether they would have succeeded otherwise.

Similarly, the carefully cultivated and managed nature of public participation and involvement in energy policy was also revealed in the expansive political rhetoric from Ottawa under the NEP but chiefly in subsequent activity in the marketplace. Under the new policy, Canadian oil companies, investors and taxpayers were encouraged to participate in risky and expensive programs of Canadianization and frontier exploration immediately prior to a disastrous market decline. The combination of policy incentives and rhetoric appeared to move Canadians in the desired direction, but the timing could scarcely have been worse. Although the federal government could not be blamed for not having the power to see into the future, nonetheless this policy venture had not adequately hedged its bets on market or economic conditions, and political goals were allowed to predominate. In the end, this attempted stage-managing of market actors and forces through policy burned taxpayers and exposed many Canadian companies to much more severe risk than foreign multinationals. Moreover, so-called Canadianization, federally defined, had been purchased at the price of severe regional divisions and dissension. Afterward it seemed, even to many earlier supporters, a bitter object lesson in the perils of economic nationalism.

While these costs need not have been automatic features of any program of economic nationalism in defence of the federal balance, they were nonetheless real hazards with which the plan described by Trudeau almost twenty years earlier would have had to contend. Since the deploying of such a policy would have to await the appropriate political "window of opportunity," it was unlikely that such political circumstances would dovetail equally well with the evolution of market forces. It appeared that these two had come together after the second 1979 petroleum price shock and the defeat of the PQ in the Quebec referendum in May 1980, but building state plans on the prospect of an unending spiral of price increases for petroleum over the decade turned out to be a reckless gamble. The NEP experience underlines the risks and hidden costs with a state plan of defending federal power through accelerated national ownership of resources and industry — at least in the lucrative but turbulent business of oil and gas exploration, production, retailing and development.

This policy venture, as well as the brief rise and eclipse of the Trudeau government's broader national industrial strategy, also underlines the limits to which a program of nationalism by a modest middle power, already beset with high levels of foreign ownership and placed beside the world's largest imperial market, will be subject. Since the economy is so heavily interlinked with that of the United States, so exposed to international market forces over commodities, including its own currency, and so vulnerable to world recession or to changes in the international trading system, there is little room in practical terms for rekindling the fires of economic nationalism. The National Policy, after all, had been laid down in a simpler and less interdependent economic world; it would be a far more challenging prospect to do the same under current modern conditions. This is not to say that the venture ought not be undertaken, but merely to record the modern, complex interplay of national policy and the international economic order. Under these circumstances, only state economic policies built upon a broad national consensus of elites and public can expect to survive. Those conditions were, by definition, missing from the Trudeau government's plan for rebalancing power against most provincial elites, whom he had come to regard as the "enemies from within."

It should perhaps not be so very surprising that a nationalist program emanating from a Liberal government in Ottawa that sought to defend federalism from the centre should have provoked a counterreaction, especially from a different nationalist regime in Quebec City or from the regional peripheries of East and West. The PQ government was especially bound to fight measures that so clearly encroached upon provincial jurisdiction and policy, just as virtually any other Quebec government would have done. The politics of language had become far too sensitive and inflamed for there to be quiet accommodation to the constitutional provisions under the charter or to the absence of any special recognition in the constitutional agreement for the province of Quebec in the country's fundamental understanding of duality. On the centre-periphery division over the constitution, economic development and energy policy, it was not simply that much of the chosen battle-ground was over certain natural resources crucial to the West and to Newfoundland and Nova Scotia, that the constitutional instruments were aimed at curbing economic province-building ostensibly in the name of an economic union that was regarded as manifestly unequal and unfair, or even that the political threat was too brazen for these new ambitious elites to swallow. A Toronto-Ottawa alliance over energy, the constitution and many of the other elements of the federal government's program was far too visible and cynical a reminder of the older pattern of metropolitan-hinterland relationships that had always been regularly held up and consecrated in the higher name of the "national interest."

There can be no doubt about the profound cynicism in which this Ottawa-Toronto alliance was regarded by dissenting provincial leaders and officials. They had become all too accustomed to pan-Canadian sermons on nationalism, which were regarded as little more than the delusionary incantations of Ontario regionalism writ large, and they instinctively doubted the soundness of any "national" programs supported once again by central Canadian leaders preaching the virtues of central-ized federalism. Trudeau had perhaps forgotten, in his enthusiasm over deploying nationalism in defence of federalism, that Canadian national-ism, though a powerful force, also carried a dubious historical baggage of distrust, certainly from Quebecers and from the people of the East and the West. Neither his own government's deficiency in representation from the West nor the open partnership with Ontario, critical in bringing about these changes, was likely to remove perennial suspicions about the regionally biased and self-interested nature of that nationalism.

It is, in fact, appropriate to ask whether this "new nationalism" by the federal Liberals in the 1980s really broke ground from earlier conceptions of Canadian nationalism, whether it managed to extricate itself from the old pattern of dominant central Canadian sectionalism, and therefore whether there really lay within it a new consensual footing for the federal state. As noted earlier, in its economic dimensions, this program of nationalism failed to provide a coherent and compelling vision for a modern Canada. There was, on the one hand, the uneasy and unhappy marriage of economic liberalism, together with its restraints on the role of the state, intended for the provincial partners in the federation; on the other, economic interventionism reserved exclusively for the federal Parliament, presumably speaking effectively in the name of all Canadians. This distorted picture, together with the supporting hymns to the sanctity and integrity of Canada's economic union and the free market by a joint Toronto-Ottawa chorus, was scarcely convincing in the face of continuing regional inequities and massive government involvement in the economy.

Any intervention, it might be argued, limits the efficiency of the national market or adds extra "costs," but there are also other values, including equity, to be considered in the equation. Public policy on economic questions means, if it means anything, the right of the state to make those determinations and to have those respected in the marketplace. The Trudeau government considered these unarguable propositions when it came to its own legislative actions affecting the national market, but it was unwilling to extend the same logic to the provinces because of their presumed provincialism and narrow self-regarding proclivities. If this version of economic nationalism and the federal state had been accepted and implemented in constitutional and policy terms, the interests of the outlying regions would be left to the mercy of the market, restrained only by the ordinances of a federal government with lopsided representation from central Canada. That was neither a new nor a particularly convincing rationale for Canadian nationalism in the 1980s.

If the economic elements of the new nationalism seemed to look back longingly in form if not in substance toward the centralized and interventionist federalism of the Macdonald era, the social and fiscal elements of Liberal nationalism returned in spirit to the postwar period of federal pre-eminence. Once again the federal state attempted to project itself forward as the senior government in defence of social policy, especially in the battle over the 1983 Canada Health Act. Not only had the Liberals attempted to reinvigorate and restore that postwar legacy, but they returned to enforce the original conditions of the shared-cost program in the health field, a question that had lain dormant for almost a generation, as the very principle of federal intrusion by this means was being vigorously debated, especially in Quebec. The same spirit of federal control and supervision could be detected in the intergovernmental struggle over EPF and higher education. After moving toward block-funding for more than a decade, there was a marked shift toward demanding a linkage in levels of increase in government expenditure and toward monitoring provincial use of federal monies on established programs. Federal demands for a share in decision-making in jointly funded programs under formal provincial jursidiction also became more insistent and confident than they would ever have been in the 1960s, especially in the delicate field of education. There was even the suggestion that the federal government might return to the older postwar practice of sending its money for postsecondary education direct to the clients in the provinces in the form of student vouchers and hence circumventing provincial governments altogether. In all of these ways, the reassertion of federal power on social policy was in many respects backward-looking and deliberately constructed to shore up a defensive and weakened federal state by drawing on select patterns in the past.

Only on the constitutional front, and then only with respect to the Charter of Rights, can it be said that a distinctively new approach was taken toward the definition of the Canadian state and identity. This constitutional injection of nationalist liberalism, built in part upon the earlier statutory efforts on bilingualism and biculturalism, drew upon traditional Quebec ideas for French-English reconciliation going back to the time of Henri Bourassa. It was, however, a radically new definition of the relationship between the two founding peoples, notably for anglophones, and yet it appeared to be taking firm root in the country as an enduring part of the nationalist program of the federal Liberals. By contrast, the other definition of the French-English duality, which had ultimately led to a powerful movement for Quebec independence under the leadership of the PQ government, appeared to be steadily sliding in popularity and interest.

On a wider plane, the enshrinement of liberalism in a new Charter of Rights can be seen as a powerful new element in the national definition of Canadians and of the liberties contained within the federal state under judicial guardianship. This element in modern Canadian nationalism and federalism is quite new and bears no resemblance to any defensive features for federal pre-eminence or national unity in earlier regimes. Indeed, it can be seen as a first major step away from the political culture of British or French imperialism for Canada, as a needed element in a vastly more diverse country composed of many races, religions and political traditions, and an alternative to the earlier complacent acceptance of parliamentary institutions and mere competing orders of government in the defence of citizen rights. This achievement, however, needs to be balanced carefully against the remaining institutions, ideologies and traditions of the country, and against the possibly double-edged effects of judicial review of the charter. Whether this grafting on of constitutional liberalism will really in the long run form an important new element of nation-building in Canada remains to be seen.

When this program of nationalism is examined from the point of view of efficacy — of successes and losses — it is striking how the newer elements, added to the old mix of defensive federal instruments and policies, proved to be the more effective. While the Canada Health Act was successfully launched and the fiscal regime tightened up, largely because these could be easily accomplished from within Parliament's own undisputed ambit of powers and because they struck cleanly at provincial governments, there were no comparable results in the larger program of economic nationalism. This ran directly into opposition from much of the private sector, the Americans, the provinces and consequently the opposition Conservatives. The program was turned back early on the constitutional level, defeated in Bill S-31, shelved in the case of a strengthened FIRA and modest industrial strategy, and successfully resisted in many other cases. Even the NEP, which got off to such a fine start, eventually fell victim to economic recession and turned out to be easy prey for the new majority Tory government. The same fate befell many crown corporations created earlier as instruments of economic nationalism, including de Havilland, the Canada Development Investment Corporation and, probably in due course, the most important state jewel of all, Petro-Canada.

The campaign over higher educational financing simply stalled in 1984, after years of tightening the financial screws and pressuring provincial governments for a federal role in this area. When Trudeau decided to opt for retirement, there was simply no political will in either of the major political parties to tackle the provinces on the issue of university financing or to push through a student voucher system. The subsequent abandonment of this forced program of nation-building by the Conservatives left postsecondary education outside the active field of intergovernmental combat, with none of the anomalies resolved; it subsequently became a target among others of the federal restraint and deficit reduction program. Though financing of the program area had suffered and would continue to do so, there was thus no progress in this part of the Liberals' agenda.

Only the liberal nationalism around human rights and freedoms was securely established, entrenched as it was in the constitution. The courts appeared to be giving the new charter, even within a few years of its enactment, a strong and forceful reading, and interest groups were well along in using litigation as a prominent vehicle in defence of their own interests. Moreover, that part of the Liberal nationalism, including the bilingual and bicultural vision of Canada, had now been assumed by all federal parties. There was good reason to think that this part of the Liberal legacy would survive and prove a new testing ground for challenging separatism and regionalism in the future.

The nationalism supporting the diverse range of policy initiatives studied in this period was broadly constructed from an amalgam of distinct elements, some of which were extensions of more or less traditional nation-building instruments and some not. In that respect, it was certainly not radical in Canadian terms to use the state to expand the economic or cultural dimensions of Canadian nationalism, although the NEP was the most ambitious effort at repatriating a sector of the economy Canadians had ever seen. It was also the first mighty sign of apparent Liberal reversal of its long-standing marriage to American foreign investment since the Second World War. Yet the selection of the energy sector as a ground for nationalism was hardly accidental — it was here where Ottawa expected the fruits of nationalist policy to directly benefit its own state-building campaign.

The comprehensive nature of the Canadian nationalism deliberately deployed in the 1980 — from constitutional to economic, social and fiscal aspects — appeared to flow from the nature of the balancing task for which it was drawn into service. Some parts of the program were of course more important than others — particularly the defusing of Quebec separatism and establishment of a new framework for future French-English relations in the country — but all were assumed to be necessary to accomplish the desired swing in the pendulum of power in the federation. It was the calculated nature of these initiatives as selective, rational and wide-ranging instruments in a politics of balancing the federation that sharply distinguished them in spirit from the zealous work of a principled nationalist.

What also marked them off — even the government-led movement for a new Charter of Rights — was the defensive character of these planned measures. Once again, more than a hundred years after the founding of the Canadian federal state, the national government felt itself so threatened by internal forces of division, by American pressures and by a faltering and incomplete process of national integration that it resorted to the old logic of defensive expansionism. That was the real meaning of the string of policy recommendations underlying Trudeau's brand of nationalism in defence of Canadian federalism, that "line of policy" that was to keep state-threatening fissiparous elements at bay. Carefully nurtured and controlled by a select circle of federal leaders and bureaucrats and without significant independent public involvement, it resembled far too much the elite-controlled, cautious and conservative route to country-building of the original founders of Canada.[8]

## Neoconservatism and the Decline of Nationalism

There were three constellations of power both within and outside Canada that were variously threatened and disturbed by this assertion of Liberal nationalism: most provinces, excepting Ontario and occasionally New Brunswick; most business interests, especially those controlled by foreign multinationals; and finally the American state. All of these potential enemies of this nationalist program were recognized by Liberal planners and were to some extent targets of it. Nor was there much delusion in the Liberals' thinking over the combined power those interests could muster against them. Trudeau, and especially his trusted associates from Quebec, recognized that they were putting their seats on the line with the planned but dramatic unilateral initiatives and that the Liberal party would be severely tested as a vehicle for this kind of program. As Prime Minister Trudeau had declared on the eve of his replacement as party leader in June 1984, their program had been implemented largely by "going over the heads of the premiers and the American multinationals" by mounting a populist appeal to the "people of Canada." Such a strategy was a perilous undertaking at the best of times, but it was virtually suicidal in bad. It was perhaps a risk only a retiring prime minister in his final years in office under a majority government would ever have entertained. As the program ran headlong into world recession hardly a year into the new government's mandate, it began to fall apart as the political props upon which it rested started to crack. By then it was becoming obvious to all that federal state-building could not be expected to be pursued successfully in the most severe economic downturn since the Great Depression.

Just as the defensive expansionism of the federal state in nineteenth-century Canada had been pursued in opposition to the potentially threatening power of the United States, the economic components of the Liberals' nation-building program virtually dictated a collision course with American interests. In that sense, even if anti-Americanism had not already been the enduring bedrock of Canadian nationalism, there would have been reason in any vigorous nationalist defence of the Canadian economy to have reignited these sentiments. As federal ministers argued throughout the late 1970s and early 1980s, this protective nation-defending function, especially over the economic and cultural life of the country, was a traditional but vital role for the Canadian federal state and one that could not be discharged successfully by the provincial orders of state.

The collision with American multinationals, entailed in the repatriation of the energy sector of the Canadian economy and the proposed tightening up on foreign ownership rules, largely explained the growing distance between the Trudeau government and the business community in Canada. However, many Canadian-owned businesses, especially those moving more successfully into export markets in the United States, would join the multinational companies in complaining about restrictive nationalist measures, and virtually all business organizations took strong exception to the interventionism essential to the federal state plan. Although there were some cooperative players from the private sector ready to play supportive roles in the NEP, thus opening up a possible alliance between important fractions of Canadian capital and the federal state, most did so uneasily and only because of the enormous policy leverage of the federal program.[9] Certainly, conditions in the 1980s did not suggest that it would be easy to resurrect the old federal-corporate alliance of Macdonald's National Policy. It is therefore not surprising that hardly a year into the Liberals' mandate former minister Don Johnston was writing the prime minister to warn him that "relationships between the federal government and the business community have never been as hostile as they are today" and urging him in the name of the party not to desert business and become a "captive of narrow social democratic interests."[10] Trudeau's reply indicated that moderate reform under a progressive banner would continue and that while the party needed "some links and supporters within the [business community]," it was perhaps unrealistic to expect "majority support from [it]."[11] This was about as candid an acknowledgment from the prime minister in May 1981 of the relative divergence of interest of these camps as can be reasonably expected, along with the related notion that only some select elements within the business community could be drawn in and treated as potential allies in nation-building.

This result was part of a gradual distancing of relations between business and the Liberal government that had been going on over the previous decade and of an assessment that broad mutuality of interests over the federal state-building program was simply not to be expected. Although the government had hoped to win over many more Canadian private interests in its fight to repatriate and redirect the energy industry and was somewhat taken aback by the extent of NEP criticism by Canadian independents, particularly because of its broad public appeal, there was no illusion about anticipated business opposition from many quarters. Similarly, while the extent of American opposition under a new administration headed by President Reagan could not have been known prior to the U.S. election, there was doubtless recognition of the flak this policy would generate there.[12]

When these interests were conjoined with the vigorous opposition of most provinces, the federal government found itself engaged in a vicious political war across many simultaneous policy fronts. It is therefore hardly surprising that from 1982 onward there were some signs of attempted accommodation — at least toward the business community, now acknowledged by the new solicitous finance minister, Marc Lalonde, as the real "engine of growth" — from an embattled federal state, considerably tempered by the ravages of recession. But by then, with the economy suffering high unemployment and dizzying interest rates and the government presiding over a mushrooming federal deficit, the Liberals' own political coalition was under considerable strain just as opposing forces were regrouping in support of the Conservative party under its new leader, Brian Mulroney. It was evident then that with the September 1984 transfer of power to the Conservatives, a new political realignment would take place in Ottawa that would no longer countenance economic nationalism, sour relations with the United States or attacks upon the provinces. These indeed became central planks of Mulroney's federalism.

Not only did the Mulroney government wish to erase the earlier federal campaign against these "enemies from within," it wished to invite them back inside the circumference of federal policymaking. In its own review of the progress in federal-provincial relations published for the First Ministers' Conference at Halifax in November 1985, the government congratulated itself for bringing the provinces back into national policymaking as "trusted partners in the business of managing the federation, partners equally dedicated to its unity and prosperity."[13] The following table was produced to demonstrate how seriously the Mulroney government was taking its new responsibility to work more vigorously with the provinces in joint policymaking to recharge again the machinery of interstate federalism. Unlike the Trudeau government's attempt to circumvent that apparatus and to pursue unilateral initiatives or to plan a centralized program of intrastate federalism with its proposals for Senate reform, the pattern of Canadian federalism had once again returned to the norm of intergovernmental negotiation with high hopes for future harmony, coordination and cooperation under new federal management. In fact, the new government's commitment to ushering in a new and more harmonious chapter in federal-provincial relations quickly led, as noted in earlier chapters, to highly accommodating though often dubious policy gestures in energy policy, offshore development, regional economic development and even in provincial representation in the jealously guarded federal field of international affairs. If rhetoric, sincerity and evidence of "good works" were enough to heal the divisions of the past and to place federal-provincial relations on a sounder footing, then this was indeed an auspicious beginning.

Although these overtures did initially produce a marked drop in hostile rhetoric between governments, there was evidence that these innocently seductive assumptions were quite incapable of shifting the often competitive dynamics of Canadian federalism onto a mutually accommodating and civilized plane. Despite the new energy agreements

## Table 6-1

### FREQUENCY OF MULTILATERAL AND BILATERAL MEETINGS OF THE GOVERNMENT OF CANADA AND PROVINCIAL GOVERNMENTS

| Participants | Sept. 1984 to Sept. 1985 | Annual Average 1980-84 |
|---|---|---|
| First Ministers | 13 | 5 |
| Ministers | 353 | 82 |
| Deputy Ministers | 72 | 45 |
| Total | 438 | 132 |

that went so far in meeting Premier Lougheed's long-standing complaints, and those of other western premiers, there was no compensating flexibility when Ottawa pleaded for the support of those premiers for the entrenchment of the principle of aboriginal rights in the Canadian constitution at the abortive First Ministers' Constitutional Conference on that subject in February 1985. With the spectre of continuing low prices for petroleum, these federal accommodations also did not silence the anti-federal rhetoric of Lougheed's successor, Premier Donald Getty. Nor did they overcome (though they may have moderated) vigorous provincial opposition to the cuts in the federal rate of increase for transfers in support of health and higher education. Perhaps the most grievous betrayal of the new accommodative spirit in federal-provincial relations came with Premier Bourassa's deliberate undermining of the federal-provincial agreement by which Quebec was permitted for the first time to sit as a party in an international gathering in Paris of *la francophonie* in January 1986.

There were no charts indicating increased government consultation with the business community after the chilly period under Prime Minister Trudeau, but if they had been unveiled, they too would have indicated a marked upswing. Business was given a prominent position in representation at the National Economic Conference held by the prime minister in March 1985, although at that time they shared the spotlight with labour and many other public interest groups. In the subsequent year when Mulroney refrained from continuing the practice, the federal government joined business in boycotting a follow-up conference organized by labour representatives. Instead the Mulroney government was listening to business representation on a range of policy issues not only through the usual consultation and lobbying, but increasingly from the "inside," so to speak — it was literally inviting business representatives inside the policymaking process as co-partners in a variety of initiatives, including comprehensive committee review of the whole range of government programs under Deputy Prime Minister Erik Nielsen and development of the government's negotiating mandate on free trade. Although there was token representation from other interest groups in the Nielsen Task Force study, there was no doubt that business was the dominant partner and could now use its own yardstick to measure the size and efficiency of the federal bureaucracy. The prominence of business in the policy process around free trade was only one of many signs of this new interlocking of business interests and the federal state: the government's program of economic renewal through private sector investment; the removal of the capital gains tax; the reduction of corporate tax rate levels; and the attack on the federal deficit principally through cutting government programs and increasing the burden on individual taxpayers. The money markets even appeared to be dictating the pace of deficit reduction by the concerted pressure that was applied to ensure that the government's projected budget deficit fell below $30 billion in early 1986.

But there were also signs that the Mulroney government's exceedingly friendly overtures to the business community, as part of its program of national reconciliation and renewal, could lead it into very rough weather. In its embarrassingly enthusiastic decision to welcome back business into the councils of the nation and foreign investors into the economy, the government proceeded to adopt much of that constituency's agenda, including the dismantling of foreign ownership controls, the reduction of taxes and royalties on energy, the removal of the back-in rights on developments in the Canadian offshore, the scaling down of government, the privatization of crown corporations, reductions in social spending, and attractive tax and other inducements to private capital. The government also appeared sympathetic to the multinationals' demand for the removal of protection for generic drugs. Moreover, it had also picked up the central recommendation of business, repeated again and again in the Macdonald Commission hearings, for a free trade agreement with the United States. Many of these measures would land the government into precarious political waters where self-comforting sermons on rebuilding trust between Ottawa and private sector elites would not prove over time to be a particularly effective political shield. Indeed, when the heat of political conflict became exceedingly intense, as with the battle over the limiting of indexation of old age pensions after the spring 1985 budget, the

Mulroney government could even find itself deserted by its business allies, as was the case when the BCNI publicly rebuked the government for that part of its belt-tightening over social policy.

The third element of the triad was no more secure. Here the Mulroney government proceeded to thaw Canadian-American relations with such rapidity that its overtures threatened to rebound negatively upon the government if the fruits of friendship proved inadequate. Measuring the policy payoffs with Washington was already becoming a deadly public relations game over a series of bilateral irritants, with acid rain and free trade heading the list. Not only was the strategy vulnerable to the political whims of the president and Congress during a particularly tough-minded imperial period in American history, but it also had to be pursued before a sceptical Canadian public with a venerable record of anti-Americanism at the root of its nationalist character. Since the free trade talks would roam over highly sensitive subject matter, much of it touching the policy fundamentals of Canadian sovereignty in the cultural, economic, social and environmental fields, it was easy to see that the Mulroney government's reconciliation program might turn out to be a time bomb with highly unpredictable and volatile effects. After all, more than one Canadian government had walked away from trade deals with the United States, even where they touched on mere tariff issues, because of the treacherous politics around the issue. Would a new and inexperienced Mulroney government, with a trade package encompassing tariff and nontariff matters, fare any better?

Given this coalition of interests, it was apparent that the program for the Canadian federal state had shifted dramatically away from the preoccupations of the Trudeau era toward economic renewal through continental integration and the expansion of the role of the market. In one sense, that was a reflex action by a Canadian government following the severe buffeting the Canadian state and economy had received from worldwide recession, a redressing of the obsessive state-driven policy instruments of the federal government aimed at separatism and provincialism over the past quarter century, and a reassertion of power by those often excluded elites who were by definition not accepted earlier by Ottawa as partners in protecting federalism and in balancing its threatened system of power relations. What appeared to go with the new alliances, however, was an acceptance of an increasingly neoconservative philosophy for the Canadian federal state, which appeared to fit uneasily into traditional Canadian Conservative doctrine and which in fact called into question many of the country's policies and practices that had developed over several earlier generations.

This neoconservatism derived strength from fears over the future economic growth of the country and over its ability to handle rapidly mounting debt. Like so many other countries in the Western developed world, Canada appeared to be entering a new period of restricted fiscal capacity, generating in its turn a politics of scarcity. Increasingly, the federal government and its allies were declaring that many of the older programs of legitimation for the modern liberal state could no longer be afforded and must be dropped or severely circumscribed under current conditions of restraint. Such a vision was not one the people of Canada were entirely ready to accept, particularly when the politics of financial restraint began to encroach upon their own programs of interest. This too was part of the broader political risk the Mulroney Conservatives had assumed with the deficit, and with its allies' recommended methods of dealing with it. The first two years of the Mulroney government was a splendid test case in the frustrating see-sawing exercise of trying to pursue that program while not entirely destroying its political base.

The first round in that ongoing battle had begun with Finance Minister Michael Wilson's November 1984 statement. He announced on the one hand a combination of budget cuts and increased energy taxes and user fees for government services, which was to trim in excess of $4 billion from the next year's budget, and, on the other, an open invitation to review the principle of universality in big-ticket items of social spending. The latter invitation was taken up with alacrity by the opposition parties and public, and the government was quickly driven back in this first round from considering the incorporation of a selective targeting approach in place of universal family allowance payments, old age pensions and the like. The cuts fell most severely upon costly programs in energy and conservation, unemployment insurance, transportation, employment support and regional economic development — many of which disproportionately injured the interests of have-not regions, especially the Atlantic provinces. But there were other targets, including Via Rail, cultural agencies and institutions, such as the CBC, and research and development programs. These cuts were justified not only on fiscal grounds, but as merely the first step in a larger process of "downsizing" the federal government (to the tune of $10 to $15 billion a year by 1990) to make way for a stronger and more competitive private sector. That broader undertaking was already clear in the government-business review of all federal government programs under the Nielsen Task Force and in the ongoing work on a program of privatizing crown corporations and selling off other excess government properties. It was in fact an initial if somewhat faltering shot at a "radical reassessment of Ottawa's role as an economic actor, cultural buttress and social benefactor."[14]

The second round came with the government's first official budget on May 23, 1985. This phase provided for increased sales, personal and corporate taxes, the closing of some tax loopholes, and more cuts in federal spending, including the elimination of 15,000 jobs in the civil service by 1990, the closing of the money-losing heavy water plants in

Cape Breton, partial deindexing of personal income, family allowance payments, old age pensions, reduction in the value of the child tax exemption by 1987, cuts in transfer payments to the provinces, and reduced grants and subsidies for industry, transport and foreign aid. There were some modest compensating benefits, especially for an improved child tax credit and job training, but by far the most important signal of the government's new priorities was the announcement of a phased-in exemption from capital gains tax up to a lifetime limit of $500,000 per Canadian. The exemption was entirely open-ended and not restricted to investments made in Canada. That was a dramatic indication of the government's wish to encourage equity investment, to "reward risk takers," to promote the accumulation of capital, while flatly declaring that financial constraints were "forcing" government to press harder on the legitimation side of the ledger. While that strategy won cautious plaudits from business leaders together with stronger demands to push on with the deficit-fighting program, it was in fact an uneasy political message to sell to the nation, especially the juxtaposition of capital gains exemptions for the well-to-do alongside increased taxes and social expenditure cuts. In the end, one part of that budget package came loose, namely, the proposal to partially deindex old age pensions, in a ferocious post-budget fight by "grey power." While that extraordinary lobby succeeded in turning the government back on that particular issue, the rest of the cuts remained in place.

Meanwhile, the privatization program of the government was proceeding both as a policy outcome of the government's broad ideological direction and as a component part of deficit-fighting. During the 1985-87 period, privatization together with sale of real property was expected to bring in more than $600 million according to government accounting methods (which merely record the difference between what Ottawa actually received for the asset and the book value assigned to it), although the transfer of cash for these properties would be much greater.[15] These sales included Canadian Arsenals, Northern Transportation, Canada Development Corporation shares, de Havilland and Canadair, but the really lucrative crown assets — Air Canada, Petro-Canada and Canadian National Railways — would, if sold, bring in much more. In this way, the government appeared to be pursuing its double objective — fighting the deficit by a direct downsizing of government, an agenda very much written in neoconservative terms.[16]

The 1986 budget on February 26 carried forward the thrust of the government's program, although this time without any embarrassing reversals over social policy. This was accomplished by pushing over to the next budget the matter of social policy, including a revamping of the unemployment insurance system after the release of the report of the Forget Commission, and by carrying on with general tax increases, the closing of more tax loopholes, and phased-in reductions in corporate and small business tax rates. The budget appeared to show an increasing shift of the overall tax burden onto the personal tax system and away from the corporate sector, while the corporate tax system was moving toward lower rates with fewer special-case tax exemptions and incentives.[17] Projections for tax revenue in 1990, for example, indicated that corporate income tax would increase by only 60.6 per cent, while personal income tax would grow by 66.3 per cent. The budget naturally won support from the business sector as the next year's deficit was projected to fall below their own well-known insistent ceiling of $30 billion, with at least two-thirds of the savings arising from strict government expenditure cuts and controls. As the finance minister proudly declared, "total program spending, including all statutory programs such as Old Age Security, family allowances and unemployment insurance, will be held to $86.6 billion — lower than last year's spending. This is the first absolute decline in total program spending in over 20 years."[18]

While the business community, in the words of BCNI president Tom d'Aquino, continued to describe the government's planned program now in its third stage as "bullish," "chapter four ... [on] social spending" promised for the succeeding year by Finance Minister Wilson was likely to be just as encouraging from its point of view.[19] Although that issue would continue to be a highly sensitive political matter, especially as polls warned of Canadians' continuing commitment to the social safety net, including unemployment insurance protection, there was increasing confidence that by adopting "an evolutionary rather than revolutionary" approach through the gradual rearranging of the tax system so that more would be taxed from those who did not really need assistance and more provided to those most in need, an acceptable balancing of political risks and benefits could be achieved.[20] The strategy had already been tried successfully with the balancing off of the phased-in reduction in the value of the universally accessible child tax exemption (for those with children) alongside the increase in the targeted child tax credit program for those families most in need. This program appeared to carry the earmarks of a progressive approach to social reform, often winning support from groups such as the Canadian Council on Social Development, while at the same time opening up the possibility of saving money and scaling back the size and scope of state activity. However, the long-term problem of that targeting approach remained: if successful, it allegedly would erode the political footings of the modern welfare state by disconnecting middle-class support for that structure. If that class started to feel "ripped off," the political foundations around the welfare state would crumble; as Leon Muszynski had noted, "the more people who benefit from social programs, the more support there is for them."[21]

In an interesting essay on the politics of the deficit done for the

Macdonald Commission, David Wolfe has shown the extraordinary linkage between this issue and the broader neoconservative program of scaling back government and balancing the books — in some respects, presenting us with a rerun in the 1980s of ideological arguments last prominently heard in the 1930s prior to the ascendancy of Keynesianism.[22] He shows that the cause for the substantial deficit growth after the mid-1970s can be placed not on irresponsible state spending, but on the discretionary tax measures introduced by the federal government after 1970, which severely reduced revenue flowing to Ottawa, together with the known cyclical effects of coping with the massive recession of the early 1980s. Yet these facts are hardly acknowledged in the current ideological debate around the deficit, which has turned more and more on the question of the "appropriate size and role of the state in the contemporary economy."[23] This simpleminded ideological equation — less government (through budget-slashing) equals a more efficient Canadian economy — has been recognized and deplored by Irving Brecher:

> As "big government" becomes more and more the target, spending restraints are bound to become more indiscriminate with justification provided less on the specific merits than on the wooly grounds of "cutting government down to size." Furthermore, budget-slashing tends increasingly to be used as a false proxy for the basic decisions required to produce a more efficient, faster-growing Canadian economy.[24]

If there remain any lingering doubts about the linked nature of deficit-fighting and cutting back the size and role of government, the release of the Nielsen Task Force report on March 11, 1986, ought to dispel them. Here again the state-reduction program was seen as a direct element in a program of revitalizing the economy. Its challenge to bureaucratic power and the public sector could hardly be clearer in the thousands of recommendations for program terminations, privatization of public corporations, staff cutbacks, and tighter and leaner government. This was an agenda written largely by business, reflecting its own philosophy and interests, and while much of it would be politically unpalatable, it nonetheless remained an important element in the Mulroney government's ongoing effort at downsizing the federal state. Together with the growing movement toward deregulation, the deliberate reining in of the power of labour, and the pursuit of continental trade, these were all signs of a changing ideological shift toward our own Canadian version of that neoconservatism already so powerful in Britain and the United States.[25]

This broad paradigm shift was already beginning to make its appearance during the latter years of the Trudeau government, although it was always then overshadowed by the remaining preoccupations over federalism and the vigorous battles over policy carried out in these terms. The moves toward deregulation, restraints on social programs, controlling inflation through wage controls and restrictions on labour, tax incentives for business investment, and even increased trade with the United States through sectoral trade agreements were already taking place under the federal Liberals, although not with the same single-mindedness and fervour that later marked the Mulroney Conservatives. Moreover, there was plenty of evidence at the provincial level, even from the new Liberal government of Quebec, that these were becoming more general concerns.

None of these ideological overtures, including the fashionable neoconservative attack on the state as leviathan, effectively disguised the fact that much of this effort was at bottom aimed at increasing capital's share of national wealth. The relative indifference to the tax expenditure component of the deficit, the centring out of costly government social services programs for deficit reduction, the efforts to reduce corporate income tax burdens, the attempt to limit the "social wage" and labour rights and to reduce or shirk environmental responsibilities were all part of an aggressive assertion of business interests during the 1980s. The adoption of dramatic tax reform measures in the United States late in 1986, apparently lowering individual tax rates while raising corporate tax levels and deleting many tax breaks, has taken on the appearance of a populist countertrend and may challenge the direction of the Mulroney government's program in the middle of its mandate. The government has announced that it will pursue tax reform with the aim of narrowing the differences between the American and Canadian tax systems. But thus far the government's general policy has been governed by a classic neoconservative economic theory that pretends it can overcome the productivity problems plaguing Western economies by pushing back state intervention, rewarding capital and encouraging tougher competition.[26] These themes were prominent elements in the Conservative program of economic recovery, even if muted in practice by the complexities of Canadian political culture and the requirements of electoral politics.

Nevitte and Gibbins argue that neoconservatism in Canada and elsewhere "involves a core set of beliefs which include a preference for down-sizing government, a belief in the efficacy of private enterprise and hence a preference for deregulating the economy."[27] In their recent survey of Canadian students, they explored a complex set of "attitudinal linkages" pointing to the presence of a "coherent neoconservative ideology" in Canada with its own "distinct political agenda." Although the results in this survey are not representative of the Canadian population as a whole and scarcely show that students are being swept up in a right-wing ideological tide, they do indicate a strong association between those identifying themselves as federal Conservatives and high neoconservative scores.[28] This result suggested that neoconservatism could "be mobilized by the party system." Recent work by Professor George Perlin of Queen's University on opinion among Conservative party convention members also shows that Canadian Conservatives, although distinct in many respect from American conservatives, particularly in their relative avoidance of religious and moral fundamentalism, are moving more sharply toward deregulation, fiscal prudence and, especially, a continentalist economic position over recent years. There appears to be less and less patience in these quarters with the politics of intervention and nationalism.[29] These shifts in opinion, along with increased institutional ties with the Republican party for technology, campaigning ideas and so on, have moved the Tory party much further away from its earlier nationalist legacy with the founding of Confederation, away from the thinking of prominent conservative theoreticians such as George Grant, and certainly some considerable distance from the Diefenbaker legacy of the late 1950s and early 1960s.

Perhaps one of the best "official" gauges of this apparent attempt to shift the social consensus in a neoconservative direction (while still holding on to much of the older Trudeau mandate of defending federalism from the centre) can be read in the September 1985 report of the Royal Commission on the Economic Union and Development Prospects for Canada (Macdonald Commission). This massive undertaking, completed after three years of data gathering, hearings, and work on an exceedingly ambitious research program, had to be carried forward in delicate fashion. Not only was the commission's own credibility, as a creature of the Trudeau government, very much in doubt as federal power shifted from the Liberals to the Conservatives virtually in the middle of its mandate, but it now had to find a way to address many of the older and pressing concerns about the functioning of the Canadian federal state in a considerably changed climate of federal-provincial relations, while remaining constantly alert to the new government-business set of preoccupations over economic policy. It resolved the dilemma by straddling and melding these two agendas together, following the Trudeau mandate essentially on its federalism proposals and the Mulroney government's mandate over economic questions, especially free trade. While that did not in every respect necessarily add up to a politically coherent package of recommendations, it at least appeared to ensure that some parts of the royal commission's corpus of recommendations would be welcomed and acted upon by the new Conservative government.

The commission's proposals concerning federalism did attempt in many ways to complete the centre-building state program of the earlier Trudeau government. No federal organ has so eloquently sought to consolidate the entrenchment of the Charter of Rights and Freedoms as a new foundation for Canadian nationality and identity. In that respect, the commission's report in its first volume is fully as lyrical (and uncritical) an exponent of the theory of nation-building through a presumed constitutional restructuring of the people's feelings, norms and consciousness as are some of its research studies on that subject. The proposals on Senate reform reject the provincialist arguments for restructuring that body and follow the Trudeau government's preference for direct regional expressions of opinion in Parliament other than those of provincial premiers or their delegates. Intrastate federalism is clearly intended to work along lines that circumvent direct provincial input into or increased control of national institutions. It also adopts the Trudeau government's earlier plan to include services as well as goods in section 121 of the Constitution Act and, after some political experience with a so-called Code of Economic Conduct aimed at protecting the economic union from the bane of nontariff barriers, to entrench and enforce these principles through the constitution. Similarly, the strengthening of federal trade and commerce powers under section 91 (2) to provide for federal regulatory power over competition and product standards is called for, along with a tightening up of federal power over the field of international trade by removing the provincial power to reject treaties affecting provincial jurisdiction and by requiring instead that these agreements meet the normal consensus expected of the amending formula. The commission even went so far as to recommend the adoption of the student voucher system, a policy change very much in line with the thinking and intended plans of the Trudeau government.

While it is true that the commission did make some modest proposals on behalf of provincial governments, and certainly did not accept either the spirit or the substance of the Trudeau government's later attempt to circumvent or downplay the institutions of interstate federalism, but rather sought to strengthen and improve their functioning, there can also be little doubt that on balance this report turned its back on provincialist rhetoric and policy. One need only spend a few hours comparing the Macdonald Commission report with the recommendations and rationale of the earlier Pepin-Robarts Task Force report on national unity, produced only a few years earlier prior to the Quebec referendum, to see how firmly the Macdonald Commission had departed from this agenda. But it is perhaps in the extraordinary preoccupation with the new canons of market rationality and language in economic and social policy that the commission really showed how sharply it had moved beyond the older competing state-based agendas in favour of the new priorities of the mid-1980s.

Here, the commission turned increasingly away from the economic strands of the Trudeau government's federalism, from its moderately interventionist and nationalist tendencies, and adopted instead a much more market-driven approach to policy. This was apparent in its cool response to the NEP, to the extensive use of crown corporations, to continued foreign ownership controls and to the very idea of a targeted industrial strategy. Instead, it placed almost unbounded confidence in the normal operation of the marketplace — especially in an open, competitive world trading system with assured Canadian links to the U.S. market — to secure and revitalize the Canadian state, society and economy. That faith undergirded its chief recommendation for a free trade agreement with the United States, just as it did much of its proposed changes in other areas, including social policy. The move toward restructuring the unemployment insurance system so that it would provide less in benefits with longer qualifying periods, and then channelling some of the savings into benefits for those ready to move out of low-employment areas and retrain as market demands indicate else-where in the country, was an excellent illustration of the new neoconservative market-driven consciousness.[30] Similarly, federal re-gional economic development programs should, according to the com-mission, abstain from all regional employment-creation schemes, leaving those to the provinces, and seek instead the improvement of market skills, productivity and interregional mobility. This was a considerable shift away from the older federal state-based responsibility for redressing regional economic disparities in the country and for preserving "place prosperity" through a combination of active national programs and policies, and a return to modest liberal (that is, market) policy parame-ters. Indeed, even provinces that carried on the work of place-specific employment measures with regional economic development grants were expected to operate from within the newer more restricted terms of the liberal Code of Economic Conduct.

Other recommendations by the Macdonald Commission on social policy show the new linked nature of social policy with the commission's larger market-driven program that aimed to encourage work incentives, mobility and adaptability, system efficiency and lower administrative costs. The establishment of a universal income security program over the graves of family allowances, child and married tax exemptions, etc., was aimed at satisfying the demands for a more targeted policy in favour of the truly needy — always, however, in such a way that disincentives to work would not arise — even if that placed the social system as a whole in a politically less secure and defensible position than it would have enjoyed under a universal system of demogrants. Yet the effect of these changes also appeared to reward mobile labour and the working poor more generously than the welfare poor and most of the very poor (those living on the street and ineligible for welfare benefits).[31] Incentives were arranged in such a way that a family of four from Cape Breton ready to move and retrain might receive up to $26,000 in transitional support, compared to a mere $7,000, plus a provincial "top up," if the same family preferred to stay in place in Cape Breton. Hence, those who appeared unwilling to face "mobility" or to undertake "adjustment" would find themselves staying poor, while the system of incentives would be arranged for others.

But certainly the commission's most important recommendation, to pursue a free trade agreement with the United States, had potentially greater implications for the containment of state activity and the release of market power than any of the other recommendations. Adopted as official policy of the Mulroney government in September 1985, it also appeared to be a better candidate for immediate political action than many of the commission's other recommendations, which so often appeared to operate outside acceptable political boundaries. Here was an image around which those who wished to recharge private enterprise and to circumscribe the state could rally, even though ironically the promise of a reduced state might well turn out to be fallacious at least in the short run.[32] This was a venture that seemingly promised to usher in a new chapter in intergovernmental and state–private sector relationships, but whose affect on the pendulum of power in the federation could only be guessed at.

### The Future of the Balance

Speculating on the future index of power — especially on the effects of a free trade agreement on the future dynamics of centralization and decentralization in the federation — is doubly hazardous. As we have seen in the power-measuring exercises conducted over the Trudeau years, not only is it exceedingly difficult (if not theoretically impossible) to grasp the elements of any index, to collate and measure them as something more than mere arbitrary aggregates or proxies for the real thing being sought, but the uncertainties over the eventual outcome of free trade talks with the United States are likely to make this kind of exercise even more dubious. Yet, as noted in chapter 1, the temptation to track the binary dynamics of the federation is hard to resist at any time, and even more so when new developments on this scale appear to enter the equation.

The common view, according to Richard Simeon, is that free trade would have a dramatic effect on the federation.[33] Any treaty that went very far in striking down nontariff barriers between Canada and the United States would obviously directly constrain the powers and policies of provinces, which now seek to limit or redirect the operation of the national or international market in their own favour. Indirectly, any movement on this international front would swiftly push the old national agenda item of freeing up Canada's own economic union forward at a pace and scale that would dwarf the results that might have been achieved by purely domestic negotiation. The treaty would dictate in continental and national terms a unity and singleness of purpose concerning both the role of the "free market" and the limits to the state's infringements of it — a social consensus that has eluded Canadian statesmen and publics over the years — and it would presumably provide for investigative and enforcement mechanisms to secure those principles. There is more than a little irony in this result, if Canada proves able to settle these issues only in a continental deal with the United States that explicitly abjures economic nationalism, while failing to achieve it by internal consent of its own peoples and elites.

If the commission is right that free trade (by eschewing the old phony calls for Canadian economic nationalism, which actually masked central Canadian dominance) will submerge the perennial and divisive Canadian debate concerning the imperial heartland of Ontario and the exploited hinterlands in federal economic policy, there certainly will be a broader consequent sense of national unity and centralization of purposes among Canadians. However, that is a claim that is, to the say the least, highly debatable. Even if the economy receives the healthy stimulus free trade will allegedly bring, and enjoys a higher level of productivity and greater wealth through the beneficent operation of the unshackled engines of free enterprise, it is by no means clear that these results will work toward enhanced national unity. As noted earlier in chapter 4, commentators have been divided over whether free trade will tilt costs toward heartland or periphery, but no one has argued very persuasively that it will promote more balance or a reduction in disparities. That after all is not one of the chief objects of a market economy, and the restrictions a free trade agreement will place upon the state will only reduce attempts to mitigate those effects or to moderate the pursuit of economic efficiency with the redistributive claims of losers and disadvantaged regions.

It is this broader implication of the free trade policy — its tendency to constrain the state, to reduce the scope of direct political involvement in the economy and to limit the responsiveness of the democratic state to domestic political pressures in both countries — that distinguishes it so sharply from a politics of economic nationalism. This policy, with its implied defence of a vastly reduced state role in the modern economy, is most compatible with neoconservative ideas for economic reform and revitalization in North America. That is why the call for "freer trade" and a "reduced state" have been twin pillars of neoconservative thought in America, championed repeatedly by the Reagan administration during the 1980s. This is, of course, a recipe for circumscribing politics and the public realm, while expanding markets and private power. It reflects a growing presumption on the part of the neoconservatives that the

operation of an expansive and interventio₁ust democracy and the pursuit
of economic efficiency are incompatible elements, a conflict which, if
economic renewal is to take place, can only be finally resolved by de-lim-
iting the state.

What does this analysis suggest about the future power index in the
federation? On the one hand, it clearly underlines the new assertion of
power by private nonstate actors, particularly business interests, which
we have noted as a prominent part of the post-Trudeau era. These interests have apparently decided to try to pursue a continental program of
economic rationalization, and if successful, they will certainly be less and
less interested in alliances with either level of the state in Canada. Not
only will many of the traditional avenues for seeking state shelter be cut
off by treaty, but the logic of the new arrangements will dictate private
sector continental strategies. Presumably, if in that respect the new Conservative government is successful in weaning Canadian business off
their addiction to state support — free them from what then deputy
prime minister Nielsen derided as their condition as "program junkies"
— there will be no reason to expect a strong economic role for the federal state. Nor for economic province-building. This is merely to note the
obverse of mercantilism as state policy: laissez-faire liberalism is hardly a
doctrine to bring on another round of competitive big government dynamics around economic state-building.

While both levels of government in the federation would be adversely
affected in terms of their use of a broad range of economic policy instruments, both the extent of the treaty provisions and especially the nature
of the exceptions permitted will affect the governments' relative freedom
of action. The effect on the power index will be determined in part by the
negotiated exceptions that may tend to free up one level of the Canadian
state more than the other or to leave important economic areas open for
one level of the federation while mostly curtailing the other. Since the
provinces and the federal government will be setting the negotiating
mandate and approving or rejecting the final product, it is unlikely, however, that either would permit the treaty to be an instrument by which
their respective balance of power in this area would be sharply upset. It
may well be that the treaty would tend to monitor and capture any federal violations of its provisions more easily and more readily than provincial or state measures, and therefore it would indirectly constrain national governments more than the subfederal units in each country.[34]

The unconventional view on the effect of a free trade agreement on
federal power and national unity may very well offer a sounder prognosis. It is difficult to see how free trade could promote centralization of the
federal state in Canada, especially since at least in theory it entails the explicit renunciation of so many state policy instruments that might be
used in the national interest. While many of these may not in fact be

ceded in the bargaining, it is quite clear that if a deal is to be struck, it must involve a significant devolution of power and authority from the state to the marketplace. These are not the conditions under which the power of the national government of the far weaker partner in the market can be furthered.

The same logic also extends to the provincial order of state, although its purpose in protecting and giving expression to a less expansive definition of political community may be considerably less challenged. Certainly for many provinces, especially have-nots, there has always been a serious limit upon their ability to pursue economic province-building and there will be little of their own ambitious programs to roll back. What may be of more concern to them will be the restraints placed upon the federal state in the promotion of regional equity or the equalizing of regional opportunity. If these are curtailed in the name of market efficiency, their own interests will be seriously threatened. For the stronger provinces, there will naturally be considerable concern over limits to provincial power over the local interests and economy, but there would at least remain the crucial policy roles of training and education.[35] While the provincial governments would doubtless suffer a setback under free trade in the range of their policy and purposes, it is also likely that they would feel these effects much less dramatically than would the federal order of state.

For those who have come to see the direct role of federal and provincial governments in the economy as frequently unwise and a source of unhealthy competition in the federation, a retreat from the economic realm by governments may be seen as a necessary prelude to economic recovery and improved national unity. That appears to be the innocent view of the Macdonald Commission. But this neoconservative posture ignores the need for controlling market power in the national interest, especially for Canada as the weaker of the two partners under the free trade treaty. One is left adrift with mere faith in the ultimate compatibility of the continental "free market" and Canadian political, economic and cultural sovereignty. As James Laxer and many other commentators, including Stuart Smith from the Science Council, have noted, this posture also ignores the successful experience with close state–private sector relationships, frequently operating in an industrial strategy, that has brought impressive economic results in many countries, most notably Japan, just as it fails to pay sufficient attention to the relatively swift and recent decline in the economic position of the United States in the world economy. America, after all, has had access to a market of over 200 million for a long time and yet its productivity hasn't improved in recent years; nor does evidence from the European Community support the notion that free trade is any panacea despite what economists often would like us to believe.[36] All of these should be warning signs against casting our fate so completely upon alluring but simple remedies.

Of course, many interests, both governmental and nongovernmental, are not prepared to put their trust in laissez-faire economic theory on matters of this importance. With the bargaining difficult and the demands very high, the prospects for impasses in the negotiations, with each government walking away from the table, are considerable, or given the political capital that has been invested in it, the outcome might be only a modest retrieval of the idea in a scaled-down treaty package. A limited sectoral agreement, removal of tariffs only (with nontariff barriers sent for further study by a bilateral consultative body) or even a government-procurement treaty might be seen as safer policy outcomes. Analysts such as Robert Young were already offering this kind of advice as "a way out of the policy box" on free trade even before the talks really got under way.[37]

Certainly, the negotiators will want to steer very carefully through politically treacherous free trade waters, for while it is becoming harder for modern economies to operate a mercantilist policy in an increasingly interdependent world, protectionist pressures are very high and the international economic order is increasingly vulnerable in part because of growing interdependence in trade, capital markets, debt and so on. Under these circumstances, modern nation-states are losing much of their ability to direct domestic economic and monetary policy, while international institutions like the International Monetary Fund or money markets are becoming very important.[38] The role of the money markets in driving down the value of the Canadian dollar and in pressuring the Conservative government to bring in a budget with a projected deficit under $30 billion in 1986 has already brought home that fact to Canadians. These conditions may provide as potentially fertile a ground for the reassertion of economic nationalism by modern nation-states as they do for ongoing liberalization. It is therefore far from clear what international economic environment Canada may face, and yet this factor may well shape much of the pattern of federalism in the future.

Meanwhile, the partisan map of the country has been redrawn in a fashion that challenges much of the conventional wisdom about Canadian government and federalism written during the 1970s. The alienation the West was said to feel from its lack of representation in the government at the federal level seemed to be temporarily removed with the election of the Mulroney government, even though with the subsequent calamitous fall in commodity prices, only partially cushioned by federal support, westerners wondered about the value of that new status. At the same time, new Liberal governments arose in the provinces of Ontario and Quebec to replace a Conservative dynasty on the one hand and a nationalist PQ government seeking Quebec independence on the other. These governments have already begun to pattern their competitive relations with Ottawa into a closer fit with traditional historic norms. Ontario seemed no longer tied into an alliance of convenience with the federal government, nor was Quebec actively pursuing the long nationalist drive it began almost a quarter century ago in the 1960 election of the Lesage government. Meanwhile, there was growing evidence that the federal Conservatives would face a much less monolithic friendly partisan group of governments in the other provinces than they faced in the first year of their mandate.

The only certainty about the future dynamics in the Canadian federation is the persistence of both change and continuity. As the various cycles and stages of Canadian federalism are reviewed over the years, these have always been present in good measure. As the country has moved from founding, to western settlement, to world wars and depression, to Keynesian economics and the construction of the welfare state, to Quebec separatism and the politics of oil, there has always been a profoundly different set of policy challenges to which the system of federalism has adapted. It may be, as Richard Simeon has argued, that these different periods of federalism have been dominated by distinct sets of policy concerns, which become paradigms around which the different patterns of federal-provincial interrelatedness have grown.[39]

Some of these agendas in various periods have seen regional or linguistic tensions exacerbated, while for others, different kinds of alignments and conflicts have been featured. While there are continuities in linguistic conflict between the French and English, regional collisions especially between producing and consuming sections of the country, and tensions with the United States, these do not always dominate or crowd out the overarching character of each phase in the evolution of the federal state. Hence, Simeon argues, with considerable force, that the older agenda over language and region that has dominated federal- provincial relations for the last quarter century is now becoming less pressing. A new agenda of concerns — possibly over scarcity, the championing of new social movements, such as the women's movement and native rights, and over the implications of the new international economic order — is emerging. It may well be wise to pay increasing heed to a growing neoconservative ideological mood, especially in English-speaking countries, a movement already having considerable impact and carrying with it a more or less coherent set of policy objectives and concerns. Which of these trends will prove to be the more forceful and exactly where they may carry the future pendulum of power in the Canadian federation is for the moment unclear.

# Notes

## Introduction

[1]For an early elaboration of that theme, see G. Bruce Doern, "The Limits of Scheming Virtuously," in G. Bruce Doern, ed., *How Ottawa Spends, 1982,* Ottawa: School of Public Administration, Carleton University (Toronto: James Lorimer, 1982): 1-36.

[2]See R.A. Young, Philippe Faucher and André Blais, "The Concept of Province-Building: A Critique," *Canadian Journal of Political Science* 17, no.4 (December 1984): 783-818.

## Chapter I: The Origins of the Liberals' "New Federalism"

[1]William H. Stewart, *Concepts of Federalism* (Lanham, Maryland: University Press of America, 1984), 20.

[2]See, for example, Alan C. Cairns, "The Governments and Societies of Canadian Federalism," *Canadian Journal of Political Science* 10 (December 1977): 695-726.

[3]Edwin Black, *Divided Loyalties: Canadian Concepts of Federalism* (Montreal: McGill-Queen's University Press, 1975), 1-7, 217-29; David Elkins and Richard Simeon, *Small Worlds: Provinces and Parties in Canadian Political Life* (Agincourt: Methuen, 1980), 1-30.

[4]See Paul Craven and Tom Traves, "National Policy, 1872-1933," *Journal of Canadian Studies* 14 (Fall 1979): 14-38; Paul Phillips, "The National Policy Revisted," *Journal of Canadian Studies* 14, no. 3: 3-13, 39-49; and John Richards and Larry Pratt, *Prairie Capitalism: Power and Influence in the New West* (Toronto: McClelland and Stewart, 1979), 148-76. For a venture into the theory of the political economy of federalism, see Garth Stevenson, "Federalism and the Political Economy of the Canadian State," in Leo Panitch, ed., *The Canadian State: Political Economy and Political Power* (Toronto: University of Toronto Press [hereafter UTP], 1977), 71-100.

[5]See H.V. Nelles, *The Politics of Development: Forests, Mines, and Hydro-Electric Power in Ontario 1849-1941* (Toronto: Macmillan, 1974), 427-95; and Christopher Alexander, *The Politics of Federalism: Ontario's Relations with the Federal Government, 1867-1942* (Toronto: UTP, 1981), 68-84. The extent of the state's "embeddedness" in modern society and political economy may now, however, cause these discrete patterns to lose something of their visibility and distinctiveness. See Alan Cairns, "The Embedded State: State-Society Relations in Canada," in Keith Banting, *State and Society: Canada in Comparative Perspective,* vol. 31, Prepared for the Royal Commission on the Economic Union and Development Prospects for Canada (hereafter identified as Macdonald Commission Studies) (Toronto: UTP, 1986), 53-86.

[6]See Donald Smiley, "An Outsider's Observations of Federal-Provincial Relations Among Consenting Adults," in Richard Simeon, ed., *Confrontation and Collaboration: Intergovernmental Relations in Canada Today* (Toronto: Institute of

Public Administration of Canada, 1979), 108-11; and Timothy Woolstencraft, *Organizing Intergovernmental Relations,* Discussion paper 12 (Kingston: Institute of Intergovernmental Relations, Queen's University, 1982), 75-81.

[7]See Sharon L. Sutherland and G. Bruce Doern, *Bureaucracy in Canada: Control and Reform,* vol. 43, Macdonald Commission Studies (Toronto: UTP, 1985), 57-80, 149-55. See also Alan Cairns, "The Governments and Societies of Canadian Federalism," *Canadian Journal of Political Science* 20, no. 4 (1977): 693-725.

[8]The classic seminal piece on province-building appeared in Edwin R. Black and Alan C. Cairns, "A Different Perspective on Canadian Federalism," *Canadian Public Administration* 9 (1966): 27-44. It has since been amplified by numerous writers on federalism. The best link of this literature to the self-interested behaviour of a market economy appears in Alan C. Cairns, "The Other Crisis of Canadian Federalism," *Canadian Public Administration* 22 (1979): 175, where the bureaucratic and economic development dimensions of province-building are given full rein. See also Alan C. Cairns, "The Governments and Societies of Canadian Federalism," in Richard Simeon, *Intergovernmental Relations and the Challenges to Canadian Federalism,* Discussion paper 7 (Kingston, Ont.: Institute of Intergovernmental Relations, Queen's University, 1979), 8-12. This literature has recently been subject to a severe attack in R.A. Young et al., "The Concept of Province-Building: A Critique." The chief defect of this literature as it relates to "province-building," according to these authors, is the unwarranted generalizations and weak empirical support for propositions underlying this imagery. No one, however, has as yet analyzed the image itself and the political theory supporting it.

[9]R.A. Young et al., "The Concept of Province-Building."

[10]Unlike a balance-of-power system in an international context which can comprise a distribution of power between a number of sovereign states, federalism understood as a "charged" but limited intrastate balance of power is always dualist in theory even if not always so in practice.

[11]See Richard Simeon, "Federalism in the 1980s," in Thomas J. Courchene, David W. Conklin and Gail C.A. Cook, eds., *Ottawa and the Provinces: The Distribution of Money and Power* (Toronto: Ontario Economic Council, 1985), vol. 1, 29-43.

[12]J.R. Mallory, "The Five Faces of Federalism," in P.A. Crepeau and C.B. Macpherson, eds., *The Future of Canadian Federalism* (Toronto: UTP, 1965), 3-15.

[13]Canada, Royal Commission on Dominion-Provincial Relations (Rowell-Sirois Commission) *Report* (Ottawa: Queen's Printer, 1940).

[14]H.G.J. Aitken, "Defensive Expansionism: The State and Economic Growth in Canada," originally published in H.G.J. Aitken, ed., *The State and Economic Growth* (New York: Social Science Research Council, 1959), reprinted in W.T. Easterbrook and M.H. Watkins, eds., *Approaches to Canadian Economic History* (Toronto: McClelland and Stewart, 1967), 183-221.

[15]"A Conversation with the Prime Minister," with Host Bruce Phillips, taped December 21 and broadcast December 27, 1981 (Ottawa: CJOH-TV, 1981).

[16]See especially Garth Stevenson, *Unfulfilled Union* (Toronto: Gage, 1979). The same thesis is followed in the later edition.

[17]As Malcolm Brown has noted, the opting-out offers continued later in 1966 and 1973 respecting hospital insurance, the Canada Assistance Plan and the national health grants, but given the reduced financial commitments, they appeared to suggest "that they were made, not in the expectation that the provinces

would accept them but for the purpose of maintaining the illusion that all provinces were being given opting-out options." Malcolm C. Brown, *Established Program Financing: Evolution or Regression in Canadian Federalism?*, Centre for Research on Federal Financial Relations (Canberra: The Australian National University, 1984), 22.

[18]See Canada, Prime Minister's Office, *Federal-Provincial Grants and the Spending Power of Parliament*, 1969, esp. 34-50. Since the latter condition of payment to taxpayers rather than provincial governments was something of a kicker to pressure provinces into such schemes, it did not attract provincial government support and was not included in the 1971 Victoria Charter. Note also the concessions to the provinces in the idea of provincial configuration of federal spending programs, the notion that provinces might alter within broad limits the particular distribution of federal benefits under shared-cost programs. See Keith G. Banting, *The Welfare State and Canadian Federalism* (Montreal/Kingston: McGill-Queen's University Press, 1982), 156-59.

[19]This was accomplished by granting Quebec a 1% tax abatement over corporate income tax and a federal grant to bring the total benefit up to $1.50 per capita.

[20]The same logic was later extended to restrict direct federal payments to municipalities. See K. McRoberts, "Unilateralism, Bilateralism, and Multilateralism: Approaches to Canadian Federalism," in R. Simeon, *Intergovernmental Relations*, vol. 63, Macdonald Commission Studies (Toronto: UTP, 1985), 102-3.

[21]Canada, Canadian Unity Information Office, *Federalism and Decentralization: Where do We Stand?* (Ottawa: Minister of Supply and Services, 1981).

[22]Richard Bird, "Fiscal Decentralization," in *Financing Canadian Government: A Quantitative Overview* (Toronto: Canadian Tax Foundation, 1979), 64, 66-67. See also Bird's "Federal Finance in Comparative Perspective," in T. Courchene et al., *Ottawa and the Provinces*, 137-78. A recent review of these and other related arguments can be found in Thomas J. Courchene, *Economic Management and the Divison of Powers*, vol. 67, Macdonald Commission Studies (Toronto: UTP, 1986), 17-30.

[23]See, for example, Michael Jenkin, *The Challenge of Diversity: Industrial Policy in the Canadian Federation*, Science Council of Canada (Ottawa: Minister of Supply and Services, 1983), esp. 49-97. A good example of this new state entrepreneurship focused on Alberta can be found in John Richards and Larry Pratt, *Prairie Capitalism*, or Larry Pratt, "The Political Economy of Province-Building: Alberta's Development Strategy, 1971-1981," in David Leadbeater, ed., *Essays on the Political Economy of Alberta* (Toronto: New Hogtown Press, 1984).

[24]Transcript of Proceedings, Prime Minister and Students of Osgoode Hall Law School, York University, Toronto, February 5, 1981, p. 4.

[25]*Canadian Industrial Gas and Oil Ltd.* v. *Saskatchewan*, 1978, 2 SCR 545, and *Central Canada Potash Co.* v. *Saskatchewan*, 1979 1 SCR 42.

[26]Constitutional Committee of the Quebec Liberal Party, *A New Canadian Federation* (Montreal, 1980).

[27]See Richard Johnston, *Public Opinion and Public Choice in Canada*, vol. 35, Macdonald Commission Studies (Toronto: UTP, 1986), esp. chap. 6, for an illuminating review of public opinion toward Ottawa and the provinces at the end of the 1970s and into the first years of the 1980s.

[28]Task Force on Canadian Unity, *Report: A Future Together* (Ottawa: Minister of Supply and Services, 1979).

[29]Prime Minister with Bruce Phillips, December 21, 1981, p. 2.

[30]Pierre Elliott Trudeau, *Federalism and the French Canadians* (Toronto: Macmillan, 1968), xxiii.

[31]Pierre Elliott Trudeau, "Quebec and the Constitutional Problem," in *Federalism and the French Canadians*, 37-38.

[32]Ibid., 39. The sentence has been slightly recast for my purposes.

[33]Prime Minister with Bruce Phillips, December 21, 1981, p. 5.

[34]See this matter treated in Reginald Whitaker, "Reason, Passion, and Interest: Pierre Trudeau's Eternal Liberal Triangle," *Canadian Journal of Political and Social Theory* 4, no. 1 (Winter 1980): 21, 23.

[35]See Pierre Elliott Trudeau, "The Practice and Theory of Federalism," first published in Michael Oliver, ed., *Social Purpose for Canada* (Toronto: UTP, 1961), reprinted in Trudeau, *Federalism and the French Canadians*, 147.

[36]Hon. Jim Fleming, "The Economics of Disunity," Speech to the Canadian Club, Vancouver, November 12, 1980, p. 13.

[37]Prime Minister Trudeau, cited in *Financial Post*, May 17, 1980. The same point is made in the research of David Elkins and Richard Simeon in 1980. They found that the emergence of the PQ government did not cause the other provinces to rally around Ottawa, nor did it appear to cause any shift in public opinion toward the centre. Instead citizen identification with Ottawa as the most important government was true only in Ontario and in the linguistic minority hostage groups in French- and English-speaking Canada. Elkins and Simeon, *Small Worlds*, 287.

[38]Prime Minister Trudeau, Ottawa News Conference, cited in *Globe and Mail*, March 16, 1982.

[39]See, for example, Elkins and Simeon, *Small Worlds*, esp. 300; Simeon, *Intergovernmental Relations and the Challenges to Canadian Federalism*, 5-15, and "The Images of Canada," *Policy Options* 1, no. 4 (December 1980/January 1981): 11-14.

[40]*Globe and Mail*, November 25, 1981.

[41]House of Commons, April 15, 1980, 33.

[42]Elkins and Simeon, *Small Worlds*, 300; Donald Smiley, "The Challenge of Canadian Ambivalence," *Queen's Quarterly* 81 (Spring 1981): 1-12.

[43]House of Commons, April 15, 1980, 32-33.

[44]Richard Simeon, "Some Observations on the Powers over the Economy," in David Conklin, ed., *A Separate Personal Income Tax for Ontario: Background Studies* (Toronto: Ontario Economic Council, 1984), 365-80; and T.J Courchene, "The Political Economy of Canadian Constitution-Making: The Canadian Economic Union Issue," *Public Choice* 44 (1984): 201-49.

[45]Hon. John Roberts, Secretary of State, Speech to Annual Meeting of the Canadian Club, Royal York Hotel, Toronto, April 24, 1978.

[46]Hon. Jim Fleming, Speech, 2.

[47]Ibid., 7, 10.

[48]Ibid., 11.

[49]Ibid., 13.

[50]Ibid., 12.

[51]Hugh Aitken, "Defensive Expansionism." That point had been recognized earlier by John Hutchinson in "Trudeau's New Trick," *Canadian Forum*, February 1981, 4.

[52]Aitken, "Defensive Expansionism," in Easterbrook and Watkins, *Approaches to Canadian Economic History*, 221.

[53]This term is derived from an early essay on this subject by Donald V. Smiley, "Canada and the Quest for a National Policy," *Canadian Journal of Political Science* 8, no. 1 (March 1975): 40-62.

[54]Pierre Elliott Trudeau, "Federalism, Nationalism, and Reason," first published in Crepeau and Macpherson, *The Future of Canadian Federalism*, reprinted in Trudeau, *Federalism and the French Canadians*, 182-212.

[55]Ibid., 188-89, 192, 193.

[56]See this matter treated, and especially Trudeau's nationalist resistance to continentalism, in Reginald Whitaker, "Reason, Passion and Interest," esp. 23.

[57]Trudeau, "Federalism, Nationalism, and Reason," 193.

[58]Jean Chrétien, Vancouver, June 29, 1981, *Canadian News Facts*, 1981, 2529.

## Chapter II: Constitutional Politics

[1]See Alan C. Cairns, "Recent Federalist Constitutional Proposals: A Review Essay," in Canadian Public Policy, no. 3 (Summer 1979): 348-65. For an excellent review of the issues and problems in "federalizing" central institutions, see Donald V. Smiley and Ronald L. Watts, *Intrastate Federalism* in Canada, vol. 39, Macdonald Commission Studies (Toronto: UTP, 1985).

[2]For a treatment of the constitutional agenda items and the distinction between the "people's package" and the "institutions package" and "powers package," see David Milne, *The New Canadian Constitution* (Toronto: James Lorimer, 1982), 50. For a superb treatment of the fallacies in the federal sales pitch for the charter, see Peter Russell, "Democratic Approach to Civil Liberties," *University of Toronto Law Journal*, 1969, 109, and "The Political Purposes of the Canadian Charter of Rights and Freedoms," *Canadian Bar Review* 61 (March 1983): 30-54.

[3]Donald V. Smiley, "The Challenge of Canadian Ambivalence," *Queen's Quarterly* 88, no.1 (Spring 1981): 1-12.

[4]Pierre Elliott Trudeau, *Commons Debates*, April 15, 1980, 32.

[5]Ibid., 33.

[6]Richard Simeon, "An Overview of the Trudeau Constitutional Proposals," *Alberta Law Review* 19, no. 3 (1981): 395.

[7]See, for example, Allan Blakeney's declaration at the September 1980 Constitutional Conference, cited in Milne, *The New Canadian Constitution*, 75.

[8]My italics. An address by the Rt. Hon. Pierre Elliott Trudeau, Confederation Dinner, Toronto, November 5, 1980, p. 8.

[9]This action was in marked contrast to the careful restrictive approach to the matter of constitutional amendment by the federal government in 1949 when Parliament carefully limited its own direct unilateral power to amend the constitution to subjects of internal concern only. Although the constitutional issues here are not identical, they do raise the same broad question of the adequacy of the federal order of government making constitutional changes af-

fecting the provinces on its own and provide two starkly opposing answers. Certainly the contention of the Trudeau government in 1980 was considerably closer to the older nineteenth-century model of a self-sufficient and paternal central government than it was to its Liberal predecessor only thirty-five years earlier.

[10]Edward McWhinney, *Canada and the Constitution, 1979-1982* (Toronto: UTP, 1982), 65-71.

[11]Ibid., 46. It may be that this author's complaint arises from an unduly romantic attachment to the American and French routes to constitutionalism and that the government's course was one to which the government was driven by sheer political realism. Popular ratification of the contents of the federal constitutional resolution in every region of Canada was by no means certain.

[12]The expression belongs to Professor Ed Black of Queen's University, cited in Simeon, "An Overview of the Trudeau Constitutional Proposals," 394.

[13]Ibid., 393.

[14]See Kenneth McRoberts, "Unilateralism, Bilateralism, and Multilateralism: Approaches to Canadian Federalism," in Richard Simeon, *Intergovernmental Relations*, vol. 63, Macdonald Commission Studies (Toronto: UTP, 1985), 71-129.

[15]This issue is taken up at much greater length in chapter 4.

[16]See the prime minister's address to Parliament, April 15, 1980.

[17]See A.E. Safarian, *Canadian Federalism and Economic Integration*, Constitutional study prepared for the Government of Canada (Ottawa: Information Canada 1974); J. Chrétien, "Securing the Canadian Economic Union in the Constitution," Discussion paper (Ottawa: Ministry of Supply and Services, 1980). For a careful review of this argument, see M.J. Trebilcock et al., *Federalism and the Canadian Economic Union* (Toronto: Ontario Economic Council, 1983). Not even the Macdonald Commission was prepared to go along with these strong economic claims. See chapter 4.

[18]Thomas J. Courchene, "The Political Economy of Canadian Constitution-Making: The Canadian Economic-Union Issue," *Public Choice* 44 (1984): 227.

[19]Only mobility rights were included in the unilateral constitutional package as part of the charter, while the other demands were wisely dropped.

[20]Alan C. Cairns, "The Canadian Constitutional Experiment: Constitution, Community, and Identity," Killam Lecture, Dalhousie University, November 24, 1983, p. 25.

[21]See Stephen A. Scott, "The Canadian Constitutional Amendment Process," in Paul Davenport and Richard Leach, eds., *Reshaping Confederation: The 1982 Reform of the Canadian Constitution* (Durham, N.C.: Duke University Press, 1984), 268.

[22]P.H. Lane, *An Introduction to the Australian Constitution*, 3rd ed. (Sydney: The Law Book Company Ltd., 1983), 4.

[23]See *Melbourne University Law Review* 14 (June 1984): esp. 366; G. Walker, *The Australian Law Journal* 59 (July 1985): esp. 364; and Leslie Zines, ed., Commentaries on the Australian Constitution (Sydney: Butterworths, 1977), 235. Thus, while Australians may seem "referendum shy" in turning down all but eight of the thirty-eight national referendum proposals put to them by the Commonwealth government since Federation, there is little warrant for arguing that they always vote "no" to centralizing initiatives.

24For an examination of this and other formulae, see Milne, *The New Canadian Constitution*, 24-32, 189-95.

25This is not the place to go into the strengths and weaknesses of the amending formula actually adopted. For critical commentary, see Garth Stevenson, "Constitutional Amendment: A Democratic Perspective," in *Socialist Studies* 2 (1984): 269-84; Stephen A. Scott, "Canadian Constitutional Amendment"; D. Marc Kilgour and T.J. Lévesque, "The Choice of a Permanent Amending Formula for Canada's Constitution," *Canadian Public Policy* 10 (September 1984).

26Alan Cairns and Cynthia Williams, "Constitutionalism, Citizenship, and Society in Canada: An Overview," and Cynthia Williams, "The Changing Nature of Citizen Rights," in Alan Cairns and Cynthia Williams, *Constitutionalism, Citizenship, and Society in Canada*, vol. 33, Macdonald Commission Studies (Toronto: UTP, 1986), 1-50, 99-132.

27Somewhat as an afterthought, rights for aboriginal peoples became added to the package of minority rights upon which the case for national unity was being based.

28See Cairns and Williams, "Constitutionalism, Citizenship, and Society in Canada."

29See Milne, *The New Canadian Constitution*, 86-88, 155-60.

30While public interventions also strengthened the language provisions, there was never any doubt that these were additions to an already toughly worded and specially entrenched section.

31A.I. Silver, *The French-Canadian Idea of Confederation, 1864-1900* (Toronto: UTP, 1982), 191-92.

32See C. Michael MacMillan, "Henri Bourassa on the Defence of Language Rights," *Dalhousie Review* 62, no. 3 (Autumn 1982): 413-30.

33Ibid., 420.

34H. Bourassa, "The French Language and the Future of Our Race," cited in MacMillan, "Henri Bourassa," 422. For extensive extracts on Bourassa's views on biculturalism, see Joseph Levitt, ed., *Henri Bourassa on Imperialism and Biculturalism, 1900-1918* (Toronto: Copp Clark, 1970).

35The legal pinnings to federal paternalism remained in section 93 and elsewhere in the Constitution Act, but the charter can only be seen as a clear repudiation of that legal and political machinery for a defence of minority rights.

36McWhinney, *Canada and the Constitution, 1979-1982*, 55-57.

37Ibid., 60.

38 Alan Cairns, "The Politics of Constitutional Renewal in Canada," in Keith G. Banting and Richard Simeon, eds., *Redesigning the State: The Politics of Constitutional Change* (Toronto: UTP, 1985), 130.

39Cairns and Williams, "Constitutionalism, Citizenship and Society in Canada," 41.

40Peter H. Russell, "The Political Purposes of the Canadian Charter of Rights and Freedoms," *The Canadian Bar Review*, March 1983, 37-38.

41Ibid., 36.

42Note that the ideological battle against the charter was taken up both by conservative defenders of parliamentary traditions like Sterling Lyon and by socialists like Allan Blakeney, who attacked entrenchment liberalism for its elitism and its tendency to curtail democratic political life. The latter argument has also been forcefully made by Peter Russell and Donald Smiley among others, and has been a constant theme in democratic struggles against conservative Supreme Court decision-making in the United States for many years. Perhaps the classic struggle in this respect was the democratic attempt to challenge the court by President Roosevelt in the late 1930s. Students of judicial review have long recognized that the theory of democracy itself sits rather uneasily with the notion of court policymaking under a charter of rights.

[43]See Charles Taylor, "Alternative Futures: Legitimacy, Identity and Alienation in Late Twentieth Century Canada," in Cairns and Williams, *Constitutionalism, Citizenship, and Society in Canada*, 183-230. This is a subtle and exceptionally richly textured argument that by a different route obliquely raises the same critical questions about the role of the charter and evolving Canadian political life and identity as those that first appeared in the work of Peter Russell in "Democratic Approaches to Civil Liberties." These are important questions, particularly where it is conceded that the modern state needs a more active citizenry with stronger positive identification to the state than ever before.

[44]See the conclusions of Howard Leeson, Roy Romanow and John Whyte, *Canada Notwithstanding: The Making of the Constitution 1976-1982* (Agincourt, Ont.: Carswell/Methuen, 1984), 250-79.

[45]See F.L. Morton, "The Impact of the Charter of Rights on the Canadian Polity," Paper delivered at the Annual Meeting of the Western Political Science Association, Eugene, Oregon, March 20-22, 1986, 7. For a more modest review of the scope and importance of the Supreme Court's decisions, see Peter Russell, "First Three Years in Charterland," *Canadian Public Administration* 28, no. 3 (Fall, 1985): 367-96. For a review of divided expectations over Supreme Court performance, see A. Wayne MacKay and Richard W. Bauman, "The Supreme Court of Canada: Reform Implications for an Emerging National Institution," in Claire Beckton and A. Wayne MacKay, *The Courts and the Charter*, vol. 58, Macdonald Commission Studies (Toronto: UTP, 1985), 37-132.

[46]The blanket use of the notwithstanding clause by the PQ, as a protest against unilateral imposition of the constitution without the consent of its government, was a temporary and limited symbolic political action, later rejected by the subsequent Liberal government. But the recent Saskatchewan measure referred to earlier is certainly a more troubling indication of the use of the notwithstanding clause for the future.

[47]Peter Hogg, "Is the Supreme Court of Canada Biased in Constitutional Cases?" *Canadian Bar Review* 57: 724; Peter Russell, "The Political Role of the Supreme Court of Canada in Its First Century," *Canadian Bar Review* 53: 576; and Peter Russell, "The Supreme Court and Federal-Provincial Relations: The Political Use of Legal Resources," *Canadian Public Policy* 11, no. 2: 161-70.

[48]Peter Russell, "The Political Purposes of the Canadian Charter," 42. Federal laws will be similarly reviewed, but the national review is still worth underlining.

[49]Cairns, "The Politics of Constitutional Renewal," 131.

[50]The incident concerned a refusal by the Senate to pass authorizing legislation for increased borrowing until it was provided with the government estimates.

[51]It is the opinion of a highly placed official in the Prime Minister's Office that Newfoundland will likely be unable to secure the required provincial consent for such an amendment. But that may turn out to be wishful thinking.

[52]This view, according to Lloyd Axworthy, former minister of transport in the Trudeau government, is now widely shared by politicians in Ottawa.

[53]Whether bilingualism can continue to operate as a national bond between the founding peoples in the face of increased development of two more and more unilingual societies — one French in Quebec, the other English elsewhere — is an interesting question for the future. It may be shortsighted to rule out the possibility that the spirit of bilingualism may still work as a basis for national unity even with the decline of linguistic minorities. That notion has not yet been given any serious thought, since it has always been assumed from the Trudeau logic that only separatism could follow from such sociological facts. But that may be a doctrinaire and misleading argument.

[54]See David C. Hawkes, "Negotiating Aboriginal Self-Government," in Peter M. Leslie, ed., *Canada: The State of the Federation, 1985* (Kingston: Queen's University, 1985).

[55]See David C. Hawkes, *Aboriginal Self-Government: What Does It Mean?* Discussion paper, Institute of Intergovernmental Relations (Kingston: Queen's University, 1985).

[56]Roger Gibbins, Paper delivered at the Canadian Political Science Association, May 1985.

## Chapter III: The Politics of Energy

[1]Alan C. Cairns, "The Politics of Constitutional Conservatism," in Keith Banting and Richard Simeon, eds., *And No One Cheered: Federalism, Democracy and the Constitution Act* (Toronto: Methuen, 1983), 47.

[2]James Laxer, *Canada's Economic Strategy* (Toronto: McClelland and Stewart, 1981), 9.

[3]See Christopher Armstrong, *The Politics of Federalism: Ontario's Relations with the Federal Government, 1867-1942* (Toronto: UTP, 1981), for an early treatment of these dynamics in Ottawa-Ontario feuds. For an excellent treatment of the politics of federalism in earlier national fuel policy, see John McDougall, *Fuels and the National Policy* (Toronto: Butterworths, 1982), and his more recent essay "Natural Resources and National Politics," in G. Bruce Doern, *The Politics of Economic Policy*, vol. 40, Macdonald Commission Studies (Toronto: UTP, 1986). For a fine account of the state-industry relationship in oil and gas and its link to federalism, see John Richards and Larry Pratt, *Prairie Capitalism: Power and Influence in the New West* (Toronto: McClelland and Stewart, 1979).

[4]On October 16, 1973, OPEC unilaterally raised the price of oil approximately 70%, from $3.00 (U.S.) to $5.11 per barrel. A further increase of over 100% to $11.65 per barrel took effect on January 1, 1974. John M. Blair, *The Control of Oil* (New York: Vintage Books, 1978), 262. For an account of the oil "price explosion" see Blair, chap. 11.

[5]Anthony Sampson quoted in Peter Foster, *The Blue-Eyed Sheiks: The Canadian Oil Establishment* (Toronto: Collins, 1979), 19.

[6]Ed Shaffer, *Canada's Oil and the American Empire* (Edmonton: Hurtig, 1983), Table 9.3, p. 197.

[7]L. Pratt, "Energy: The Roots of National Policy," *Studies in Political Economy*, no. 7 (1982): 38.

[8]This measure, adopted by the Diefenbaker government on the recommendation of the Borden Royal Commission on Energy, was the central feature of what was rather incongruously labelled the National Oil Policy. For discussions of the NOP, see John McDougall, *Fuels and National Policy*, 96-97; Shaffer, *Canada's Oil*, 160-63; and James Laxer, *Oil and Gas: Ottawa, the Provinces and the Petroleum Industry* (Toronto: James Lorimer, 1983), 8-9.

[9]Imperial Oil, *Annual Report*, 1972, p. 8.

[10]In 1974, if Ottawa had permitted the domestic price of oil to rise to the world price of $12.50 per barrel, equalization payments in that year would have risen from $1.4 billion to $3.4 billion. See A. Breton, "The Federal-Provincial Dimensions of the 1973-74 Energy 'Crisis' in Canada" (Toronto: Institute for Policy Analysis, November 1975). If, as under the former scheme, oil revenues were fully included in the calculation of equalization payments, even Ontario would become a "have-not" province eligible to receive federal grants. Instead the equalization formula was amended so that only a portion of additional energy royalties beyond 1973-74 levels would be included. See D.V. Smiley, *Canada In Question: Federalism in the Eighties*, 3rd ed. (Toronto: McGraw-Hill Ryerson, 1980), 169-70. In 1981 legislation was introduced in Parliament that effectively barred Ontario from receiving equalization payments, a measure deplored by the Economic Council of Canada (ECC) Report, *Financing Confederation* (Ottawa, 1982), 22-23.

[11]During the 1970s the difference between the domestic and world price of oil was relatively modest. In 1978 the differential was $3 but by 1980, after the Iranian oil crisis', it had risen to about $20 a barrel. Federal expenditures on oil import substitution, approximately $1.4 billion in 1976-77, would rise to over $3 billion in 1980-81. See G. Bruce Doern, *How Ottawa Spends Your Tax Dollars: Federal Priorities 1981* (Toronto: James Lorimer, 1981), 64, 74.

[12]Some commentators have emphasized the role of the NDP in pressuring the Liberal minority government to adopt a more interventionist energy policy, especially with respect to establishing a national petroleum company. See, for example, Laxer, *Oil and Gas*, 53-54. Pratt's assessment that, while NDP pressure "certainly influenced the timing of the decision," it cannot claim to have "fathered" Petro-Canada, is probably accurate. Certainly, as Pratt points out, the Liberals "did not hesitate to carry through the decision after obtaining a parliamentary majority in the 1974 election." L. Pratt, "Petro-Canada," in Allan Tupper and G. Bruce Doern, eds., *Public Corporations and Public Policy In Canada* (Montreal: Institute for Research on Public Policy, 1981), 109.

[13]The Bertrand report estimated excess profits of the major oil companies operating in Canada at $12.l billion between 1958 and 1973. Robert Bertrand, Director of Investigation and Research, Combines Investigation Act, Department of Consumer and Corporate Affairs, *The State of Competition in the Canadian Petroleum Industry* (Ottawa, 1981). Foster took issue with the report's conclusions. See Peter Foster, *The Sorcerer's Apprentices: Canada's Super-Bureaucrats and the Energy Mess* (Toronto: Collins, 1982), 260-62.

[14]For an account of the oil companies' campaign of misinformation, see Laxer, *Canada's Economic Strategy*, 108 ff. The federal government's response to the information problem was twofold. Aside from establishing Petro-Canada as a "window on the industry," it passed the Petroleum Corporations Monitoring Act of 1977-78, which provided access to detailed information on oil and gas companies' activities in Canada. See Doern, *How Ottawa Spends Your Tax Dollars: 1981*, 72.

[15]There was a remarkable shift of capital to the oil and gas industry during the 1970s. In Canada "the oil industries' 1980 after-tax profits were 29.7 per cent of all non-financial industries' profits, as compared with 15.3 per cent in 1972; at the same time the return on shareholder's equity had risen to 21.4 per cent in 1980 as compared with 14.9 per cent for other non-financial industries, while the return on capital employed was 14 per cent in the oil and gas industry as against 10.7 per cent in other non-financial industries." David Crane, *Controlling Interest: The Canadian Gas and Oil Stakes* (Toronto: McClelland and Stewart, 1982), 14. The large foreign oil companies were poised to accelerate diversification into nonresource sectors, thereby threatening even greater foreign domination of the Canadian economy. See Crane, *Controlling Interest*, chap. 10; and Department of Energy, Mines and Resources (EMR), *The National Energy Program* (hereafter *NEP*) (Ottawa: EMR, 1980), 19, 22. Furthermore, as the value of the assets of the oil and gas industries soared so too did the potential cost of Canadianization. See *NEP*, 19.

[16]Pratt argues that the foreign majors relying on internally generated earnings and generous federal government incentives "were able to pursue a virtually self-contained strategy of expansion in Canada .... The tendency towards furthur concentration in the oil production sector, the high barriers to entry in the downstream refining and marketing sector, the shift to high-cost capital intensive projects, and the exclusionary and monopolistic control of land, technology and markets by the majors — all of these restricted the participation of Canadian capital in the most dynamic and profitable area of the economy." Pratt, "Energy," 47.

[17]*Foreign Ownership and the Structure of Canadian Industry: Report of the Task Force on the Structure of Canadian Industry* (Watkins report) (Ottawa: Privy Council Office, January, 1968); *Eleventh Report of the Standing Committee on External Affairs and National Defence Respecting Canada-U.S. Relations* (Wahn report), Second Session, 28th Parliament (Ottawa: Queen's Printer, 1970); Government of Canada, *Foreign Direct Investment in Canada* (Gray report) (Ottawa: Information Canada, 1972). For critical discussions of Canada's industrial strategy (or lack thereof), see Laxer, *Canada's Economic Strategy*, chap. 5; and Glen Williams, *Not for Export: Toward a Political Economy of Canada's Arrested Industrialization* (Toronto: McClelland and Stewart, 1983), chaps. 7, 8. For a more orthodox diagnosis of Canada's industrial ills, which contests the thesis of "deindustrialization" (cf. Laxer, *Canada's Economic Strategy*, 127-29), consult Economic Council of Canada, *The Bottom Line: Technology, Trade, and Income Growth* (Ottawa, 1983).

[18]Barbara Jenkins, "Reexamining the 'Obsolescing Bargain': A Study of Canada's National Energy Program," *International Organization* 40, no. 1 (Winter 1986): 145. This study tests a prominent theory of delayed state challenges to multinational-company control after investment costs have been sunk, first enunciated by Raymond Vernon in his *Sovereignty at Bay* (New York: Basic, 1971).

[19]Clark, influenced by the party's right wing and concerned about his own credibility, pressed for policies to honour the Tory commitment to privatize Petro-Canada. He was handicapped by stern resistance from many quarters — the majority of his own inner cabinet, bureaucrats in EMR and, the final arbiter, public opinion. The result was a confusing succession of half-hearted proposals that were quickly pounced upon by both opposition parties. See Jeffrey Simpson, *The Discipline of Power* (Toronto: Wiley, 1980), 159-74.

[20]The Conservative and NDP parties, for example, had flirted with the idea of Quebec national self-determination in the late 1960s; now there were charges that Joe Clark was soft on Quebec separatism. Perhaps the charge was fiercest when Clark was seen to be working with known PQ supporters in order to dislodge the federal Liberals' grip on Quebec.

[21]From a speech by Trudeau in Halifax, January 25, 1980. Cited in Foster, *The Sorcerer's Apprentices*, 138.

[22]G. Bruce Doern and Glen Toner, *The Politics of Energy* (Toronto: Methuen, 1985), 61. Chapter 2 in this work is an excellent overview of the anatomy of the NEP decision, showing the complex mix of personalities, concerns and ambitions that played a part in the decision. Although the political nature of the program is clearly recognized, and used effectively to refute Peter Foster's thesis of bureaucratic domination over the policy in *The Sorcerer's Apprentices*, it does not for our purposes adequately describe the policy's links to Trudeau's philosophy of federalism and the use of nationalism to preserve and enhance both the federal state and its threatened system of power relations.

[23]Gillies complained later about the bureaucrats' success at blocking the new government's plans on energy. The paper prepared by the department for the Clark government ended up arguing the merits of a continuing state corporation in the field despite the known position of the Clark government on the matter; that paper produced divisions in the Clark cabinet between right-wing and left-wing elements. For a review of the role of the bureaucrats and of the department's secret policy paper, see Foster, *The Sorcerer's Apprentices*, chaps. 9-12.

[24]So eager was Gallagher to serve the Canadianizing policy goals of the federal program, gobbling up foreign companies while assuming a massive debt load, that the recession forced Dome Petroleum into near bankruptcy. The company only now survives at the sufferance of nearly fifty banks to which it is indebted.

[25]Consultative Task Force on Industrial and Regional Developments from Major Canadian Projects, *Major Canadian Projects, Major Canadian Opportunities* (Blair-Carr report) (Canada, 1981). The report advocated strict Canadian sourcing requirements for future megaproject development. The political appeal of this industrial strategy was that it appeared to ensure benefits to all regions of the country. With the fall in oil prices, however, this scheme collapsed.

[26]*NEP*, 1.

[27]The blended price is the "weighted-average cost" of conventional domestic oil, more costly oil from nonconventional sources, and foreign oil purchased at the world price. Oil imports to eastern Canada continued to be subsidized, but the federal government through the Petroleum Compensation Charge (PCC), a charge levied on domestic oil at the refinery gate, shifted the cost from the Canadian taxpayer to the Canadian consumer. *NEP*, 30. This budgetary "sleight of hand" reduced accounted federal expenses on oil import compensation from $2.7 billion in 1980-81 to only $350 million (est.) in 1981-82. See G. Bruce Doern, "Spending Priorities: The Liberal View," in Doern, *How Ottawa Spends Your Tax Dollars: 1981*, 50.

[28]Under the NEP the price of domestic oil from conventional sources was strictly controlled while imports were purchased at the higher world price. In September 1980, for example, the domestic price was $19.57 per barrel while the world price was $38.85. *NEP*, 4. In 1980-81 and 1981-82 the federal govern-

ment, through the PCC, paid out $3,161,707,159 and $3,438,229,608 to subsidize imported oil. *Globe and Mail*, June 30, 1982.

29*NEP*, 25.

30Though it is true that Ontario paid marginally more than the world price for western oil during the lean years of development in the 1950s and 1960s, the support was not nearly so vast nor the gap between the domestic and international price so wide as it had become by the 1970s. It might also be noted that there was a valuable industrial spinoff in Ontario from the development of the western Canadian petroleum industry. See Laxer, *Oil and Gas*, 9.

31Pratt argues "that the essential purpose of Canadianization is to mobilize the larger pools of Canadian capital and to lower their costs of entry into the oil and gas sector." Pratt, "National Policy," 49. There should be no surprise about this interpretation, since the government had made Canadianization a priority objective of the NEP second only to security of supply. *NEP*, 2.

32In July 1981 Finance Minister MacEachen asked the major Canadian banks to restrict the rate of financing of Canadian takeovers of foreign firms. "By July, 1981, ten Canadian companies had spent $66 billion to acquire subsidiaries of foreign petroleum companies. The resulting strain on the current account balance and on the Canadian dollar impelled the government to slow down the speed at which its own policies were working." Stephen Clarkson, *Canada and the Reagan Challenge* (Toronto: James Lorimer, 1982), 77-78.

33See especially Melville Watkins, "In Defence of the National Energy Program," *Canadian Forum*, June-July 1981; Laxer, *Oil and Gas*; and Pratt, "Energy: The Roots of National Policy." There is a surprising consensus among left commentators that strengthened federal power is the instrument by which Canada is to escape its status as a dependent, semi-industrialized nation. For dissenting opinions, see Cy Gonick, "NEPMEN and Other Nationalists," *Canadian Dimension*, August-September 1981; and Phillip Resnick, "The Maturing of Canadian Capitalism," *Our Generation* 15, no. 3 (1982). Resnick, in particular, attacks the centralist bias toward a bureaucratic, statist model of socialism and the left's insensitivity to long-standing regional disparities.

34M. Watkins, "In Defence of the NEP," 8.

35*NEP*, 108. See Table 3-4 for a review of the revenue share of industry and governments both before and after the NEP.

36Transcript of Peter Lougheed's address to the Province of Alberta in reaction to the federal budget, October 30, 1980.

37Alberta's manoeuvre was designed to press Ottawa financially by increasing the consumption of expensive imported oil and consequently the cost of import subsidies. The ploy misfired, however, when Lalonde, utilizing the new Petroleum Compensation Charge, simply adjusted the price of oil at the refinery gate. The extra burden was dubbed the "Lougheed levy."

38National Energy Program, *Update* (Ottawa: EMR, 1982).

39In September 1981 the expected revenue split was 29% for the federal government, 35% for the province and 46% for the industry. NEP, *Update*, 77.

40Given that the federal share of revenues had risen so substantially, Laxer's assessment that the feds had "capitulated" and Alberta had scored a "huge coup" is most questionable. Laxer, *Oil and Gas*, 152.

41Note, however, that with the new price increases total revenues had increased substantially. Alberta's actual dollars received were then higher than those projected prior to the program even if its relative share was much less.

[42]*NEP*, 15.

[43]Between 1949 and 1974 total petroleum and natural gas revenues collected by Alberta were $4,402,000. In 1975 alone, with higher prices and a new tax regime, royalties were $1,387,000, i.e., 24% of total revenues collected since 1949. Alberta Department of Mines and Minerals, *Annual Report 1975*, 41.

[44]See Alastair R. Lucas and Ian McDougall, "Petroleum and Natural Gas and Constitutional Change," in Stanley M. Beck and Ivan Bernier, ed., *Canada and the New Constitution: The Unfinished Agenda* (Montreal: Institute for Research on Public Policy, 1983), 11-12.

[45]See J. Peter Meekison, Roy J. Romanow and William D. Moull, *Origins and Meaning of Section 92A: The 1982 Constitutional Amendment on Resources* (Montreal: Institute for Research on Public Policy, 1985); and Nigel D. Bankes, Constance D. Hunt and J. Owen Saunders, "Energy and Natural Resources: The Canadian Constitutional Framework," in Mark Krasnick, *Case Studies in the Division of Powers*, vol. 62, Macdonald Commission Studies (Toronto: UTP, 1986), 53-138. However, there has been a considerable political expansion of provincial power over natural resources in this amendment, a theme taken up by Marsha Chandler, "Constitutional Change and Public Policy: The Impact of the Reource Amendment (Section 92A)," *Canadian Journal of Political Science* 19, no.1 (March 1986): 103-26.

[46]M. Watkins, "In Defence of the NEP," 8; Pratt also argues: "The political centralism of the NEP has also been a source of grievance in the West, and not merely with provincial governments and regional business interests.... Such discontent should not be dismissed by the Left as merely the mutterings of a handful of parvenu millionaires." Pratt, "National Policy," 29.

[47]Resnick, "The Maturing of Canadian Capitalism," 15. "To the extent that the NEP pre-empts native land claims and undercuts the bargaining power of groups attempting to link land claims to programs of regional economic development and political autonomy, Liberal energy policy represents a regression — a throwback to an earlier, discredited era of colonialism." Pratt, "National Policy," 29.

[48]*NEP*, 20.

[49]*NEP*, 45.

[50]Ibid. Cf. John McDougall, *Fuels and the National Policy*, 14.

[51]These principal features of the NEP remained intact despite considerable opposition from industry and provincial governments. Compensation for back-in rights and some other concessions were later made to the industry. The Ottawa-Alberta agreement of September 1981 also substantially altered the pricing regime and revenue-sharing among the contesting parties. See NEP, *Update*.

[52]These and other issues are extensively treated in a recent book, J.D. House, *The Challenge of Oil: Newfoundland's Quest for Controlled Development* (St. John's: Institute of Social and Economic Research, Memorial University of Newfoundland, 1985).

[53]At a Liberal fund-raising dinner in St. John's, Trudeau suggested that Peckford was "power-hungry" and "anti-Canadian." Trudeau stated, "If he wants control of the offshore and the fisheries simply for the sake of having more power for himself and his government, then he's acting in his own interest, not yours." *Vancouver Sun*, May 6, 1981.

[54]John McDougall, *Fuels and the National Policy*, chap. 8.

<sup>55</sup>G. Bruce Doern, "The Liberals and the Opposition: Ideas, Priorities, and the Imperatives of Governing Canada in the 1980s," in G. Bruce Doern, ed., *How Ottawa Spends* (Toronto: James Lorimer, 1983), 2-4.

<sup>56</sup>John McDougall, *Fuels and the National Policy*, 11.

<sup>57</sup>Larry Pratt, "Energy, Regionalism, and Canadian Nationalism," *Newfoundland Studies* 1, no. 2 (Fall 1985): 188.

<sup>58</sup>M. Taschereau, Administrator, Canada Oil and Gas Lands Administration, in testimony to the Standing Senate Committee on Energy and Natural Resources, May 15, 1984, cited in Ibid., 189.

<sup>59</sup>Ibid., 191. The PIP system was, also almost from the beginning, so open-ended it was an administrator's nightmare: there was considerable misuse of the program by companies to backstop costly capital investment ventures and by deliberate fraud; the costs moreover had to be contained early on by requiring ministerial approval on the drilling of wells exceeding $50 million.

<sup>60</sup>In his study of Canadian-American relations in the Reagan era, Clarkson lists the concessions made by the Canadian government. "In May 1981 [Ottawa] offered compensation for the back-in and amended the industrial benefits legislation to ensure competitive conditions for foreign suppliers. In July it asked the banks to help slow down the rate of takeovers. In February 1982 it dropped plans to give Canadian controlled firms preference in gas exports. In April Marc Lalonde announced he would not proceed to give Canadian oil companies the power to force out their foreign shareholders." Clarkson, *Canada and the Reagan Challenge*, 80. A detailed treatment of industry response to the NEP is provided in chapter 6 and of provincial responses in chapter 7 of Doern and Toner, *The Politics of Energy*.

<sup>61</sup>Barbara Jenkins, "Re-examining the Obsolescing Bargain," 155.

<sup>62</sup>"Petro-Canada's marketing system in Western Canada showed a volume gain of 12% in 1980 following replacement of the old Pacific signs with those carrying the new Petro-Canada logo, compared with an average of about 4% for the industry." Pratt, "Petro-Canada," 142.

<sup>63</sup>This tangible evidence of Ontario support for NEP goals is discussed in Doern and Toner, *The Politics of Energy*, 279-81.

<sup>64</sup>Pratt, "Energy, Regionalism, and Canadian Nationalism," 183.

<sup>65</sup>The Liberals received perhaps the finest accolades for their strategy when NDP theorists like James Laxer stood ready to salute Trudeau as a latter-day John A. Macdonald. Cy Gonick was quick to pour acid on such infatuations with Liberal statecraft, but the left's fascination with the new Liberal nationalism was widespread nonetheless. Gonick, "NEPMEN and Other Nationalists." It was perhaps because of these dangers that Phillip Resnick attempted to draw a distinction between state-building ("Bonapartism") and the left's larger commitment to democracy and workers' rights. Resnick, "The Maturing of Canadian Capitalism."

<sup>66</sup>If the Canadian left wish to build support outside their traditional power base, established labour in central Canada, then they must rethink their position on federalism. Strengthened federal power is not an unqualified blessing and will be resisted in the regions. This will be especially true if reform of national political institutions like the Senate proves to be relatively timid. A strong federal redistributive power must be dissociated from political centralization if national distributive justice is to be reconciled with regional political autonomy.

<sup>67</sup>It was well known in Liberal circles that party strategists like Jim Coutts felt

that the party must move left and occupy more of the nationalist and progressive planks of the NDP program. See Christina McCall-Newman, *Grits: An Intimate Portrait of the Liberal Party* (Toronto: Macmillan, 1982), chap. 3.

[68]Peckford, who called an early election on the offshore issue, won a resounding victory, taking forty-four of the fifty-two seats in the provincial legislature. Lalonde charged Peckford and the Tories with resorting to "outright lies" in the campaign and said the election results changed nothing as far as Ottawa was concerned. "Our principles remain the same," he said, "We have no new proposals to put forward." *Canadian News Facts*, 1982, 2678.

[69]See G. Campbell Watkins, "A Hockey Stick, Boomerang or Downhill Schuss — What Future Pattern for World Oil Prices?" Mimeo. (DataMetrics Limited, Calgary, n.d.), for a thorough treatment of these issues and their effect on oil prices.

[70]In April 1982 Alberta announced a $5.4-billion program of lower royalties and other tax benefits to aid the oil and gas industry. Ottawa followed with a $2-billion "relief package" unveiled in June. The federal changes included "temporary relief through a reduction in the effective rate of the Petroleum and Gas Revenue Tax and a holiday on the incremental oil revenue tax; longer term relief from the PGRT, especially for producers with $2 m. or less in production income; and higher prices (to a maximum of 75 per cent of the world price) for oil found between Dec. 31, 1973 and Dec. 31, 1980." Jennifer Lewington and Jeff Sallot, *Globe and Mail*, June 2, 1982.

[71]Pratt, "Energy, Regionalism, and Canadian Nationalism," 179. The work by Helliwell et al. is "The National Energy Program Meets Falling World Oil Prices," *Canadian Public Policy* 9, no. 3 (September 1983): 284-96.

[72]The severity of the fiscal crisis was evident when, from November 1981 to June 1982, the projected federal deficit rose from $10.5 billion to $19.6 billion. In June 1982 Finance Minister MacEachen estimated forgone federal revenue due to falling international oil prices at $1.5 billion. Hon. Allan J. MacEachen, *The Budget, 1982* (Ottawa, 1982).

[73]Barbara Jenkins, "Re-examining the Obsolescing Bargain," 160.

[74]At that time, Peckford was prepared to accept that the provincial share of resource revenues should become less than that of Canada after ceasing to be a have-not province. See Bruce G. Pollard, "Newfoundland: Resisting Dependency," in Peter M. Leslie, ed., *Canada: The State of the Federation*, 97-98.

[75]Peckford Address, Canada-Newfoundland Offshore Agreement, St. John's, February 11, 1985, pp. 2-3.

[76]House, *The Challenge of Oil*, 304.

[77]Statement of the Hon. Pat Carney, Minister of Energy, Mines and Resources, on the Atlantic Accord, February 11, 1985.

[78]This was the language of Roy Romanow, former attorney general of Saskatchewan, in an overview of natural resource management for the Second Banff Conference in 1985. See Roy Romanow, "Federalism and Resource Management," in J. Owen Saunders, *Managing Natural Resources in a Federal State* (Toronto: Carswell, 1986), 10.

[79]John D. Whyte, "Issues in Canadian Federal-Provincial Co-operation," in Saunders, *Managing Natural Resources*, 335.

[80]Jean-Paul Lacasse, "Oil and Gas Revenue Sharing: Beyond Legal Foundations and Constraints," in Saunders, *Managing Natural Resources*, esp. 81-83. The

same point is made by Robin Boadway in his essay in this collection, "Economic Implications of Revenue-Sharing Alternatives," 103-20.

[81]See John McDougall's proposal for such a program of national unity in "National Resources and National Politics: A Look at Three Canadian Resource Industries," in Doern, *The Politics of Economic Policy*, 163-219.

[82]Peter A. Cumming, "Equitable Fiscal Federalism: The Problem in Respect of Resources Revenue Sharing," in Mark Krasnick, *Fiscal Federalism*, vol. 65, Macdonald Commission Studies (Toronto: UTP, 1986), 72.

[83]Ibid., 73.

[84]The federal take through the corporation tax would be considerably reduced, especially if Alberta continued to apply high royalty rates to the industry. That had been a concern of the federal government for many years and helped explain their final resort to the PGRT. See Trudeau's complaint to Premier Lougheed about this matter in 1974 in David G. Wood, *The Lougheed Legacy* (Toronto: Key Porter Books, 1985), 153. It was therefore logical that Energy Minister Carney would have demanded provincial reductions in royalty rates in return for the gradual removal of the PGRT.

[85]Mary E. MacGregor, "Macroeconomic Impacts of the Western Accord," *Western Economic Review* 4, no. 3 (Fall 1985): 98.

[86]This was of special concern to Husky Oil with its dramatic new find in the Hibernia field in November 1985.

[87]See, for example, *The Politics of Energy* and their essay in Allan M. Maslove, *How Ottawa Spends, 1985: Sharing the Pie* (Toronto: Methuen, 1985).

[88]Larry R. Pratt, "Natural Gas: Canadian Adaptation to North American Market Instability," *Western Economic Review* 4, no. 3 (Fall 1985).

[89]In fact, not too much should be read into the Reichmann–Petro Canada deal and Conservative Canadianization policy. As chapter 4 will show, the new Conservative direction was toward the encouragement of foreign ownership in the Canadian economy.

[90]*Globe and Mail*, October 31, 1985, B1.

[91]See Doern and Toner, *The Politics of Energy*, and "Energy Budgets and Oil and Gas Interests," in Maslove, *How Ottawa Spends, 1985*.

[92]That policy retreat is, in the judgment of John Whyte, unlikely to stick, especially as demands for federal economic regulatory activity continue to mount. See Whyte, "Issues in Canadian Federal-Provincial Cooperation," 332.

[93]Doern and Toner, "Energy Budgets and Oil and Gas Interests," 85.

[94]President of Trilogy Resource Co., a junior company, cited in Glen Toner, "Stardust: The Tory Energy Program," in Michael J. Prince, ed., *How Ottawa Spends, 1986-87: Tracking the Tories* (Toronto: Methuen: 1986).

[95]Romanow, "Federalism and Resource Management," 8.

[96]See Larry Pratt, "Energy Policy," in Canadian Union of Public Employees, *The Facts: Rebutting the Macdonald Commission* (CUPE, March-April, 1986), 63-67.

[97]See G. Campbell Watkins, "A Hockey Stick."

## Chapter IV: Economic Policy

[1]See Doern and Toner, *The Politics of Energy*, 2.

[2]See, for example, Jeanne Kirk Laux, "Global Interdependence and State Inter-

vention," in Brian W. Tomlin, ed., *Canadian Foreign Policy: Analysis and Trends* (Toronto: Methuen, 1978).

[3]L. Rangarajan, "The Politics of International Trade," in Susan Strange, ed., *Paths to International Political Economy* (London: George, Allen, and Unwin, 1984), 130.

[4]Canada had a trade deficit in manufactured goods with every major trading partner; it imported a higher proportion of its imports in manufactured form than other major OECD countries; and the proportion of its work force employed in manufacturing had been declining since 1960. See Glen Williams, *Not for Export: Toward a Political Economy of Canada's Arrested Industrialization* (Toronto: McClelland and Stewart, 1983), 86 ff.

[5]See Michael Bliss, *The Evolution of Industrial Policies in Canada: An Historical Survey*, Discussion paper no. 218 (Ottawa: Economic Council of Canada, 1982).

[6]The best and earliest outline of the two ideological options competing for Canada's attention as industrial policy models — technological sovereignty and free trade — can be found in Richard D. French, *How Ottawa Decides: Planning and Industrial Policy-Making 1968-1980* (Toronto: James Lorimer, 1980), 96-104. For a comprehensive and fairly faithful outline of the free trade argument, see the Macdonald Commission, *Report of the Royal Commission on the Economic Union and Development Prospects for Canada* (Toronto: UTP, 1985), vol. 2, part 3, chap. 9. The supporting research background papers for the commission are also a valuable introduction to this subject. See in particular D.G. McFetridge, *Economics of Industrial Policy and Strategy*, vol. 5, and G.B. Doern, *The Politics of Economic Policy*, vol. 40, Macdonald Commission Studies (Toronto: UTP, 1985).

[7]See, for example, Jeffrey Simpson's analysis of the Mulroney government's adoption of early liberal doctrine in the *Globe and Mail*, September 6, 1985.

[8]It is doubtful that any previous Canadian government had been particularly hostile to foreign ownership, although some measures had been introduced to respond to pressures in that direction over the previous decade. As Michael Bliss has argued, belief in the beneficent role of foreign capital in the Canadian economy had been a truism for every Canadian government at least prior to the 1970s.

[9]See, for example, Christopher Armstrong, *The Politics of Federalism* (Toronto: UTP, 1981), 85-112. For an excellent and more contemporary account of these interactions over the issue of federal tax reform and the mining industry in the early 1970s, see M.W. Bucovetsky, "The Mining Industry and the Great Tax Reform Debate," in A. Paul Pross, *Pressure Group Behaviour in Canadian Politics* (Toronto: McGraw-Hill Ryerson, 1975), 87-114.

[10]See, for example, J.H. Dales, *The Protective Tariff in Canada's Development* (Toronto: UTP, 1966); H.V. Nelles, "The Ties that Bind: Berton's CPR," *Canadian Forum*, November-December 1970; P.J. George, "Rates of Return in Railway Investment and Implications for Government Subsidization of the CPR: Some Preliminary Results," *Canadian Journal of Economics* 1, no. 4, (November 1968); and Ken H. Norrie, "The National Policy and the Rate of Prairie Settlement: A Review," *Journal of Canadian Studies* 14, no. 3 (Fall 1979).

[11]These relationships, particularly as they apply to Anglo-American patterns, are given a brief but early treatment in Harold Innis, "Economic Trends in Canadian-American Relations," in Harold Innis, *Essays in Canadian Economic History*, ed. Mary Q. Innis (Toronto: UTP, 1956), 233-41.

[12]See, for example, Cairns, "The Other Crisis of Canadian Federalism," *Canadian Public Administration* 22 (1979).

[13]Ibid., 176, 178.

[14]Ibid., 184.

[15]Douglas Brown and Julia Eastman, "The Limits of Consultation: A Debate among Ottawa, the Provinces, and the Private Sector on Industrial Strategy," Queen's discussion paper, 1981, 15-28, 79-86, 101-4.

[16]See Anthony Careless, *Initiative and Response: The Adaptation of Canadian Federalism to Regional Economic Development* (Montreal: McGill-Queen's University Press, 1977), 165.

[17]See Williams, *Not for Export*, 103-28. Paul Phillips in his "The National Policy Revisited," *Journal of Canadian Studies* 14 (1979/80): 3-13, advances an interesting argument in defence of the original National Policy; he is considerably harder on Liberal governments in the twentieth century for their abandonment of national policy in favour of a continentalist economic program heavily reliant on American multinationals than he is on the Macdonald policy.

[18]"Overall foreign control of non-financial firms amounted to 36 percent of total capital employed in 1970, 26 percent in 1981. In all major industrial sectors, the proportion of assets controlled abroad has declined since 1970....In 1970, Canadian direct investment in the USA amounted to 15 percent of U.S. investment here, but this proportion doubled by 1979. Since 1975 Canadian direct investment in the USA has increased five-fold." See R.A Young, "Last, Worst Deal," *Policy Options* 6, no. 6 (July 1985). The most extensive and useful study of these patterns can be found in Jorge Niosi, *Canadian Multinationals* (Toronto: Between the Lines Press, 1985). He found that "86 per cent of Canadian investment in foreign countries was accounted for by sixty-five companies, each with more than $25 million invested outside Canada (65 per cent of the total was accounted for by only sixteen companies, each with more than $100 million invested in foreign countries.)" Moreover, apart from impressive size, most Canadian multinationals are "leaders in highly concentrated domestic oligopolies." Niosi, 170.

[19]See Susan Strange, "The Management of Surplus Capacity: Or How Does Theory Stand up to Protectionism 1970 Style?" *International Organization* 33, no. 3 (Summer 1979).

[20]See Garth Stevenson, *Unfulfilled Union* (Toronto: Gage, 1982), 104-26; and A.E. Safarian, *Canadian Federalism and Economic Integration*, 1-46.

[21]See, for example, Abraham Rotstein, *Rebuilding from Within* (Toronto: James Lorimer, 1984); H.G. Thorburn, *Planning and the Economy* (Toronto: James Lorimer, 1984); Michael Jenkin, *The Challenge of Diversity*, vol. 50 (Science Council of Canada, 1983); and many other publications by the Science Council and by the ECC.

[22]See Jean Chrétien, *Securing the Canadian Economic Union in the Constitution* (Ottawa: Supply and Services, 1980).

[23]See Pierre Eliott Trudeau's New Year's address on the eve of the application of wage and price controls.

[24]See Trebilcock et al., *Federalism and the Canadian Economic Union*. The same study argued that the bulk of the distortions were induced by the federal government. The Macdonald Commission also concluded, after careful review of the evidence, that the economic effects of these measures were not unduly

worrisome at this time: "despite recent expressions of concern that the econo-my is becoming increasingly balkanized and fragmented, the Canadian eco-nomic union generally functions effectively. Goods, capital, services and people move relatively freely within the Canadian common market," vol. 3, 135.

[25]Macdonald Commission, *Report*, vol. 3, 109-23.

[26]See French, *How Ottawa Decides*, esp. 96-132.

[27]See, for example, John N.H. Britton and James M. Gilmour, *The Weakest Link: A Technological Perspective on Canadian Industry Underdevelopment* (Science Council, October 1978).

[28]See Jenkin, *The Challenge of Diversity*, 169-81.

[29]Clarkson, *Canada and the Reagan Challenge*, 2nd ed., 18-21.

[30]S. Carr and S.R. Blair, Co-Chairmen, *Major Projects Task Force*, June 23, 1981 (Re-port from Commission of FMC of November 1978).

[31]Savoie notes that although "impressive in absolute terms, this figure represents only 10 per cent of total projected capital investments in Canada in the 1980s and 1990s." Donald J. Savoie, *Regional Economic Development: Canada's Search for Solutions* (Toronto: UTP, 1986), 127.

[32]See Donald Savoie for a skilful treatment of GDAs as a less combative form of federal-provincial economic development in *Federal-Provincial Collaboration: The Canada New Brunswick General Agreement* (Montreal: Institute of Public Adminis-tration of Canada, 1981), esp. 151-67. See also the complementary treatment of the GDA approach by J. Stefan Dupré, "Reflections on the Workability of Exec-utive Federalism," in Richard Simeon, *Intergovernmental Relations* (Toronto: UTP, 1985), esp. 11-15.

[33]Savoie, *Regional Economic Development*, 71.

[34]Ibid., 73. See also G. Bruce Doern, "The Tories, Free Trade, and Industrial Ad-justment," Table 2:1, in Prince, *How Ottawa Spends, 1986-87*, 81. DREE estimates for 1983-84 fell, for example, below their 1981-82 levels. See *The National Fi-nances, 1982-1983*.

[35]See, for example, Kenneth McRoberts, "Unilateralism, Bilateralism, and Multilateralism: Approaches to Canadian Federalism," in Simeon, *Intergovern-mental Relations*, 102.

[36]The Caisse guideline contrasts sharply with the Alberta Heritage Savings Trust Fund rule which restricts ownership in a single company to a 5% voting ceiling. See K.J. Huffman, J.W. Langford and W.A.W. Neilson, "Public Enterprise and Federalism in Canada," in Simeon, *Intergovernmental Relations*, 140.

[37]Alan Tupper, *Bill S-31 and Federalism of State Capitalism* (Kingston: Queen's Uni-versity, Institute of Intergovernmental Relations, 1983), 34.

[38]K.J. Huffman et al., "Public Enterprise and Federalism," 144.

[39]McRoberts, "Unilateralism," 112.

[40]Ibid., 104.

[41]Dupré, "Reflections," 24.

[42]Normally, as the polling work by LeDuc and Murray indicates, Canadians are timorous ationalists, but they did move from a majority view against Canadianization of energy in the fall of 1980 prior to the NEP to a massive 70% support for such a program in the winter election period of 1980. By 1983, sup-port for this "motherhood" goal had dropped to 55%. There is also evidence of dropping support for nationalist measures on foreign ownership in general. See Richard Johnston, *Public Opinion and Public Policy in Canada*, vol. 35, Mac-

donald Commission Studies (Toronto: UTP, 1986), 172-76. See also L. LeDuc and J.A. Murray, "A Resurgence of Canadian Nationalism: Attitudes and Policy in the 1980's," in A. Kornberg and H.D. Clarke, eds., *Political Support in Canada: The Crisis Years* (Durham, N.C: Duke University Press, 1983).

[43]This excludes the constitutional conference on aboriginal rights also held within six months of the government's assumption of office.

[44]"Mulroney targets francophobia, Quebec on anniversary," *Globe and Mail,* September 6, 1985, 5.

[45]For an interesting treatment of the francophone elites and the state, see Alain G. Gagnon, ed., *Quebec: State and Society* (Toronto: Methuen, 1984). See also Michael D. Behiels, *Prelude to Quebec's Quiet Revolution: Liberalism Versus Neo-Nationalism, 1945-1960* (Kingston/Montreal: McGill-Queen's University Press, 1985), 110-20.

[46]See Jeffrey Simpson, *The Discipline of Power* (Toronto: Macmillan, 1984).

[47]The actual figure was certainly no more than $155 million but could well be less when all of the details of the complex deal were factored in. This decision indicated that the government was moving away from any attempt to preserve the long-standing struggle for a Canadian presence in the aerospace industry, in favour of promises of jobs and a world product mandate for the new Canadian branch plant of Boeing Corp. This policy venture indicated the kind of economic logic behind the Conservative plans for recovery under free trade and increased foreign investment.

[48]See *Financial Post,* November 10, 1984, 8-9.

[49]See P. Foster, "Strong Politics," for an excellent review of the Trudeau government's later attempt to bring the board of the CDC to heel and to make it serve its intended public policy mandate. The same article explains the later creation of the CDIC.

[50]See Allan M. Maslove, "The Public Pursuit of Private Interests," in Allan M. Maslove, ed., *How Ottawa Spends: 1985: Sharing the Pie* (Toronto: Methuen, 1985), 1-29; and Michael J. Prince, "The Mulroney Agenda: A Right Turn for Ottawa?" in Prince, *How Ottawa Spends, 1986-87,* esp. 23-24.

[51]*Regional Economic Development: Intergovernmental Position Paper,* June 1985. This memorandum arose because of the willingness of the federal government to put regional economic development on the agenda of the First Ministers' Conference in February of 1985, and to set the respective ministers to work on the preparation of a working document to guide all governments. In practical terms, the end effect was to continue the ERDA agreements with the provinces, and to make them vehicles for federal-provincial cooperation.

[52]See Donald J. Savoie, "Barometer Falling," *Policy Options* 7, no. 3 (April 1986): 28-29.

[53]See Table 1.4 in Maslove, "Public Pursuit of Private Interests," 24.

[54]See Prince, *How Ottawa Spends, 1986-87,* 53. It may, of course, be too easy to use a simple expenditure indicator as a measure of government commitment in this area. Indeed up-front expenditures may not really be part of an effective solution to such policy. The government would doubtless argue that although cuts were being made in this envelope, their regionally sensitive national policies, especially in energy, were, in all but name, sizeable contributions to regional development policy. While that may seem a plausible argument, it is likely no substitute for direct federal financial support for targeted programs in many have-not provinces.

[55]Ibid., 43.

[56]See Clarkson, *Canada and the Reagan Challenge*, 2nd ed., 83-113.

[57]Gorse Howarth, *Financial Post*, February 9, 1985.

[58]The expression comes from a confidential document of Allan Gotlieb, Canada's ambassador to the United States, as quoted in the *Globe and Mail*, November 4, 1985.

[59]See Stephen Clarkson, "Why Bother to Debate Canada's Foreign Policy?" *Globe and Mail*, May 24, 1985.

[60]See French, *How Ottawa Decides*, 96.

[61]See Craven and Traves, "National Policy, 1872-1933," 14-38.

[62]J.L. Granatstein, "Free Trade between Canada and the United States: The Issue That Will Not Go Away," in Denis Stairs and Gilbert R. Winham, *The Politics of Canada's Economic Relationship with the United States*, vol. 29, Macdonald Commission Studies (Toronto: UTP, 1985), 11.

[63]John A. Macdonald, House of Commons, March 7, 1878, 862, cited in Ibid., 17.

[64]Granatstein, "Free Trade between Canada and the United States," 36-43.

[65]See, for example, Gary Clyde Hufbauer and Andrew James Samet, "United States Response to Canadian Initiatives for Sectoral Trade Liberalization," in Stairs and Winham, *The Politics of Canada's Economic Relationship*, 179-205.

[66]See Glen Williams, "Symbols, Economic Logic, and Political Conflict in the Canada-U.S.A. Free Trade Negotiations," *Queen's Quarterly*, Winter 1985.

[67]Since the BCNI is so heavily dominated by the leaders of foreign multinationals, it is questionable how reliable an indicator it is of an "indigenous" business perspective on this matter.

[68]R.A. Young, "Last, Worst Deal," *Policy Options* 6, no. 6 (July 1985).

[69]See Bruce G. Pollard, "The Year in Review: 1983," chap. 6.

[70]See "Assessment of Direct Employment Effects of Freer Trade for Ontario's Manufacturing Industries" (Toronto: Ministry of Industry, Trade and Technology, November, 1985); "Canada-U.S. Free Trade: U.S. Perspectives and Approaches," Edward Nef Associates (Toronto: Ontario Ministry of Industry, Trade and Technology, September 1985); and "Assessment of Likely Impact of a U.S.-Canadian Free Trade Agreement upon the Behaviour of U.S. Industrial Subsidiaries in Canada (Ontario)," Dr. Jack Baranson, Illinois Institute of Technology, for the Ontario Ministry of Industry, Trade and Technology, September 1985.

[71]John Crispo, *Globe and Mail*, December 17, 1985.

[72]For a treatment on the expansive possibilities of case law around trade and commerce, see H. Scott Fairley, "Constitutional Aspects of External Trade Policy," in Mark Krasnick, *Case Studies in the Division of Powers*, vol. 62, Macdonald Commission Studies (Toronto: UTP, 1986), esp. 7-18.

[73]*Globe and Mail*, November 30, 1985.

[74]Ibid., November 8, 1985.

[75]Macdonald Commission, *Report*, vol. 1, 357.

[76]Abraham Rotstein, "Hidden Costs of Free Trade," *International Perspectives*, July-August 1985, 5.

[77]R.J. Wonnacott, *Canada's Trade Options*, prepared for the ECC (Ottawa: Information Canada, 1975), 171. The reverse argument on behalf of the peripheries can be found in H.E. English, " 'National Policy' and Canadian Trade," in *Inter-*

*national Perspectives,* March-April 1984.

[78]Charles Pentland, "North American Integration and the Canadian Political System," in Stairs and Winham, *The Politics of Canada's Economic Relationships,* 118.

[79]Richard Simeon made this point in a stimulating address on "Federalism and Free Trade" at the University of Toronto, January 13, 1986. I am grateful to him for raising so many thought-provoking issues that have strengthened my own work.

[80]R.A. Young, "Last, Worst Deal."

[81]Rotstein, "The Hidden Costs of Free Trade," 6.

[82]The sensitive sectors to be defended by a required review of foreign takeovers lie in business activity "related to Canada's cultural heritage or national identity"(section 15). This section would certainly cover industries related to publishing, film, video and audio production. If an investment in this area is not considered to be a "net benefit" to Canada, it would be blocked, or if implemented earlier, divestiture would be required (section 24).

[83]Giles Gherson, *Financial Post,* October 12, 1985.

[84]This issue of the compatibility of a free trade deal between Canada and the United States and these countries' simultaneous pursuit of multilateral trade under GATT is a vexing and difficult question. It was fudged by the Macdonald Commission in its apparent attempt to straddle both sides of the fence, but it is probably fair to say that the commission came down more firmly on the side of a bilateral deal with "guaranteed access" to a world-class trading bloc than it did for the multilateral vision. In an interesting commentary, Wayne Gooding accused the commission of using a "blatant piece of double-think" in this respect. *Financial Post,* September 14, 1985. Japan and Europe certainly appeared to be watching the experiment with concern and interest.

[85]Hyman Solomon, *Financial Post,* February 15 and January 25, 1986.

[86]William Coleman in his work for the Macdonald Commission argued for stronger business involvement in policymaking and even saw this input as a potential enhancement of democracy. Needless to say, that line of argument is not compatible with my own, particularly in the light of his admission that business interest groups poorly represent the regions of Canada. See William D. Coleman, "Canadian Business and the State," in Keith Banting, *The State and Economic Interests,* vol. 32, Macdonald Commission Studies (Toronto: UTP, 1986), 267-68, 282.

[87]*Globe and Mail,* September 27, 1985.

[88]On that score, the Macdonald Commission was as sanguine as ever — it declared breezily that hardly any measure could have as happy and healing an effect on regional disparities and discontents as free trade.

[89]Doern, "The Tories, Free Trade, and Industrial Adjustment Policy."

[90]Macdonald Commission, *Report,* vol. 3, 425.

[91]Ibid., vol. 1, 71.

[92]Michael Jenkin, *The Challenge of Diversity.*

[93]Ibid., 180.

## Chapter V: Fiscal Federalism and Social Policy

[1]The expression belongs to former finance minister Donald Macdonald, more recently chairman of the Royal Commission on the Economic Union and Development Prospects for Canada, cited in David B. Perry, "The Federal-Provincial Fiscal Arrangements Introduced in 1977," *Canadian Tax Journal* 25, no. 4 (July-August 1977): 429.

[2]See Thomas Courchene, "The Fiscal Arrangements: Focus on 1987," in an excellent comprehensive review of fiscal federalism and power in Canada in a recent publication by the Ontario Economic Council: Thomas Courchene et al., eds., *Ottawa and the Provinces*, vol. 1 (Toronto: OEC, 1985), 4.

[3]See A. Milton Moore and J. Harvey Perry, *The Financing of Canadian Federation: The First Hundred Years* (Toronto: Canadian Tax Foundation, 1966), 1. Only Ontario with its developed municipal property and income taxes had advanced into this taxing field.

[4]Ibid., 2.

[5]Ibid., 119.

[6]J.C. Strick, *Canadian Public Finance* (Toronto: Holt, Rinehart and Winston, 1973), 97.

[7]See Robin Boadway, "Federal-Provincial Transfers in Canada: A Critical Review of the Existing Arrangements," in Mark Krasnick, *Fiscal Federalism*, vol. 65, Macdonald Commission Studies (Toronto: UTP, 1986), 7; and Robin W. Boadway, *Intergovernmental Transfers in Canada* (Toronto: Canadian Tax Foundation, 1980).

[8]It is worth noting that the standard "principled" rationales for federal involvement in these fields can in no way really account for the changing patterns of intergovernmental financial arrangements over recent decades. These can only be adequately explained by reference to larger political forces. See Allan M. Maslove and Bohodar Rubashewsky, "Co-operation and Confrontation: The Challenges of Fiscal Federalism," in Prince, *How Ottawa Spends, 1986-87*, 114-16.

[9]Thomas Courchene has proposed in fact a blend of these two approaches in his two-tier scheme of equalization for Canada. See Thomas Courchene and Glen Copplestone, "Alternative Equalization Programs: Two-Tier Systems," in Richard Bird, ed., *Fiscal Dimensions of Canadian Federalism* (Toronto: Canadian Tax Foundation, 1980).

[10]See, for example, Thomas Courchene, *Equalization Payments: Past, Present and Future* (Toronto: Ontario Economic Council, 1984); and Robin Boadway and Frank Flatters, *Equalization in a Federal State: An Economic Analysis*, ECC (Ottawa: Minister of Supply and Services, 1982).

[11]No one has spelled out the centralizing political implications of this federal construction of the welfare state better than Keith G. Banting in his *The Welfare State and Canadian Federalism* (Montreal: McGill-Queen's University Press, 1982). See also Keith Banting, "Federalism and Income Security: Themes and Variations," in Courchene et al., *Ottawa and the Provinces*, 253-76.

[12]See Claude Morin, *Quebec versus Ottawa: The Struggle for Self-Government 1960-72* (Toronto: UTP, 1976).

[13]*Attorney-General for Canada* v. *Attorney-General for Ontario* (Unemployment Insurance Reference) [1937] A.C. 355.

[14]See E.A. Driedger, "The Spending Power," *Queen's Law Journal* 7 (1981): 124-

34; and J.E. Magnet's alternative views in *Constitutional Law of Canada*, vol. 1 (Toronto: Carswell, 1985), 408-11.

[15]See Peter Hogg, *Constitutional Law of Canada*, 2nd ed. (Toronto: Carswell, 1985), 126.

[16]See Breau Committee, *Fiscal Federalism in Canada*, 38.

[17]The government had already placed a 15% ceiling on its increased contributions to postsecondary education earlier in 1972, and another on medicare costs in 1975.

[18]See, for example, the alternative views for contentious fiscal federalism in Courchene, "The Fiscal Arrangements," 3. Not many observers noticed, however, that the federal intention to cut back the transfer payments to the provinces appeared as early as 1980, well prior to the recession and the ballooning federal deficit.

[19]Courchene recognizes that the movement over the Health Act cannot easily be squared with the politics of restraint. Ibid. Nor can the deliberate linkage of recent fiscal federalism with decentralization of power, the breakdown of the "fiscal relations model" of negotiation or the policy thrust in higher education be explained in that manner. For an analysis of the impact of this extension of the "counter-offensive against provincialism beyond the constitutional review and into the fiscal domain," see Stefan J. Dupré, "Reflections on the Workability of Executive Federalism," in Simeon, *Intergovernmental Relations*, 1-32.

[20]For a review of the link between federalism and predominant social paradigms, see Simeon, "Federalism in the 1980's," in Courchene et al., *Ottawa and the Provinces*, vol. 1, 29-43.

[21]See R.M. Burns, *The Acceptable Mean: The Tax Rental Agreements, 1941-1962* (Toronto: Canadian Tax Foundation, 1980).

[22]See J. Stefan Dupré, "Reflections on the Fiscal and Economic Aspects of Government by Conference," *Canadian Public Administration* 23 (Spring 1980): 55.

[23]This provision underlined the obvious difficulties stemming from the close interlocking of federal tax policy and provincial revenues under the tax-sharing arrangements. This issue later became a highly contentious element in the politics around EPF in the 1980s. For an exchange of views on that particular issue, particularly as it affects higher education, see the articles by Malcolm Taylor and David Milne in the September and October 1985 issues of *Policy Options*.

[24]ECC, *Financing Confederation* (1982), 62.

[25]Canada, Health Services Review, *Canada's National-Provincial Health Program for the 1980s* (Ottawa, Department of Health and Welfare, 1980). Special commissioner: Emmett M. Hall.

[26]J. Stefan Dupré, "Reflections on the Workability of Executive Federalism," 18. The committee was established on February 5, 1981.

[27]See Richard Simeon, "Fiscal Federalism in Canada: A Review Essay," in *Canadian Tax Journal* 30, no. 1 (January-February 1982), for an excellent review of the Breau Committee and fiscal federalism.

[28]For a review of public participation during the constitutional process, see Milne, *The New Canadian Constitution* (Toronto: James Lorimer, 1982).

[29]Rod Dobell, "The Consultation Process: Prospects for 1987 and Beyond," in Courchene et al., *Ottawa and the Provinces*, vol. 2, 153-54.

[30]The equalization formula was first to be altered by using Ontario as a standard for measuring a national average for purposes of equalization, a decision that would immediately remove the need to equalize oil and gas revenues in the formula and the necessity for the earlier "Ontario override" clause excluding it from equalization grants. The government later accepted the provinces' proposal for a five-province average as the standard.

[31]I am indebted to Bruce Pollard for his fine work, *The Year in Review: 1983*, Institute of Intergovernmental Relations (Kingston: Queen's University, 1984), for much of this material.

[32]Rodney Dobell, "The Consultation Process," 148. Prophetically, that linkage in fact appeared later in the Johnson report on postsecondary education. See A.W. Johnson, "Giving Greater Point and Purpose to the Federal Financing of Post-Secondary Education and Research in Canada," Report to the Secretary of State, February 15, 1985.

[33]Dobell, "The Consultation Process," 148.

[34]See David Falcone and Richard J. Van Loon, "Public Attitudes and Intergovernmental Shifts in Responsibility of Health Programs: Paying the Piper without Calling the Tune?" in A. Kornberg and Harold D. Clarke, eds., *Political Support in Canada: The Crisis Years*, 225-51. See also Morris Barer, Robert G. Evans and Greg Stoddart, *Controlling Health Care Costs by Direct Charges to Patients: Snare or Delusion?* (Toronto: Ontario Economic Council, occasional paper 10, 1979).

[35]This and much other information related to this issue has been generously provided by Raisa Deber and Steve Heiber of the University of Toronto, who are currently working on a book-length manuscript on the Canada Health Act. For an excellent introduction to some of the politics around the issue, see Steve Heiber and Raisa Deber, "Banning Extra-Billing in Canada: Just What the Doctor Didn't Order," an essay submitted to *Canadian Public Policy*, July 1986.

[36]Canada Health Act, section 15 (1).

[37]See Heiber and Deber, "Banning Extra-Billing in Canada."

[38]See, for example, Greg L. Stoddart, "Rationalizing the Health-Care System," 3-39, and William G. Watson, "Health Care and Federalism," 40-57, in Courchene et al., *Ottawa and the Provinces*, vol. 2. See also Raisa B. Deber and Eugene Vayda, "The Environment of Health Policy Implementation: The Ontario, Canada Example," in G. Knox, ed., *Investigative Methods in Public Health*, vol. 3 of *Oxford Textbook of Public Health* (Oxford: Oxford University Press, 1985).

[39]See, for example, Thomas Courchene, Stefan Dupré, Rodney Dobell and the health specialists in Courchene et al., *Ottawa and the Provinces*. Dupré claims that the bill, although responsive to interest group pressures, is at bottom an attack both on constitutional morality and economic rationality.

[40]The Agricultural Instruction Act was introduced as early as 1913, while the Technical Education Act of 1919 and the Vocational Education Act of 1931 quickly followed. The federally controlled Royal Military College at Kingston, Ontario, was established as early as 1876.

[41]In 1960 an agreement was finally worked out with Quebec that permitted the province to make the grants to its universities while Ottawa provided Quebec with the required revenue by ceding additional tax room.

[42]See Peter Leslie, *Canadian Universities, 1980 and Beyond: Enrolment, Structural Change, and Finance* (Toronto: AUCC, 1980).

[43]J.W. George Ivany et al., *Federal-Provincial Relations: Education Canada* (henceforth *FPR:EC*) (Toronto: OISE Press, 1981), 54.

[44]Fox, cited in Ibid., 57.

[45]The same was true of other measures to protect and expand Canadian publishing, the Canadian arts and the communication system. Apart from CRTC directives, one of the most notorious ways of furthering the Canadianization objective was the federal practice of complaining publicly about separatists in the Quebec media. This even provoked a full-scale investigation by the CBC of its Quebec network in the mid-1970s.

[46]Desmond Morton, "Canadian Universities and Colleges: After the Power Trip, Priorities," in H.A. Stevenson and J. Donald Wilson, eds., *Precepts, Policy, Processes* (London, Ont.: Alexander, Blake Assoc., 1977), 186.

[47]Paul Axelrod in his *Scholars and Dollars* (Toronto: UTP, 1982) shows the close relationship between the expansion of higher education in Ontario and expectations of economic payoffs; he also shows that provincial elites were deeply involved in expanding education in order to further their own public purposes. Provincial governments, anxious to pursue economic development strategies, were careful to see that Ottawa's initiatives in higher education did not conflict with their own economic and other priorities.

[48]The provinces were also expected to accept as part of this package the other fiscal proposals of the government, including the termination of the revenue guarantee.

[49]Camille Laurin, the Quebec minister of education, bitterly denounced these initiatives as an attempt "to render postsecondary education a sort of shared jurisdiction," an interference with institutional autonomy and an attack on the "most deeply attached" jurisdiction of the Quebec government upon which the identity and cultural distinctiveness of the Quebec people depended. Letter to the Secretary of State, March 3, 1982.

[50]Peter Leslie in his massive study of *Canadian Universities, 1980 and Beyond*, conducted for the AUCC, marked this issue as one of central concern for the future of universities in Canada.

[51]See David Milne, "Act for Education," *Policy Options* 6, no. 1 (January 1985): 34-36, for a brief explanation of the draft act.

[52]These energy agreements were fiscally threatening not only for the cession of actual or future federal government taxes and royalties, but also for the distorting effects of the provisions in the Atlantic Accord that aim to slow down cuts in equalization that would ordinarily have followed the receipt of offshore royalties for Newfoundland or any other province operating under the same agreement.

[53]*Globe and Mail*, December 14, 1985.

[54]I am grateful to Steve Heiber for his cooperation and assistance with the legal issues around the Canada Health Act.

[55]For a brief review of the issues and case law, see Andrew Petter in *Globe and Mail*, February 20, 1986.

[56]Eric Alan Moyes, "A Critical Analysis of the *Canada Health Act* and Its Impact on the Administration of Health Care in British Columbia," Report for the Master of Public Administration degree, University of Victoria, August 1984, 47. In an earlier case on related issues, however, Dr. Mercer, who was not granted standing in his application for a declaration against the constitutional validity of the federal Medical Care Act, was nonetheless given the views of the trial court

judge on his constitutional claims. The trial court judge stated that if he had to decide the issue he would find that the conditions imposed by the state "in no way regulate or control medical practice within the province" and that the argument of "economic coercion" against the province of Alberta through the spending power was not tenable. See *Mercer* v. *A.-G. Can.* (1972) 24 D.L.R. (3d) 758 (Alta. C.A.) affirming [1971] 3 W.W.R. 375 (Alta. S.C.).

[57]Courchene, "The Fiscal Arrangements: Focus on 1987," 3.

[58]Breau Committee, *Fiscal Federalism in Canada*, 32.

## Chapter VI: Public Policy in the 1980s

[1]See, for example, David Wolfe, "The Politics of the Deficit," in G. Bruce Doern, *The Politics of Economic Policy*, vol. 40, Macdonald Commission Studies (Toronto: UTP, 1985); and Cy Gonick, "The Deficit," *The Facts*, CUPE, 8, no. 2 (March-April 1986): 14-20.

[2]Inis L. Claude, *Power and International Relations* (New York: Random House, 1962), 14-16. There are obvious differences between the theory and practice of international politics and those conducted within a nation-state, even a federally organized state. These differences usually form the first chapter of study in any text or program in international politics and need not detain us here. However, there are useful similarities in these patterns of relations. This is certainly the case with the politics of balance, of preserving equilibrium, of applying counterweights to state power. As we will see, that concept has played its part in the theory and practice of international relations for centuries, though a domestic variant of the idea within federal states is only now being recognized. At these points, it makes some sense to recognize the linkage (with due regard to the continuing radical difference between intrastate and interstate politics) and to explore the interrelationships. That is the reason for carrying federalism as balance of power further than is customarily done here and for examining it both as an ideology and practical strategy with the Trudeau government.

[3]See Richard Bird, *Financing Canadian Government*, 56-68, and Richard Bird, "Federal Finance in Comparative Perspective," in Courchene et al., *Ottawa and the Provinces*, 137-78. This method of calculation of the changing pattern of power in Canadian federalism, together with other rough measures, had already appeared earlier in the writings of Trudeau prior to his assuming the office of prime minister, and it can be concluded that he was already comfortable with this approach to measuring the balance. Moreover, there was a booming literature on measuring patterns of centralization-decentralization in federations through public finance data, including especially the work of Albert Breton and Anthony Scott, *The Economic Constitution of Federal States* (Toronto: UTP, 1978).

[4]Bird, *Financing Canadian Government*, 64, 67. A recent study of this complex issue in relation to various economic indictors is Thomas J. Courchene, *Economic Management and the Division of Powers*, vol. 67, Macdonald Commission Studies (Toronto: UTP, 1986). In the end, after reviewing Canada in comparative context, he was driven to the existential "logic" of balance, expressed differently in every country and at different times, rather than a simpler "formula approach" to the question of centralization and decentralization. These are matters that cannot be treated in one-dimensional terms.

[5]Claude Morin, *Quebec versus Ottawa: The Struggle for Self-Government, 1960-72,* trans. from *Le Pouvoir Québécois ... négociation* (1972) and *Le Combat Québécois* (1973) (Toronto: UTP, 1976).

[6]Preston King, *Federalism and Federation* (London: Croom Helm, 1982).

[7]Ibid., 57, 61, 67.

[8]The criticism over the insufficient basis of popular support and involvement was an important part of the reviews over the post-1981 constitutional settlement — see, for example, Keith Banting and Richard Simeon, *And No One Cheered* (Toronto: Methuen, 1983) — and it could just as easily be extended to the whole panoply of Canadian nationalist policy of the late Trudeau era. Indeed, the complaint goes much further than the exclusion of the broad public from the nationalist program, but also extends to Parliament, to members of the Liberal caucus and even to excluded cabinet ministers. Donald Johnston, president of the Treasury Board under the Trudeau government after 1980, was especially bitter about the exclusion of ministers from key decisions of that period, including the NEP and the subsequent expansion of Petro-Canada through the acquisition of Petrofina. See Donald Johnston, *Up the Hill* (Montreal: Optimum Publications, 1986), chaps. 2-4.

[9]Doern and Toner, *The Politics of Energy*, 106-8, 205-53.

[10]Johnston letter to the prime minister, cited in D. Johnston, *Up the Hill*, 62-65.

[11]Letter of reply from Prime Minister Trudeau to D. Johnston, cited in Ibid., 65-66.

[12]See Clarkson, *Canada and the Reagan Challenge*, esp. chap. 3.

[13]Government of Canada, *Progress Report on Federal-Provincial Relations*, Annual Conference of First Ministers, Halifax, November 28-29, 1985. Table 6-1 appeared on p. 16 of that document.

[14]Giles Gherson, *Financial Post*, November 17, 1984. This extensive review, along with many others at the time, reveals the extent to which the neoconservative agenda of reducing government — "taking the scalpel to leviathan" — was already a well-understood feature of the program, attested to by many ministers, including Robert de Cotret.

[15]Dunnery Best, *Financial Post*, March 8, 1986.

[16]For an interesting critical review of the privatization program from a business perspective, see Christopher Waddell, "Privatization Pratfalls," *Report on Business Magazine*, April 1986, 50-56.

[17]Corporate exemptions had permitted, for example, Northern Telecom, a company with sales of $3.3 billion and profit of $325 million in 1983, to escape paying tax altogether, along with Shell Canada and others. Effective rates of tax paid by large corporations had fallen from an average of 18.2% in 1977 to 14.3% in 1981. Tax deferrals had also grown sharply, reaching a total of $24.2 billion in 1980 alone, and there was some doubt whether these would ever be paid. See H.A. Crooks and Peter Raymont, *Special Economic Report, Canadian Business* 58, no. 1 (January 1985): 38-77. Corporate tax data appears on pp. 69-70.

[18]*Securing Economic Renewal: The Budget Speech*, February 26, 1986, 7.

[19]Business had less to worry about on this score, since it was also reputed to be serving in an advisory capacity on budget cuts as well as program rationalization under Erik Nielsen's task force. See *Globe and Mail*, November 10, 1985.

[20]See, for example, both Hyman Solomon and Giles Gherson, *Financial Post,*

March 8, 1986. The d'Aquino citation appears here.

[21]David Wolfe and Leon Muszynski, program director of Metro Toronto's Social Planning Council, cited in H.A. Crooks et al., *Special Economic Report, Canadian Business,* 76. See also James J. Rice, "Politics of Income Security: Historical Developments and Limits to Future Change," in Doern, *The Politics of Economic Policy,* 221-50.

[22]Wolfe, "The Politics of the Deficit," 111-62.

[23]Ibid., 138.

[24]Irving Brecher, "Beyond Budget Slashing," *Policy Options* 6, no. 3 (April 1985): 6.

[25]This theme is also taken up as an important element in the Mulroney government initiatives in Prince, *How Ottawa Spends, 1986-87.* For a brief review of these and other related themes in the "stale" thinking and language of Prime Minister Mulroney, see Mark Abley, "Talking Tory," *Canadian Forum* 63 (March 1984): 7-13.

[26]See Leo Panitch, "The Tripartite Experience," in Keith Banting, *The State and Economic Interests,* vol. 32, Macdonald Commission Studies (Toronto: UTP, 1986), 83.

[27]Neil Nevitte and Roger Gibbins, "Neoconservatism: Canadian Variations on an Ideological Theme?" *Canadian Public Policy* 10 (December 1984): 385. For a treatment of the politics of scarcity and neoconservative themes respecting Canadian federalism, see Thomas O. Hueglin, *Federalism and Fragmentation* (Kingston: Queen's University, Institute of Intergovernmental Relations, 1984).

[28]Nevitte and Gibbins, "Neoconservatism," 388. The results also showed significant linguistic divisions with higher neoconservative scores for anglophones than francophones, and sizeable regional variations, with Alberta, Ontario and British Columbia acquiring the highest scores and Newfoundland and New Brunswick the lowest.

[29]Professor Perlin presented these general results, including a shift toward increasing hawkishness on foreign policy matters, in an open seminar on conservatism at the University of Toronto in January 1986. His findings are to be published soon.

[30]This recommendation was heavily influenced by the research and arguments of Thomas Courchene and others, which had for some time claimed that many of the income security programs had the effect of reducing economic efficiency, increasing dependency and retarding the necessary adjustment of have-not regions in the country. See Thomas J. Courchene, "Avenues of Adjustment: The Transfer System and Regional Disparities," in *Canadian Confederation at the Crossroads* (Vancouver: Fraser Institute, 1978), 145-86; and his subsequent work for the commission. It was also presaged by the DRIE document, "Policies for Industrial Adjustment," 1983.

[31]This was the conclusion of James Rice after reviewing the commission's recommendations in this area. Seminar on Macdonald Commission's social policy, Workshop on Public Policy, University of Toronto, February 1986.

[32]See Doern, "The Tories, Free Trade, and Industrial Adjustment Policy."

[33]Richard Simeon, "Federalism and Free Trade." Much of the following analysis draws upon his views. For later treatment of this topic by Simeon, consult Peter M. Leslie, ed., *The State of the Federation, 1986* (a forthcoming publication of the Institute of Intergovernmental Relations, Kingston).

[34]Simeon, "Federalism and Free Trade."

[35]Ibid.

[36]See André Blais, *The Political Sociology of Public Aid to Industry*, vol. 45, Macdonald Commission Studies (Toronto: UTP, 1986), esp. chap. 2.

[37]See R.A. Young, "A Way out for Mr. Mulroney," *Policy Options* 7, no. 4 (May 1986): 3-8.

[38]See David Calleo and Susan Strange, "Money and World Politics," in Susan Strange, ed., *Paths to International Political Economy*,(London: Allen and Unwin, 1985); and Loukas Tsoukalis, *The Political Economy of International Money: In Search of a New Order* (London: Sage, 1985).

[39]See Richard Simeon, "Federalism in the 1980's," in Courchene et al., *Ottawa and the Provinces.*

# Index

362

Oil and gas, *see* Energy.
Oil Import Compensation Charge, 108
Ontario, *see also* Central Canada — extra-billing, 196 — free trade, 145-46, 148-49, 152-54, 159 — position on Bill S-31, 133
Ontario Medical Association (OMA), 196
*Operation Dismantle*, 59
Opting out, *see* Conditional grants; Quebec.
Organization of Petroleum Exporting Countries (OPEC), 18, 72-74, 95, 112
Ottawa Valley Line, 74

Parti Québécois (PQ), 14, 20, 36-37, 97 — government of, 132, 187, 214
Peckford, Brian, 90, 94, 99-100, 101
Pentland, Charles, 154
Pepin, Jean-Luc, 21, 129
Pepin-Robarts Task Force, 21, 231
Perlin, George, 230
Peterson, David — federal energy policy, 110 — free trade, 148-49, 152, 153, 158, 159 — government of, 202
Petro-Canada, 76-79 passim, 87-91 passim, 93, 100, 104-11 passim, 113, 124, 130, 217, 226 passim — Clark Conservatives' plan to "privatize," 71, 80, 57, 139
Petroleum and Gas Revenue Tax (PGRT), 108, 113, 114, 115, 192
Petroleum Compensation Charge, 108
Petroleum Incentive Program (PIP), 90, 92, 110, 111, 113
Pitfield, Michael, 79
Postsecondary education, 16-17, 184-91, 193-95, 217 — in British Columbia, 189 — spending cuts, 189-90, 193, 222 — student aid, 191, 194, 216, 217, 231
Power Corporation, 80
Pratt, Larry, 93
Prentice-Hall Canada, 143, 156-57
Prince Edward Island Comprehensive Development Plan, 132, 207
Provigo Inc., 133

Quebec, *see also* Separatism — Bill

S-31, 133-34 — free trade 148-49 — Liberal party, 21 — the Mulroney government, 65-68, 139 — national self-determination, 20-21, 36, 48-56 passim — nationalists' concept of cultural duality, 48,-56 62, 216 — opts out of federally led social programs, 16-17, 171, 175, 186, 215 — postsecondary education, 186, 187, 209 — referendum, 20, 23, 27, 36, 50-56 passim, 97, 210
Rabinovitch, Bob, 79
Reagan, Ronald, 136, 148, 158, 220, 224 — administration of, 92, 234
Regional economic development, 124-25, 131-35, 140-41, 232-33 — and free trade, 154
Regional Economic Expansion, Department of, 18, 124-25, 131-32, 135
Reichmann family, 111, 113
Reisman, Simon, 152, 158
Rémillard, Gil, 66
Robarts, John, 21, 176
Roberts, John, 29
Romanow, Roy, 114
Rotstein, Abraham, 154, 155, 156
Rowell Sirois Commission, 11, 123, 165, 169
Royal Commission on the Economic Union and Development Prospects for Canada — on the Charter of Rights and Freedoms, 48, 57, 231 — on free trade, 119, 145-46, 151, 153, 160, 230-33 — on the NEP, 232 — on regional development, 128, 141, 232 — on social policy, 194, 232-33
Russell, Peter, 58
Ryan, Claude, 21

Safarian, A.E., 44, 126
Sampson, Anthony, 73
Saskatchewan — natural resources, 20, 98, 114 — position on Bill S-31, 133
Savoie, Donald, 140
Science Council of Canada, 128, 130, 236
Separatism — provincial, 15-19, 115, 210 — Quebec, 14, 23, 29, 32, 41,